Classism For Dimwits

Long ago it was said that "one half of the world does not know how the other half lives." That was true then. It did not know because it did not care. The half that was on top cared little for the struggles, and less for the fate of those who were underneath, so long as it was able to hold them there and keep its own seat. ~ Jacob Riis, *How the Other Half Lives*

Contents

Introduction

" 'Status quo.' Latin for the mess we're in." ~ Jeve Moorman

Much has been written and said about poverty over the last three decades. Most of what has been said or written has come from those who have never personally suffered from classism and the social injustice of poverty. Their writings and opinions are from the perspective of being on the outside looking in, often through the bias of middle class lenses. The only two authors that I am aware of that have actually written about poverty from the trenches with an insider's experience and perspective are Barbara Ehrenreich and Dr. Donna M. Beegle.

Classisms For Dimwits is written by someone with significant insider experience — mine. Hence, many of the examples which I use and cite are drawn from my own personal life experiences. While writing this book, a trusted friend and mentor – Michael J. McFadden – who is a published author from an upper-middle class background with an Ivy League education under his belt, helped with some of the editing. I am grateful to him for his feedback.

I would also like to personally thank Karl Kaun, Matt Janovic and his mother Billie Meyers for paying for a necessary ophthalmologist exam and covering my travel cost after my initial glaucoma diagnosis while poor, uninsured, long-term unemployed and struggling as an upcoming writer; Jack and Coley Martin for their moral support, friendship, treasured gifts of books and my first horseback ride; Peggy McPherson for her badly needed and greatly appreciated emergency donation towards my heating needs during the winter of 2010-2011; Betsy Leondar-Wright for reading my previous writings on class matters and inviting my participation on her site, Classism.org; Michael Parenti for his encouragement of my work as a poor and struggling author coming up from the underclass, Lawrence Porter of CAUS for fighting the good fight against unaffordable utility rates and utility shut-off related casualties; and Timothy M. Conley of Logan County, West

Virginia for sharing his extensive knowledge of the historical facts about the settlement of West Virginia during the 1700's, its separation from the state of Virginia, and chronological events surrounding the Matewan Massacre and the Battle of Blair Mountain. And most importantly, Donnie E. Homan, Sr., the only man who loved me, stood by me, and cared enough to support me in my work. None of us are an island who "did it all on our own."

I do not hold a PhD (couldn't afford grad school). Nor have I written about social injustice from an outsider's point of view. I am not a policymaker, social worker or a bureaucrat working for a government agency that manages the poor. I have written from an insider's view and first-hand life experience. *Classism For Dimwits* is very much in-your-face, up front and personal. I do not sugar coat things. That is my style. I make no apologies for that.

Chapter 1

"Justice is better than chivalry if we cannot have both." ~ Alice Stone Blackwell

I was abandoned by my mother on a cold, rainy, windswept November night in 1969 when I was barely 2 years old and thereafter raised by my grandmother. When I was 13, my grandmother died. I was orphaned. My uncle and his wife stole my inheritance, sold the house I was raised in out from under me, and left me to fend for myself on the streets of Philadelphia as a 13 year old girl with absolutely nothing.

I was eventually taken in by my older half-sister whom I scarcely knew because we were not raised together. She was a street-smart high school drop-out who worked very, very hard for very little money and no health benefits as a waitress. We lived in a run-down tenement in a Philadelphia ghetto.

Most teens get fake ID's so they can buy alcohol and party. I got a fake ID when I was 14 just so I could get a job in order to afford food and a place to live. I worked delivering newspapers and in fast food restaurants making minimum wage, which was $3.35 an hour throughout the early through mid 1980's. There weren't very many "respectable" or legitimate job opportunities for women and girls that paid a living wage then. The only living wage "job" available to me as a very poor girl was strip dancing.

I endeavored to maintain a cool distance between myself and others at school because I lived in daily fear that my precarious situation would be discovered by the authorities – which would have landed me in the foster care system with total strangers who might have been abusive at worst or negligent at best.

Although my sister and I both worked, we were always one $10 rent increase away from eviction. We often went hungry and had utilities shut off for lack of enough income to afford rent, food, gas, and electric. A phone was a luxury we had to do without. We never had medical or dental care. We were often confronted by men, especially landlords and employers, who tried taking advantage of us because we were poor young girls on our own trying to survive in a man's world, trying to make it in a society where poor women and girls are disposable. We were vulnerable.

The first job I tried to get that paid above federal minimum wage that was not in fast food or waitress work was a job in a local furniture factory known for hiring vo-tech students. I was 15 years old at the time. The owner suspected that I was desperately poor because it was not typical for a girl in high school to seek out that type of work. He told me I could have that $4 an hour job that I desperately needed if I agreed to have sex with him. He was old enough to be my grandfather, and he was a "community pillar."

I told him if I had to be a whore for a $4 an hour job, he could shove it up his ass. Without mincing words, I told him that if all I could expect to get was forced into prostitution just to survive simply because I was a poor girl, I could do better than what he was offering because a streetwalker can make $40 an hour and not have to worry about getting fired.

The price I paid for maintaining my dignity and pride was not getting the job that I desperately needed in order to survive. My sister and I ended up homeless as a result of me not getting that job under honorable terms because getting sent home poor and empty-handed without that job translated to being unable to pay the rent after our landlord raised it.

Our landlord owned two thirds of all the rental units in Philadelphia. He propositioned my sister. He told her if she agreed to what was tantamount to a trade of sexual favors, specifically a blow job, he wouldn't raise our rent. My sister refused. Our rent got raised. We were evicted because we couldn't afford it. Nobody cared how we were supposed to live, where we could live, or if we would live.

In the context of a middle class person's life, men are responsible family providers and protective fathers; trusted mentors, and loving husbands — but only towards the women of their own social class. It's been my personal observation and experience that middle class men only use poor women for temporary comfort until "something better" comes along: we're only good enough to be "Miss Right Now", never good enough to be "Mrs. Right." In the context of the reality of dire poverty in which I lived, men were not nice. Men were bullies, liars and cheats who would do and say anything to get what they wanted from poor and vulnerable women and girls – without caring whose lives got ruined in the process. Men only used women for what they wanted and then kicked them to the curb with nothing afterwards. Women and girls got dumped if they got pregnant and had to fight to the death for any meager amount of child support – which they usually didn't get. In my world, men were not trustworthy: they were liars, selfish guttersnipes, and they were abusive and cruel.

As a matter of personal survival, I had to be a hard-ass in order to scare men away so they would think twice before trying to take advantage of me. It was my sole defense as a poor and vulnerable orphan girl in a white male world ruled by avarice and injustice created by a system of unearned privileges.

The anticipation of dating boys, falling in love, getting married, living happily ever after and raising a family in a home of my own seemed like an unattainable dream. It was a fairy tale to me. In the context of my life, love didn't exist. True love and romance happened for others; for the "pretty people" from privileged homes, people who were part of society – not those like me who existed on the margins unnoticed and unwanted. Love and romance happened for the girls lucky enough to be born pretty, and those whose families protected them from the users, the liars, the cheats, and the abusers. But that was not my reality in the "Other America."

I went to vo-tech in high school. I gained experience in painting, cement finishing, drywall finishing, plastering, and laying block. After graduating from high school, I worked for several non-union contractors and usually had to chase them down in order to get paid. Although there was a subsidized job placement program specifically to serve disadvantaged youths and adults at the local Private Industry Council (PIC) office which was funded and administered through the Comprehensive Employment Training Act (CETA), its funds were eliminated during the Reagan years. The few jobs available through PIC went almost unanimously to the dislocated union factory workers from Mack Trucks, Bethlehem Steel, and Phoenix Apparel. The downwardly mobile middle class workers received priority in job placement over those with the least amount of economic security and opportunity in the community.

Good jobs available for poor young women without college degrees were practically non-existent after the unionized garment factories and textile mills closed as the era of globalization was ushered in during the 1980's. For poor girls like my sister and I, the employment opportunities were either to work (even if we were sick) 90 hours a week at minimum wage jobs with no benefits, or work as strip dancers. Poor girls who didn't even have slim figures and semi-good looks going for them couldn't even fall back on exotic dancing gigs in order to survive.

My sister and I separated when she met and subsequently married Prince Not-So-Charming, an ex-felon with a high paying construction job. He took her far away from me and all she knew. He ended up abusing her after isolating her (she had no drivers' license or car) in their rural home in Sciota Township in Pennsylvania's Pocono Mountains, far away from the public transportation and jobs in Philadelphia. She died from ovarian cancer one week after her 40th birthday in April of 2001 two weeks before I graduated from college at the age of 34. I was the first in my family to ever graduate from college.

Meanwhile, in the early days while Prince Not-So Charming was wooing my sister, I got accepted into the local plasterers and painters union when I was 22. I finally got a chance for a job that paid a middle class wage without having to take off my clothes, or without having to chase down fly-by-night non-union contractors for my money.

I knew the insecurities and deprivations of poverty in the richest country in the world where nobody gives a damn about poor women.

Poverty is isolating because nobody cares about you, and no matter what you try to do to better yourself people look down on you and judge you. You can't afford to participate in anything. You have very limited opportunity for positive social interaction and building networks of resources into your life. It is isolating because almost everybody else is cruel to you, abuse you, and exploit you because you're at a disadvantage. And they expect you to just suck it up and take it because when you're poor, you don't have a choice – especially if you're a poor white female.

After getting into the plasterers' union in 1989 (the first woman to do so), I wanted to do everything humanly possible to attain security in my life so I'd never again be hungry, homeless and without the means to get dental and health care if I needed it. I knew that if I owned where I lived, no greedy slum landlord could proposition me in exchange for doing me the "favor" of not raising my rent beyond what I could afford. Having enough money meant having health care and not having to take any shit.

I saved every penny I could after the rent and utilities were paid. My furniture was "curbside special." I lived on Ramen Noodles and generic macaroni and cheese dinners. All of my clothing (except underwear and socks) came from Goodwill or the Salvation Army Thrift Store. Within a year of joining the union and living frugally, I had saved enough money to buy a small 2-unit apartment building in the same neighborhood my sister and I had once lived as poor renters when we were teenagers. I paid cash on the barrelhead for the property.

A week before my 24th birthday in May of 1991, my plan for building economic security came to a crashing halt – literally. An uninsured driver ran a red light and plowed into me while I was driving to work. My truck was totaled, my back was broken in four places, and both of my knees were smashed. In an instant, I went from earning $19 an hour and facing a bright future with a sense of hope for economic security to not being able to work and earn anything at all. The doctors didn't think I'd ever be able to walk again; at least, not without a walker or a cane. I can walk now, but I am unable to stand for long periods of time. I cannot walk any significant distances, and I can't lift a lot. I have poor balance and cannot manage very well on ladders. The accident left me unable to work in anything that I was suited for by educational level and experience. I only had a high school diploma and experience as a strip dancer and as a journeyman plasterer and painter in the skilled construction trades.

I tried to get help from welfare after my savings ran out, but I was denied because I didn't have children. I applied for social security disability (SSDI) but I was denied on the grounds that I had not yet had enough time in the workforce to contribute enough credits into the social security system. I was too young when I became disabled and had not gotten a chance to get established in life with a sufficient work history. I applied for SSI, and was denied that on the grounds that I wasn't "disabled enough." The people at the social security office referred me to the Pennsylvania Office of Vocational Rehabilitation (OVR) for assistance with retraining and job placement in a new line of work that I could do, despite my permanent physical problems from the car accident.

My OVR caseworker was indifferent to my needs and problems. He told me to go to college for a degree in math and computer science because that's where all the jobs were. He said that if I wanted OVR's help with job placement after having to start all over as a disabled woman, I had to follow his advice and vocational retraining plan to the letter. He dismissed my concerns that I might not be able to be academically successful due to my dyslexia and lack of a college prep background during my high school years.

I didn't think I could be successful in college, especially in a major that required taking a lot of extremely difficult math and computer programming courses when I was not computer literate. I had never even turned on a computer, much less used one or programmed one. This OVR "vocational retraining expert" trivialized my situation and invalidated my realistic concerns. His response to all of my concerns was an off-handed dismissal of "You'll just have to try harder. It will take you a little longer than everybody else, but that means you'll just have to work a little harder."

It took me *a lot* longer and I had to work *a lot* harder. The obstacles of a physical disability and a learning disability were enormous. But they paled in comparison to the barriers created by the conditions of poverty and a very real – not imaginary – lack of adequate help and support. I finally graduated from college when I was 34 with a Bachelor degree in mathematics and computer science and a minor in physics.

But I never got a chance for a good job. I never got a chance to go to grad school. I never got a chance to re-enter the workforce at a stable career because I was considered "too old", lacked "experience", I didn't have the "right image", I was "too fat", or "overqualified." I never was able to make it out of poverty, despite super-human efforts to do so.

Poverty meant not having enough food. Poverty meant not having hot water to bathe regularly. The college gymnasium was my *only* resource for bathing so I wouldn't have to walk around dirty and smelly. Poverty meant being penalized on my grades by professors because of not having any money for reliable transportation or car repairs so I could get to and from school. Poverty meant not having a computer or other school supplies needed for the acceptable and timely completion of assignments. Poverty meant no access to decent dental care so I wouldn't lose my teeth and having to face potential employers with missing, broken, or rotting teeth. Poverty meant having all of my time sucked up and wasted by all the social agencies that supposedly help the poor, but do nothing except give you a big run-around and deny you badly needed help — that's what middle class social workers and welfare caseworkers are paid to do. Poverty meant having no free time because every waking minute of my day was spent on struggling just to survive and make it through one more day. Poverty means living in constant and utter economic terror with no end in sight and no hope. It also means living in terror of the phalanx of law enforcement professionals who owe their middle class jobs to kangaroo courts that grease the skids of the fast-track for the cradle-to-prison pipeline for the poor.

The vast majority of "experts" who have studied poverty and written about it have never had to live it. Their professional opinions are from the vantage point of an outsider's perspective that is tainted with class bias. They're prone to making judgments about the behaviors and "choices" that may not make sense in the context of middle class people's lives, but which make all the sense in the world for those struggling in poverty.

Classism For Dimwits is not written from a outsider's condescending point of view, from a more privileged position in life. It is written from an insider's very real life experience. It is proof that you can struggle against tremendous odds and do "all the right things" in life and still remain poor, kept down and stuck at the bottom because, despite popular belief, we do not live in a meritocracy. We do not have a true "free market", and we do not live in a "classless" society with liberty and justice for all.

Chapter 2

"The laws of capitalism, blind and invisible to the majority, act upon the individual without his thinking about it." ~ Che Guevara

When we talk about justice, we must first ask ourselves what justice means, what justice is. Justice is formally defined according to Merriam-Webster as:

Justice: 1. The quality of fairness, of being just. 2. The principle of moral rightness; equity. 3. The upholding of what is just, especially fair treatment and due reward in accordance with honor, standards, or law. 4. Conformity to truth, fact, or sound reason; conformity to moral rightness in action and attitude. 5. The state of being unbiased.

Now the short version of the definition of justice is fairness and equity in action. In order to be in a position to question the justice system, we first need a firm grasp of the working definition of what justice really is. Once we have a solid comprehension of the meaning of the word "justice", then we must examine all that pertains to it. There is crime and adjudication and there is also social justice (or lack thereof) which goes hand in hand with the justice system, the economic system, and every aspect of our social mores. These concepts cannot be easily separated. The biggest saboteur of justice is classism.

Privilege is about how society accommodates you over others who are not being accommodated. It's having unearned advantages that you think are "normal." Privilege is a "knapsack" of stuff you're not forced to think about, let alone deal with.

Classism is defined as any form of prejudice or oppression against people based on their actual or perceived socio-economic class.

Social stratification refers to the division of society into layers (strata) whose occupants have unequal access to social opportunities and rewards. People in the upper strata enjoy power, prosperity, and prestige that is not available to other members of society. People in the lower strata endure penalties that members of higher strata in society escape.

A **social class** is a large group of people who rank closely to one another in wealth, power, and prestige. The consequence of social class position is far reaching. Consider dating and marriage. Children, teens, and adults tend to seek out those who act, speak, and dress like themselves. They seek others who have a set of shared cultural values and life experiences. The upper class arranges social events such that upper class children only meet and interact with other upper class children.

Social exclusion is defined as the inability to exercise the social rights of citizens to a basic standard of living and as a barrier to participation in the major social and occupational opportunities of the society. Sociologists Dale Parent and Bonnie Lewis observed that social exclusion is the product of flaws in the system that creates disadvantaged for certain segments of the population[1]. There is no group in America that is more socially excluded than the poor.

What do poor people do without that everyone else takes for granted? The short answer: basic human needs and socially approved necessities, including the opportunity to participate in life. Social exclusion occurs where different factors combine to trap individuals and communities in a downward spiral of disadvantage. A 1999 British working paper identified four dimensions[2] of social exclusion:

1. Job market exclusion

2. Exclusion from adequate income or resources

3. Goods and services exclusion

4. Exclusion from social participation and relationships.

Service exclusion was divided into two main areas:

---

[1] *Southern Rural Sociology*, Vol. 19, No. 2, 2003, pp. 153-175

[2] *"Social Security, Poverty, and Social Exclusion: Evidence From the Poverty and Social Exclusion Survey of Britain."* (Karl Ashworth, Sue Middleton, 1999)

1. Exclusion from basic household utilities, either because of disconnection or using less than minimally needed because of lack of money.

2. Exclusion from local services, public and private, either because they are not available or because the poor cannot afford them (e.g. DSL Internet)

Exclusion from social participation and relationships was treated in three main areas:

1. Exclusion from participation in social activities because of lack of money
2. Deprivation of support in times of need
3. Disengagement from civic life

When you don't have enough money to afford food, housing, clothing, and life-sustaining utilities; you don't have money to be able to go out. Being unable to afford to go out eliminates opportunity for building social networks and makes it impossible to date and hopefully, find the marriage partner of your choice and raise a family. In the age of the Internet, online dating was supposed to open horizons for meeting people who don't live near you. But lack of money makes it impossible to travel in order to meet your date in person after initially meeting and finding common interests online. Even having hobbies costs money – something that the middle class and rich take for granted that the poor do not have.

What sort of social opportunities could you afford to participate in if you were jobless, unemployable, and had no income? What about if you were on an extremely low fixed income such as social security or SSI?

How does classism affect the innocent hopes, dreams, and aspirations of children? That is a tough question, but it is one that merits some serious discussion. I was entering my "rite of passage" into teenagehood when I was orphaned and consequently, poor thereafter. Before my grandmother (who had adopted me) died, I had a solidly middle class childhood if you only consider access to books (but nothing else) as the hallmark of middle classdom.

But I was not like all the other "normal" middle class children in my neighborhood. First, I was Jewish. Second, I didn't know my father. I had a mom who lived less than two miles away who never bothered with me after she abandoned me when I was 2 years old on a rainy, cold, windswept November night in 1969. Although that happened 39 years ago as of my writing this book, I can vividly remember every painful detail as if it happened yesterday. My grandmother, and my uncle and his wife never answered the tough questions. They simply told me that my father was already married to another woman when he and my mom had a tryst – of which I was the unintended result.

The other "normal" middle class children in my neighborhood had both a mom and a dad. Their parents *wanted* them. The only exception was Karen and Shelly Pervallo whose parents were divorced, and they lived with their mom in their grandparent's house. I, on the other hand, rarely heard from my mother and certainly never heard from my father. I didn't even know who he was and that caused me untold shame and guilt which haunted me throughout my life – even though the circumstances of my birth were clearly not *my* fault, and certainly not *my* choice.

I became very cynical at an early age. Raised to believe in God and take the Torah to heart, I decided to bargain with God, like Abraham did. I prayed to God with the utmost sincerity. I vowed to keep all 613 *mitzvot*[3] and be a flawless child if only He would make my mother want me and accept me, and bring me a dad as well – so I would be loved, wanted, accepted, and "normal" like all the other children and be a part of society; and be somebody who counted. And I meant it. I wanted to be good enough so that God would hear me and answer my questions and my prayers. I lived up to my end of the bargain – a tall order for any child, Jewish or not.

---

[3] Hebrew: *mitzvot* = commandments

I avoided eating *treif*[4]; I rarely spoke in order to avoid *loshon hara*[5]. I was seen and unheard by the adults. I never gave my grandmother or schoolteachers reason to scold me. Even when other children's parents were rude and mean to me and said nasty things about me behind my back because of the circumstances of my birth, I was mindful to always display the most well-behaved and politest of dispositions to them no matter how petty, thoughtless, and cruel they were towards me.

But God never answered my prayers. By the time I was 8 years old, I began to question the existence of God. I reasoned that if God was real, He didn't care about me and had abandoned me just like my own mother had – He had bigger and better things to worry about than an unwanted "accident." It didn't matter how good I was or how well-behaved I was. My belief in God waned at an age when most children still believe in Santa Clause and the Tooth Fairy. Since I didn't buy into religion, I also didn't buy into miracles. I had a very jaded view of life for as long as I can remember.

Internet blogger Jennifer Kesler, a.k.a. "BetaCandy", wrote a blog dealing with the ramifications of privilege on underprivileged children. One poster posed the question of how poverty and classism affects poor children on Christmas. I examined my own feelings and memories from my childhood about God. Either God didn't care about me if He was real, or maybe He wasn't any more real than Santa Clause.

I asked others who were born into poverty and who had to deal with poverty at Christmas time as children. Like God, here is Santa Clause who is supposed to be a good guy instead of an asshole bigot. Santa Clause is supposed to be impervious to financial constraints. What does it do to poor children in a rich country whose classmates throw it in their faces about all the great stuff they got for Christmas when everyone *knows* that it is only the very naughty children who don't get anything, or

---

[4] Hebrew: *treif* = forbidden foods pursuant to Mosaic kosher dietary law.

[5] Hebrew: *loshon hara* = "evil speech", gossip. The worst sin in Judaism is to speak badly and falsely about others, to gossip about others. The power of life and death is in the tongue.

who get socks and underwear? In a competitive culture where we're judged by what we have, this is devastating.

Some who grew up in poverty remember their parents telling them the truth from the beginning: that there is no such thing as Santa Claus. Other children get lots of nice things because their parents are lucky enough to have good jobs to be able to afford to buy them all the nice things that make life fun; while poor children get nothing. When you're poor, all you get is shit – and shoved in it.

Some who grew up in impoverished single mother households had painful associations with the holidays. They dreaded Christmas because every Christmas they saw all the pretty lights, decorations, and elaborate store displays with all the great stuff that they knew they could never have. Going to sit on Santa's lap was a waste; they never got anything they wanted anyway.

They were confronted with having all these nice things thrown in their faces knowing full well that the time of year had come once more to go to the neighborhood community center where some fake Santa would dole out a used, unwrapped gift that was some other child's discarded toy to poor kids at the center. They were expected to be grateful for cast-offs that they didn't want in the first place. Poor children know that others whose parents have "important" jobs, plenty of money and nice homes get cool stuff. They see that some have everything while they have nothing, and then they're ridiculed at school for having nothing.

At a young age, kids start asking adults tough questions: Why doesn't everybody have nice stuff? Why doesn't everybody get to "win" at least once? The usual response is, "That's just the way it is. Life's not fair." That may shut the kid up, but it won't shut off his brain.

Children know that the adults make all the rules. Children therefore conclude that the adults don't care about life being unfair. And they don't understand *why* the adults don't care about life being unfair when everything they're exposed to at school is based on rules made by adults that stress the concept of fairness. Don't copy answers off another student's test because that's not fair. Don't cheat at playing sports because that's not fair. Don't take another child's toy because that's not fair. Yet, they see adults behave in ways that are anything *but* fair. Morals are developed. Kids learn morals from what they see adults do, not from what adults tell them to do. It is from adults' *behavior* that the critical moral value of fairness is learned.

Poor kids get resentful of middle class peers who throw their privileges in their faces. They get angry at their moms because even though their moms work very hard for very low pay, there isn't enough money to live decently, never mind any extra money for fun and nice things. They get angry at the society which has unfairly excluded their parents from a share in this nation's prosperity.

They quickly become cynical because they see that adults say one thing and then do another when it comes to fairness. They see that for no reason other than misfortune of birth, they're not entitled to have any hopes and dreams. All you get is your hopes and dreams shattered because no one with the power to make life a little bit fair wants to do so. They learn that no one cares if they're cold and hungry. They see that poor people get told to "stop whining", go suffer silently somewhere out of sight and out of mind. Angry, resentful kids develop apathy for the society that has rejected them, and become recalcitrant. Instead of addressing the injustice of poverty and classism, the privileged classes opt to build more prisons to deal with angry kids who grow up into angry adults.

Those who are not benefitting from society because they've been marginalized are viewed as a threat, as "the Other." Society is indifferent towards their plight and often views them with loathing and fear. Mainstream media, right-wing talking heads of questionable credibility, and biased pseudo-intellectuals from billionaire-funded right-wing think tanks have all done their part to set up the "undeserving" poor as "the Other", as "trash" who are living undeservedly well off the largesse of "good" and "hard-working" middle class people who played by the rules that the rich contrived. The media peddled classism like a drug dealer hawking his wares, enticing the unwitting prey into an addiction.

The sea of middle class professionals who romanticize, fetishize, and demonize the poor also took up the baton and led the parade of poor-bashing. Their Ivy League PhD's give them automatic credibility and respect for their insipid drivel amounting to how we need to "fix" the defective poor, which infers that those trapped in poverty are to blame for their problems caused by a system that was not of their making.

People in poverty are the proverbial "turtle on the pole" — we did not get trapped there solely on our own. But the media and the Commissariat — the professional/managerial class — refuses to talk about that. The professional class is rewarded with token privileges and comforts as long as they serve the interests of those who endow their academic department chairs and fund their research. Like the corporate-owned media, they are well-kept lapdogs that are not likely to bite the hand that feeds them. The few leftist scholars who have dared to speak out and write the truth found themselves professionally alienated, blacklisted, harassed by the FBI (a component of the national security state), framed up on bogus criminal charges, and even murdered ("official" reports often don't comport with the actual forensic evidence).

Meanwhile, "experts" like Ruby Payne and Milton Friedman are hailed as celebrities and geniuses of social and economic policy, and are employed by think tanks who serve as part of the Praetorian guard which protects the interests of the rich. They present quasi-Ayn Randian word salads with a few grains of truth marinated in false and circular logic. They spoon-feed contempt for the poor like cake to the masses and society swallowed the bait — hook, line, and sinker.

Social engineering by the entertainment industry has also played an underestimated role in this. Radio personalities like Rush Limbaugh openly call for cutting food stamps saying that poor children should "learn how to dumpster dive" if they're hungry. Television and Hollywood depict the poor as uneducated, brutal and vicious monsters while depicting those from the middle and upper classes as pretty, nice, intelligent, and as heroes. Case in point: Wes Craven's horror film "*Nightmare on Elm Street*".

The 1980's cult classic horror film's villain, Freddy Kruger (played by Robert Englund), was not handsome and well-dressed. He was horribly burned and wore a trademark ratty red and olive green striped sweater, a crumbled fedora hat that had seen better days and a hand-made metal glove with razor knives for fingers which he used to murder the town's children by slashing them to death. Freddy Kruger wasn't the bank president, the high school principle, or any other "community pillar" in the fictional upper-middle class suburban hamlet of Springwood. He was a transient who (before his fiery death by vigilante justice), was the janitor of the local power plant and he lived in the boiler room where he worked. His victims were middle class children. Angry and resentful in death, Freddy returned to kill Springwood's teens in their dreams. The underlying message was that Freddy Kruger (who had no family or status) murdered children out of rage-driven class envy against the "nice" people in society. The heroine, Nancy Thompson (played by Heather Langenkamp), was the police chief's daughter. No hidden messages there, right?

Another example is the 2003 B-rated horror film *"Wrong Turn"* – a blood and gore packed thriller set in Greenbrier County, West Virginia. The villains were three grossly deformed cannibalistic inbreds who prey upon the young, pretty, middle class college grads stranded by an automobile accident on a deserted back road in the heart of Appalachia. The film's producer Stan Winston said he "wanted to create monsters that were very realistic", that medical texts were used to get "information about deformities and psychosis common in insular rural areas where inbreeding is prevalent" (too bad he didn't investigate the British royal family!). But the real monsters are Hollywood big shots that villainized the people of West Virginia. The governor of West Virginia should have sued the makers of *"Wrong Turn"* for slandering his entire state's populace by promoting loaded stereotypes depicting the people who live in Appalachia as psychotic cannibalistic retards.

Most people say that movies are only entertainment. So was *Song of the South*, which got banned. If a Disney cartoon promoting racism isn't acceptable, movies promoting classism shouldn't be either.

We all need some form of entertainment. But what we get to choose from is limited to the selections presented to us. If it's not on the menu, it's not an option. The entertainment industry targets white, heterosexual men from the middle to upper-middle classes. Games, movies, and TV shows do not need objectification or themes of classism in order to appeal to the public and make a buck. It's a deliberate choice to diminish those who are marginalized. Diminishing marginalized groups dehumanizes them and preserves a status quo of unfair advantages derived from unearned social class privileges.

Take for example the Elder Scrolls game Oblivion with its superior graphics. There are no overweight characters. There are no children or pregnant women in any role, never mind in the role of a key character. In order to get information needed to complete many of the quests in the game, your character must sometimes bribe poor homeless minor characters (none of which are young, thin, and "attractive" looking) in which your character says, "Have a coin, beggar" which is met by the response, "Thank you kind lady/sir." What we choose for entertainment is not necessarily what we want; it's what we get to choose from. Restricting options restricts choices. And what we want is shaped by what's available.

When those who are more fortunate fear or despise those on the margins as "the Other", they develop an attitude of "why should we help *those* people?" Those who have been socially and economically excluded are not seen as being a part of society. They are not valued or acknowledged and those who are better off would rather forget them and pretend they don't exist.

British sociologist Peter Morrell opined during a 2001 conference on poverty about the social exclusion of the poor, saying that the poor need to be included in society and "not just fobbed off with hand-outs." While it is true that those struggling in poverty need to be socially included in society, it is also true that adequate social support for meeting basic physiological needs cannot be left out of the equation. Economists have yet to derive an economy that works for everyone's benefit in society. Therefore, it is fair to say that "hand-outs" will be necessary because there will always be those who are unemployable and who still need (and deserve) to be able to live with dignity.

Older people and those who are limited because of medical problems or disabilities are not going to be able to improve their lives if nobody will give them a chance for a job that they *can* do. And it is necessary that such a job pays a living wage – especially if a debt load of college education was one of the prerequisites for the job. The long-term unemployed (who are mostly the middle-aged) need much better social support when they're systematically left out because there are not enough jobs to go around for everyone.

Society treats the long-term unemployed as if there is something wrong with them. They're viewed as defective by society due to the misconception that if they were not personally deficient, they wouldn't have been passed over by employers. People look down on the long-term unemployed as if their inability to get a job was solely their fault; that they failed to "retool" and keep a "positive attitude" even though their lives are falling apart, that they failed to "make the right choices" – not that something is wrong with the job market or that changes need to be made in our superficial society which discards those who aren't sexy-looking 20-something year old "eye candy."

The long-term unemployed are bombarded with the message of "you must be doing *something* wrong if no one is hiring you." Age, appearance, weight, gender, and disability discrimination is not recognized as a significant part of the problem. Middle-aged and/or overweight women earn an average of 12% less than their thinner, prettier peers (who *still* only earn 72 cents for every dollar earned by white men), and are unemployed for much longer periods of time. Those who didn't luck out in the gene pool crap shoot for looks, body type, and weight; and those who committed the sin of aging are the last socially acceptable group to abuse and discriminate against[6]. It is legal and

---

[6] In 2004, ABC's show "20/20" investigated appearance discrimination in the job market and confirmed that "lookism" leaves "unattractive" jobseekers at a disadvantage in hiring; they're penalized by as much as 12% less in earnings than their more attractive looking co-workers.

acceptable to discriminate against the overweight and the toothless for jobs, thanks to social engineering by mass media. Although appearance discrimination has devastating economic, psychological, and social consequences, its victims have no legal recourse.

The "body fascism" that is so prevalent in the US job market is also becoming a serious problem in Great Britain as well. Researchers from the University of Strathclyde[7] found in their 2005 study that most women (and some men) can actually become unemployable because they're not sufficiently "good-looking". Women who are poor and unable to afford healthy foods, fitness club memberships, liposuction, good dental care, and Botox shots are especially vulnerable to being denied jobs for being "too ugly" or "too fat." This appearance-obsessed culture pervades all areas of service sector employment, from the ivory towers of academia to banking to call centers. The extent of the problem faced disproportionately by middle-aged women and/or overweight women with below-average looks made the limelight with the case of Laura Zubulake, a 44 year old Wall Street executive who was fired in 2001 by her employer, UBS Warburg, because she was "old and ugly." Although Ms. Zubulake was awarded $15.5 million in damages on the grounds of age and sex discrimination, most job discrimination victims never get anything at all.

The Strathclyde study was based on a survey of 150 bosses and 128 male and female employees working in service industries, including hotels and restaurants. Dr. Singh, an expert on women and businesses, said [of the Strathclyde study] that "in the US, you have to be perfect."

The impact of weight and appearance discrimination was brought to the forefront of the public's attention in 2004 when *20/20* investigated appearance discrimination in the job market. The show hired four people: two men and two women. Both genders were represented by one very attractive looking person and one average to below-average looking person to test the effects of physical attractiveness in job interviews. The four "job seekers" were all given identical credentials

[7] Karl Ashworth and Sue Middleton, University of Strathclyde 2005 study on "unattractiveness" and its socio-economic penalties.

and experience and trained to act and speak in the same manner, leaving their looks as the only differentiating factor. For both genders, the very attractive looking candidate was offered the job and treated better while the less attractive looking ones didn't get hired.

An earlier study in 1998 done by Biddle and Hamermesh tracking the careers and earnings of lawyers found that earnings discrepancies based on appearance were present. Biddle and Hamermesh determined that the more attractive looking attorneys were billing at higher rates, not billing more hours. This indicated that attractive looking attorneys were paid more for doing the same amount of work as their less-attractive looking colleagues. Looks determine earning opportunity, and who can afford good looks is an unearned social class privilege. There is no meritocracy when one is judged "unworthy" for a job, fair pay, and dating and marriage opportunities based solely on their looks when everyone does not have the same advantage of birth or the financial resources to take care of their appearance.

Since the poor and the working class can't afford expensive cosmetic surgery to correct physical flaws that society has deemed unacceptable, those on the bottom socio-economic rungs don't have the ability to invest in getting the "right" image. They don't have access to quality dental care, including dental implants and crowns or even dentures so they don't have to face prospective employers with an appearance that will cause them to be rejected. Looks matter a lot. People treat you according to the way you look in all aspects of society. Looks and social class status go together like peas and carrots. For women who are fat or who have dental problems, lack of money to correct those problems is a social, economic and marital death sentence.

Our plutocratic culture also treats its upper-middle class males according to their status based on the upper class WASP-defined physical attractiveness of the women they have on their arm at conferences, political events, and quasi-social business meetings at the country club.

No male of the status-seeking middle class wants to be caught dead in public with "the fat girl" or the "plain Jane" with dental problems or severe acne who is a "3" on a "10" scale. His boss, peers, and even his own family will disrespect him and say, "What are you doing with *that* when you can get better?" He will suffer social repercussions if he doesn't dump Miss Frumpy Fatso. He will be silently passed over for promotion up the executive pipeline. He will be denied partner at the law firm or uninvited to a critically important upscale university faculty dinner event where making the "right" impressions on the "right" department heads and others determine one's consideration for a coveted tenure track position.

An aspiring status-seeking man in our culture of "get ahead at all costs" who can't land that "9" or "10" 20-young babe is considered a "loser" if all he can get is the "5" or "6." Such men are frequently referred to as "beta" males and they comprise about 80% of the male population. Therefore, they're most likely to be "pump and dump" types which helps explain part of the poor single mother problem since most women aren't Angelina Jolie. In our society, women are valued solely on their looks.

What does it say about a society that discards its unattractive, overweight, pregnant, and older people? Why isn't this shallow cruelty acknowledged in discussions concerning those who have been sentenced to poverty due to appearance/age/weight discrimination in the job market and passed over for dating and marriage? Isn't it fair to say they end up poor through no fault of their own if they're left on the shelf, and left unable to earn any money to support themselves while they're also begrudged medical and dental care and adequate income support so they can live independently with a little bit of dignity?

Like appearance discrimination, poverty profiling in hiring practices is legal. Since it is socially accepted, nobody sees it as a problem and they don't see why it's wrong. Instead, everyone in mainstream society blames those suffering in poverty due to long-term unemployment by saying that there is something wrong with them. Adding insult to injury, those who have been reduced to poverty due to long-term joblessness and/or failure to land an economically stable husband are told by everybody else to "stop complaining because nobody wants to hear it."

What does it do to a person to deny them an equal opportunity in our economy? What effect does it have on a person who is denied the right to participate in society, and then told that it's their own fault if they're not making it? How would you feel if you were being excluded? What if you weren't getting your basic needs met and everybody else told you to shut up because "nobody wants to hear it?"

Victims of discrimination and social exclusion will only tolerate so much before things come to a head. The Watts riots in south central Los Angeles and the IRA bombings and retaliation against British oppression in Northern Ireland are two examples of that on a macro level. For too long, disenfranchised groups suffered in poverty and were told to suck it up and take it; to "stop complaining because nobody wants to hear it" until one act of social injustice too many proved to be the spark that ignited the tinderbox.

Class shapes values, customs, norms, and communication styles. These things determine how people act, speak, and dress in social settings, schools, and workplaces. Class also correlates to rates of mental illness[8]. As social class decreases, mental illness and stress-related sicknesses increase. The higher level of stress associated with constant deprivation of basic needs and social exclusion is a major reason for higher rates of mental illness among the lower social classes. Nothing is more chronically stressful than the poverty trap and lack of opportunity for social mobility to improve one's life.

Class shapes educational opportunity and educational experience. Teachers in public schools are mostly from middle class backgrounds and therefore, they relate more positively with students whose backgrounds mirror their own. Class shapes the political climate

---

[8] A national survey in 1994 showed that people who earned $19,000/year or less were twice as likely to suffer depression or anxiety disorders than those who earned $70,000/year or more.

and voter turnout. People vote in accordance with their socio-economic class interests. Class also shapes American jurisprudence.

People from the lower classes don't commit more crimes, but their crimes are often exaggerated and reported in a one-sided slant by the media and result in harsher punishment. A poor man who passes bad checks to get money for the rent or who steals a loaf of bread because he is hungry and desperate will serve several years of hard prison time, whereas the CEO who embezzles millions and bankrupts the corporation he was entrusted to run, ruining thousands of lives in the process, gets sentenced to a "white collar" prison that is more like a country club than a penitentiary — *if* he's convicted. Nowhere is the power differential due to classism more obvious than in our criminal justice system.

Those in the higher social classes tend to view the police as "protectors" charged with keeping law and order in society. The police are agents who serve them and protect their interests: their property. In contrast, those from poverty often see the police as jackbooted, fascist, militaristic thugs who are out to get them and who will liberally use violence that wouldn't even be legal at Guantanamo.

On Monday, May 13th 1985 two weeks before I graduated from high school, a feat in and of itself in a rough Philadelphia school district, my sister sent two of her friends, Steve and Pete Dedoljce (two more members of society's "throw-away" caste) to meet me at my high school. Wild-eyed with panic, Steve shouted, "Mayor Goode lost it, man! He's blowing up the whole fuckin' city!" I was 17 years old and not quite able to process what Steve and Pete were telling me. It didn't sink in until I was about half way home.

The powers-that-be were so determined to fulfill a decade-long vendetta against MOVE (a leftist group with a majority black membership), that the risk of collateral damage no longer mattered. I didn't know if my sister and I still had a place to live, or if everything but the clothes on our backs had gone up in flames.

Less than a mile from our apartment building, the Philadelphia police department eagerly acting on the orders of Mayor Wilson Goode dropped a C-4 bomb on the home of MOVE leaders John and Ramona Africa at 6221 Osage Avenue moments after the police Commissioner shouted through a bullhorn, "*Attention, MOVE! This is America!*"

The tactical assault which left 6 unarmed adults and 5 children dead turned the surrounding neighborhoods into a war zone: 61 homes were destroyed by the explosion and fire, leaving close to 300 people homeless. The C-4 bomb that turned the home of John and Ramona Africa into a 2,000 degree inferno started a string of fires among the Powelton Village row homes. When MOVE people tried to escape the blaze carrying their animals and children, they were driven back into the burning house by gunfire from the police who emptied 10,000 rounds of ammunition into the home at the occupants. The fire department stood by and refused to douse the flames, causing the fire to spread, on order of the police. Only two MOVE members survived: 29 year old Ramona Africa, who escaped with third degree burns over much of her body. She crawled through a basement window carrying 13 year old Birdie Africa.

Although our place was unscathed, the city was under siege. Police on horseback chased and trampled everyone in those poor areas, especially black people, and beat them with night sticks. Several black kids whose faces I recognized from one of the surrounding neighborhoods were shaking in terror, hiding in the hallway of our apartment building. We sat with them, all of us just holding onto each other and crying, because we were afraid, too.

Being poor street urchins ourselves, we instinctively knew to avoid the police because poor white "throw-away" kids are not treated much better than poor black kids by the authorities. Even though a poor white girl is not typically the primary target for malevolent police brutality like poor black kids are, it is nonetheless demoralizing and frightening to witness it or be caught in its midst because it sends the message, "this is what we'll do to *you* if you side with "those people" or step out of line in *any* way."

Before Philadelphia's first black mayor, Wilson Goode, marshaled the might of the notoriously corrupt and violently fascist

Philadelphia police force in the incendiary climax on May 13th, 1985, repressive attacks against MOVE had been carried out by the police since Frank Rizzo was Police Commissioner (1968-1971) and subsequently mayor (1972-1980). Rizzo, a proud male chauvinist and racist, began his career as a Philly cop who rose through the ranks to Commissioner during an era when the "City of Brotherly Love" of over a million people had not one single woman or minority on its police force.

Like so many other tough guys who are among the ranks of society's "winners", Frank Rizzo got his foot in the door by virtue of unearned privilege: white male privilege. And like so many of his ideological peers who believed that poor women should be kept barefoot and pregnant and denied equal opportunities and that blacks need to be kept down and "in their place", Rizzo rejected the notion that women and minorities should get equal social and economic rights. He was voraciously committed to safeguarding middle class white male privilege by forcibly keeping poor people under the heel of patriarchal capitalism's boot. And being a cop gave him the legal authority to do it.

When MOVE had their home on 33rd Street in the racially diverse impoverished North Philadelphia neighborhood where I had lived for many years, they were subjected to routine harassment and brutality from the police force under Rizzo's command. MOVE resisted the injustices of poverty and discrimination imposed by capitalism. They were the marginalized poor and largely non-white precursor to today's trendy affluent liberal vegan movements and animal rights groups. They were doing then what Food - Not Bombs and PETA does now, except they weren't upper-middle class college students.

MOVE promoted a non-materialistic lifestyle, stressing vegetarian diets and daily exercise, they grew vegetable gardens with organic compost, rescued stray dogs and sheltered them, and heated with firewood as a response to PGW's unaffordable gas utility rates that were out of reach for the poor *before* deregulation. MOVE also did what the charitable machinations of "free enterprise" capitalism failed to do: they provided mentoring and nutritious community meals for poor hungry neighborhood kids and they strove to solve the problem of gangs and crime arising from the despair that crushing poverty brings. MOVE was also very vigilant in their protests of racial discrimination, pet shops and the zoo where animals were exploited and mistreated. Their activity was deemed "anti-American", "militant black nationalist" and "Communist", resulting in police harassment and arrests for picayune violations that middle and upper class people would never even get a scolding for, much less arrested. MOVE's protests also prompted fatal attacks by the authorities who often targeted MOVE members' babies and pregnant women — in the name of "maintaining law and order."

During his position as Police Commissioner, Frank Rizzo publicly bragged that his cops made "Attila the Hun look like a faggot", claiming that the Philadelphia police force could "invade Cuba." Rizzo was elected mayor in 1972 for his "tough on crime" stance which really meant "protect middle and upper class white male privilege." Rizzo initiated police assaults against MOVE on May 9th 1974 resulting in two pregnant MOVE members, Janet and Leesing Africa, miscarrying after being beaten by cops and jailed without food, water or medical attention for 24 hours.

On April 29th 1975, police dragged pregnant Alberta Africa from her holding cell, pinned her to the concrete floor, and stomped on her stomach and kicked her repeatedly in the groin until she miscarried. On March 18th 1976 after seven MOVE members were released from jail and were being welcomed by their community and family members in front of their home, the Philadelphia police rolled up and set upon the unarmed crowd of men, women and children. MOVE members tried to defend themselves, but they were outmanned and outgunned by the Philadelphia police. One MOVE member, Janine Africa, who had recently given birth, was hurled to the ground and stomped on by police while she was holding her three week old newborn, Life Africa. Police stomped on the baby too, crushing its fragile skull.

Not one member of the Philadelphia police force was ever arrested for the murder of little Life Africa. The Philadelphia police department denied the murder even happened, saying that there was no proof that the baby ever existed since there was no official birth certificate on file with the Pennsylvania Bureau of Vital Records (registering births was not automatic in Pennsylvania in the 1970's).

Throughout the repressive violent attacks by the Philadelphia police, the mainstream establishment news media was sympathetic to the police and painted MOVE as a group of "armed and angry black radicals" and "militant Communists", ignoring the vicious beatings of pregnant women and newborn babies resulting in broken bones and death. The establishment media never cared when it was *poor* women and babies being bludgeoned by police, especially poor women and babies of color.

In response to mainstream media's deliberate effort to demonize a populist movement of economically marginalized people and racial minorities while refraining from reporting the repressive acts committed by jackboot terrorists in uniform, MOVE took matters into their own hands out of desperation. They constructed a platform in front of their home and took turns as guards, and told their side of the story by speaking through megaphones to make sure everybody heard what they otherwise wouldn't through KYW news radio and other local news media.

Mayor Rizzo escalated the conflict in 1978 by ordering the Philadelphia police to seal off a four-block perimeter around the MOVE home in North Philly, blocked food supplies from coming in, and shut off the water supply to the neighborhood. Sympathetic people from outside of this embargo zone were mercilessly beaten up by police and arrested when they tried to bring potable water and food to the pregnant women, nursing mothers, and children inside the MOVE home. The federal authorities finally stepped in after the 60 day siege and starvation blockade, putting pressure on the Philadelphia police for its violations of civil rights. Police relented on the condition that MOVE members leave their home, and preferably leave the city. Growing impatient with the time it was taking a grassroots group of poor people without the resources that middle class people take for granted, the Philadelphia police once again took matters into their own hands.

On August 8th 1978 under Rizzo's order, the home of MOVE members John Africa, Ramona Africa, Delbert Africa, Mike Africa, Sr., Merle Africa, Phil Africa, Eddie Africa, Chuck Africa, Debbie Africa, Janet Africa and Janine Africa in the heart of poverty-stricken North Philly was besieged by demolishers and police armed with grenades and tear gas. Hundreds of cops clad in riot gear accompanied by bulldozers and cranes began demolishing their home while the people, including small children, were trapped inside. MOVE members barricaded themselves in the basement, in fear of their lives as their home was being demolished over their heads, terrified of a racist police department that previously and indiscriminately used deadly force on pregnant women and babies.

Mayor Rizzo got the Philadelphia fire department to aid in the attack by setting water cannons on the MOVE home, flooding the basement until the water reached over six feet deep. Frightened women held babies and MOVE's rescued/adopted animals above their heads so they wouldn't drown in the deluge. Philadelphia police expended 2,000 rounds of ammunition into the home, aimed toward the basement towards the direction of screaming women and children. Policeman James Ramp was shot in the melee. Although MOVE was blamed for that, it was physically impossible for anyone to take aim and shoot upwards from a basement filling with gushing water that was sending railroad ties (used as fencing) careening like missiles through the basement window. KYW reporters Larry Rosen and John McCullough recalled the shot that killed Ramp coming from a third floor window across the street, seeing an arm holding a gun. Nevertheless, MOVE was blamed for the officer's death.

When the police finally forced MOVE out of the basement, they took the kids and viciously beat the adults. At a press conference later that same afternoon, Mayor Rizzo openly declared his intent to kill every last MOVE member to get rid of them, vowing to "put them in the electric chair" and pull the switch himself. Eight of the "MOVE 9" remain in prison to this day; one died in prison. They're serving sentences of 30-100 years each on charges relating to conspiracy and third degree murder for the death of Officer James Ramp. It should be noted that the same newspapers that ran impassioned headlines about the officer slain in the line of duty never once used the power of the pen to inform its predominantly middle class readership of the brutal beatings administered to poor pregnant women and the stomping death of a newborn infant by the police.

When you're poor and resistant to state-sponsored terrorism and a classist, racist, misogynistic system, you can be assaulted with impunity and have your baby stomped to death, and then get convicted and imprisoned for the crimes committed against you by a fascist, militaristic police force.

Former Black Panther member and famous black journalist Mumia Abu-Jamal had been documenting and reporting the truth about police brutality against MOVE. He was the *only* journalist who wrote the truth about the level of police repression targeting marginalized people and leftist groups that agitated for social and economic justice for the poor. He paid the ultimate price for his integrity: he was framed for the shooting death of Philadelphia police officer Daniel Faulkner in 1981 and convicted by an all white middle class jury and sentenced to death by Judge Albert Sabo who assured the Philadelphia police department that he would help them "fry that nigger."

Mumia Abu-Jamal remains on death row today where he still writes. He used his literary talent to muster international support. Dignitaries from France and other European nations called for Mumia's conviction to be vacated and for Mumia to be released. It's no secret that the poor young black man who had an FBI dossier since the age of 14 for simply using the power of the pen to be a "voice for the voiceless" was framed and remains America's most famous political prisoner on death row.

When you're poor but educated, you are a nemesis to the privileged classes whose interests the police protect and serve. Law enforcement was created to protect the interests of private property from the property-less, and guard the wealth of those who have benefited from a legacy of unearned privilege that enabled them to acquire that wealth and property. The justice system is designed to incarcerate and kill in the interests of privilege. On the most benign level, it is a system of cronyism designed to bleed the poor for their last dime through a system of fines. When you're poor, the policeman is not your friend.

Anatole France once said that "the law, in its majestic equality, forbids the rich as well as the poor to sleep under bridges, to beg in the streets, and to steal bread." Out of one hundred interviewees from the lowest income quintile from three different municipalities in three different states, 87% responded that they were pulled over and harassed by police who had managed to find *something* to fine them for. They were not speeding or driving recklessly. But they lived in the "wrong" areas. Their cars were "beaters." They were targeted for living while poor. The police didn't care about the hardships that fines impose on those in poverty; if paying the fine in order to avoid drivers' license suspension or jail for nonpayment of the fines translated to going hungry, not paying the rent (resulting in eviction), and having utilities shut off.

There is very good reason for poor people to mistrust the police. Policemen are the Praetorian guard for the middle and upper classes who despise and fear the poor. Police see the poor as easy targets for fines and trumped up charges because the poor can't afford to fight back (thanks to eliminated funding for legal aid for the poor). Being poor means an automatic label of "criminal." When you're poor and live in a ghetto, you're automatically presumed to be guilty of something. Most of the crimes committed by the poor are illegal drug sales out of economic desperation and lack of any real job opportunity.

While welfare and subsidized housing was cut for the poor, spending for incarceration burgeoned. Public spending for the prison industry went from $33 billion in 1990 to $216 billion in 2010, an increase of 660%. The largest increase in incarceration rates for the poor happened under Clinton's watch when "welfare as we know it" ended. During the 1990's the federal corrections budget increased by $19 billion while the federal budget for subsidized housing under HUD was slashed by $17 billion.[9] A nation that discards its poor to "balance the budget" for more money than it costs to help the poor does not practice the "personal responsibility" it preaches. Our society really hates the poor and will spend money to destroy the poor before spending that same amount to help the poor. This was done in the name of "law and order" as poverty itself was criminalized.

For example, take a semi-skilled $8 an hour worker who loses his job to globalization. Unemployed and alienated by a society that doesn't care and blames him for his poverty, he turns to the drug economy or other illegal means of survival. He gets arrested, incarcerated, and given a new job at 22 cents an hour in prison. He went from worker to unemployed to criminal to convict laborer. The only winner is big business. AR-210-35, the Civilian Inmate Labor program, is the goose that lays golden eggs for wealthy corporations. There's no unionizing, no strikes, no unemployment benefits, no workers' compensation, and no social security taxes for businesses to worry about. Inmates across the US do data entry for Chevron, take telephone reservations for TWA, and raise livestock. They also make electronic components, waterbeds, and lingerie for Victoria Secret.

When poor people can't pay their traffic tickets, they get picked up on a bench warrant and sent to jail – which costs them their jobs (if they're employed) and/or custody of their children. The more jails that have to be built to warehouse poor people for failure to pay fines or delinquent child support in addition to the drug offenders, the more money in federal tax dollars goes to the communities where prisons are built. Someone benefits from these contracts. But it's not the taxpayers and it's certainly not the poor. The beneficiaries are businesses using prison labor, private prison corporations, and the investor class who own shares of stock in those with vested interests in our for-profit prison-industrial complex. There are two corporate behemoths that dominate the privatized prison industry in the US: Corrections Corporation of America

---

[9] James Carroll, "The Prison Boom Comes Home to Roost", *The Boston Globe*, November 8th 2010

and GEO Group (formerly known as Wackenhut)[10]. These two outfits control 75% of the for-profit prison industry.

Many state and county prisons even charge inmates money for basic needs ranging from medical care to soap, toothpaste, toilet paper, and use of the prison law library. Many prisons also charge "room and board." Berks County prison in Pennsylvania charges inmates $10 per day to be there. The only way inmates can meet these "obligations" is if they have friends and family who are willing and able to put money on their commissary books, and if they work under the prison's contract with private industry for the average inmate pay of 22 cents an hour. Although the government cannot technically force inmates to work in private industry jobs for less than the federal minimum wage, inmates are forced to do so by proxy.

The incarceration industry is a growing nightmare of forced slave labor, disenfranchisement, and state repression to isolate large segments of the poor while building up large reactionary forces to repress those at the bottom. As of December 1999, 1 in every 143 US citizens was incarcerated[11]. Assuming incarceration rates remain the same, an estimated 1 in every 20 Americans can expect to be incarcerated during their lifetime. For black men, the rate is greater than 1 in 4. There is a noticeable correlation between the growth of the prison-industrial complex and the flight of capital. Ever since the Reagan-Bush, Sr. era of the 1980's and early 1990's, the working class has been besieged with union-busting, corporate deregulation, dismantling of civil rights, and the flight of capital seeking the havens of cheaper labor markets. The gaping economic chasm created by the jobs exodus in nearly every community across the United States was quickly filled by the illegal drugs economy, courtesy of the Mafia in league with the CIA.

The prison-industrial complex is very profitable for the middle and upper classes that have stock portfolios, the owners of investment

[10] *"The Prison-Industrial Complex and the Global Economy"*, Linda Evans and Eve Goldberg, 1999.

[11] Beck, Allen J., PhD, and Paige M. Harrison, US Department of Justice, Bureau of Justice Statistics, Prisoners in 2000. (Washington DC: US Dept. of Justice, August 2001), pp. 1-2

brokerage firms, and hedge fund managers. Investment firm Saloman Smith Barney is part owner of a Florida prison. American Express and GE are vested stakeholders in private prison construction in Oklahoma and Tennessee. Telecommunication companies also jumped on the prison contract bandwagon. AT&T, Sprint, and MCI profit enormously off the backs of the poor families of inmates via price-gouging with the hyper-inflated prison telephone system rates that are billed to inmates' families when the prisoner calls collect (which is the only way prisoners are able to call anyone on the outside).

Prisoners and their families are effectively cut off from communication due to the excessive rates. Since inmates are usually shipped to prisons hundreds of miles away from their home communities, and since inmates' families are mostly from the ranks of the poor; prisoners are unable to maintain any meaningful contact with their partners and children. Unaffordable prison phone rates sever what fragile ties remain, destroying the poorest and most vulnerable families.

The poor are easy targets because they're vulnerable. They create a ready supply of "raw material" to fill prisons as society's solution to poverty while creating a lucrative growth industry of incarceration-for-profit that enriches America's investor class. But being targeted by the police is not the only way the criminal justice system is patently biased against the poor.

Consider jury selection. The majority of jurors in criminal trials return guilty verdicts based on the belief that the police would not have arrested someone if they weren't guilty of something. Middle class juries usually side with the police. They see the police as "their kind." It's unfathomable to them that the police routinely plant evidence, sell illegal drugs stolen from police evidence lockers, or withhold critical evidence from defense attorneys despite increasing reports exposing police corruption and prosecutorial misconduct.

Under the US Constitution, when you're arrested and charged with a crime you are entitled to representation by a lawyer and one will be appointed for you if you cannot afford one. You are also entitled to a trial by a jury of your peers. However, juries are largely middle class. What makes sense in the context of a middle class person's life is different than what makes sense in the context of the lives of those struggling in poverty. A defendant's actions, choices, and mannerisms may be wrongly interpreted due to social class differences in the life experiences of the middle class and the poor.

Can you *really* get a fair trial and impartial treatment in the courts with deeply entrenched classism? If you are from a culturally deprived home on the "wrong side of the tracks" and can't afford the "right image" and the jurors are all middle class, are those jurors *really* your peers when you're "not their kind?" How can they render an unbiased verdict when they look down on you due to lifelong social class conditioning by the media and highly credentialed policy "experts?"

How often are homeless people chosen for jury duty? How many migrant farm workers have been selected for jury duty? How many jurors that get selected live in subsidized housing scraping to survive on food stamps and a meager $600 a month SSI check?

The "war on drugs" and the mandatory minimum laws for drug related offenses is another example. It is perfectly okay for the medical constabulary, in exchange for sweetheart deals with pharmaceutical companies, to prescribe drugs to the public with well-known dangerous side effects. But it's not okay for the drug dealer to sell a "street" drug like marijuana that has been proven effective in the treatment of glaucoma with less harmful side effects in addition to other practical uses such as making paper, clothing, and hemp-crete.

When you're from the higher social classes, you can afford to get prescription antidepressants, painkillers, and tranquilizers to help you cope with inordinate amounts of stress in your life. The well-heeled can develop dangerous pharmaceuticals and obtain patents for drugs like Zyban, Chantrix, Viagra, Vioxx, Xanax, Ritalin, and Prozac and get even richer as a result. But the poor marijuana dealer gets to go to prison. They don't reap monetary rewards from price-gouging the public with runaway drug prices, or enjoy the residual benefits of patent and trademark rights. They get their few meager personal possessions seized under RICO laws. No royalties for them!

The phony war on drugs is really part of a concerted effort by rich corporate interests to subdue a potentially restive populace; a pre-emptive strike. Lock up poor people before they get angry. Target and imprison those at the bottom of the socio-economic ladder. The war on drugs has not diminished drug use. But it has taken millions of unemployed and disenfranchised young people off the streets and created a burgeoning prison population to feed the prison/industrial complex – which has been bolstered with "Three Strikes" laws and mandatory minimum sentencing. The war on drugs is really a war on the poor.

It isn't only the drug laws that are classist and which disproportionately hurt the poor. Any offense punishable by fines has a disparate impact on the poor compared to the effect those fines have on those who have resources. Laws such as Zoning and Code Enforcement which allow for unaffordable fines and unreasonable compliance timeframes are set up specifically to target and punish the poor.

When your choices are paying the gas bill so you don't freeze to death in the winter and can have hot water to bathe with, or paying the water/sewer/refuse bill so your water isn't shut off and your garbage pick-up cancelled, buying materials and supplies to repair the exterior of your house is not high on the priority list. There are no local volunteer organizations in Erie, Pennsylvania that assist low income older homeowners with code violation correction repairs. Lower income homeowners are unable to afford to bring their homes out of disrepair within the 30 day timeframe mandated by the Office of Zoning & Code Enforcement.

A $300 fine issued by the magistrate for zoning/code violations is an annoying inconvenience for someone in the middle class with a decent income. But for someone who is on a very low fixed income of less than $1,200/mo struggling to pay their $525/mo mortgage and escrow payment, a $300 fine for failure to comply with code corrections within 30 days is an unjust hardship.

It is hard to afford a $525/mo mortgage payment on an older, modest, inner-city home with such a low fixed income. But it's even harder to afford rent for a crappy apartment where you are one rent increase, one sickness, one car breakdown, or one job loss away from eviction and homelessness. When you're struggling just to afford food, utilities, Medicare co-pays, and a mortgage for a humble home in the poorer side of town, being slapped with a $300 fine triggers an avalanche of problems that can be a life and death matter.

Being told by a callous magistrate that you must pay that fine — foregoing your rent/mortgage payment (resulting in homelessness), foregoing food and going hungry, or foregoing a utility bill resulting in winter heat shut-offs because if you can't pay the fine you go to jail — is *not* justice. It's cruel and unusual punishment. It's deliberate indifference. For someone who is elderly or disabled on a very low fixed income, that fine causes far more hardship than the "crime" warrants. But for someone in the middle class, that same $300 fine is a mere nuisance.

Non-uniform enforcement of housing code laws is classism. Municipalities do not enforce these laws fairly. They do so by "selective enforcement[12]." In Erie, Pennsylvania where I live, wealthy slum landlords who own multiple rental properties are rarely, if ever, penalized – especially if they're Italian, male, middle class, and well-connected. Low income homeowners such as the elderly or disabled get the book thrown at them without any consideration for the reality of their situations on extremely low incomes. Conversely, it is the rental properties of rich slumlords that tend to pose the most health and safety hazards. But wealthy slumlords have plenty of money to afford legal appeals.

Since magistrates tend to be from the upper-middle class, their social networks include wealthy influential businessmen. If you are a

---

[12] Selective enforcement in code/zoning laws means that your neighbor might be able to get away with violating the same codes that you get fined for, while you get harassed by code officers and fined by the magistrate. Selective enforcement is based on the premise that the citations and fines were the result of an "anonymous complaint" where you're denied the right to face your accusers.

struggling self-employed entrepreneur in a small town who might threaten market share competition from one of the local big shots, and that big shot is the magistrate's golfing buddy and part of a privileged good ole boy network, your wealthier competitor can use his social ties with the magistrate to cause you undue harassment and unaffordable fines for zoning and code violations.

Magistrates also look down on the poor. They're not impartial adjudicators. Being too poor to be able to pay a fine for a summary offense is a greater crime than embezzlement or murder. They don't care that the poor senior citizen or disabled person will face homelessness as a result of unaffordable fines for code violations on their humble homes that they can't afford to remediate. They also don't care about poor renters who have to live with substandard plumbing, rodents, and vermin in rental units owned by greedy slumlords.

I have personally experienced social class bias with respect to Erie's selective enforcement of code and zoning laws, and the kangaroo court of a magistrate known for forcing poor people to pay unaffordable fines for code violations at the expense of going hungry and losing their homes under threat of going to jail for non-payment of fines. Although I cannot prove it, I suspect that Magistrate Lafaver's golfing buddy wanted to grab my property for a fire sale price and saw economically abusing me through the city's zoning and code enforcement office as a means to an end.

When you're struggling just to keep from losing your modest home, trying to survive with one or more utilities shut off because of not having any money (or a chance to earn any money) to pay the bills, home repairs take a backseat. We just didn't have the money to get all the code violations fixed within the 30 days we were given by Joe Cilladi, the City of Erie Code Enforcement Officer who harassed us unjustly. It should be noted that since issuance of citations from code enforcement is selective and not uniformly applied, there are other properties on our street in far worse shape whose owners have not been harassed and fined into destitution like we were.

Selective enforcement also means that the low income homeowner being harassed by Code Enforcement is denied the right to face their accuser and know who called and filed the complaint with Code Enforcement, and denied the right to challenge malicious prosecution.

We can't even afford to have our gas service restored so we can have heat in the winter, hot water to bathe, and cooking. When you're choices are between paying the mortgage (or rent), your electric and phone bill while hoping your water isn't shut off next, money for code violation corrections isn't on the radar. But those with power, authority, and privilege don't care. They're selfish. They've got theirs – tough shit if you don't have yours.

My husband is 25 years older than me. He is in his sixties and is disabled with a heart condition. He also developed a hernia which he has not been able to get treated because he is a cardiac patient on Medicaid and Medicare. I have no healthcare at all. Being poor, our health needs don't get taken care of. Even if we had the income to afford our basic bills and food plus enough left over to buy the materials and do all the work ourselves, his health problems make it impossible. When my husband tried explaining our situation at the hearing to appeal the crushing code violation fines Magistrate Joseph Lafaver sneered, "Mr. Homan, I don't care about your health problems or your money problems. The law is the law."

The magistrate put us on a payment plan for the fines for a monthly amount beyond what we could afford on our extremely low income. We just couldn't pay – unless we opted to starve or end up homeless by taking it from the mortgage payment. A state constable was sent out with bench warrants to arrest my husband, a senior citizen on heart medications with back problems and a hernia. He could die in jail for all that magistrate and the City of Erie Code Enforcement and Zoning Office cares. This is one of many crimes of poverty in what is supposed to be a free country where no one is unjustly oppressed based on race, sex, age, religion, or socio-economic status.

Our nation's founders did not envision a country where you could be put into an early grave from being made to suffer undue hardship caused directly by malicious prosecution and legal harassment just because you're poor. But our founders apparently never lived in Erie, PA – a small Mafia town ran by a handful of greedy rich Italian good ole boys that control everything from who gets a chance for a job, who gets no opportunity at all, and who gets crushed with unaffordable building code fines and then thrown into jail for being unable to pay without the right to face the accuser in court.

Class privilege is being one of the fortunate sons who create policy and laws that crush the poor and most vulnerable while violating the law themselves. It should be noted that the justice system rarely prosecutes wealthy slum landlords who force poor tenants to live in squalor. I challenge anyone to prove that this is fair and just when it reeks from the stench of classism.

Class shapes our perspective and attitudes. The higher one's social class, the greater chance there is for personal success, and therefore more reason for optimism and a positive attitude. If something gets broken, there is money or access to credit to fix or replace it. Everything always works. For people in poverty, nothing works out.

Poor people face teachers who alienate them and schools that can't teach them. They face employers who won't hire them so they won't be poor. They face police who harass and abuse them. They face doctors and dentists who won't treat them because they're uninsured and can't pay for care — they've been priced out by our for-profit healthcare system. They face social agencies that don't help them and encounter caseworkers who don't care – they're paid the same salary whether you get helped or not. The poor live near stores that can't sell to them because they can't afford anything. They are constantly confronted by the luxuries, wealth and social acceptance enjoyed by others that they don't get a fair chance to obtain.

Classism is the elephant in the room that everyone pretends doesn't exist. It is present in our houses of worship, our living rooms, the job market, and even in the check-out line in the local supermarket. America is a classless society, we are told. We are told that we all have an equal opportunity to succeed if we only try hard enough, work hard enough, and live right. But we are told wrong.

Classism is the last legally permissible, socially acceptable barrier in access to jobs, housing, medical and dental care, and fair adjudication. Classism is a very destructive prejudice that promotes and perpetuates social injustice against others. Call a university women's basketball team a "bunch of nappy-headed ho's" like Don Imus did you will be called on your racism and sexism. Wealthy black Texaco junior executives complained of racism when white junior executives referred to them as "jellybeans" and they won a substantial damage award on grounds of racial discrimination.

But when poor whites are called "uneducated", "trailer trash", and denied adequate employment opportunities as punishment for their conditions of poverty, this is somehow okay. Poor whites are marginal people – the only group in America that it is legal to discard and pillory for every conceivable social ill. Two words are proof of that: Lyndie England.

Lyndie England grew up in poverty in Fort Ashby West Virginia – a whistle stop town with one 7-Eleven, two bars, an ice cream joint and no job opportunities other than a filthy poultry plant where management cuts corners to boost profits at the expense of worker safety and public health. Corporations like Pilgrim's Pride can get away with compromising the quality of the chicken you buy and the safety of its workers when they're the only employer in a town full of poor whites that have been economically left behind. The median annual family income for Fort Ashby is $32,375, but half of Fort Ashby's residents earn far less.

Lyndie England's father is a CSX railroad utility worker; he earns roughly $1,500 per month, excluding overtime. No one in the family has a college degree. Lyndie's sister, Jessie, came close but had to quit halfway through her first semester at Potomac State College in

Keyser, West Virginia. The England family lives in a trailer on a $200/month gravel and dirt trailer park lot. On hot, humid summer days, the odor of manure from the neighboring farm permeates their neighborhood and home. Lyndie England had only one opportunity to *maybe* have a future, one chance to be able to travel, one chance to be able to afford a college education and escape the trailer park life of poor white trash hell: the military. She enlisted at the age of 17.

Unlike America's fortunate sons and daughters, poor young adults like Lyndie England only have the military as their sole opportunity for travel abroad. Lyndie's itinerary didn't include a trip to the Louve in Paris or the Swiss Alps. It was a trip to the middle of a war zone in the oppressive desert climate of Iraq. The sights she got to see were not the works of Holbein, Peter Paul Rubens, or Picasso. Her experience did not include tasting the finest of foods and wines while relaxing on the French Riviera or basking on the beaches in Monaco. Instead, her daily sustenance was MRE's.[13] She lived without creature comforts not knowing if every day would be her last. The sights she saw were that of her "battle buddies" getting blown up and those responsible in the *jihad* insurgency cells get off scot-free after being arrested by American and Iraqi authorities, tried in corrupt Sharia courts run by mullahs who hold women and non-Muslims in less esteem than camel dung.

Lyndie England was a very naïve girl from a backwater Appalachian town barely out of high school. At 19, she married a shy, quiet reserved man her age. She was easy prey for an older man like Sgt. Charles Graner: a fellow Abu Ghraib guard, a higher ranking soldier and a very worldly man who is 14 years older than she. Unknown to Lyndie at the time, Grainer had a history of violence dating back to Operation Desert Storm in the early 1990's. After his tour in the first Gulf war, he was hired as a corrections officer at SCI-Greene – a maximum security prison in rural southwestern Pennsylvania. SCI-Greene is hell on earth in the heart of God's country. While working as a prison guard at SCI-Greene, Graner and other guards tortured inmates and put a razor blade

---

[13] MRE: Military jargon for "Meals Ready to Eat."

in a prisoner's mashed potatoes. Graner also beat up his ex-wife, dragging her by her hair across their bedroom floor.

But Lyndie never knew about that side of Charles Graner. She saw the charming, outgoing, protectorate side. He followed Lyndie around and paid attention to her, acting like he really cared about her. She saw him as an alpha male "protector" with whom to entrust her safety and life in the violent and dangerous war zone in occupied Iraq. Lyndie saw kids her own age getting their arms and legs blown off by IED's (improvised explosive devices) from Iraqi insurgency cells. Graner was a social predator that saw the malleable 20 year old Lyndie as someone he could easily use and manipulate. Add to the fact that the military is truly a man's world founded on principles of intense misogyny, extreme homophobia, and white supremacy and you get the recipe for the perfect storm. That perfect storm was Abu Ghraib. The acceptance of women into the military ranks has not changed the misogynistic culture of that institution. The military instills in all of its soldiers a hatred of those who speak with funny accents, who are not white, not American, not male, and not straight.

Unlike a normal job in America, questioning or refusing to obey an order (no matter how ridiculous) from a higher ranking soldier in a combat zone is grounds for a court martial and time in the brig – military prison. When Sgt. Graner ordered Lyndie to hold that leash as he snapped the picture that was seen around the world and pose on cue with naked Iraqi prisoners, she did as she was told by her superior. In Lyndie's case, her superior was the 35 year old man who swept her off her feet, talked her into divorcing her husband, and having a relationship that eventually resulted in the pregnancy and birth of Lyndie's baby, Carter, whom Graner denies paternity and child support.

But the real question isn't why Lyndie England was so easily manipulated into participating in torture in a bloody desert war zone halfway around the world. The real question isn't why Charles Graner conned Lyndie into divorcing her husband in order to have his baby that he later decided he didn't want. The *real* question is *why* the general in charge of that operation passed on orders that violate the Geneva

Convention – orders that only subordinates would take the fall for – and why military intelligence *wanted to* put a known sociopath with a history of violence in charge of Iraqi prisoners at Abu Ghraib when he (Graner) and the others were Reservists who lacked professional training in proper interrogation protocol.

Graner was specifically assigned to that detail because he had a "commanding voice." When Grainer showed pictures documenting his abuse of the Iraqi prisoners to people from the CIA, the FBI, and military intelligence, they said, "Good job! Keep up the good work because we're getting great results." They gave Graner a letter of recommendation for what he was doing.

After the famous leash picture leaked out to the media and all over the Internet, Lyndie England and Charles Graner were prosecuted in military court. Each received a prison sentence, loss of duty pay, and a dishonorable discharge which will follow them for the rest of their lives. Lyndie England and Charles Graner should be held accountable for their actions. But we must seriously question the system that created this perfect storm; a system that started an unconstitutional war to secure more wealth and power for the multinational oil and natural gas cartels and their financiers – the world's bankers.

It is the poor from the ranks of "the other America" that are sent to war to protect the interests of capital and lose their sanity, their limbs, and their lives while the affluent remain coddled and secure in their status, wealth, and privilege. And it is discarded Americans from "the wrong side of the tracks" who take the fall for obeying the orders of their superior officers. The government and the wealthy that own it thinks nothing of exploiting desperate and naïve kids – they're a surplus.

Underprivileged young adults are promised generous sign on bonuses and a chance have their college education paid for by the military. They're promised medical and dental benefits. They're used as pawns for the purpose and agenda of America's wealthy, and those who occupy the highest ranks in government which only serves the interests capital.

The torture at Abu Ghraib and our government's refusal to adhere to the Geneva Convention and agree on the definition of "torture" is disturbing. The scandal of Abu Ghraib is an indelible stain on the face of America. But why is the public *not* outraged about the classism behind the Abu Ghraib scandal? Lyndie England was prosecuted for her role in Abu Ghraib prisoner abuses, sentenced to prison and dishonorably discharged, going down in history as the "trailer trash torturer." But Lt. General Ricardo Sanchez, who was in charge of operations in Iraq (including the protocol at Abu Ghraib), was rewarded with the rank of Brigadier General!

Rich and powerful men in positions of authority with affluence and social class privilege in our society – generals, CIA officials, and (former) Secretary of Defense Donald Rumsfeld – hid behind a poor, disenfranchised, learning-disabled 21 year old single mother from a West Virginia trailer park. Wealthy, powerful men running the show were the ones responsible for launching an illegal war, giving the orders, for altering the definition of the word "torture" to suit their agenda, and for scapegoating society's marginal people in the name of "fighting the war on terror."

It would be interesting to see if the outcome for Lyndie England would have been different had she looked like Angelina Jolie or Sharon Stone. Would the public have had more sympathy for her? Would she have been deployed to Iraq in the first place? Being lucky enough to be born beautiful provides the only hope for poor girls from the bowels of America's underclass for making it in a middle and upper class WASP male dominated society. The not-so-pretty girls can always join the military – no one cares if poor, ugly looking women are offered up as cannon fodder.

When poor women lose their teeth from lack of money and insurance to get dental care, our society ridicules them and denies them even the lowest paying jobs as cashiers because of how they look; perpetuating a vicious catch-22. You can't get dental care if you're poor and don't have a good job with health and dental benefits, but you can't get even a crappy minimum wage cashier job where you must face the public if you're unable to get regular dental care. When you have to walk around facing everybody with visibly decayed or missing teeth, everyone judges you. They assume that you're a drug addict. They assume you didn't care enough about yourself to exercise personal hygiene. They think you were too "uneducated" or "lazy" to brush and floss properly – not that contaminated drinking water, lack of proper nutrition, a real lack of access to health and dental care and a lack of opportunities for good jobs with benefits is why you couldn't get dental care. Being able to take care of your health and appearance is a social class privilege.

In Pennsylvania, poor Medicaid recipients cannot even get dentures in the event of losing their teeth from years of lack of access to dental care due to poverty. Medicaid classifies dentures as "cosmetic" – thus, not "medically necessary." Whoever made that policy has obviously never tried eating, speaking, or getting a job in order to climb out of poverty while having to face everyone without teeth in an image-oriented job market in our appearance-obsessed society.

Medicaid programs in post-Welfare Reform America are administered by the states who receive TANF block grants with federal guidelines that stipulate specified mandatory bare-bones dental benefits for only certain populations under the poverty level. As of 2005, only 6 states provided reasonably comprehensive dental benefits to poor adults while the rest only provide emergency treatment (extraction) or no dental benefit at all. Pregnant women over age 21 who are on Medicaid can only get dental care in 22 states.

Even for those in the lower-middle class who have jobs with some dental benefits, dental care is often financially out of reach. Most, if not all, dentists refuse to treat patients without being paid the patient's portion of the bill up front — even with emergencies where someone is in obvious pain and at risk of dying from infection. If you don't have enough income to qualify as creditworthy, you can't qualify for the CareCredit dental loans to pay for care, which leaves the poor and near-poor out in the cold with *no* care. The only dental treatment poor people can get is getting their teeth pulled. Medicaid won't pay for a denture or anything else deemed "cosmetic", like a crown or a dental implant.

In our society, being poor is enough of a reason for everybody else to look down on you. Being poor and having visibly decayed, missing, or broken teeth is even worse. You can't even get a minimum wage job without health and dental benefits as a supermarket cashier or any other low-paying job where you're facing the public when you have to go around looking like that; because in our society, missing or rotting teeth means that you didn't take personal pride in your appearance. What "normal" person doesn't care about how they look enough to take proper care of themselves? Missing and decayed teeth make it impossible for poor women to get any job, and everybody else judges you, treats you badly, and you get marginalized.

During Congressional hearings on passing the Welfare Reform Act of 1996, Maria Brand of the Federal Health Resources and Services Administration, Office of Rural Health Policy said, "There's a lot of pain. There's a lot of disfigurement. People can't even get jobs if they have bad teeth. No one is going to hire a person who as to hold a hand over their mouth when they talk because their teeth are so bad."

Barbara Evans Fleishauer, the West Virginia Delegate from the Office of Rural Health agreed, adding during the agency's evaluation of Welfare Reform that dental problems was the leading factor in preventing the poor from getting jobs.

But "lookism" fueled by our for-profit health and dental care system isn't the only way middle and upper class white males enjoy unearned social class privilege while poor women in our society are kept down and oppressed.

In the US, a woman is physically abused every 9 seconds according to the US Crimes Statistics. Women are more frequently the victims of domestic abuse than they are victims of any other physical crime. 42% of murdered women are killed by an intimate male partner. 50% of all homeless women and children are destitute and homeless because of domestic violence and the social control exerted by men over women. The constraints of few available jobs, no public transportation in rural areas – in addition to hiring discrimination against women in well-paying "non-traditional" jobs and pay discrimination — compound the difficulties victims face in permanently leaving their abusers. Ours is a society that always blames the victim instead of holding the aggressor accountable for their actions. We have a rich white male dominated society, so men have a sense of entitlement to always get their way at others' expense. They think they have the God-given right to dominate women and treat us any way they please, expecting that we should just suck it up and take it and never challenge their "authority" and unearned privileges which causes women to be poor. And poverty is a form of violence.

Our allegedly classless society looks down on the poor; berates and belittles them and tells them that their suffering is their own fault. Poor people are just expected to just suffer quietly and prostrate themselves before their "betters" in exhibition of how grateful they are for [insert cast-off of choice here]. Our society is a classist one; not a classless one. The basic tenets of classism hold that:

1. If you are poor, it is your own fault (if you're white).
2. If you're poor, it's because your character is deficient in some way.
3. If you're poor, you're a thief.
4. If you're poor, it's because you're stupid and uneducated.
5. If you're poor, it's because you're lazy.
6. If you're poor, it's because you chose to be poor.
7. If you're poor, it's because you didn't try hard enough.
8. If you're poor, it's because you didn't plan better.
9. If you're poor, it's because you had too many children that you couldn't afford (poor people breed like rabbits, don't ya' know?)
10. If you're poor, you lack proper manners.
11. If you're poor and female, you're sexually promiscuous (i.e. "easy")
12. If you're poor, you're a threat to society.
13. If you're poor, it's because you're unskilled and/or uneducated.

14. If you're poor, it's because you're an amoral primate lacking in self-discipline to control the urge for immediate gratification.

How many times have you observed rude disapproval when a customer in the supermarket swipes his or her ACESS debit card to pay for their groceries with food stamps? Perhaps you were one of those who barely concealed your contempt and judgmental attitude. I have lost count of how many middle and upper class people complain about welfare recipients eating from the largesse of society's "producers", buying fresh produce and healthy cuts of meat with their food stamps benefits. But when food stamp recipients buy cases of reduced price Coca-Cola and junk food, everyone complains about the imprudent use of food dollars paid for by the middle class taxpayers.

It should be noted with irony that the well-off who complain about food stamp recipients are often the same complainers who blame their own skyrocketing healthcare costs on the poor dietary habits of "welfare people" who buy cheap processed foods with their food stamps. The middle class complainers allege that the poor people's choices in cheap foods leads to obesity, diabetes, high cholesterol, and high blood pressure – which translates to higher health insurance premiums for everyone else in society.

But the reality is that those scraping to survive on food stamps must stretch what little they get in food stamps so they can eat at least once a day for an entire month. Healthy organic foods cost twice to three times as much as Monsanto's genetically modified (GMO) produce and meats and dairy foods contaminated by recombinant bovine growth hormones (rBGH). The ability to afford healthy food that doesn't cause obesity, diabetes, and ovarian cysts should not be a social class privilege. "Big Ag" giants like Monsanto that dominate the global food market get a free pass; poor food stamp recipients get crucified. Poor people reduced to having to rely on food stamps because of a rigged job market rife with age, gender and appearance discrimination in an unjust society just can't win.

As I write this book, the price of gasoline has risen to well over $3.00 per gallon. Crude oil has skyrocketed to over $100 per barrel. The result of high fuel prices is higher food prices since food is shipped to supermarkets by truck. An AOL newsflash has warned that a box of Cheerios or Corn Flakes is expected to reach $7.00 a box. Cheerios and Corn Flakes are hardly what one can consider high class food. But given the direction this country is headed with stagnant incomes for those at the very bottom compounded by excessive job losses and less jobs to go around for everyone who needs and wants a job, the only ones who might be able to afford to eat at all will be the wealthy.

I am not optimistic that enough people will do anything about it to force accountability on those rich corporations responsible for price-gouging the public anytime soon. Blinded by classism, it is easier for the middle and upper-middle classes to scapegoat the poor – America's most despised and marginalized group. Especially poor whites.

Internet blogs about the $7.00 per box cereals are nothing but one big bash-the-poor fest. People fortunate enough to be able to afford computers and high speed Internet access in their homes have the luxury of spare time to play Billy Bad-Ass from behind their computer screens, hammering out their two cents on blogs attacking those whose incomes are so low that they qualify for food stamps. The vitriol of these posts by bloggers shows how deeply ingrained classism is in this country.

12-19-2007 @ 3:28 PM

Jessica, Bossier City, IA said:

I agree doc...im sure shes enjoying the food stamps and welfare though...gee, must be nice to sit at home and make babies all day and let the government pay for it all.

Momofwings...curl up in a ball and rot

12-21-2007 @ 9:13 AM

Terri said:

"rich kids food"? Give me a break! I have seen those with food stamps eat better than most middle class people!

Instead of directing their resentment at the greedy powerful corporate interests that are responsible for unaffordable food and fuel prices, middle class people attack the poor. Just look at the stereotypes of poor women on food stamps evidenced in these two posts. Most people think poor women on welfare live it up and do nothing except procreate for recreation.

What they refuse to acknowledge is that the poor single mother on welfare was probably a "plain Jane" who didn't have the luxury of being able to take her pick of the available men. She thought she could trust that one man who swept her off her feet and made her feel desirable, wanted, and love only to find herself abandoned by the co-conceiver of her child after he conned her to gain her trust and get into her pants – and then bailed ship because he didn't want to stand by her through the pregnancy, birth, and raising of that child as a mate and father; even though he "loved" her enough to have sex with her knowing that pregnancy could result. And sadly, most of these women probably didn't even get a hell of a good orgasm out of the deal; they just got stuck holding the bag - literally.

Condoms break. The Pill is not infallible. Many women cannot get the Pill because of pre-existing medical conditions. Tubal ligation is typically not afforded by the medical constabulary to women as a contraceptive choice if the woman is under age 35 and hasn't had at least two children. Pregnancy and childbirth often has devastating (and often permanent) damaging and disfiguring effects on women's bodies, and poses a significant risk to women's health including death[14] during labor and birth – a fact that is lost on men because they're superficial, shallow, and selfish. They only care about themselves; getting what they want.

[14] According to the 2004 WHO Report, the US has the highest maternal and infant death rate among the first world nations. The infant and maternal mortality rate in Detroit is the same as that in Mozambique.

Then they spend an inordinate number of years trying to get out of paying child support because *they chose* to discard their baby's mother like a cheap disposable commodity.

Lose your figure and ruin your body from pregnancy and childbirth and you lose your value in our male-dominated society as well as your desirability as a marriage partner. You can die in childbirth or end up permanently maimed or disabled as a result, but men don't care. Men might occasionally care about their children, but most of them don't give a damn about the women who make the ultimate sacrifice to carry and bear their progeny with all the pregnancy side effects, risks, and excruciating pain that childbirth entails – even at peril to their own health and lives. All men want is the status of "eye candy" on their arm, a fuck trophy that does not require their financial support, devotion or commitment. Women are disposable, especially poor women. After all, there are always hot young babes working as exotic dancers in order to survive to entertain them, and porno starlets on the Internet porn sites that are pleasing to the eye, right? The vilification of poor single mothers by society after they've been abandoned by the co-conceivers shows society's lack of value for women and non-appreciation for all the sacrifices women are forced to endure; all which ensure white male middle/upper-middle class privilege.

What these welfare-bashing Internet warriors ignore is that a significant percentage of food stamp recipients are long-term unemployed people who were formally middle class and others are the working poor who never made it to the middle class. The paychecks and benefit-less jobs of the working poor do not lift them out of poverty.

Millions of Americans with skills and post-secondary educations desperately want adequate employment but have found themselves on the outside looking in due to age and appearance discrimination. Many others work but don't get a middle class wage, let alone health benefits, paid vacation, and paid sick time. They don't enjoy the privilege of a good job with any security. Many work full time hours in various services industries but get paid almost nothing because of being paid commissions-only without a base salary. In some retail operations, in insurance or financial services sales, you get paid only if you get a sale regardless of how many hours you worked for nothing. Others work in services fields that rely on tips – which cheapskate customers often fail to give. They think that workers relying on tips are making enough to not need a tip, or they blame the workers they cheat out of tips to justify their own selfishness.

Here are some facts about food stamp recipients:

- There is an 8 step process to go through in order to get approved for food stamps.
- In 2005, 25.7 million people received food stamps.
- 40% of all food stamp recipients live in households with an earned income.
- Only 15% of those on food stamps collected TANF (full welfare benefits) in 2005.
- 54% of the households receiving food stamps have small children. The rest are elderly or disabled on extremely low fixed incomes, or are very low income workers without children, whose incomes are well below the federal poverty line of $7,600/year for a single individual. (Picture yourself trying to live on $7,600 a year!)

Nothing angers me more than people that can afford to go out, who have good jobs with health and dental benefits, nice homes and the latest style clothing; who can afford lobster and shrimp, and exotic vacations bitching about some poor food stamp recipient who buys fresh produce and meats. I wish I had it so rough. The last time I had lobster was on my wedding day. We went to Red Lobster after our small private wedding commenced in the magistrate's office in McKean, Pennsylvania in Erie County on July 3rd, 2003. It's been so long since I had lobster, I've forgotten what it tastes like.

My husband Donnie is 25 years older than me. He worked very hard for very low pay all his life in a foundry until a workplace accident left him permanently disabled with back problems. The most he ever made was $9.28 an hour. I was 36 when we married after a two month courtship. I still had hopes at that point that my hard-won college education would open doors of opportunity for me in the job market so I wouldn't be a destitute disabled woman with nothing; so I would have a chance for something resembling a normal life. But that never happened for me.

My husband would love to be able to enjoy shrimp once a year on the holidays. But we can't afford it so we do without this small holiday luxury. It's a sad, terrible, crazy day when you can't even have one small bit of joy and happiness to enjoy on the holidays in the twilight of your life after a lifetime of paying your dues and struggling for so many years.

We don't have money to buy birthday gifts, anniversary gifts, or holiday gifts for anyone – not even for each other. We haven't been able to afford anything in a very, very long time. Holidays are a particularly painful reminder of just how little enjoyment we get out of life compared to those who are not poor. I struggle and have aggressively sought adequate employment to no avail, held back by dental problems, I make such little money (about $30-$100 per month in royalties from my self-published book sales) that we qualify for food stamps. Poverty, the lack of hope, and seeing the chance for any opportunity grow slimmer and slimmer; destroyed our health, our marriage, and our lives.

If those who are lucky enough to have good jobs and lives of relative comfort and security think we're really living large as jobless food stamp recipients, I challenge them to trade places with me for a year — I'll gladly take their good-paying job with dental benefits and a decent paycheck and they can keep my goddamn food stamps.

I'll gladly work at their jobs and enjoy the respect, economic security, and social participation commensurate with their upper-middle class paychecks. I'll buy the organic health foods I would prefer, get good dental care, and get an "extreme makeover[15]" so I can presentable.

[15] The Associated Press ran a headline in June 2006 citing that the number one high school graduation present given to girls is lipo-sculpture and breast augmentation. Cosmetic surgery is a choice available to those who have money, not for poor people.

I'll travel and experience some cultural enrichment. I'll take a vacation and see what it feels like to be able to relax (for once). I'll live in their nice house that's not in disrepair and have the ability to entertain friends and enjoy the activities and social acceptance that accompanies middle to upper-middle class life.

I'll live their nice life of the American Dream while they get a taste of mine - the American Nightmare of poverty and deprivation; of living in a ghetto in a cramped house where there's no heat in the winter and everything is falling apart and nothing works, but there's no money to get anything repaired. They'll get an idea of how it feels to try to get a job in order to climb out of poverty when the very location of where they live is held against them by potential employers and staffing agencies. They'll gain some insight of what it's like to have no hope of ever succeeding in life, of ever having any of the health, comfort, and security that having enough income buys. They'll get a taste of what it's like to have everybody else in society look down on them and judge them unfairly just for being poor.

Such an exchange would give the judgmental, condescending, status-driven middle class snob some understanding of how it feels to be put down, marginalized, and socially; to be labeled as a "deviant" or as a "criminal." It would open their eyes to the fact that our so-called meritocracy society is really a myth. After even one month of having to live like that, they will never again envy the "leisurely" life of a food stamp recipient and bitch about how great poor people in America have it on their tax dollars – guaranteed!

Classism is not restricted to the ritual abuse and humiliation of food stamp recipients in the supermarket check-out lines. The handling of rescue efforts in the face of natural disasters is also a blatant example of classism in our society. Look at the attitudes of the middle and upper-middle classes towards New Orleans' poor that were stuck in their own sewage for five days at the Superdome in the wake of Hurricane Katrina. Those survivors had no cars, no money for bus tickets and hotel rooms, and no one to take them in. They were told to go to the Superdome to wait for a rescue effort that was not forthcoming. Look at how these survivors were treated by law enforcement personnel, FEMA, and the mainstream media.

Fox News and CNN painted these survivors as "looters", and even falsely claimed that these "looters" were shooting at rescue personnel. The only "looting" I saw on the televised hurricane coverage were survivors who broke into stores to get food, diapers, baby formula, juice, bottled water, and perishable medicines such as insulin. Hurricane Katrina caused widespread power outages. Thus, perishable items were claimed as a total loss by those respective business owners who filed claims for those losses with their insurance carriers – regardless if the items were left to spoil in the sweltering heat or commandeered by stranded survivors. Business owners got compensated either way.

The governor of Louisiana gave a standing order to the National Guard and local law enforcement personnel to "shoot to kill" these "looters" so they wouldn't capitalize on the disaster by stealing large screen TV's. But what the mainstream media did *not* report was that Blackwater's soldiers of fortune were contracted by the Department of Homeland Security to "protect FEMA rescue workers" and had been deputized by Louisiana's governor.

Blackwater mercenaries sporting M-4 assault rifles, black garb, and wrap-around sunglasses were granted legal authority to use lethal force. They were dispatched onto the streets of New Orleans with "shoot to kill" orders[16] in order to "confront criminals and stop looters" in direct violation of the Posse Commitatus Act and the US Constitution.

Lorrie Beth Slonsky and Larry Bradshaw, two EMT's from California attending an EMT continuing ed conference in New Orleans when Hurricane Katrina struck were among the stranded "looters." Their personal account of what happened was very different from the mainstream news reports that falsely said the poor (and overwhelmingly black) Katrina survivors were shooting at their rescuers and stealing high tech goodies. When Slonsky and Bradshaw and other stranded survivors

---

[16] Eyewitness account of Jeremy Scahill, author of "*Blackwater Down*", who was in New Orleans covering the rescue effort for *Democracy NOW!.org.*

attempted to escape New Orleans on foot along the only route not flooded out, they were fired upon by sheriffs at the Gretna Bridge. Their group, which included old and disabled people in wheelchairs as well as poor women with infants, was subsequently chased and threatened at gunpoint by SWAT teams. Their makeshift shelters were destroyed by law enforcement personnel while they were waiting to be rescued near an overpass after it was evident that they would not be allowed to cross the Gretna Bridge to leave New Orleans.

By Slonsky and Bradshaw's account, it was the intent of the wealthy that those with no way out were to be deliberately prevented from escaping; and instead, left to die from lack of food, water, medical care, and exposure to the elements. The hurricane might have been an "act of God", but the disaster of the "rescue effort" certainly was not.

It was intended by the privileged that the underclass of New Orleans should die; if not from the storm that had been predicted several days in advance by NOAA[17], then by deliberate prevention of their escape – by force of gunpoint, if necessary. That is why Blackwater mercenaries (who were paid $350 per diem) were dispatched to New Orleans before FEMA rescue personnel and the Red Cross arrived on the scene. The tab for Blackwater's "services" provided under contract with the Department of Homeland Security to protect the interests of New Orleans' privileged class was billed at $950 per day – paid for by the US taxpayers.

Independent journalist Jeremy Scahill observed while covering the Katrina disaster in New Orleans, that there was no food or drinking water distribution, no Red Cross, no humanitarian relief – but there were plenty of well paid burly mercenaries. Blackwater mercenaries are opportunistic killers: they're young (and mostly white) middle class males who are self-centered, without a conscience, driven by greed and lust for life on the edge.

It should also be noted for the record that several charities pocketed much of the cash donations given by the public at large who

[17] NOAA = National Oceanic and Atmospheric Administration

thought their donations would reach those in need. Charities operate under the auspices of IRS Code §501(3)c. Executive directors of these benevolent organizations get the lion's share of cash donations and tool around in luxury cars and socialize at exclusive country clubs. Money that is *supposed to* go to the poor gets eaten up in administrative costs of running the charity – mostly for lavish executive compensation. Meanwhile, the poor are often turned away empty-handed.

Wealthy New Orleans businessman James Reiss brought in Israeli mercenaries from Instinctive Shooters to guard Audubon Place: the elite gated community that is home to New Orleans' wealthiest and most powerful citizens. Instinctive Shooters is an Israeli firm that recruits exclusively from the ranks of Israel's IDF. The poor of New Orleans weren't told to eat cake; they were threatened with a lead diet. In the immortal words of Jeremy Scahill, it was "Baghdad on the Bayou."

This was not a harmless error on the part of government at the local, state, or federal level. *Someone* anticipated that destitute survivors might try to reach the Gretna Bridge and wanted to prevent their egress. Those Gretna sheriffs were already assembled and waiting on the Gretna side of that bridge with their guns cocked and loaded before the Lorrie Beth Slonsky, Larry Bradshaw, and the other survivors arrived there. *Someone* had ordered those sheriffs to be there, and they were not dispatched to roll out the welcome wagon and then have everyone sit around holding hands and sing "*Koom-Bye-Ya.*"

One of the sheriffs who insisted on anonymity candidly told the EMT's that they had received orders from higher up to ensure that Gretna did not "turn into another Superdome." These were code words for "if you're poor, we won't let you live." Why would those in power have any reason to fear society's poorest, those who were least able to fend for themselves? Greed. The affluent did not want hordes of poor survivors traversing their neatly manicured lawns, banging on their doors begging for help that they had no intent to provide.

There is no incentive for the privileged classes to help the less fortunate when they view the poor are sub-human and as "useless eaters." In our society of "ME ME ME", killing the poor is a patriotic virtue cloaked in romanticized ideas of "rugged individualism" and worship of the "self-made man."

This phenomenon occurred repeatedly throughout history. At the end of World War II after the Allied Forces liberated the Nazi death camps and brought the Nazi war machine to its knees, the handful of sick and starving Jewish Holocaust survivors tried to return to their homes that the Nazi SS illegally expropriated. They found strange new occupants in their former homes who threatened to shoot them. Many displaced Jews had to go to the Displaced Persons camps where they were issued one set of ill-fitting clothes and languished in absolute poverty while awaiting the goodwill (that was often not forthcoming) of strangers to help them relocate to Palestine or to the United States. Some were able to build economically successful lives after World War II with the help and support of social connections and family. But many were not that fortunate, and remained in poverty until they died.

Many Holocaust survivors had no network of comfortably-off family or friends to help them rebuild their shattered lives – their friends and relatives had been gassed and burned into oblivion in the ovens at Auschwitz, Sobibor, Treblinka, Belzic, Majdanek, and Chelmno. The few who were able to escape the horrors of Naziland were only able to flee with the clothes on their backs. Their money, parcels of food, and extra clothes were confiscated by the SS. They escaped by night and fog to America – only to find that wealthy bosses of the American Jewish Relief Agencies had no interest in helping the poor who had narrowly missed going up the chimney at Auschwitz-Birkenau.

Holocaust survivors Gerhard and Ursula Falk, both retired professors in their late eighties, recounted their experiences of coming to America in the 1930's. Having had the privilege to study Talmud with them at a Buffalo, New York synagogue, they befriended me and helped me understand classism and how it affected me as a Jewess who had been a dispossessed orphan, starting out in life from behind the 8-ball. Like the Falks, I always felt like an outsider, never really belonging anywhere and never quite fitting in. But unlike the Falks, college and grad school was put financially out of my reach by inflated tuition and slashed aid which held me back as a poor woman.

The Falks arrived here as children before Nazi-occupied Europe's remaining Jews were forcibly deported under SS gunpoint to the sealed ghettos of Łodz, Lublin, Krakow, Warsaw, and Minsk in Poland which were really holding pens pending the implementation of Hitler's "Final Solution." Gerhard was ejected from a Philadelphia synagogue on his first Yom Kippur in America because he was homeless, destitute, and lacked the money to buy a ticket to attend the High Holiday services for the Day of Atonement. Ursula was ridiculed as a 10 year old child by a wealthy American Jewish businessman who basically called her a beggar and made a big scene of offering her a piece of peanut brittle *after* he invited her family to his home for the traditional weekly Sabbath meal. Ursula spoke very little English, but understood Yiddish perfectly.

Her "benefactor" sang loudly in Yiddish, "*Schoen ist das Zigeunerleben Forio, sie wollen nur nemmen and gor nischt geben Forio*." (Translation: "Beautiful is the life of gypsies for they only want to take, but give nothing."). Dr. Ursula Falk, retired author and psychotherapist, remembers the sting of his insult to this day, over 70 years later.

Holocaust survivors were blamed for their own poverty. Poor Jews are rejected by non-Jews who think "Jews have all the money" and ostracized by their co-religionists in the American Jewish community. In synagogues, which are largely run like little oligarchies, poorer congregants are not supported properly with *tzedakah*[18] and are often shamed and humiliated by other Jews who are more fortunate. Poor Jews are not made to feel welcome at most synagogues and are never elected to serve on boards and committees. To be poor and Jewish in America is to be a non-person.

[18] *Tzedakah*: Hebrew, meaning charity. It is a commandment to give to charity and help support those unable to support themselves for whatever reason.

Throughout history, the privileged classes have always been selfish and hateful toward the dispossessed. As with the survivors of Hurricane Katrina, destitute Holocaust survivors were blamed for their own poverty. Judgmental questions of "*why didn't you just leave?*", "*why didn't you try to help yourself?*", and "*why didn't your people do something about it?*" accusing the poor of New Orleans for being the authors of their own misery were hurled at poor Jewish Holocaust survivors. Demographics and time may change, but attitudes of greed and self-importance do not.

The petit bourgeoisie never cared and wanted to help. They say it's "not their responsibility." They don't feel obligated to do their part to eradicate social injustice by breaking down systemic barriers and dismantling harmful stereotypes that keep the poor miserable, exploitable, hopeless, and stuck at the bottom with no chance for a decent life.

The middle class won't admit that for the years they enjoyed good jobs with medical and dental benefits so they could have decent lives, others got deprived and suffered in poverty without decent wages, health and dental care. For those lucky enough to get a middle class job, others did not get a chance for that job – someone who needed it just as badly, if not more so. Someone else who was desperately poor got their hopes and dreams ripped away from them.

In a capitalist society where the economic law of supply and demand does not operate in a vacuum, where markets are artificially manipulated by the rich and powerful, there exists unearned privilege for certain members of society at the expense of others.

Chapter 3

"Poverty is the worst form of violence." ~ Mohandas Ghandi

Callousness towards the poor is justified by various fundamentalist religious dogmas. The fundamentalist Christian view is extremely conservative and holds that poverty is a punishment for sin, that it is God's will. It's an excuse used to justify cruelty and abuse. It is less about worshipping God and more about worshipping yourself. It's patting yourself on the back for gains obtained through a system of unearned privileges while convincing yourself that you're entitled because God says so and you deserve everything you got, even if you got it at someone else's expense. If your "god" says that it's okay to profit at the expense of the poor, if your "god" says that it's okay to exploit the oppressed for personal gain and that the suffering of those you've oppressed is "god's will"; then you and your "god" need an attitude adjustment. But a small few of the more enlightened Christians embrace a liberation theology that correctly views poverty as a structurally determined outcome.

Unitarian minister Reverend Lynn Thomas Strauss summed up the following myths and facts about poverty and classism in the following sermon:

"I want to believe that equality can exist alongside significant differences. But the evidence is slim. Our country is split along socio-economic lines. This is why people hide behind gated communities…Set forth by sociologist C. Wright Mills in 1959, these myths still hold power and keep class differences, class struggle, and class pain quiet and unacknowledged:

Myth #1: The US is a classless society.

Myth #2: We are all equal in the eyes of the law.

Myth #3: We are essentially a middle class nation.

Myth #4: We are all getting richer.

Myth #5: Everyone has an equal chance to succeed.

People without healthcare know that ours is not a classless society. Service men and women who joined the military as a ticket to a college education know that this is not a classless society. Innocent people on death row know that all are not equal in the eyes of the law."

In order for everyone to have an equal chance to succeed, then everyone must necessarily start out in life with the same resources, the same social personal support, and abilities. Do those who lack the personal safety net of a family to turn to in times of need have an equal chance of making it in society as those who have family? There's a big difference in "consequences for bad choices" made by those who have family to bail them out compared to those who have no family, or whose families are abusive and won't help them.

Do those who have physical disabilities really have an equal chance for a good job and some economic security as those who have no health problems? What about those with low IQ's or those who have learning disabilities?

In the "new economy" a college education in addition to good looks and the "right image" are requirements for women to get any kind of job that pays a living wage. Where does that leave the woman who is not able to be academically successful in college or the young girl from poverty with visibly decayed or missing teeth? Where does that leave women who didn't luck out in the gene pool crap shoot regarding body type and looks who cannot even date nice men and hope to marry her way out of poverty? What about women who are pregnant, or middle-aged, or overweight? What about the older woman who was out of the workforce for several years and has no recent employment references who finds herself economically left out because companies only want to hire and promote young people in good jobs?

White male high school drop outs and ex-felons get more opportunities to make more money than women with clean records and

Bachelor's degrees in the hard sciences. White male high school drop-outs and ex-felons get chances for good jobs in male dominated fields that don't require college degrees which *still* discriminate against women such as construction, tool and die making, heavy equipment operator, and freight management. Men can be butt ugly, stupid Neanderthals and get a lot more chances for decent paying jobs with benefits and security than unattractive looking women because "women's jobs" are more image-oriented. Women are judged solely on their looks. Can we honestly say that *everyone* has an equal chance to succeed in our society?

What most people fail to grasp is that lack of opportunity and income to afford life's basic needs is the primary structural cause for poverty – not lack of education, or "poor choices." But most people are too selfish to care. They would rather promote the notion that if you're poor it's your own fault for failing to get an education or for making all the wrong choices in life because that's the answer that lets *them* off the hook. That's the answer that makes *them* feel better. But it doesn't gel with the fact that there are many poor people who *did* get educations despite enormous obstacles only to still not get chances. Plenty of people avoided having unplanned pregnancies, avoided drug and alcohol use, and were careful to do "all the right things" – yet still remained poor. I know because I am living it. Poverty is not "God's will." Poverty is the scourge of man-made social constructs that set up and maintain systems of unearned privilege which accord benefits to some at the expense of others.

If an education and marketable skills were truly the answer to climbing out of poverty, then middle-aged women like me who obtained educations and attempted to re-enter the workforce wouldn't be jobless, unemployable, and poor.

Armchair experts and neocon talking heads say that the disabled poor are undeserving of social support and economic help because they "failed to plan better." By planning better, they mean having a personal disability income replacement insurance policy (DI) which pays 67% of your gross pre-disability wages for a set number of years up to age 65, tax-free. But what Rush Limbaugh, Bill O'Reilly, and the rest of

America's class bigots don't consider in their narrow view of life is that the ability to obtain personal DI coverage hinges on three factors: your occupational hazard class, pre-existing medical conditions, and your income.

When I was younger and working as a strip dancer and a union plasterer, my occupational hazard class did not meet underwriting guidelines to qualify for a personal DI policy. Many other workers were in that same boat.

Waitresses, massage parlor workers, truck drivers, seasonal farm workers, and custodial staff who are exposed to bio-hazardous waste materials in medical facilities also have trouble qualifying for a DI policy. For many more Americans, pre-existing medical conditions that could cause them to be terminated also disqualifies them for DI coverage. Lastly, the level of income isn't enough to be able to qualify for a policy based on underwriting guidelines, or enough to afford the premiums. When you are paid so little that you barely have enough to afford a roof over your head, utilities, and food, there isn't any money left to afford the luxury of a DI policy. Medicaid, SSI and food stamps are often the only sources of income support for those who end up prematurely disabled (and hence, unemployable).

Everyone has heard about the plight of uneducated laborers who remain poor despite working exceedingly hard and the low-paid waitresses who remain poor despite busting their asses while having to rely solely on tips. But there are plenty of white collar workers with educations who are extremely poor. Most working in commissions-only paying sales jobs are poor, with 85% earning $15,000 a year or less[19].

Not only must you have a college degree which costs a lot of money, you must usually obtain expensive licenses (insurance, real estate, or NASD Series 7 &66) that also cost a lot of money. In order to get these licenses, you are required to pass difficult state proctored exams and take ongoing continuing education courses and exams - which are all costs that come directly out of your own pocket. You have to be able to

[19] Barbara Ehrenreich, *Bait & Switch.*

afford the proper clothing and the "right" image to be able to get a sales job. Try finding the right clothes at Goodwill when you're a plus-sized middle-aged woman. Meanwhile, you get paid nothing for all of your time, education, and licensing because you only get paid if you get a sale. Commissions-only pay means exactly that: No base wage and no benefits.

After earning my bachelors degree at age 34, the only job opportunities I was offered were commissions-only paying sales jobs selling insurance and financial products and services (mutual funds, stocks, annuities, etc.) – no base salary and no health benefits. In order to be allowed to work selling financial products and services, you must pass the NASD Series 7 & 66 exams and get those licenses. You must also qualify for fidelity bond and pay for Errors & Omissions Insurance (E&O) – a malpractice insurance for insurance and financial sales people. The companies you sell for don't pick up the tab for this – *you* have to.

The Series 7 & 66 exams are so difficult that over 80% of the candidates fail and must retake the test a second time in order to pass. It is an exhaustive 6 hour test. I passed it easily on the first try in only half the allotted time. Renewing my NASD Series 7 & 66 licenses every year would have cost me at least $200 in continuing education fees each year plus the $1000 NASD annual renewal fees, had I been able to afford to keep those licenses after 9/11.

In order to be successful working in a commissions-only paying job in finance or insurance sales, you need to be socially connected to people from the higher socio-economic classes. You need to be a member of the club. You are also expected to have an extensive network of well-to-do family and friends (and their associates) to sell to. Being educated and knowing your stuff isn't enough. If you can't afford expensive tailored suits, Prada shoes, a fancy car, and dental care to keep your teeth, you don't stand a chance of making it. It takes a lot more than just an education, skills, the proper credentials, and hard work when starting out with absolutely nothing because nobody buys from somebody that doesn't look successful.

And if you're not a thin, young, beauty queen, you have an even harder time getting sales and you won't find a work environment that is very supportive. The "pretty people" get all the plum accounts assigned to them by management. Workers over age 30 are lucky to be able to get a job, and are constantly reminded of that in every way they're treated on the job by management. Workers over age 40 trying to re-enter the workforce are discarded and often not hired at all. If you're disabled, however minimally, you can forget it.

The company that hired me after I re-entered the workforce at age 34 upon graduating from college was an investment brokerage firm. I still had enough front teeth left then so if I didn't smile, nobody would know I was "poor white trash." For the five months I worked there until 9/11 abruptly truncated that career, I made enough to be able to live – as long as my student loans were in deferment. After 9/11, I was out of a job. I could not collect unemployment because stockbrokers and other commissions-only paid salespeople are considered "executive level" contract workers – exempt from the safety net of unemployment benefits. I did not qualify for any free career retraining under the Trade Adjustment Allowance (TAA) that those who lost jobs due to plant closures can get. All I had to live on was what little money I was able to save (after paying for the basics of food, transportation, utilities, and a roof over my head) during my five month stint as a broker. And for those five months, my commissions-only pay for putting in 80 hour work weeks trying to get sales was less than the 40 hour a week paycheck of a janitor at GE.

After a 4 ½ year long fruitless job search during which I had no income at all, we were reduced to having to apply for food stamps and Medicaid. Our gas and electric were both shut off. I tried self-employment. But I had no money to start any kind of viable business with. I inquired about getting a loan as a disadvantaged woman from the local SBA office, only to find out that only a few certain businesses can qualify for that: manufacturing and food service. I did not have a background in either.

I had prior experience in the plastering and drywall trade, but there were no SBA loans available to start a construction business in order to hire able-bodied tradespeople. I had experience in exotic dancing, but a "gentleman's club" was not the sort of business that would qualify for SBA money. I gained the knowledge, licenses and experience in the financial services industry for selling stocks, options, bonds, mutual funds, and various types of insurances ranging from personal lines to commercial property and casualty lines.

But start up money for an independent insurance agency was not available because selling workers' comp, auto, and property insurance didn't meet SBA guidelines for "qualifying businesses." Additionally, in order to start an independent insurance agency, one needs to have E&O insurance as a condition of getting appointed by carriers to sell their insurance products. Someone without 5 or more years experience won't get underwritten by E&O carriers except through the surplus lines market – which means premiums that cost triple the average going rate. The premiums for E&O obtained through the excess and surplus lines market for a start-up insurance agency runs about $3,900 a year – money that is out of reach for someone who is poor enough to qualify for food stamps.

Being poor and unable to pay even the basic utility bills, I had bad credit; so I couldn't qualify for any type of financing in order to get start-up capital in order to "create my own job" by starting my own business. All I had was my education, my insurance and NASD licenses, a computer, and a commercially-zoned home in a poor urban neighborhood.

My husband sold his dump truck for far less than what it was worth. I sold my house in the ghetto that I previously had before getting married at a loss in order to get his mortgage caught up which had gone into foreclosure. What little bit of money that was left went for the $3,900 premiums in mandatory E&O coverage so I could "create my own job" as an independent insurance agent with my office in my living room. No one gave me a chance and hired me at any of the 4,800 places I had applied for jobs over the span of 4 ½ years after 9/11 because of being a chubby middle-aged woman with dental problems. I had no opportunity.

I had to buy office equipment, expensive specialized software, and pay for high-speed Internet. If the proceeds from the sale of my former house and my husband's dump truck would have been enough to pay off our house completely, I would have done that instead of trying to start a business with no income to live on, teeth rotting out of my head, and trying to meet expenses while trying to get a business off the ground.

After getting appointed by two non-standard carriers, AIG and Farmers, I let every used car dealer in Erie know I was in business.

Selling auto insurance is a rough racket. Working for commissions only when you're poor and need security is just too hard. Even though auto insurance is mandatory in almost every state (except New Hampshire), customers let policies cancel for nonpayment of premium when money is tight – hoping they won't get caught driving without insurance. When people let their policies cancel for whatever reason during mid-term, the agent is back-charged what little bit of commission pay they got from the carrier for the policy sale. Additionally, auto insurance carriers charge the poor commissions-only paid agent $8 a clip for every MVR and CLUE[20] report that the agent is required to run before the sale of an auto insurance policy can take place.

If the MVR and CLUE's come back with any traffic tickets or showing a claim for any accidents, the quoted rate increased dramatically. As a result, many people simply walk out without buying the auto insurance policy and the agent is not paid for their time. So you not only end up working for free, you're also charged by the insurance carriers out of your pocket for the mandatory MVR and CLUE reports! Imagine going to your job that you have had to incur up front out of pocket expenses for, then working a full-time work week only to have the company take back 95% of your paycheck that you need in order to

[20] MVR: Motor Vehicle Report compiled by each state Dept. of Motor Vehicles for every licensed driver. CLUE: Comprehensive Loss Underwriting Exchange, a national database of records of claims filed by insureds for losses.

live. Trying to start your own business after not getting any chances for a "real" job, without any financial cushion until you can build a big enough clientele base to be successful, is a recipe for guaranteed failure.

No matter what I tried to do, no matter how hard I worked, no matter how many hoops I've jumped through, I'm still poor. I still have to rely on food stamps. I still have to suffer without basic utilities. I still can't get health and dental care after almost an entire lifetime of never having had any. I have no hope of ever being able to save anything for my own old age. I still can't even begin making payments on my student loans for that almighty college degree that was supposed to be my ticket out of poverty. I still can't afford anything that makes living life worthwhile. I got nothing for all my efforts except poverty, suffering, and doing without.

As far as getting a better job (or any job at all), that's only possible if someone is willing to hire you and give you a fair fighting chance. I've tried very aggressively to get a good job so I could climb out of poverty and repay my student loans but couldn't get anything because no one ever gave me a chance. I was denied opportunities because I am a middle-aged woman. I was denied opportunities because the disabling car accident at age 24 left me with a work history gap of over a decade – leaving me with no recent employment references when I tried to re-enter the workforce in my 30's. I was denied opportunities because of having bad credit as a direct result of being poor. I was denied opportunities because of having to walk around with rotting and missing teeth throughout my 20's and 30's. I couldn't afford dental care, nice clothes to have the "right" image, and I lived in the places I could afford: poor areas.

I'm not poor because of making "poor choices." I'm not poor because of not trying hard enough – there isn't much I haven't tried. I'm poor because I never got a fair chance in my entire life and by the time I had something to possibly get a chance with, I had lost most of my teeth from a lack of access to dental care.

Like millions of other women struggling in poverty due to job discrimination and lack of enough living wage jobs for everyone, I was unable to break out of the Catch-22 that poverty in America imposes. Having had no dental care for almost all of my life because of being poor, my only dental care was getting badly decayed and broken teeth extracted, one at a time. Throughout what should have been the best years of my life, I suffered the social and economic repercussions of poverty with having to face people with missing and rotting teeth and jagged stumps of what were once nice teeth that could have once been saved if only I could have afforded dental care. Even dentures were financially out of reach for me.

Dental implants cost between $2,500 — $3,500 per tooth, and in the event of a problem during the procedure, the $2,000 — $3,000 dental implant can turn into a $15,000 bill (due at time of treatment) for one single tooth replacement. For me, it might as well cost a million dollars.

Being poor all my life, I couldn't afford fillings, root canals, and porcelain crowns that I needed in order to keep my teeth and look normal while I was still young so I could get a good job and have something resembling a nice life. By the time I graduated from college at age 34, most of my teeth were gone except for 6 front teeth upper front teeth and 10 lower teeth. I couldn't eat fresh fruits and vegetables because I couldn't chew them. I also couldn't smile or open my mouth too wide when trying to speak naturally. In a society where the only jobs available to women tend to be very image-oriented and working with the public, my chances for getting anything close to a living wage jobs were zilch.

While enduring a 4 ½ year long job search as an "outsider" after moving to across the state to Erie in 2002 when I could no longer afford housing in my home town of Philadelphia after losing my briefly held brokerage firm job as a result of 9/11, the remaining few teeth I had started to go bad.

Like others in poverty, I had no choice. I had little to no access to dental care and for the brief 90 days I was able to get Medicaid as a destitute childless adult with a slightly less poor but disabled husband on less than $1,000/month social security. The only dentists within 100 miles of us who accepted Medicaid were abusive and made no secret of their contempt for the poor.

By the time I reached my mid-30's, I had only 2 upper front teeth left and 8 on the bottom. Except for my husband, everybody else treated me like total shit because of how I looked with almost no teeth left. Unsolicited remarks of *"well if you would have brushed and flossed correctly, you wouldn't have lost your teeth"* and similar personal value judgments from those who have never had to go without dental care what poor people endure every day — while we're lectured by our middle class abusers for not having the "correct" attitude and accused of "having a chip on our shoulder" for telling off self-centered, inconsiderate assholes.

I eventually gave up trying to get a job. Between the disadvantages of gender, a physical disability that wasn't "disabling enough" for me to get even a $600/mo SSI check, a work history gap of almost 5 years with no middle class references, poor credit due to poverty, having almost no teeth left by the time I was 36 years old, I had no chance to climb out of destitution to reach poverty, let alone reach the lower-middle class.

For several years, my husband and I collected scrap metal and salvaged old appliances from other people's garbage for the metal. Whenever we found discarded wiring from homes that had been remodeled, we felt lucky. But stripping and cleaning enough copper wire to get $100 from the salvage yard took more than 2 weeks of our time working steadily at it for about 8 hours every day. Being a poor person is the hardest job in the world.

Despite my husband's health problems and my own physical limitations, we worked very hard. We tried our very best with the hand life dealt us. But we never made it out of poverty. We both sacrificed, scrounged, scraped and sold what few things we had between the two of us on eBay so that by the time I was 40 I was *finally* able to afford the extractions of my last 2 upper teeth, 3 root canals and crowns on my remaining lower teeth, and an upper denture (all at a cost of $8,000). And by the time I was finally able to afford the luxury and privilege of being able to look normal, I was "too old" for any employer to want to hire me in what few jobs that are available to middle-aged women with any kind of physical disability that doesn't require standing for long periods of time or lifting.

And through it all, very few people treated me like a human being. Nobody offered any kind of real helping hand by the way of dental care before it was too late for me, before I'd be too "overqualified" for a job that I *could* do and was more than willing to do if only given a chance. Being poor is a lifetime of no choices while being told by everybody else that your poverty is a "choice" because America is the "land of opportunity." Land of opportunity my ass. Poor women with severe dental problems from years of cheap unhealthy food bank food and a lifetime lack of access to decent dental care get no opportunity, no matter how hard we work and how much we try.

I had taken civil service exams for various entry level positions in local and state government agencies for which I was qualified by virtue of my education. I was called for an interview twice when my name came up on the civil service list. The first entailed traveling across state from Erie to Lancaster Pennsylvania. In order to afford the travel to go for the job interview, I had to forego paying the mortgage for that entire month because I had no income and my husband was only getting $772 a month in social security early retirement, of which $541 had to pay for our combined mortgage and escrow payment. When I was called for the interview, I explained my situation: I could not afford to travel across state if I did not have a realistic chance of getting the job if there were several other applicants being considered. We couldn't afford to forego the mortgage payment to travel for a pig in the poke. I was told that I was the only candidate being interviewed because my name came up on the list.

But the civil service human resources person had lied to me. After arriving for the interview, I found four other applicants also waiting to be interviewed for that one single job opening. I learned that one of those candidates already had an instant “in” for the job – he was a veteran and had veteran’s preference and he was already a civil service employee, which gave him automatic seniority rights to the job over any other candidate. He got the job. I got sent home poor and empty-handed with nothing. I felt like a fool for trying in the first place, for believing the human resources person who assured me that I wouldn’t be making an unaffordable trip across state for nothing, and for thinking that I had a chance.

The second civil service job interview that I was called for was for an entry level bookkeeper for Erie County Office of Children & Youth. The interview was held in the administration building of the North Warren Hospital for the criminally insane in Warren County; a two hour drive from my home in Erie.

When I arrived, I found that the interviewer was from India and could barely speak English. He could not pronounce my name and frustrated at his own ineptitude, he muttered, “Names aren’t important anyway.” He led me down a corridor to a conference room where two other women were seated. They were to co-interview me with him. The whole set-up was a tag team approach specifically designed to put the job applicant on the defensive.

He already had my résumé out on the table. Looking at it without making any eye contact with me, he said, “I see you haven’t had any work experience since 1991.” I replied that I had struggled with extreme poverty and overcame a disability in order to get a college education and earn my degree so I could re-enter the workforce in a new career, and that should count for something. He refused to acknowledge that. Then he said, “I see you are self-employed, but that doesn’t count as work experience. That only means you are unable to work well with others.”

That was the final straw. If anyone thinks that taking abuse from the inconsiderate public in order to MAYBE get a sale and earn a measly commission selling auto insurance is some sort of hobby instead of work, they’re on drugs – and if not, they ought to be.

Instead of recognizing that I have valid work experience from having to resort to self-employment for lack of any other opportunities, this interviewer wasted my time and insulted me. Instead of acknowledging that at least I was trying to do *something* as opposed to begging for spare change on a street corner, he belittled my efforts in the face of so much adversity. He dismissed my self-employment "job" as proof that I was personally deficient; unworthy of a chance for a stable job with benefits and some security.

You can't just "get a better job" when no one will hire you and give you a chance. Even though I tried very hard in life and did "all the right things", I'm still not good enough. I'm still unworthy. I'm still poor and unable to support myself without any hope of being able to live with a little bit of comfort, economic security, and dignity. My arms have grown tired of reaching for a "carrot" that will always be out of my reach.

It is beyond disingenuous for middle and upper class people to accuse the poor of not wanting to work when being jobless and poor means not having teeth, not having your health, not having good food, and being socially rejected. People are social creatures. Everybody wants acceptance. Everybody wants to fit in. In our society, being accepted, wanted, and respected are attached to employment and socio-economic status. To be denied jobs, to be rejected for conditions of poverty not of your making while you're denied dental care so that every last door of opportunity is slammed shut in your face is the cruel reality of classism in America.

I got no reward for trying more and working harder. I struggled for three years trying to make my self-employment venture work. Unaffordable fuel and energy prices killed my business when customers let policies cancel for non-payment of premiums and I got back-charged by the carriers as a result. I never got the opportunity to make a lateral career move into a salaried position in management or in claims adjusting with the carriers whose insurance products I sold. I'm still poor.

When all you get is beaten down into the ground time after time by everybody else no matter how hard you've worked and how much you try, you begin to lose hope. Trying harder is futile because it's like beating your head against a brick wall. When all you get for all your efforts is told "well, you just have to try harder" only to never get anywhere anyway, there's no incentive to try harder. For those who say that "we make our own luck", it would be nice if they would send me the recipe.

As long as I am denied chances for jobs because of age, sex, disability, appearance/weight discrimination and poverty-profiling, I'll never be able to climb out of poverty and fend for myself economically. I am poor for the same reason that most other poor people remain trapped in poverty in America – the richest country in the world. I live in a society that doesn't care. I live in a society that hates its poor. I live in a society that accepts the social and economic injustice of sex, age and appearance discrimination; a society that perpetuates classism while trying to pretend classism doesn't exist. Not everyone really has an equal chance to succeed and blaming it on "poor choices" is bullshit.

Poor choices alone on the part of the individual are not the sole cause of that individual's circumstances. The same "poor choices" and mistakes made by poor people are made by people in the middle and upper classes, yet the outcomes aren't the same. So if making the wrong decisions throughout life is the cause of poverty, then why are the end results different for those in the middle and upper classes who make those *identical* mistakes? And what exactly are these "poor choices" that the middle and upper class claim are the sole cause for poverty?

Those without financial means can't afford to "choose" to go to college. There are not enough jobs for all of those who already have college degrees anyway. Women without money and/or middle class family support can't afford the most reliable contraception to prevent pregnancy, or an abortion in the event of contraceptive failure. People with physical disabilities and medical problems did not make the "poor choice" to be disabled and unable to get a job. People with low IQ's or learning disabilities didn't choose their mental abilities. Those who didn't inherit nice bodies, good teeth and good looks didn't choose their gene pool. Those who were born into poor or dysfunctional families lacking academic and emotional support did not choose their parents. Poor women can't afford to "choose" to terminate an unintended pregnancy so they're not sentenced to poverty for life.

Those who are being economically excluded didn't get a choice – employers who have the power to decide who gets a chance and who does not made that choice. Job applicants are rarely given a chance to explain to potential employers that the reason they have rotten/missing teeth, bad credit, and work history gaps is due to prolonged periods of involuntary unemployment. Instead, such job seekers are merely rejected without any reason given other than the position has been filled. Usually, rejected job applicants are simply ignored. But in a job market where there are far more job seekers than there are jobs, those who are the most disadvantaged for getting a chance know the reasons why: age, sex, looks and poverty profiling with credit checks.

The reason given by employers for basing hiring decisions on a job applicant's credit was stated by a local K-Mart human resources manager who insisted she remain anonymous, "People with poor credit, especially the poor, are more prone to steal or be irresponsible." When you're poor, you don't get much of a chance to work your way out of poverty – you can't even get the chance to work!

If you can't get a chance for a good job, you certainly can't get any money to set aside and save for a rainy day. When you're poor, every day is a rainy day. But even if you were one of the lucky ones who enjoyed a secure job with health and dental benefits and a middle class wage for 15 to 20 years during which you could save money after paying for food, transportation, housing, utilities, and health care, it is highly unlikely that your savings would be sufficient to weather a period of prolonged unemployment lasting longer than one year. But when you've never had a chance to join the ranks of the middle class to begin with, your situation is even more precarious. To be poor (whether working or not), is to live in the "Other America" where it is a luxury just to be able to meet your basic needs, never mind have money left to stick in a savings account or a 401(k).

Most working class people don't get paid enough to afford enough food and heat in the winter. They are living paycheck to paycheck. Exponential increases in the number of working people turning to charity food pantries[21] and soup kitchens are proof that working harder, getting educations, and trying harder is not a guaranteed escape from poverty. There are *some* rare Horatio Alger cases but they're the exception, not the rule. According to Temple University sociology professor David Elesh, there are 52 million Americans who are working poor – most whom must rely on food banks. In 2002, one quarter of all low-income families[22] with one full-time worker was food insecure and housing insecure. As of 2007, over 37 million Americans[23] (12.5% of the population) were below the federal poverty line.

There are millions of middle-aged people who previously enjoyed high paying jobs in technology and finance fields before those jobs were off-shored en masse in the late-1990's/early-2000's, leaving them jobless and unemployable in their 40's and 50's. The losses of those white collar jobs followed the exodus of the good paying manufacturing jobs thanks to NAFTA and GATT. They previously had the incomes to be able to save money and afford comfortable middle class lives. They did "all the right things" and saved well but found that due to age discrimination in the job market, they couldn't get another job no matter how much they invested in "retooling" themselves and upgrading their skills. Those who remained jobless after the exhaustion of their unemployment benefits were no longer counted as unemployed – even if they were still jobless.

There are also plenty of middle-aged people who had never gotten any chances for the good life at all, even though they got

---

[21] Pennsylvania food banks report:
http://www.pafoodbanks.org/PARF_Site/Archived_Articles/Trainer

[22] USDA, Mark Nord, M. Andrews, S. Carlson. *Household Food Security in the United States, 2007.*

[23] US Census Bureau. Carmen DeNavas-Walt, B. Proctor, C. Lee. *Income, Poverty, and Health Coverage in the United States:2007*

educations and other training. Getting a job when the game is rigged in class-stratified society is more about whom – not what – you know.

When marginal people try to compete in a society that has routinely excluded them, they lose out to those who have historically benefited and who feel entitled to continue benefitting at others' expense. But no one wants to acknowledge this because then they would have to admit that they haven't won life's social prizes and rewards fair and square. They prefer to pat themselves on the back, revel in their successes, and tool around with bumper stickers on their cars reading "He who dies with the most toys wins." [Fact: He who dies with the most toys is still nonetheless dead.]

I will never forget another experience in my own fruitless job search in 2004 at the local PA Career Link Center when I tried to get an application for Penelec, the local electric utility company. Penelec was hiring meter readers. The starting wage was $18 an hour plus medical and dental benefits. That was certainly a job I *could* do and more than willing to do, *if* given the chance. Penelec was only taking applications through the PA Career Link office so that was the only way to get an application submitted. But I was denied the chance to even apply by the intake worker at the Career Link office who was in charge of the Penelec job applications.

This middle class bureaucrat flat out refused to give me an application – even though I was registered with Career Link and I was desperately poor and jobless. She told me, "No one owes you a job." I responded by telling her that it was my understanding that the US Constitution guarantees all citizens the right to life, liberty, and the pursuit of happiness. Being denied an equal chance to get a job that would enable me to support myself and get my basic needs met is being denied the right to life. Without adequate income, one cannot get food, clothing, medical/dental care, utilities, and shelter. Being unjustly denied an equal access to the very resources that I need in order to survive is a violation of my Constitutional rights and my human rights.

I explained to her that the US Constitution covers "all citizens" and that "all citizens" meant everyone – not just the privileged ones who feel they're the only ones entitled to get good jobs at the expense of poor people who need a chance, too. I told her to read the US Constitution and the Bill of Rights; that it says "We the People" – not "we the privileged classes", and definitely not "we the filthy rich multinational corporations." Being too poor to be able to live because of being denied opportunities was a deprivation of my right to life. There is no liberty in starvation, homelessness, and lack of access to health and dental care. There is no freedom in debt peonage. There is no justice in poverty.

Most middle and upper class people don't get it. That civil servant paid from taxpayer dollars which fund budgets for state agencies (including staff health and pension benefits), didn't get it. She took her comfortable middle class life, her secure job and all its benefits for granted. She got hers, regardless if anyone in poverty ever got a chance to get theirs. Apparently, only well-connected middle class people are entitled to good jobs – poor people who've been marginalized and socially excluded despite doing "all the right things" in order to be deserving of a chance can just starve, suffer without health and dental care, and go die under a bridge somewhere for all anybody cares. Welcome to America – the "land of opportunity."

In our "no pea" shell game of a job market, unemployed middle-aged workers are preyed upon by all sorts of "experts" who make the long-term unemployed feel as if their descent down the death spiral of poverty is their own fault. They're told by financial "experts" to plan better. They're coerced into spending money they can't afford or don't have on job coaches, "success" seminars, and extreme makeovers to fix their looks to make themselves more marketable[24]. It's a high-priced crap shoot in a casino economy where the house always wins. Those who can't afford expensive and drastic measures in order to *maybe* get gainfully re-employed are told that their lack of resources is their own fault for not saving enough money.

[24] http://www.todaysworkplace.org/2003/08/21/confusing-job-market-for-older-workers

The reality is that not all those who've been shoved out of the job market in their 40's earned enough money while they were young to be able to afford to save anything. Many never got chances for good jobs. Many have student loan debt and children to support. Many are also trying to help elderly parents who are poor and unable to live on what they get from social security.

Many middle-aged workers who previously enjoyed high paying jobs that enabled them to save well could not save enough money to live on for 20-25 years until they can collect social security (if social security will even be there for them). They would have needed to be able to save between one and two million dollars[25] in order to maintain solvency in the event of being unemployable at mid-life. How is that possible when most didn't get good jobs with security and health benefits right out of high school at the age of 18? How do you save a million dollars when you're poor and suffering from dental problems during your younger years while hoping to get a chance for a good job?

Age and disability discrimination has infected the job market like a contagious disease. Many found they couldn't get another job despite following the advice from all the "experts" who counseled them to be "upbeat." They're told if they're not able to get another job, it's because they don't have a positive attitude. How can anyone expect those suffering job loss combined with middle-age related health problems and bankrupting medical bills plus decimation of savings; to walk around displaying the sunniest of countenances and Pollyanna attitudes when their lives are being flushed down the toilet due to age discrimination in the job market? Regardless of what the "experts" claim, these issues cannot be solved with counseling and anger management.

Discarded middle-aged workers who previously had middle class jobs have had to prematurely cash in their 401(k)'s at steep penalties just to be able to pay their mortgages and buy food. Most couldn't afford to maintain their health coverage under COBRA. Any savings they had

[25] Amount needed to have in savings projected by financial planners like Suze Orman to be adequate enough to last 20-25 years during which you have no employer-paid health and dental benefits.

could not realistically be expected to last them for more than a year. And it is not uncommon for older workers to endure a period of joblessness for 3 years or longer. Given that, I challenge the credibility of armchair experts who contend that poverty and lack of opportunity is the fault of those who are poor.

According to ExecuNet, an Internet-based career services center for executives, age discrimination has increased in the last five years. ExecuNet conducted a survey of 200 of its participants of which 80% attribute these past five years of lay-offs to being age-biased, putting older workers at even greater risk for old age poverty. The Equal Employment Opportunity Commission (EEOC) reported that age discrimination complaints during the first quarter of 2001 was the highest since 1995 – an increase of 15%. Lisa B. Song of Knight Ridder News Service reported that a recent survey of 200 IT managers conducted by business technology magazine *Information Week* showed that only 2% of the IT managers surveyed would hire a job applicant with more than 10 years experience.

It is not only the middle-aged discarded worker who is at a disadvantage. What about young people who have the intelligence to succeed academically but who are from dysfunctional and impoverished families? What about those from poverty who are first generation college students? For them, odds of being able to successfully complete a college degree program are overwhelming. There is no social support for them. Poor whites face the additional barrier of everyone else assuming that just because they're white, they're middle or upper-middle class and if not, it must be because they're personally defective.

Immigrants attempting to get college degrees and good jobs get sympathy, help, and support because English is not their primary language and many are refugees. Minorities are recognized as deserving of help because it is assumed that past and present effects of racial discrimination served to make them poor. But if you're white and poor, you're invisible. Conventional wisdom holds that your white privilege should have sufficed to lift you out of poverty and that your poverty must be of your own making – even if you're disabled. The only sympathy poor whites get is in the dictionary - between "shit" and "syphilis." Any benefits conferred by white privilege are diminished by lack of class privilege.

It is not enough to get a college degree in order to have a chance. There are fewer and fewer jobs to go around for everyone than before NAFTA, GATT, and CAFTA. This is why the nepotism of social connections; and age, gender, and appearance is more of a determinant than ever in who gets a good job and who does not.

The pro-globalization trade policies set in motion since the 1980's resulted in the massive exodus of middle class American jobs. These policies undermined all of the workers' rights and gains realized during the 1940's through the 1970's when the majority of Americans could realistically aspire to the ranks of the middle class. 2008 reports from the US Department of Labor show that there are 100 job applicants for every job. Following the recipe of doing "all the right things" doesn't get you a job – it gets you an admission ticket to the "No Pea" shell game of scrambling for a small slice of an ever-shrinking pie.

Those with the most chances of getting hired in good jobs are those who have an "in" by knowing the right people, moving within the right social circles, living in the right neighborhood, having resources to live on while "paying your dues" working for nothing, and having a university degree from the right schools. The advantage of money and social connections goes a long way. More often than not, it is unearned social class privilege that determines employment opportunities. And it is our socio-economic status that defines our social connections. Classism plays a powerful role in defining our social networks. It is a major factor in making or breaking career opportunities, and navigating the back-biting minefield of "office culture."

If you can't afford a car or the "right image" of a nice smile, nice clothing, a nice physical appearance (i.e. thin and young), and the ability to fit in socially; your chances for success are slim – even if you manage to land the job. Education is not enough by itself to guarantee a chance to reach for the brass ring of middle classdom.

For every success story like that of Dr. Donna Beegle, a single mother who overcame generational poverty to earn her PhD and enter a rewarding career, there are millions of other poor women who also got educations but who were not able to escape "the other America." They never got the right opportunity before something really bad happened to them, stopping them dead in their tracks.

Contrary to popular belief, there isn't enough help for those who need it. Many poor people gained educations and skills against the overwhelming odds of poverty. But when they have to face potential employers with visibly decayed or missing teeth, health problems, ill-fitting thrift store clothing, no car, no phone, an address in the wrong part of town and poor credit, they found door after door of opportunity slammed shut in their faces. These critical factors are ignored by the talking heads, the self-proclaimed "experts", the politicians, the Ivy League policy makers at think tanks, and by society. Whether anyone admits it or not, luck matters. It's not how well you run the race; it's where you start from in the first place.

Conservative and liberal politicians alike tout the virtues of "Enterprise Zones" as the answer to job creation in pockets of urban poverty. Enterprise Zones are designated by government as economically blighted areas for which generous tax credits are given to large corporations to set up operations there. The experts claim that Enterprise Zones are the key to renewal and economic revival. What none of the experts and policy makers admit is the fact that the jobs created in these Enterprise Zones never go to the poor local residents who live in those areas; regardless of their educations and qualifications and desire to work.

An impoverished area of Brooklyn, New York known as Red Hook was designated by the government as an Enterprise Zone which brought an influx of construction and retail jobs. But virtually none of the poor jobless Red Hook residents were offered any of the jobs; even if they had the skills, education, or prior experience to be able to perform the essential functions of the jobs. One contractor hired lower-middle class blacks from a middle class neighborhood to fill the security guard positions. When he was questioned as to why he didn't hire any of the poor jobless people from the immediate vicinity, he replied, "What? You want me to give jobs to *those* people who are probably out to steal from me!" His attitude is not unique among employers. This attitude towards the poor and the hiring practice of poverty-profiling has been prevalent for decades. It only became a major problem when it began happening to middle class people.

Another method that employers use in poverty-profiling for weeding out job applicants is in the job application process itself: requiring the disclosure of your social security number on job applications – even if you have already submitted a résumé. You must not only disclose your social security number on job applications, you must also sign the job application. Signing the job application grants automatic consent (as a condition of applying for the job) to the employer to do background checks and pull your credit report. If you refuse to disclose your social security number on the job application, your application gets tossed. It's a no-win situation for those struggling to get good jobs in order to escape poverty.

Your credit report not only shows your credit score (FICO score) which ranges from 350 to 800, it also lists all information about you. A FICO score below 620 is considered poor credit – a dead give-away that you're probably low-income. Other information listed on the very top of the credit report is your date of birth – which allows employers to discriminate against you for a job based on your age and get away with it. Your credit report also lists your address because auto insurance companies and utility companies regularly report your payments every month to the major credit bureaus. It lists the address for where utility service is provided and whether or not it is a residential or a commercial address. Whether or not you live on the "wrong" side of town is obtained from your credit report.

Medical bills incurred from an illness or injury is also listed on your credit report. That would indicate a possible medical condition or disability which would give the employer medical information about you not related to the job that would result in your being discriminated against for the job. This information is used in poverty-profiling, and in age and/or disability discrimination; all of which is used in the employer's decision to illegally deny you an equal opportunity for a job – without you being able to prove it.

Requiring the disclosure of your social security number on job applications is not to ensure you're a legal resident or citizen of the United States. Employers could ensure Form I-9 compliance[26] by requesting a copy of your drivers' license, state issued non-driving photo ID, and a copy of your birth or marriage certificate. There is no valid reason for employers to force job seekers to disclose their social security numbers on job applications and pull credit reports. Use of the ubiquitous credit score is common practice among all employers today – even big box retail stores which pay \$6 - \$7 an hour with no benefits. Poverty is a life sentence when your socio-economic status is used against you for getting a chance for a job that pays a living wage. Poverty-profiling is a legal time-honored method of discriminating against women and minorities for everything from good jobs to decent housing.

As recently as 2004 the same situation occurred when Wal-Mart was building their new store three blocks from my house in Erie's impoverished central/east side. Local black community leader and civil rights activist Gary Horton raised a huge stink on the local television news station WJET-24 so that job seekers from my neighborhood (which has a 68% poverty rate) got a fair chance to apply for any of the \$6 an hour jobs at the new store. These were low paying jobs without health or dental benefits. Wal-Mart, the nation's largest retailer, sought to profit from the patronage of local poor residents while denying those same people a chance to work there. A \$6 an hour job without benefits is nowhere near enough to lift someone out of poverty, but it's still better than absolutely nothing.

Levi Hipp, the general manager of the new Wal-Mart, confirmed to me that it was Wal-Mart's corporate policy to not hire poor people in most need of a job because "the majority of the poor lack work ethic and

---

[26] Federal Form I-9 is to verify that you are legally allowed to be employed in the United States as either a citizen or resident alien.

might steal." Refusal to hire local poor people for local jobs is universal in all types of jobs. Middle class snobs tell the poor to "just pack up and move" if where you live is preventing you from getting a job. But being able to "pack your stuff and move out" requires money – something poor people without jobs don't have.

In 1989, poor jobless locals were excluded from good-paying jobs when the Lehigh County Prison in Allentown, Pennsylvania was given federal grant money to refurbish and expand its facility in order to accommodate federal prisoners. All of the construction jobs, which paid prevailing wages, were filled by middle class white males from out of the area while local apprentices, skilled tradespeople and vo-tech graduates stood in soup kitchen lines — hungry, jobless, and homeless. This happened after the closing of Allentown's Mack Trucks, Bethlehem Steel, Trojan Powder Company, and Phoenix Apparel during the 1980's.

Lehigh County, especially Allentown, was disproportionately affected by the closings of the steel mills and all of the local textile and garment factories. Thousands of local middle class residents were thrown into joblessness and poverty. Many were over the age of 35 so going to college when they lacked the appropriate academic preparation in high school many years prior, made no sense for them. The majority of the new "Information Age" computer jobs were being given to younger people who graduated from college at age 22 or 23. The few dislocated manufacturing workers who struggled (often without success) to get college educations at an older age — after being told to do so by all the "experts" — were at an unfair disadvantage due to ageism, lack of support, and academic deficits.

Lack of a high school college prep background and years away from the classroom were not the only barriers faced by the older learners who attempted college after the loss of their union manufacturing jobs. The older students were socially excluded from study groups and various other learning opportunities outside of class by their younger college classmates as well as by administration policies. The older students also had to frequently juggle the obligations of families and menial jobs around the expectations and assignments of elitist professors who never considered the needs of older students. While there was a loosely organized support group for these non-traditional aged students, very few of them had the luxury of time to participate in the group. Older students had no mentors.

Older learners also faced unreasonable and unsympathetic professors who held that the older students "should have thought about college when they were younger" instead of going to work in the factories. Older learners who weren't getting a free ride on football scholarships or from the bank of mom and dad were not welcome at college. Excluded and ridiculed by the younger students and marginalized by elitist professors, older students had no academic support network available to them. For all the talk by "experts" who claimed "you can achieve anything if you try hard enough", making older learners feel inadequate if college was too hard for them, no one offered any support. In sum, the game was rigged.

The situation was far worse for socio-economically disadvantaged jobless people who had already been having a tough time before the better jobs vanished, pitting them in competition for "survival jobs" against middle class job seekers. If things were bad for formerly middle class blue collar union workers, they got infinitely worse for the poor as competition for crumbs at the bottom grew even fiercer. The poor got no sympathy from the "yuppies"[27] who told them that their poverty and lack of job opportunities was their own fault because they "chose" to forego a college education when they were younger in order to work in the factories instead. Yuppies forgot that if it weren't for good-paying union jobs, their parents would not have been able to buy homes send them to college. Do you deserve nothing except hunger, lack of health and dental care, preventable disability and premature death from poverty simply because you lost out in capitalism's zero-sum game when you never really had a chance in the first place?

After the industrial jobs vanished leaving thousands jobless and unemployable, the next bootstrap for the poor got sliced. Private Industry

---

[27] "Yuppies" is slang for Young Urban Professionals; particularly the greedy self-centered college-educated upper-middle class.

Council (PIC) of the Lehigh Valley, the agency in charge of administering the now-extinct Comprehensive Employment & Training Act (CETA) program which provided federally subsidized low-paying jobs to socio-economically disadvantaged people, lost its funding under Reagan. Furthermore, former union factory workers with at least *some* economic security and trappings of middle class life were given precedence for job placement at PIC – shoving out the poorest of the jobless who weren't getting unemployment benefits and who had never had any chances at all for getting any work experience. CETA was designed to aid the most disadvantaged unemployed job seekers get jobs; not those who already had resources, work experience, and a cache of middle class resources built into their lives.

This was the "brave new world" I entered as a high school graduate in 1985. I was one of countless underprivileged young adults in need of job placement through PIC who got "crowded out." I was from an inner-city ghetto where the premature death rate from suicide, drug overdose, and drive-by shootings was higher than the rejection rate for admissions to MIT or Cal Tech.

While the middle class workers from the closed plants deserved and needed jobs, the most underprivileged job seekers who were the intended target of the CETA program had the most pressing need because they didn't have anything. They didn't have stable middle class families. They didn't have any resources built into their lives. They didn't have any middle class references. They didn't have nice homes in the "right" neighborhoods. They didn't have decades of secure middle class employment in order to build a safety net to see them through hard times. They had no chance to get a life. They had nothing. Compared to Allentown's poor, those displaced union workers from Bethlehem Steel, Mack Trucks, and Phoenix Apparel were rich!

Those middle class workers who got preference in job placement at PIC also complained about the jobs PIC gave them as if they weren't good enough. They didn't work very hard or show appreciation for getting those jobs at the expense of the poor who had the greater need but who got shoved aside. To the middle class former union factory worker, the entry-level jobs through CETA weren't good enough.

Poor high school graduates just entering the workforce from disadvantaged backgrounds would have been extremely grateful for the low-paying PIC jobs that the middle-class workers with entitlement attitudes took for granted. Middle class spoiled brats who had enjoyed decades of high wages and benefits held their noses high while taking the "handout" of subsidized job placement through CETA while having the moxy to put down poor women on welfare. Those on the bottom socio-economic rung with the greatest need for those subsidized jobs were left out in order to take care of the middle class. The thanks we got for "taking one for the team" was Slavefare (Workfare) and the Welfare Reform Act of 1996.

I was 22 years old at the height of this major economic upheaval during the late 1980's. Whenever there were decent paying entry level jobs offered by employers who didn't require a college degree, i.e. local utility company jobs, it was middle class former manufacturing workers (mostly white men) who always got hired – not the poor and disadvantaged job seekers.

I was a poor young woman with a skilled trade who was perceived as a threat by the men in the white male dominated construction industry. The men viewed women like me as "trying to take away a man's job." The men felt they were more entitled to being able to afford food, health and dental care, and a roof over their head than a poor woman with no husband and no family to rely on. I was subjected to comments, "Why don't you get a husband?", "why don't you get a waitress job instead?", and "what's a pretty thing like you doing working in *this* job?"

Ironically, poor young women out on their own are not considered too "pretty" by these self-centered male chauvinist pigs to have to lose teeth from poverty due to job discrimination. Poor women weren't "too pretty" to be abused and exploited in the seedy sex industry. Poor women weren't "too pretty" to have to work in low-wage nurse's aide jobs lifting heavy patients without help and risking injury, cleaning up patients' shit and piss, wiping asses and changing bedpans all day long, and suffer physical assaults by nursing home residents who frequently lash out and hit the staff. I'd like to see men work for the paltry pay nurse's aides get for working in that environment –having to work a hell of a lot harder than men in the construction trades unions.

That would be a joke, considering most of these tough men can't/won't actively support and take care of their women during pregnancy, labor and birth. They gag uncontrollably at the prospect of having to change their own baby's soiled diaper once in awhile. The prospect of "let down reflex" causing them to be accidently sprayed a little bit with their wife's/girlfriend's breast milk is enough to make men lose it. Then there's the issue of women being discarded by their men after pregnancy and childbirth ruined their bodies because men – being the shallow, selfish, superficial pigs that they are – can't stand making love to the women who suffered damage to their bodies to bear men's brats. Men cringe in revulsion at the sight of stretch marks, saggy breasts, crinkly loose stomach skin and "mommy pouches". No wonder difficult labors caused by emotional trauma, post-partum depression, and childbirth related PTSD[28] is on the rise.

And of course, none of the middle class men I worked alongside with in construction offered to belly up to the bar and marry me, love me forever, treat me right, and financially support me (and any potential children) for the rest of my life. Most were too selfish to give any woman the benefits of commitment.

Poor women who are totally on their own can't make it on a benefit-less "pink collar" waitress job because women do not get to pay less than a man to live. That loaf of bread costs a woman the same as it does for a man. I needed to be able to earn enough to be able to eat, afford health and dental care, housing, utilities, and clothing until Prince Charming came along – which only happens in fairytales.

---

[28] PTSD: Post Traumatic Stress Disorder; severe depression and anxiety caused by emotional and physical trauma; suffered by combat vets and women who have had traumatic birth experiences.

That is a slim prospect for socio-economically disadvantaged women. But it was an impossible prospect for a poor woman who didn't have the good fortune to be one of the "pretty people" born with the perfect body type and good looks. Had I been fortunate enough to be one of the "hotties" able to land a middle or upper class man who would have cared enough to marry me and lift me up from poverty; I would have been branded a "gold digger" and a "whore." (Think: Anna Nicole Smith)

Middle and upper class men who straddle the class divide by dating and marrying poor women are often reminded by their families that their girlfriend isn't good enough for them, that she's "beneath him." We're judged by others for what we have, who our family is, where we live, what our parents do for a living, and what resources we have to bring to the marriage table. Dating and marriage prospects for poor women are very, very limited.

Poor women lack the same social and cultural experiences of middle and upper class women because lack of money is a barrier to social participation. Middle and upper class men rarely marry down in socio-economic class. They seek partners who have similar financial worth and shared cultural and social experiences to bring something of value to a marriage. They don't want a partner deemed a liability because of being underprivileged from the bottom socio-economic class. Meanwhile, poor men often see wives as an unaffordable commodity or an added expense that they don't want. Proper marriage and raising a family is a luxury reserved for the middle and upper classes; a luxury that is out of reach for poor women.

In our materialistic consumer-driven society, marriage is viewed in the same light as any capitalist venture. Everybody wants the winners. Nobody wants to be dragged down socially and economically by one of society's "losers." This fact escaped the logic of politicians, talk show "experts", and conservative think tanks who promoted cutting aid for the poor and redirecting those funds to faith-based initiatives that "teach marriage" to poor single mothers. Most men are too selfish to marry and support poor women – let alone poor women whose bodies are already "damaged goods" from pregnancy and giving birth to someone else's child.

Far more poor women would have better chances for marriage if the barriers of classism and job discrimination in our society were dismantled. No one advocated programs to teach middle and upper class men to marry the poor women they used for casual sex while they string poor women along – only to discard them anyway. Re-educating selfish, commitment-phobic men would have solved more of the poverty and single motherhood problems than punishing poor women and children.

How many middle and upper class men got poor women pregnant after having unprotected sex and then dumped them without even paying for an abortion and swearing that the baby wasn't theirs? How many of these men beat the system and forced poor women to pay the unaffordable cost for a paternity test that she couldn't afford while not getting a dime in child support? How many of these men left poor women to fend for themselves and their children on meager and inadequate welfare benefits, to be judged and socially persecuted for the rest of her life – and the child's life – because of *her* "poor choice" to have a baby she couldn't afford?

How many anti-abortion terrorists can afford to take time off from work to blockade abortion facilities, picket Planned Parenthood clinics that offer contraceptives at zero/reduced cost, as they call the women trying to enter those facilities whores and murderers, and stalk and kill doctors? How many of these zealots are white males with good jobs and plenty of money who will never know what it is to be poor, abandoned, and pregnant and uninsured in a vulture capitalist society that discards poor women? How many middle/upper class white male "pro-lifers" married and supported a poor, deserted pregnant woman seeking an abortion to give her and the baby a chance for a decent life, to give her and some other man's child unconditional love and support? How many of these privileged zealots also voted for politicians who eliminated welfare for poor single mothers while shooting down abortion coverage under healthcare reform and killing universal health care bills like HR 676?

Women don't get pregnant by themselves. The co-conceivers (men) responsible for these pregnancies are never the ones who are impoverished from pregnancy and childbirth. It's not men that endure risk, pain and disfigurement from childbirth. They don't face job loss and inability to get another job due to pregnancy and gender discrimination in the job market. They're not the ones suffering consequences for playing the love 'em and leave 'em game.

Middle and upper class women have access to a wide array of contraceptive choices to prevent unwanted pregnancies. If a contraceptive fails, they have the resources to pay for an abortion so that their lives aren't destroyed by a medically risky or unwanted pregnancy. Poor women don't have options since the Hyde Amendment stopped Medicaid funding for abortions in 1976 – even when the pregnancy is the result of a rape.

Poor women do not have the same opportunities socially, politically, or economically as everyone else in society. Poor women can't win no matter what. Poor women who aren't "Barbie dolls" are at the worst possible disadvantage for getting good jobs and for finding a marriageable man who is willing to give them the benefit of a commitment. In our class-stratified society, middle-aged and/or overweight women are passed over for job opportunities in favor of thinner, younger "eye candy."

After moving to Erie from Philadelphia in the wake of the devastating economic tsunami caused by 9/11, I applied for a job at the Erie American Express office. I already had six months experience and all of my licenses. I had mastered hedging and difficult restricted stock sales and foreign currency options contracts back in Philadelphia. I spoke on the phone with Scott Cable, the branch manager. He sounded very eager to hire me because I was a candidate who would be ready to hit the ground running.

But when I had the face-to-face interview his attitude toward me changed. Upon seeing that I wasn't a thin, 20-something year old "Barbie doll" and instead saw that I was a chubby plain-looking 36 year old woman, he wrote across the top of my résumé "DO NOT HIRE – TOO FAT" as I sat across the desk from him.

He didn't get the memo: I wasn't applying for the position of "trophy wife" or Victoria Secret lingerie model.

Every time a poor woman who is overweight and/or middle-aged gets turned away and denied a chance for a job she's qualified for and desperately needs to support herself; it means going home poor and empty-handed, unable to afford life's most basic necessities. It means one more attempt at climbing out of poverty through hard work is sabotaged by someone with unearned privilege who wields the power of deciding who gets hired and who does not.

It is easy to criticize poor women who didn't luck out in the gene pool if you're a member of the privileged classes, a member of the favored group, or lucky in winning the looks lottery. But the fact is that poor women who are struggling just to afford food and shelter don't have money to help them where genetics and cell biology failed them. When your choices are buying cheap foods loaded with starch, sugar, aspartame, MSG, and recombinant bovine growth hormones (rBGH) and other toxins so the family can eat at least one meal a day for an entire month; or buying healthier food which costs three times as much and won't feed a household for a month, guess who loses out. Since local organic farmers don't accept food stamps, poor people have no choice – they can't buy healthy organic foods that aren't infused with hormones, antibiotics, and other toxins.

When your choice is paying the overdue water bill or the past due electric bill, money for plastic surgery or even a YMCA membership doesn't exist. Given these facts, ask yourself honestly how poor women struggling with their weight can realistically "do something about it" when money dictates what choices are available. How are poor women supposed to climb out of poverty when they're left out of the dating and mating scene, and denied good jobs because of their weight and looks in a male dominated society that only values women for their looks and body type according to a Caucasian standard of beauty?

Being a middle-aged woman means facing an uphill battle to remain slim because of the effects of childbearing and hormonal changes associated with aging. In a society that worships its Angelina Jolies and that discards its unattractive, its overweight, its pregnant, its infirm, and its old; poor women who lost out in the physical attractiveness department also lose out in love, life, and in the job market. Media moguls have done more than their fair share to perpetuate this venomous brand of classism through social engineering for profit and preservation of *unearned* upper class white male privilege.

Wealthy dentists, doctors, and surgeons don't donate their services to poor women in need of improving their life chances by improving their looks and bodies in our image-oriented society. And women should not have to go under a plastic surgeon's knife in order to be "worthy" anyway because we're all beautiful in our own right. As long as people need to eat in order to live, the Food Mafia (Monsanto) really has no incentive to forego any of their profits – they don't care if their genetically modified "Frankenfoods" are the direct cause of increasing cancer rates, obesity and diabetes among the poor and working classes. Big Ag has a vested interest in unhealthy foods: they're in bed with Big Pharma. They profit from the increasing obesity epidemic. Being able to "do something about it" concerning weight problems, health problems, dental problems, and looks is a social class privilege not enjoyed equally by everyone in our society.

What options does this leave for poor women who aren't thin enough, pretty enough, and young-looking enough to be hired in white collar jobs, or to find decent men who will marry them and support them?

America was a very hostile place for the poor entering the mating game and the 1980's job market driven by "voodoo economics." It got worse over the last 25 years. The Welfare Reform Act of 1996 and the elimination of many social support programs in tandem with NAFTA and the massive jobs exodus fast-tracked our current economic disaster today.

But who voted for presidents and congressmen that eliminated funding for subsidized job placement programs under CETA? Who elected leaders that fast-tracked NAFTA and subsequently signed it? It was the upper-middle class and the rich, and teams of corporate lobbyists that shaped this economic landscape. The elected officials who were supposed to represent the citizens of this country sold the lower socio-economic classes down the river.

The poor have no say in the main factors that causes poverty: the lack of enough job opportunities for everyone, job discrimination, and lack of a real safety net. The poor are always told it's their own fault for not being smart enough, good enough, or hardworking enough in order to get ahead. They're told that their poverty is a "lifestyle choice" that they could change if they really wanted to. We need to really examine the definitions of "equal opportunity" and "choices" and then honestly ask ourselves about the choices available to those who are stuck in poverty.

Lack of enough opportunity, social inequality, and exploitation are the main factors that cause poverty. The "ghetto taxes" that go in tandem with lack of incomes keep people poor. Ghetto taxes are the extra fees, taxes, and miscellaneous costs that the poor are forced to pay for in order to get the same goods and services that the middle and upper classes get for less. Examples include bank fees, fees at check-cashing joints, and usurious rates at pay-day lenders.

Low-income drivers living in high poverty areas pay 30% more for auto insurance[29] than their middle class counterparts, given equal driving records, cars, age, and gender. Basic utilities such as electric and gas for heating, cooking, and hot water cost the poor more. Their rates are determined by their credit scores and neighborhoods in which they live. Poor people are penalized with unaffordable security deposits; reconnect fees, and monthly rate surcharges for their inability to afford their most basic bills. Consequently, the poor are forced to pay 30% -

[29] Source: IIAB, the national association of Independent Insurance Agents and Brokers.

50% more[30] for basic utilities on far lower incomes than the middle and upper classes have.

When you're surviving paycheck to paycheck (if you're even lucky enough to have a job to begin with) there's no "extra" money to save. You can't afford to keep a minimum balance in a checking account because you're budgeted to the penny. You must constantly choose which basic necessity to do without. You check your account balance at the ATM machine to see if you have enough money to cover the purchase of bread, eggs, milk and laundry detergent. The dozen eggs and loaf of bread is all you'll have to eat until you get your food stamps a week from now and you have no food left in your home at all. Your ATM slip shows that you have $20. You buy your few meager items and swipe your debit card only to find that your purchases put you in the red by a dollar, which will result in a $38 overdraft fee, unless you do without something. You ask the cashier to take back the detergent that you *really* needed because you ran out two weeks ago and have no clean clothes. You go home with the food that you must ration until you get your food stamps — clean clothes that don't stink are a luxury.

Another example: You take a load of scrap metal (that took two weeks of your time to salvage) to the junkyard, so that you can afford the $6 co-pay Medicaid charges you for your heart medicines and diabetes pills that you need just to live every month. The junkyard pays you with a check. Since the check is drawn from the same bank as your checking account, there shouldn't be any "holding period" on the junkyard check you deposit. Two weeks later, you get an overdraft charge notice in the mail from your bank. Your $6 Medicaid co-pays ends up costing you $38 for 8 medicines, a total of $304 in overdraft fees, putting you in the hole unable to pay your rent or mortgage or any utilities because your low monthly fixed income was eaten up by bank fees. This puts you on a downward spiral of falling even further behind on everything else, resulting in eviction, foreclosure, and utility shut-offs. For people struggling at or below the poverty level, overdraft fees add up to well

---

30 *"The High Price of Being Poor"* (Matt Fellowes, the Brookings Institute, July 23rd 2006)

over a thousand dollars over the span of one year and can make a life or death difference.

Being smug because you have plenty of money doesn't make you better than the poor; it makes you a jerk. The system is broken and needs to be fixed. Price-gouging those who have the least money to afford anything while claiming the rich "earned" theirs is excusing theft. Setting up straw man arguments as an excuse to begrudge America's poor anything doesn't make it right. Those with plenty say America is the "land of opportunity", but they forgot to add "for cutthroats and crooks." They talk about the constitutional right to pursue happiness while forgetting the poor who are crushed underfoot and denied that right.

Denying help to America's poor and reinforcing classism by saying "the poor here are rich compared to the poor in 3rd World nations" doesn't fly. There may be some truth to that, but that's like saying that the slave being beaten five days a week doesn't have it bad because he's not getting beaten seven days. Countless Americans who are among the poorest of the poor live in "tent cities." They have nowhere to bathe, brush their teeth, or wash their dirty clothes. They can't get jobs because they have no phone and no place to live. They go hungry and die for lack of health care, if they don't die from exposure in the elements first. It's a vicious catch-22. When Americans who are struggling in poverty complain, they're told to "shut up and stop whining" because the poor in 3rd World nations have it so much worse.

The destitute and homeless are routinely chased, and their makeshift shelters and few meager clothes are destroyed and bulldozed by police. They're left with nothing but the clothes on their backs, living as internally displaced refugees. The poorest of the poor have no healthcare. They can't vote because they lack a residence – a requirement to be able to register to vote in most states.

Poor Americans routinely have their poverty and pain invalidated; disregarded by elitist pseudo-intellectuals (who have *never* been poor) who point to the 3rd World and say "you don't have it *that* bad." A race to the bottom still ends at the bottom.

No matter what country you live in, if you can't get any job opportunities that you need in order to support yourself (or your family) and you are forced to do without the basic needs of food, water, clothing, shelter, and healthcare – you are poor. When you're deprived of being able to benefit and participate in the society in which you live, you are poor. Those struggling in poverty in America are always dismissed with "shut up, you whiner." Just because being poor in America is not the same as being poor in Nairobi doesn't make poverty in America okay.

If 3rd World nations' governments enforced the laws prohibiting human trafficking, prosecuted corporate abuses, abolished "honor killings", and eradicated policies that allow women to be treated as male property; then 3rd World poverty would be "nothing", too. Why should America's poor have to suffer when poverty here and abroad was caused by greedy rich people? Does invalidating the experiences of America's poor improve the lives of the poor in 3rd World countries? When Doctors Without Borders and Remote Area Medical come to downtown Los Angeles to treat a fraction of America's poor, isn't it time to recognize 3rd World poverty here?

Someone who isn't getting a chance for a job has no money to be able to live. Someone who is hungry and doing without life-sustaining utilities, suffering without medical and dental care; and someone who is homeless living in a "tent city" in the United States of America should *not* have to live in the slums of Mumbai before getting acknowledged and helped. A poor American who dies from poverty is just as dead as other nations' poor who die from poverty. What is US citizenship worth if citizens are denied their basic human needs and the opportunity to participate in the workforce and in society?

America is a 1st World nation. It is supposedly the best and richest country in the world. The fact that babies and poor pregnant women here have the same infant mortality rate as those in Mozambique (the poorest country in the world)[31] is a compelling reason to start recognizing poverty in America. Ignoring our poor by measuring "poverty dicks" doesn't help *any* nation's poor.

American capitalism emphasizes low taxes for the "winners" and rugged individualism. That's why the US has always had a relatively large number of poor people, while the middle and upper classes deny that America's poor have it bad compared to those in 3rd World countries. Fact: we have 3rd World poverty in the US, but nobody cares about Americans who are poor and not making it. They dismiss the poor and claim that they're always "somehow able to make it."

The 45,000 poor uninsured Americans who died last year for lack of access to medical care didn't "make it." Those who lose their low-paying jobs and end up in "tent cities" aren't "making it." The countless more poor and uninsured who end up blind from glaucoma due to lack of access to medical care, or who lose limbs from diabetes complications because of a lack of access to nutritious food, safe housing and preventive medical care aren't "making it." And the victims of poverty who died directly as a result of government-approved Benign Neglect masquerading as a botched rescue effort in the aftermath of Hurricane Katrina didn't "make it."

There is no excuse for discarding our marginalized, for refusing to create strong safety nets while diminishing opportunities for our disenfranchised; or for discarding our pregnant, our disabled and our elderly. America's poor are not 100% responsible for the poverty in 3rd World nations. Corrupt fascist governments in bed with greedy multinational corporations are. Poverty and social inequality in America are 100% the responsibility of Americans.

[31] 2004 World Health Organization Report to the United Nations

Chapter 4

"The function of freedom is to free somebody else." ~ Toni Morrison

People with money, family, resources and social capital have choices. They have options that are not available to those without money and resources. They have some choice over how they will live, and *if* they will live as opposed to dying prematurely for lack of access to medical care or lack of inclusion in a disaster escape plan. Recall those who died during and immediately after Hurricane Katrina: those who couldn't leave because they lacked the resources to do so. Having choices is a luxury the poor often don't have.

The rich create the poor and then cannot stand to look at them. Our media-addicted world saw the prosperity gospel's mask ripped off the face of America in the wake of Hurricane Katrina. Everyone knows that anyone who had the means to evacuate just drove out of town. There's a well-illustrated dividing line right there. Rather than enact any redistributive policies that would uplift the poor, America's middle and upper classes decided to justify cruelty and hatred towards the poor. Louisiana state representative Richard Baker (R-LA) said to well-heeled lobbyists, "We finally cleaned up public housing in New Orleans. We couldn't do it, but God did."

Former US Congressman Rick Santorum (R-PA) said that he felt that those from the poorest of the poor that managed to survive the Category 5 hurricane should be punished for not evacuating, even though they lacked the means to do so. On September 6th, 2005 just days after Katrina struck, "pro-life" conservative Christian Rick Santorum said:

> "I mean, you have people who don't heed those warnings and then put people at risk as a result of not heeding those warnings. There may be a need to look at tougher penalties on those who decide to ride it out and understand that there are consequences to not leaving."

More penalties indeed…for those least able to fend for themselves: poor women who were pregnant and ready to deliver (therefore unable to travel) when Katrina struck, as attested to by former Royal Marine Daryl Hill who owns a New Orleans hotel. Of the poor deemed in need of extra punishment for being poor, female and pregnant, Daryl Hill said:

> "This far outweighs anything I saw when I was with the British forces in various hostile areas. The lack of support we've had, the lack of supplies flown in. Now they're starting to arrive, but it has taken over a week. I think there should have been a much quicker response from the hierarchy. I saw a young lady, she had just given birth and she had to carry her newborn over her head. The water was up to her breasts and she was just walking through the water crying for help."

Evacuating was not an option available for those who were disabled, without a car, or otherwise unable to drive. Those who were poor and unemployable due to being pregnant without a car, money, and credit cars had no way to leave. Those who lacked the money to afford even a Greyhound bus ticket didn't have the option to leave. If you are disabled, your $600/mo SSI check is not enough to afford a place to live plus utilities and food anywhere in the United States unless you can get subsidized housing under HUD Section 8. And the waiting list to get Section 8 housing is an average of 10 years.

If you cannot get anything but jobs that pay minimum wage or less because of age, sex, disability, or appearance discrimination and a lack of enough jobs for everyone that needs one and wants one, you cannot afford to live – let alone have the resources to actually have the choice to leave. A car in good repair, gasoline, and a few nights' worth of motel costs plus food all cost money, something that poor people of New Orleans didn't have in order to weather a catastrophe intact. The poor of New Orleans who could scrape together the money for a Greyhound bus ticket were stuck because bus service was suspended the day before Katrina made landfall. No matter what, those with the least money and resources were prevented from being able to leave.

The affluent people from the French Quarter certainly didn't offer to come down into the impoverished 9th ward with their SUV's to give the stranded victims a ride out of the danger zone. Safe shelter elsewhere to avoid the path of nature's violent fury was not an option for those lacking money, credit cards, or social capital. What choice did the poor who were left stranded at the Superdome really have?

America really hates its poor — especially poor pregnant women. According to the US Department of Health & Human Services and the most recent US Census records 84% of those in poverty are women. A country that claims to be Christian that opposes abortion because of its "pro-life" values hates the poorest of the poor — unemployable and poor pregnant women whose condition prevents travel and who have no means to fend for themselves and evacuate a natural disaster — cheerfully enacted abusive social and economic policies against them amounting to "extermination by imposed destitution."

Right-wing television talk show host Bill O'Reilly of *"The O'Reilly Factor: No Spin Zone"* said that poverty and being left to die in a hurricane all boils down to choice,

> "If you choose to not get a college education and choose to not work hard, you won't get ahead and if a natural disaster strikes you will be left behind. It's not the government's job to bail you out."

In the world according to Bill O'Reilly, if you don't do "all the right things" you will be poor, terrible things will happen to you and it's not society's responsibility to help you because it's your own fault.

How does this explain the poverty and misfortune of those who *did* do "all the right things" who got left economically behind? The answer is that it doesn't. It's merely an excuse for greedy self-centered people to be cruel and selfish toward the poor. It's the mass line used to cover up the class line. Reality check: choices are determined by money first and foremost, and secondly by the support network one has in their life.

Like his middle class audience, Bill O'Reilly and other right-wing talking heads don't grasp the idea of a pyramid scheme; much less recognize one right underneath their noses. There has to be a large number of people at the bottom. Can *everyone* be rich? Can *everyone* be middle class? Most poor people can't make it out of poverty in the pyramid scheme of capitalism; otherwise nobody would serve the burgers and the coffee, or change the bedpans, or take out the trash, or clean the toilets in all the office buildings where those with the "important" jobs work. And no one would be the poor jobless and unemployable "case files" to justify middle class welfare caseworkers' jobs. And because of this system, the majority of the middle class hates the poor while they go about their lives, consoling themselves for being better than "those people" at the very bottom that aren't "their kind."

Capitalism works like a Ponzi scheme. If you don't accept that then there's no point in discussing solutions for those stuck at the bottom. Getting an education and having the "correct" attitude won't guarantee you a ticket out of poverty and into the middle class when you started out far behind the 8-ball in an environment that penalizes you for being unable to afford health care, the "right" image, and not having the "right" social connections to jump start your life. Some from the very bottom do succeed, but most won't be able to no matter how hard they work and how much they try. A large part of that has to do with the gender division of labor and the devaluation of "women's work", especially motherhood. Another part has to do with middle class insecurity. This works out very nicely for those who don't want to compete (or have their children forced to compete) on a level playing field for the good jobs, doesn't it?

Occasionally, a few individuals in poverty make it if they're lucky, and if they're not slapped with a disabling injury or illness while struggling to climb out of poverty and if they get a chance *before* anything bad happens to them to eliminate all chances and hope. And much of that hinges on health problems created by the limited food choices that the poor have available to them.

Adam Drewnowski, the director of the Center For Obesity Research at the University of Washington, wrote about the choices poor people have regarding healthy foods. He wrote about the correlation of poverty to obesity in terms of restricted choices due to restricted food dollars that the poor have. In his 2007 article[32] in *Epidemiologic Reviews*, Drewnowski states:

> "Low-income shoppers on a constrained budget, the very group these programs target, often make a rational decision in the supermarket to buy the most energy-dense foods limited dollars can afford. And, in the American supermarket, it just so happens that you get more calories per dollar from soft drinks than fruit juice, from refined grains than whole grains, from frozen French fries than fresh broccoli. In other words, the foods, beverages, snacks or diets said to promote obesity were, in every case, inexpensive. What epidemiologic research seems to have shown, fairly consistently, is that obesity is most closely associated with habitual consumption of low-cost foods."

When middle class people sermonize the poor about "making the right choices" while calling their condescension "advice", they ignore the reality that the poor must live in. As Adam Drewnowski said, "saying to low-income people, *'Why don't you choose to eat a healthy, nutritious diet?'* is not much different from saying *'Why don't you choose to live on Park Avenue?'* Choice has little to do with it."

It's amazing that the privileged classes, who have a tendency towards credentialism and its implication of expertise, choose to conveniently ignore the published findings of a well-credentialed world-renowned leader in obesity prevention when his findings don't fit comfortably within the Blame the Poor paradigm. Being poor means you either go without entirely, or go to food banks and soup kitchens and hope you can use half of the donated non-perishable foods they give you.

---

[32] "The Real Contribution of Added Sugars And Fat To Obesity", Adam Drewnowski, *Epidemiologic Reviews*, vol. 29, 2007. © 2007 by Johns Hopkins Bloomberg School of Public Health.

The Blame the Poor crowd really doesn't care what the poor eat, or *if* we eat. It's all about blame and feeling superior while they pat themselves on the back for donating sugary cereals, pasta, powdered milk, and macaroni and cheese mix to food banks and soup kitchens — convinced that they've "done their part" while blaming us for eating unhealthy crap because we're "ignorant", after telling us how "grateful" we should be for those donations from our "betters.

These are frequently the same people who look down their regal noses at those of us who get a little bit of food stamps and chastise our food shopping choices, without taking into consideration that a lot of poor people don't have the same resources as they do to be able to shop at a Wegman's, or buy in bulk from a Whole Foods co-op that's not within walking distance.

Once you factor into the equation the difficulties faced by those who don't have a car and who must walk or take the bus, you have to consider the limited number and weight of things that can be toted on a bus ride from the supermarket. Kansas city, Missouri is one example of a large city that has only very limited bus service that doesn't even cover the entire metro area. Of course, the sanctimonious class will contrive the most impressive polemics to blame the poor by saying that we should be "smart enough" to move to cities like NYC or Philadelphia that have something resembling a public transportation system — even though there isn't a bus stop in front of everyone's home and having to walk a half a mile to the nearest one isn't necessarily possible for those encumbered by very small children, or the elderly, or those with physical disabilities who can't hoof it even a quarter mile while loaded down with heavy grocery bags.

Transport makes an enormous difference when you're poor. You have frozen items, dairy products and other perishables that need refrigeration quickly. Potatoes and oranges alone are hard enough to buy and transport in bulk since they're heavy, never mind the liquid products. When was the last time you had to trudge on foot for a mile or two, negotiate out-of-the-way and time-consuming bus rides, with heavy grocery bags in hand and a toddler in tow? Can you imagine trying to do it as someone with a disability, or as a frail older person? It's not like there's a Whole Foods co-op in every ghetto and trailer park. And it's not like local organic farmers accept food stamps at their roadside produce stands so the poor can buy from them rather than buy food at their local Wal-Mart.

It doesn't matter how many valid points are raised, or how many credentialed experts publish findings regarding the barriers faced by the poor for getting everything from healthy food to decent housing to proper clothing to educations to jobs. The Selfish Class will never change their minds. They are invested in blaming the poor. They gain from blaming the poor. And unfortunately, some of the ugliest displays of classism that poor people have to live with every day come not only from conservatives, but also from liberals who claim they care about us. That "caring" often translates to progressives using the poor as their poster child to further their own political agenda, which never seems to include room at the table for us.

The US Social Forum (USSF) held in Detroit from June 22nd - June 26th 2010 was billed as "a space to come up with people's solutions to the economic and ecological crisis." Its mission statement on its website states that the USSF provides opportunities to "learn from each others' experiences and struggles, share our analysis of the problems our communities face, build relationships, and align with our international brothers and sisters to strategize how to reclaim our world."

According to a young low-income white female activist, Meg Couture, the USSF excluded poor people whom the conference was supposed to be about. It also denied the existence of poor whites, focusing only on the struggles faced by people of color, making classism as invisible as the poor who were excluded by a series of logistical and event planning negligence.

US Social Forum: A Sour Taste of Classism July 30th 2010, Meg Couture

A month has gone by since I experienced my first-ever social justice conference, the US Social Forum (USSF) in Detroit, and I've been trying to erase my memory of that time ever since. The lack of logistical planning we experienced had a classist effect that seemed antithetical to the forum's message, and I was left with such a bad taste in my mouth for the progressive left that I will carefully reconsider attending any conference in the future.

The forum was to be a space where social justice groups and grassroots organizations from around the country could come together and share visions for a better world. A place to connect, to network, to hold workshops, and peoples' movement assemblies — my idea of a good time. Maybe it was the term "grassroots" that I was drawn to. To think that I would be surrounded by thousands of other people like me — from a low-income, working poor, or middle class background, and be able to relate to their work and my work for change — was something that I was looking forward to. Unfortunately, it was people like me who were to be left out.

As soon as we arrived, we were moved. Originally, we were to have an apartment 8 miles from COBO Hall (the center of events), but were moved 7 miles further out. The distance normally would not be a big deal had we driven here, or if we had had the money for a taxi or the Smart bus. That first day, the COBO shuttle never showed up, and we had to locate the local bus stop. After an hour long bus ride into the city being harassed by an early morning reveler, we arrived just in time to catch the afternoon session of workshops.

We decided to skip public transportation for the rest of the week.

The reality is, if we had the money to stay in the nearby hotel, we would have been able to experience what the USSF had to offer: workshops, evening events, breakout sessions, and a close proximity to food. But being low-income, we had to choose the cheapest method of housing possible in order to attend the forum at all.

The result was that we were placed on the outskirts of Detroit with no shuttle bus to take us back and forth, no access to food, and no way to change our situation. We often got to the workshops late, had to limit ourselves to attending workshops in COBO Hall since transportation elsewhere wasn't guaranteed, and left us stranded in our apartment every night since the only bus back to our housing was at 4 (or maybe 5) PM.

Our socio-economic status truly impacted our experience. Those staying in the center of the city had more means and were able to get around with ease. They were able to attend events happening after-hours, and could go get something to eat if they so desired. The low-income conference goers were placed on the outskirts. We spent our days wondering how we were going to make it back to our housing, whether or not we'd be able to attend the workshops we wanted, and generally stressed out about the whole situation, making it nearly impossible to focus on all the good that came out of the forum.

The experience was a lesson for me as much as it is a lesson for the planners at the US Social Forum. In our work to create a more just society, classism needs to be brought to the forefront of our discussions. It seems to be an "ism" that is left out of many conversations, or merely alluded to in conjunction with racism and sexism, among many others. With over a thousand workshops to choose from, there was only one that focused on class as the main topic and ironically, there was no shuttle.[33]

Progressives wonder why so many poor whites vote against their own interests, or opt out of voting entirely. They speak of the poor as misguided children who don't know what's best for them. When neither political party really cares about the poor, does it really matter?

Many say that the War on Terror should have been ended so that more money could be spent on helping the poor. Yet, the snobbish, condescending, and downright arrogant attitudes that often emanate from upper-middle class liberals that they like to call "advice" shows those of us in poverty that even if the wars would have never happened, nothing would change. Most upper-middle class progressives are eager to shove the poor out of sight and out of mind, far away from their college campuses, their smoke-free cocktail lounges, their black tie dinner parties, and let the poor continue to suffer while blaming them for their plight.

Discussing poverty within the framework of unearned privilege and classism isn't popular. It's divisive. And in order to be true to their professed principles, every liberal would have to stand up against these injustices and that isn't as much fun as putting on goofy costumes to

---

[33] "US Social Forum: A Sour Taste of Classism", Meg Couture, *Classism Exposed*, July 30th 2010. http://www.classism.org/us-social-forum-a-sour-taste-of-classism.

attend anti-war rallies where they can praise one another for being socially conscious people. But those of us in poverty are not supposed to talk about that because that makes the middle class feel uncomfortable. How dare *we* come along with our visibly decayed/missing teeth, our overweight bodies in our Wal-Mart clothes with our straggly hair and mangy looks and make the beneficiaries of class privilege feel bad? How dare we reproach them by our very existence!

Instead, we're supposed to be content with the lack of concern and action after being rendered invisible and discarded. During the 2008 presidential election campaign, the words "Joe the Plumber" and "Main Street" were spoken no less than 28 times by presidential candidates while the word poverty was spoken only once, and then it was merely tangentially in the framework of the working poor; which infers that the economically excluded and socially marginalized jobless poor don't exist. The growing numbers of Americans living below the poverty line that would trade places with "Joe the Plumber" in a heartbeat if they could only get the chance were totally ignored. "Main Street" is code-speak for "middle class."

It's extremely offensive and classist that the concept of "Joe the Plumber" and "Main Street" is used to insulate the middle class from the suffering of those who are far worse off. We always hear the battle cries of *"Why is the government destroying the middle class?"* and *"The middle class is under attack!"* and variations thereof — implying that "destroying the poor is perfectly okay, but stepping on middle class toes is crossing the line."

David Treuer once said that language does not merely convey thought, it creates fact. The political elite, who are elected by middle class voters, aspire to be part of the owning class — the very same wealthy class that views the needs of the poor as a social drain. Note that the word "entitlement" is used as a derogatory weapon that is never aimed at the Pentagon, which loses more money in its sofa each year than what has been spent on social programs for the poor over the last 40 years.

Tax breaks essentially pay corporations to ship jobs out of America to the lowest and sleaziest bidder to places like Indonesia and El Salvador where workers are paid 15 cents an hour; lowering the tax base and stressing what's left of our threadbare social safety net and adding to the deficit. There's a double standard: the Golden Parachute for the rich and government officials at the top of the economic ladder, and the Lead Anchor standard for those on the lower bottom rungs.

Why is it okay for the poor to be crushed underfoot, suffering in misery and deprivation with higher disability rates, higher maternal and infant mortality rates, and lower life expectancies — due to lack of access to medical care and other basic human needs — than people in many 3rd World nations, while only the grievances of the middle class matter?

If it's not acceptable to destroy the middle class, then it's not acceptable to destroy the poor. If it's not OK for middle class women and girls to be forced to work in the seedy sex industry under exploitative, dehumanizing and degrading conditions with no social security credits and other benefits due to job discrimination and lack of equal opportunity for living wage jobs with dignity, *why* should it be OK for *poor* women and girls? If it's not OK for your wives and daughters, it's not OK for *us*. If it's not OK for middle class boys and men to fight in imperialist wars (that only serve the interests of the very rich) only to get blown up, maimed, and killed; then it's not OK for *our* men either.

For over 30 years that fascist right-wing politicians (whose generous salaries, perks, travel expenses, Cadillac health care, and $90,000/year retirement benefits are paid for by the public) worked to dismantle laws and social programs and safety nets that benefited the working class and the poor; the poor were promised a share of the pie if only we'd quietly wait our turn, hats in hand, after Reagan's trickle-down economics first benefited the rich and the middle class. But we never got *our* turn.

During every debate during the discourse on universal health care, provisions in health care reform bills that would have helped the poor were jettisoned in the name of "compromise." Those of us in poverty were cast aside after the middle class got what they wanted. We're sick and tired of being appointed to "take one for the team." (And no, we will not "shut up and stop whining", thank you very much.)

We stand on the precipice of irreversible catastrophe to humanity in terms of economic casualties. We have an over-privileged overclass of economic terrorists on Wall Street pulling the strings of their stooges in Congress and members of the presidential cabinet like Steny Hoyer (D-MD) who advocated cutting social security and Medicare along with his partner in crime, Al Simpson, the head of the Catfood Commission, who called the social security program a "milk cow with 310 million tits." Of course, both of those spoiled rich dirt bags enjoy the high life off of the public tit. Maybe it's time we pry our greedy arrogant lawmakers' mouths off of *our* tits and let them go try and make a living selling overpriced Amway detergent.

It's no secret that conservatives don't give a damn about the poor because they wear their contempt for the poor as proudly as if it was a Congressional Medal of Honor. But comfortably off liberals have deepened the class divide by alienating the very people who once comprised their core. There are millions of people living on the edge of destitution in this country. It is contemptuous to look at them and say, "sorry for your luck, but sacrifices must be made because there's just not enough resources for everybody" as if it's *their* responsibility to fall on their swords to save the planet. It smacks of elitism; especially when affluent people leave a much larger carbon footprint while never feeling the pinch of regressive taxation that is politely couched in terms of "environmental responsibility."

The middle class can afford $10 for a single energy-conserving light bulb and brand new energy-efficient appliances; the poor cannot. What do liberals think they're accomplishing by promoting policies that hurt the poor while doing nothing to alleviate poverty and inequality? This shows that liberals really don't care about the poor, because they ignore the impact of their proposals on those least able to afford to shoulder the burden. Misguided liberals have a lot more in common with neocons than traditional Democrat party core values. This places the poor firmly at the bottom of every pile and then tells them that it's their own damn fault that they're poor.

It never crossed their minds that some people don't do more — be it using expensive energy-efficient light bulbs and appliances, getting a college education, or buying healthy organic locally grown foods — because they *can't*. For the poor, nothing is "easy."

It's easy to tell poor people to get college degrees in order to be "worthy" of good jobs so they won't be poor because they're "uneducated." But rubbing our noses in the turd of capitalism — a system <u>not</u> of our making under which we've had the <u>least</u> power to help ourselves — that has kept us down and trapped at the bottom, and telling us how uneducated we are isn't going to open minds that would otherwise be receptive to striving for something much better...such as a better educated populace, for starters. The problem is that there are only so many jobs. And telling someone to get a college education is easy when you're not the one with a vested interest in their student loan debt or their academic success. Although there are meager Pell Grants, most of the costs connected with getting a college education must be covered by student loans. Then there are issues of economic support with housing, transportation, food, and health and dental care. This is especially critical for non-traditional aged students who don't have the support of mom and dad to fall back on in an emergency.

Non-traditional aged students are not likely to get any scholarships. They are also not likely to live on campus in dormitory housing with a meal plan while being able to live at home with parents rent-free in between semesters.

When I transferred my Associates Degree from Lehigh Carbon Community College to Kutztown University in September of 1997, I was 30 years old and disabled. I had no means to support myself because of injuries to my knees and back. I can't even work at wage jobs such as cashier or video store clerk that require employees to stand for their entire shift. I wasn't "disabled enough" to qualify for income support from SSI. Yet I was disabled enough to qualify for vocational retraining and job placement through Pennsylvania Occupational Vocational Rehabilitation (PA OVR). But PA OVR really didn't help me with anything.

Living in a poverty stricken Allentown neighborhood, I did not live near any other college students attending Kutztown University, located in Berks County, the next county west from me, whom I could have car-pooled with. There was no public transportation going from Allentown to Kutztown University, 26 miles away. Going to college to better myself meant I needed reliable transportation, my own car. I did not have mom and dad's car to use. I did not have a mom and dad. I had a 15 year old unreliable used car. When my car broke down during my junior year in the middle of the semester, I was out of luck. I didn't have the $400 to pay to get my car fixed.

Being without an income and struggling to live on student loan refund proceeds (about $2,000 per year), I couldn't qualify for a credit card or a small personal loan from a bank or credit union to pay for the car repair. My gas and electric were both shut off. My only access to a hot shower was the university's gymnasium facility. On days that I didn't have classes, I ate at the local soup kitchen that served cheap meals to the destitute. On days I had classes, I went hungry — I had no food, no money to buy any and no way to cook it. These are just *some* of the hardships I suffered while trying to "pull myself up by my bootstraps." Sorry, but nobody has the right to lecture me on how I "need to make sacrifices" so I won't be poor as if I haven't already suffered and sacrificed enough.

I was not living like this as a healthy young kid as part of an "understanding poverty" project, or as a journalist that was temporarily "slumming it" for a story. I had to live like that for over a decade as a physically disabled woman with health problems and no end in sight.

I had no family to turn to for help at all. I went to every social agency, every charity, listed in the phonebook and begged for help so I could get my car fixed and not lose out on getting the education that was supposed to be my ticket back into the workforce. Not having transportation and being unable to get to class meant being penalized on my grades by administrative disenrollment. I had nowhere to turn. And the help I desperately needed was not forthcoming.

I called my OVR caseworker and explained the situation since OVR helps disabled people with money to pay for assistive/adaptive technologies needed to complete a vocational training/college education and job placement plan. Transportation is important "technology" for getting to and from school and for applying for jobs. If OVR could cough up $65,000 for a van outfitted with special controls for a paraplegic to have transportation for school, I figured OVR could help me with a $400 car repair bill so I'd have transportation for school. My caseworker said he would "see what could be done and get back to me."

Meanwhile, I had missed several weeks of classes and fell too far behind to be able to catch up. I tried to get help from all the other agencies to get my car fixed. But I got nowhere. None of them helped with things a car repairs. Welfare wouldn't help me because I didn't have kids. The Welfare Reform Act of 1996 essentially eliminated aid for poor adults without kids. After missing too many classes, I got a letter from the college stating I would be disenrolled from my classes by the professors for failing to meet the school's attendance requirements. I called every one of my professors, explaining my situation. Nobody helped, nobody cared. If I couldn't magically find the money to get my car fixed in order to get to classes; oh well, too bad I lose – again.

Those who are responsible for making rules that govern academic institutions are from the middle and upper classes. These people had never been destitute, without any support or resources. When they made the rigid attendance requirement rule and administrative disenrollment, they did not think about how it would affect the most underprivileged students who struggle against all odds within a system that was set up against them from the start. Their rules were based on the premise that all college students are young non-disabled 18 year olds right out of high school who come from middle class families with resources. And most typical aged college students either live in dormitories on campus or in fraternity housing nearby within walking distance. As such, attendance rules were designed to penalize immature spoiled kids who might be tempted to blow off too many classes from too many frat parties.

It never crossed the policymakers' minds that not all students are non-disabled, 18 year old middle class kids who live on campus; that some students are poor older adults who must commute. The policymakers see life through class biased lenses. They didn't consider the needs of the older student with obligations of jobs and families, or that some of these older learners are disabled and living in deep poverty without family support or any resources built into their lives. They think they are being fair by making inflexible rules applicable to everyone, no matter the circumstance. But is it really fair to treat everyone based a false assumption of equal resources, assets, and support networks? The same people who put down the poor for being uneducated are the same ones who are responsible for erecting insurmountable barriers that prevent the poor from succeeding in getting educations and realizing their full potential.

I was down to the wire by four days for getting my car fixed and being able to salvage my grades by preventing administrative disenrollment for attendance problems when the OVR caseworker finally got back to me just to say, "Unfortunately, OVR can't help you with the car repair. Don't you have family who can help you?"

It floated right over his head that I had no family to help me, or I wouldn't have begged for help from him in the first place. As a result of not getting helped, I was disenrolled from my classes. My grades were penalized from being administratively disenrolled resulting in an automatic failing grade assigned per class, regardless of what my grades were up to that point – all for lack of resources to get my car fixed. I lost my financial aid eligibility as a result of the administrative disenrollment, and had to wait a year before I could appeal and re-apply and get reinstated to be able to resume my education.

Another setback that resulted from being disenrolled was that I couldn't get the last two upper level math courses I needed in order to graduate. These courses were only offered once every three semesters (once every year and a half), and often cancelled due to lack of enrollment. If less than six students enrolled, the class was cancelled. These math courses also had to be taken sequentially and were prerequisites for other required courses. The only options for students who needed those cancelled math courses were:

1. to pick them up at a more expensive private college and transfer the six credits back to Kutztown in order to complete the degree program and graduate, or;
2. Try to persuade the Kutztown math professors who taught those respective courses to offer the courses on an Individual Instruction (I.I.) basis.

The first option was not a choice available to me because I had to rely solely on financial aid to pay for college. The guidelines for Title IV monies (government need-based student aid) state that you cannot get financial aid to pay for tuition at more than one school at a time. If most of your coursework and credits towards graduation are at one college, you cannot get tuition assistance to pay for one or two classes at a different school. To exercise the first option, I would have had to come up with the money out of pocket for taking those classes at the local private college – which would have cost me $2,000 that I did not have and had no way to scrape up. When you're a poor woman without any income or any way of getting any money, a $2,000 tuition price tag for two classes might as well be $2 million.

The second option was denied to me by Kutztown University's elitist, self-centered professors. Since Kutztown University is one of the universities that comprise the state university system in Pennsylvania, full-time tenured professors are represented by America's most powerful union of state civil servants. Under the professors' right to "academic freedom" in their union contract, they were not obligated to offer students the required-but-cancelled courses under I.I. They got to decide which students they would offer coursework under I.I. to and which ones they wouldn't. A student who must rely on financial aid has no recourse through the university's administrative procedures and complaint system if they're inadvertently discriminated against as a result of this.

The math department had the most inflexible bunch of professors in the entire university. The only students they offered the option of getting those cancelled class under an I.I. basis so the students could graduate were traditional-aged, middle class students with straight A's. As an older woman struggling with extreme poverty and a physical disability, plus having to cope with dyslexia, I wasn't worth their time. They still got their $90,000 a year salaries and health, dental and pension benefits regardless if I got an equal opportunity to get an education and graduate or not. All was right in their little world.

The elitism in the halls of academia's Ivory Tower was made plain by now-retired math professor, Dr. Kiyu Sam Park who told me that "only middle class kids with proper family support really belonged in college."

So where does that leave someone who is from a poor family or who has no family at all? Where does that leave the economically disadvantaged non-traditional aged student?

The message could not have been more blunt: Poor adults weren't ever meant to be included in universities, despite the rhetoric of bettering yourself by getting a college education in order to be worthy of a chance for a job that would lift you out of poverty. It was one more lie, one more empty promise, one more con job spouted by the "haves" to the "have nots." Get a college education so that you will be able to get a job and if you don't, your poverty is all your own fault — but we won't *let* you actually get that education. The unionized professors within the Pennsylvania State University System saw themselves as "gatekeepers" whose sacred duty was to keep the poor and marginalized from getting *any* opportunity.

My graduation was pushed behind by two years as a result of the administrative disenrollment, which was really punishment for being poor and without family and support. If I had family that could have helped me, or any way to get the money to get my car fixed, I would not have been caught up in the quagmire of cancelled classes I needed in order to graduate and re-enter the workforce while the economy was still robust – and while I was still young enough to get a chance for a good job so I could afford food, a home, medical and dental care, and repay my student loan debt.

I finally graduated two years behind schedule after sending a flurry of formal complaints threatening to sue on the grounds of *collateral estoppel* by certified mail to the Chancellor, who oversees all Pennsylvania colleges within the state university system. The end result was that the administration at Kutztown University was forced to take action. They offered me a compromise: they would allow me to graduate by substituting a Visual Basic programming class and an upper level physics class in lieu of the two cancelled upper level math classes.

Now, having one's college graduation pushed back by two years (or more) may not be a huge problem if you're 18, 19, or 20 years old. But I was in my early 30's and trying to re-enter the workforce after a disabling car accident took me out of the loop at age 24, leaving me without any recent employer references. I could not afford to have my college graduation pushed behind. Nor should I have had to fight all the way to the state Chancellor's office and threaten lawsuit to get the cancelled courses issue resolved. That's not what I agreed to when I signed on the dotted line, mortgaging what was left of my future to the tune of $38,000 in order to get an education. I had a hard enough life as it was.

The final slap in my face came when my OVR caseworker told me that OVR wouldn't hold up their end of the bargain. They couldn't help me with job placement because it had taken me "too long to get through college" and get my degree. I had struggled through hunger, cold, rotting teeth, lack of utilities and a computer that professors expected everyone to have, and a knockdown drag-out legal fight in order to get my degree. I did more than hold up my end of the bargain.

All I got for all my efforts is a mountain of student loan debt, no job, no chance for being able to get a job, no health care, and no hope.

Telling the poor to "make sacrifices" by getting an education while making it impossible for them to do so is beyond egregious — especially when classist policies compound the despair of poverty and put the promise of an education opportunity far beyond reach.

Classism is deeply entrenched in academia. The unfair advantages enjoyed by fraternity members which are exclusively affluent white males, are *not* enjoyed by students who are excluded from the Greek system. Meanwhile, disabled students requiring any accommodation from professors get begrudged anything that gave them a level playing field. They're accused of getting "unfair advantages" over non-disabled students. But professors and college administrators have no problem with the unfair advantages that fraternity "brothers" get that the rest of the student body does not.

Fraternity members got copies of mid-term and final exams from which to prepare in advance of the test. Knowing *exactly* what questions to study in advance for extremely difficult and extensive exams is an enormous advantage that isn't far removed from cheating. The "advantage" of extended time afforded to the dyslexic for exam taking, or the "special treatment" of take-home exam-equivalent assignments for the wheelchair bound student who cannot physically access the building, pales in comparison to the fraternity members' advantage of getting exam copies with the correct answers prior to the test! Some of the "best and brightest" who screech "it's not fair!" about accommodations for the disabled have a 2 year old's concept of "fair." "Fair" isn't treating everyone the same; "fair" is everyone getting what they need.[34]

There is no genuine meritocracy. Our society's competitive capitalism is as competitive as shooting fish in a barrel – those who own the barrels and the guns get all the fish while the rest of us are overcharged for fishing rods and then prevented from casting our lines.

---

[34] Dr. Rick Lavoie, FAT City Workshop

The middle and upper classes don't want those of us who are at the bottom to really have an equal chance in life for realizing our full potential, and for improving our lives in this shambolic meritocracy. By keeping the poor and marginalized down and "in their place", the middle and upper classes get to keep their privileges and secure unjust enrichment and opportunities. Every poor person is their "place-keeper."

Society's "winners" ignore the fact that the only reason that dollar in their wallet has any value is because it's not in someone else's. Here's the most painful and ugly truth that most middle class people won't face: the only way to assist you in achieving your goals and aspirations is to create and maintain a system of unearned privileges which ensures that many, many others are actively prevented from reaching the same position as you, whereby you would lose your position of relative status, wealth, and supremacy — which is what your ego really craves. It's against the petit bourgeoisie interest to allow that wealth to "trickle down."

For those lucky enough to get a middle class job, someone else did *not* get the chance for that job – someone else just as deserving and who needed it just as badly, if not more so; someone who was desperately poor who had hoped for a chance that they never got. It's a zero sum game[35].

The only job opportunities I was offered after earning my hard-won degree in mathematics and computer science were commissions-only paying sales jobs without benefits or base salary. As author Barbara Ehrenreich points out in her book *"Bait & Switch"*, 85% of those working in commissions-only paying jobs earn less than $15,000 a year. In fact, most earn somewhere around $10,000 a year, before taxes, job related expenses (you need to have the right clothing) and licensing fees. There was no way I could support myself having to work like that, never mind repay my student loans which went into default after my last allowable deferment expired.

[35] Zero sum game: situation where the amount of "winnable goods" or resources is fixed; whatever is gained by one can only result from an equivalent loss by another.

As a 40 year old woman with a significant gap in my work history and no recent employer references, the only hope I might have had at climbing out of poverty and into the middle class would be if I could have pursued grad school and earned a PhD, or gone to law school.

With defaulted student loans on my record because of not getting a chance for a job, and grades that were penalized by the administrative disenrollment, I could not gain admittance into a doctoral program on a fellowship which includes a modest living stipend. Had I not been penalized for conditions of poverty, I would have graduated with a cumulative GPA of 3.7 despite my dyslexia, instead of a GPA of 2.9. Had my professors been fair instead of being self-appointed "gatekeepers", I would have been able to graduate on schedule. My grades would not have suffered from the administrative disenrollment, and I would be Dr. Jacqueline Homan today. And I probably would not be a poor, unemployable middle aged food stamp recipient reduced to near-destitution.

The few people like Dr. Donna Beegle who managed to earn advanced degrees and climb out of poverty were able to do so because there was help and a support network in their lives – and luck. It's a whole different ball game you're poor, female, disabled; and have no family, no help, and no support network. When the only support system you have are government agency caseworkers that don't care and can't/won't/don't want to help you when you're in a poverty related crisis, you can't just "pull yourself up by your bootstraps."

According to capitalism's winners, poor people without any support, any family, and any money just need to "try harder." Bill O'Reilly said that it's not society's obligation to help those who are unable to make it on their own. Rush Limbaugh says the same thing.

The gospel according to Bill O'Reilly holds that poor migrant farm workers who pick fruits and vegetables for less than the federal minimum wage from dawn to dusk don't work hard enough, they aren't trying. The gospel of Bill O'Reilly says that those unable to get college degrees from lack of money, lack of intellectual capacity, lack of proper primary education made the choice to be society's losers. It must be nice to be a rich white male like Bill O'Reilly, who's never been discriminated against into poverty and the welfare office.

What "choice" to work hard does someone have who is denied employment opportunities because of dental problems, and poverty profiling in hiring practices? What about sex/age/disability/appearance discrimination? What choice do you have as a disadvantaged job applicant if you're always denied chances for jobs after jumping through all the hoops and incurring college debt in order to be "worthy" of a chance? Who *really* gets choices? It's the employers' choice to offer you a job; not your choice when you don't have a guaranteed right to a job.

Frequently, the employer's decision is based on nepotism – especially in corrupt small towns like Erie, Pennsylvania where greedy rich cliques have everything all sown up and no one else can get a chance for anything. In order to get a job with any of the employers who pay a middle class wage with offer health and dental benefits, including municipal jobs, you have to have an "in" – a family member who had/has a job with the city, and being Italian helps. Although people want to point to the present situation of America's job losses due to NAFTA, the truth is that male dominated trade unions and other "good ole boy" networks artificially manipulated local economies to maintain a sizeable underclass in order to keep middle class workers docile and suppress wages for those among the working poor that are fortunate enough to have any job.

The Northwestern Pennsylvania Manufacturers Association banded together to keep new businesses and industries out of Erie and Crawford Counties during the economic heydays. An automobile plant wanted to relocate here to Erie, bringing with it enough jobs so that Erie would have had a full employment rate – jobs with health and dental benefits and a living wage so that no one in Erie would have been poor because of being economically left out during Erie's better times, not even poor women. But the local good ole boy club killed that.

Now that Erie is so impoverished in the wake of NAFTA, the city tries to make up for its budget shortfall by fining the crap out of poor jobless people for code violations on their homes that they can't afford to correct because eating and not having their utilities shut off for inability to pay the bill takes precedence over home improvement projects. Anyone who thinks we have a meritocracy apparently never lived in a Mafia town run by greedy powerful cliques who destroy others' opportunities and lives while ridiculing and belittling the poor whom they've kept down.

As of the writing of this book, an entrepreneur who wanted to bring a tires-to-energy plant to Erie is being stonewalled. The plant would have brought 400 badly needed jobs to Erie, jobs that pay at least $10 an hour to start with health and dental benefits.

Erie is a small city where half of those with jobs make less than $15,000 a year without health and dental benefits. The poorest are left out of getting chances for any jobs at all while suffering utility shut-offs in the middle of winter and scraping to stretch their food stamps. The 400 jobs from the proposed tire plant would have been a God-send. It seemed like a win-win situation. All the poor folks that can't afford to pay through the nose to get rid of their old tires would be able to take them to the plant which would convert those tires to fuel and energy, which would help those struggling to afford heat and electricity. And 400 poor people without jobs, without hope, and without enough food or a decent home would finally get a chance for a job to make a living. But wealthy and powerful interests kept that from happening. The poor who wanted good jobs got no choice to "work hard to get ahead" – they're not even getting a chance to work, period.

Since Pennsylvania is an "Employment At-Will" state, employers can easily circumvent the Americans with Disabilities Act, the Civil Rights laws, and the Family Medical Leave Act. "At-Will" effectively lets employers get away with discriminating against job applicants because in an "At-Will" state, employers do not have to give a reason for refusal to hire, or for firing workers. Employers get away with discriminatory hiring practices against those with medical problems who are in need of jobs by making it a requirement that they must stand for their entire shift as cashiers or video store clerks – minimum wage jobs with no benefits.

"At-Will" also gives employers a free pass to terminate pregnant women when they have to stop working in order to give birth and recover from childbirth, even though they're supposed to be protected under the Family Medical Leave Act. Parents who must take time off from work because of a sick child are told to choose either their child or their job — not a real "choice" when daycare or schools make parents pick up a sick child, leaving parents no one else to watch their child while they go to work.

The "At-Will" clause allows employers to fire you without giving you a reason – and then they fight your unemployment benefits claim. The end result is that you are out of a job and can't even collect any unemployment. Proving unlawful job discrimination in an "At-Will" state is next to impossible because the law 100% favors employers. They can discriminate against you for your gender, age, race, medical problems, and for social class.

After several years of trying to get a job and not getting a chance, you lose hope and eventually give up. That's what happened to me after I had moved to Erie where "outsiders" aren't welcome (unless you're well-off).

By 2004, my small savings had run out. My gas and electric was shut off for lack of income to pay the bills. I was still jobless despite aggressively trying to get a job. A local call center, Teletron, was hiring 18 year old high school students for $10 an hour jobs soliciting college grads for student loan consolidations. Teletron declined to hire me – three times.

The 20-something year old human resources manager said that if the company was interested, she would call me. Apparently, Teletron didn't want to hire a middle-aged woman living on the poor side of town who had a long work history gap due to several years of joblessness, even though I had an education, wanted to work, and desperately needed a job that paid a living wage with health and dental benefits. I wasn't considered a "good fit" due to my age alone: I wouldn't socially fit in with the middle class high school kids that made up Teletron's workplace.

Teletron's CEO/President Joyce Cavutto had been quoted in the Erie Times News saying, "Anyone in Erie can get a good job [at Teletron] if they want one and if they're willing to get an education." I seethed with rage at the lies used to make poor middle-aged people look like asses. Here I sat, needing a job and wanting a job and I had an education, but I got denied a chance for a job at her company three times! I fired off a letter to Ms. Cavutto demanding to know where *my* chance for a good job was. In my "put up or shut up" letter, I told her that I have a university degree, professional licenses, sales experience, and a computer background – yet no one at her company saw fit to hire me due to apparent age discrimination and poverty-profiling. I challenged Ms. Cavutto to let me have a chance for a job at her company since she publicly stated in an article on the front page of the *Erie Times News* that "anyone can have a job at her company" if they want to work and have an education.

Although my letter didn't result in a job, it gave me immense satisfaction. When you're poor and have nothing, you've got nothing left to lose. Ultimately I was forced to apply for food stamps and Medicaid when my husband ended up hospitalized due to his heart condition. After a long, knock-down, drag out procedure of appeals through bureaucratic red tape, he was approved for food stamps and Medicaid due being a low income senior citizen not yet Medicare eligible. As a woman without any income, I was only eligible for temporary Medicaid for 90 days.

As Medicaid recipients, we were eligible to be enrolled in the Ion Health Plan, a Medicaid HMO offered at no cost only to Medicaid recipients. The Ion rep came to our home to sign us up. She looked around, her eyes scanning our living room, stopping at my university degree and honor roll certificate hanging proudly over our fireplace mantle. She asked my husband how it was possible that we were so poor that we qualified for food stamps and Medicaid when I had a college education. I told her, "You can't get a good job if no one gives you a chance." She asked if I had a résumé and if so, she would gladly take it to Ion's office. I appreciated that help wholeheartedly. I followed up with phone calls over the course of several months inquiring of my job application status, but heard nothing.

Nine months later, November 22nd 2004, I was *finally* called by a new sales manager hired at Ion Health. By that time poverty had taken its toll on me. I had only two of my upper front teeth left after years of poverty and no dental care. I was without electric and without gas heat, hot water, and cooking. I was *very* interested in the job. I was ecstatic when the new Ion sales manager, Mike Quirk, called me offering me the job as an Ion marketing rep after what was, at that time, a fruitless 3 year aggressive job search. But my hopes of being able to climb out of poverty and onto the rung of a lower-middle class job were short-lived.

A tight knit clique of middle class women (and I use that term loosely!) ruled the roost at Ion Health. And they saw to it that I wouldn't have a chance to keep my job. Since my husband and I had both been Medicaid recipients and Ion health enrollees, these women *knew* I was from the underclass. They knew I was "poor white trash" from the very first day on the job by my ill-fitting clothes (unable to afford the "right image") and the fact that I didn't join them for expensive take-out lunch from a local overpriced deli because I couldn't afford it.

Danise Gilkinson, the ring-leader of this office clique, approached me on my first day saying, "You know they are having a sale at Kauffman's this weekend. If you can't afford to buy anything right now, maybe you could wear a sweater over your skirt and just let your jacket hang open because it's too tight the way you're wearing it." Since I suffered that dreaded middle-age weight gain during my period of joblessness, I could no longer fit into the three suits I owned. I had only one skirt and two blazers to wear that met the company criteria of either black or tan colored skirt suits. I didn't have the money to buy clothes until after I'd gotten a few paychecks under my belt. And before buying clothes, I had to get my car inspected since use of a personal vehicle was a job requirement. Not wanting to come across as someone who can't play well with others, I simply told her I would get some clothes when I got paid. I should have told her to go to hell.

Danise and her cronies targeted me because I didn't have a nice hairdo and manicured nails – money for the beauty parlor was something I never could afford. They criticized me for brown bagging my lunch instead of joining them for take-out food.

Danise's sidekick Cindy embarrassed me by exclaiming in front of the other reps, "But you can get the cheapest sandwich for only $10. *Anyone* can afford *that*! Why do you bring lunch in that silly little plastic lunchbox? It looks so unprofessional!" (Was I supposed to bring my lunch in a Prada tote?). I could not afford to blow what amounted to $50 a week on take-out lunches. Getting my car fixed so it would pass inspection, and getting my gas and electric utility services restored took precedence. New clothes, beauty parlor hairdos, restorative dental work, and take-out lunch would have to wait awhile.

When you're poor and struggling to climb out of poverty, all you get is put down and kept down. You're told every day that you don't belong; that you don't fit in and that you don't deserve a chance. Being Jewish and poor compounded the difficulties in a town that is predominantly Catholic due to its heavy Italian and Polish population.

Being the only Jew at Ion Health, I didn't fit in where all my co-workers were Polish Catholics. Poles have along-earned reputation for being extremely anti-Semitic. My Jewishness came up during small talk between Danise and myself while we were driving together to do a field appointment. Danise reacted by choking, spewing a hot spray of coffee across the windshield as she exclaimed, "You're *Jewish*!?! You shouldn't be poor and need a job *here!*" Like most people, Danise thought that being Jewish meant being rich. The reality is, however, that there are plenty of very poor Jews.

While en route to a field appointment with Cindy (Danise's sidekick), I got unsolicited "advice" from Cindy, who said I "needed to do something" with my hair and "get a manicure" because I didn't have the right "professional image." She said I looked like a "hill nigger", to quote her vernacular. I asked her what a "hill nigger" was and she answered, "Poor white trash people that don't live right. You know - the ones who don't take care of their hair and let their teeth go to hell. Trashy whites who have ratty houses with ratty mismatched furniture and who stink after firewood because their gas was shut off."

Cindy was talking about people like me: people for whom dental care is unaffordable and out of reach; for whom trips to a beauty parlor is an unthinkable luxury. Cindy was putting down poor people for not having nice things that weren't hand-me-downs and people whose modest homes were in the "wrong part of town", unfit for middle class visitors. The same poor people that these back-biting bitches insulted are the same people whose poverty provided *them* with *their* middle class jobs as Ion Medicaid HMO marketing reps.

I had only been working for 4 ½ days when I was abruptly fired on the morning of December 4th 2004 by Ion's company lawyer Jeri Bolten – for no reason. I asked her why I was fired. I felt I deserved to know why I was deemed unworthy of a job. Jeri Bolten retorted that I was not entitled to a reason – Pennsylvania is an "At-Will" state. I had to hand over my company-issued coat and was unceremoniously escorted past the rest of the workers to the door like a criminal. I had to trek across the company parking lot in the bitter cold with no coat to my car.

I was shocked because I worked hard and exceeded company goals. The daily enrollment requirement for reps was 25. I had averaged 60. I was never late. I always did what I was told. I put in extra hours without extra pay in order to go the third mile, picking up co-worker's slack. I didn't sell anyone out or kiss anyone's ass. When I was humiliated for my poverty by Cindy and Danise, I sucked it up and took it – in the name of being a "team player." Yet, I ended up jobless and poor. Having only worked for one week, I was ineligible to collect unemployment benefits because I did not have enough time or earnings in order to qualify. I was just out of a job and poor.

I was not fired for not working hard enough or for incompetence. I was not fired for dishonesty or unreliability. I was fired because I was "poor white trash" – I was unable to afford the costs of "getting on the team", and therefore unable to fit in with a middle class clique.

I cried all the way drive home, dreading having to tell my husband that our hopes and dreams for climbing out of poverty were shattered like a glass menagerie. I was devastated. Everything I was raised to believe in was a lie. Living frugally, doing "all the right things", staying out of trouble with the law, avoiding unplanned pregnancy, shunning vice, getting a college education and professional licenses, and working my ass off while eating more than my fair share of crow was not enough to make me worthy of a ticket to even the bottom rung of middle class America.

Being able to get a good job and be successful at keeping it is all about fitting in socially. It's who you know, where you live, being able to afford the "right image", and what status symbols you have so that you are welcomed as a "member of the team." Getting ahead is not about hard work or skills in a meritocracy. It's all about fitting in and being socially accepted in a class biased nepotocracy.

When you don't own the means of production in this so-called "ownership society", you can only work hard if those who *do* own the means of production give you a chance, hire you, and let you work and pay you a living wage for your time. When the ownership and control of capital and the opportunity to work is determined by people with higher socio-economic status than you, you don't have the "choice" to work hard and get ahead. They're holding all four aces – you're holding none. They have all the choices – you do not. When you are at a disadvantage you have no control over your earnings, or the "choice" to work hard. The only thing you have ownership of is your time.

Being willing to work is not the main ingredient in the recipe of economic success in America. You can be willing all you want, but it means nothing when no one gives you a chance. Just getting a chance is a privilege.

Education and transportation to jobs is not enough to give people in poverty an equal chance for getting (and keeping) a good job.

Speaking in "formal register" and all the rest of Ruby Payne's "hidden rules" bullshit does not build a bridge out of poverty. It is not the poor who need to be "fixed"; it's the greed, entitlement, and self-importance of the egotistical middle and upper classes.

Classism, like racism and sexism, is learned. I will not take anything away from the indefensible social injustice of racism suffered by poor blacks because they are my comrades in poverty. But it is imperative to make white poverty visible. White people living in extreme poverty have been excluded from the great table of diversity. White people struggling in poverty are the only group that can be ignored or publicly degraded. Dr. Donna Beegle asks readers in her book *"See Poverty, Be the Difference"* to think about what it does to a person who lives in a society where it is okay to call him or her "trash."

What hope do poor people have when they're always denied decent jobs for being "poor white trash" because they can't afford the right clothes, the luxury of a nice smile without missing or visibly decayed teeth, and the "right" residence – even though they struggled and overcame considerable obstacles to get educations or other training? What impact does this have on their life chances? What toll does this take on someone emotionally?

What does it say about a society that condones discrimination and openly calls its least fortunate members "trash"? When any group of people is labeled "unworthy", they're not seen as human beings. When we no longer view other people as human beings, we lose our humanity. When we lose our humanity, it's easier to see and target others as something that is disposable, as "lives unworthy of life" – which has an ominous meaning for those of us who are familiar with the politics of eugenics and genocide.

The term "poor white trash" is the only permissible hate speech in America. It dates back to the 1820's as a disparaging moniker used by blacks (both slave and free alike) to insult the local poor working class whites in the Baltimore and Washington, DC area – major shipping ports which held slave auctions. The phrase registered contempt and disgust because "trash" means something that must be permanently disposed of. It illustrates sharp hostilities between social classes and groups who are essentially competing for the same fixed number of resources – the same jobs, the same social opportunities, and even the same marriage partners.

Harriet Beecher Stowe's internationally famous classic *"Uncle Tom's Cabin"* contains an entire chapter devoted to "Poor White Trash". Stowe explained that the slave system produced "*not only heathenish, degraded, miserable slaves, but it produces a class of white people who are, by universal admission, more heathenish, degraded, and miserable.*" Stowe's book claimed that slavery locked up opportunities and productive farmland in the hands of a few obscenely wealthy planters and business owners, leaving average ordinary whites to struggle for subsistence. Stowe wrote, "*Without schools or churches, these miserable families grow up heathen on Christian soil, in idleness, vice, dirt, and discomfort of all sorts. They are the pest of the neighborhood, the scoff and contempt or pity even of the slaves. The expressive phrase, so common in the mouths of Negroes, of "poor white trash", says all for this luckless race of beings that can be said.*"

The wealthy Southern cotton aristocracy, many whom were jumped up bog peasants from Ireland, claimed that it wasn't lack of opportunity or access to schools or churches that made poor whites inferior and deserving of contempt. Pro-slavery apologists and the elite on both sides of the Mason-Dixon Line claimed that the "depravity" of poor white trash originated from the "tainted blood" that ran through their veins. One refined Southern gentleman (whose name escaped posterity) said on the eve of the Civil War in 1860 that "everywhere, North and South, in Maine or Texas, in Virginia or New York, they [poor whites] are one in the same and have...one in the same origin; namely the poor-houses and prison cells of Great Britain...there is a great deal more in blood than people in the United States are generally inclined to believe."

This "bad blood" idea promoted by the rich, who have sucked the life-blood out of every civilization since the fall of Troy, Sparta, and

Ancient Rome, spawned Manifest Destiny and the American eugenics movement – from which the Nazis learned so well.

The rich have always been obsessed with the sexuality and reproductive capabilities of poor whites that they viewed as a threat and an encroachment on their resources. The "great unwashed" had to be culled and eugenics was touted as the "humane" way of doing that.

By the 1890's eugenics gained popularity and was sponsored by America's elite, garnering social acceptance as a pseudo-science for eliminating the "unfit" by forced sterilizations and later, by mass extermination (Holocaust) in Nazi-occupied Europe. Those specifically targeted and deemed "unfit" by eugenicists were America's rural poor whites. They were judged as "feebleminded, sexually immoral, and criminal" by inherited genetic trait. Eugenicists whipped up frenzied anxieties about sex, class, gender, and race which mobilized politicians and civic leaders into action. Countless forced sterilizations were carried out on men and women whose sole crime was belonging to the class termed "poor white trash."

In the notorious US Supreme Court case *Buck v. Bell*, prominent eugenicist H.H. Laughlin testified without ever having met Carrie Buck, that it was his "expert opinion" that Carrie Buck was "part of the shiftless, ignorant, and worthless class of anti-social whites of the South." This loaded charge was leveled against Carrie Buck because she gave birth to an out-of-wedlock daughter and as a result, was involuntarily committed to the Virginia Colony for Epileptics and Feebleminded by her foster parents J.T. and Alice Dobbs in March of 1924.

The Virginia Colony for Epileptics and Feebleminded was the largest institution of its kind. It opened in 1910 and served as a convenient dumping ground for society's unwanted: Virginia's poor whites, teens from broken homes, and others deemed socially inadequate. Colony officials enthusiastically carried out their task of weeding out those whom they felt would contaminate the purity and soundness of the white race.

H.H. Laughlin was the Superintendent of the Eugenics Record Office[36], the data repository for the eugenics movement in America. He dedicated his entire career to lobbying for (unconstitutional) legalized forced sterilization. Laughlin sought to eliminate within two generations, the genes of what he called "the submerged tenth" – the most "worthless one tenth of our present population." He passionately claimed that his proposed model sterilization law in 1922 was designed "to prevent the procreation of persons socially inadequate from defective inheritance, by authorizing and providing for eugenical sterilization of certain potential parents carrying degenerate hereditary qualities."

By the 1930's, over 30 states had sterilization laws based on Laughlin's "model". Many states cast their legal eugenical sterilization laws net even wider to encompass whites who were blind, those with poor eyesight, the deaf, "imbeciles", and those who were poor and unemployed.

The case of Carrie Buck and other "poor white trash" eugenics victims remain an indelible stain on the annals of American jurisprudence. *Buck v. Bell* is the poster child for rich white men's hatred for poor white women.

We now know the facts about this case. Carrie Buck and her daughter Vivian were not "feebleminded." And Carrie Buck did not get pregnant due to her own sexual immorality. Her pregnancy was the result of a rape committed by J.T. Dobbs' nephew Clarence Garland. J.T. Dobbs had Carrie institutionalized to shield the Dobbs family from embarrassment. Since Dobbs was an affluent white male and Carrie was a "disposable" poor white girl, society discarded Carrie Buck. No one cared about the truth of Carrie's rape, forced pregnancy, wrongful incarceration, nor the injustice of the permanent sterilization performed on her without her consent at the Colony.

The state of Virginia issued a formal apology in 2002 to the family of Carrie Buck and the other victims who were forcibly sterilized during one of the darkest chapters of American history. But an apology

---

[36] Sponsored and funded by the Rockefeller and Harriman families.

does not compensate for the irrevocable loss and anguish caused by the privileged classes against American eugenics victims – who were overwhelmingly "poor white trash."

As in the late 19th and early 20th centuries during the eugenics heyday, poor white women bear the brunt of society's scorn today – in addition to the cruelty of economic, physical and emotional abuse at the hands of their fathers, husbands, boyfriends and employers. One needs only to open their eyes to see the injustices caused by punitive policies that target the poor. There is nothing harmless about the term "white trash" and all of the images it conjures of inbreeding, drug addiction, welfare mothers, "redneck" men who beat women up, and the belief that poor whites are "uneducated."

Poor white trash means being invisible and denied opportunity. It's a life sentence for a crime you didn't commit. It means can't win, no matter what you do. Poor white trash is about scars that will never heal.

Access to education and behaving responsibly is only part of the equation. Access to jobs, income support, decent health and dental care, housing, and proper nutrition is critical. Without these, education and the promise of adequate employment is futile. When someone in poverty gets an education, our society expects them to move forward, get a good job and help themselves. But they cannot help themselves if they are constantly punished for their conditions of poverty; if they are denied jobs for being unable to afford to fit in. What do you think this does to poor people? What does it do to tell them repeatedly that they "don't have it bad" and that their poverty is their fault for "not trying hard enough"?

Only 7% of low-income people are able to obtain Bachelor's degrees by the time they're 26 years old. Many others did not obtain a college degree until later – only to be rejected by potential employers for being "too old" to be considered for a job and starting out in new careers. In corporate America, especially in the computer, math and science fields, "too old" is as young as 35. The majority of America's poor people never complete college. If those who *did* earn college degrees are punished for their poverty, how did education cure *their* poverty?

When middle and upper class people in corporations, staffing firms, and community organizations see job applicants with missing/visibly decayed teeth, they see someone who is "defective." They assume that people with dental problems are "too lazy and uneducated" to brush and floss properly. Most people are prone to dental caries, some more than others - no matter how meticulously they brush and floss. But the outcome for middle and upper class people prone to dental caries is different that the outcome for poor people.

Middle and upper class people have sufficient incomes and access to employer group health and dental benefits. They can get cavities treated before they get out of hand. Poor people, whether Medicaid eligible or not, do not have that option. Most dentists won't accept Medicaid. Dentures aren't covered. Qualifying for "Care Credit" is not an option for poor people because low incomes go hand in hand with bad credit, so they don't qualify for this specialized credit line to pay for a comprehensive dental treatment plan. Not having to walk around with broken/missing/visibly decayed teeth is a visible class marker in our "classless" society.

Dental problems aren't the only pressing health need that the poor can't get resolved in order to boost their employment chances. Since only a small percentage of poor people are Medicaid eligible, vision care is also an urgent unmet need. When you can't see but can't afford an eye exam, eyeglasses, and glaucoma treatment, you're not employable. People who have never been extremely poor for any length of time think there is "all this help out there", but there isn't. When rent/mortgage and utilities eat up two thirds of your monthly income, there is no "extra" money for a trip to the eye doctor. Being able to see isn't a luxury you "earn." You can't help yourself if you can't see.

Bill O'Reilly, Sean Hannity, Rush Limbaugh and others who say that the poor just need to pull themselves up by their bootstraps, make better choices, and get college educations need a reality check. But they won't stop pedaling classism from their radio and television pulpits because promoting hatred for the poor made them rich. They're invested in blaming the victim. Imagine if they actually had to work for (less than) a living. Gee – what a concept!

Chapter 5

"In societies that worship money and success, the losers become objects of scorn." ~ Michael Parenti

Claiming that the poor aren't motivated and don't value education is another myth. It's a cropped and Photoshopped view of the real picture. The public school system is imbued with middle class customs and values. It's an intimidating environment for poor children. Poor children are not made to feel welcome in the middle class education system. They're made to feel unworthy because they can't afford the things they might need in order to participate in school activities, programs, and assignments. The message they get is that school is a place where they don't belong.

Most teachers come from the middle class. Middle class teachers and kids marginalize poor kids. Middle class kids become teachers' pets, class presidents, voted "most likely to succeed", editors of school newspapers, captains of football teams and cheerleading squads, and high school valedictorians. Poor kids are labeled, cast aside, or shunted off into special ed classes.

Dr. Donna Beegle did a study in 2000 that primarily focused on those who grew up in generational poverty and, against all odds, achieved academic success. She was motivated to conduct her survey because she wanted to bring attention to the social injustice of poverty. She herself had escaped generational poverty – a family of over three generations of illiterate migrant farm workers who worked hard in the back-breaking thankless job of picking fruits and vegetables, but never made enough money to attain basic economic stability. Conditions and pay for migrant farm workers has not improved since Donna Beegle's childhood. According to a 1998 US Department of Labor report, migrant farm workers are paid an average of $7,500 a year. They don't get unemployment benefits, credit towards an old age social security benefit, health insurance, or workers' compensation.

Although small progress has been made in diminishing the educational barriers of race, sex, and disability; class is the one barrier that continues to be ignored. Dr. Beegle's study was a sobering one.

Most of the poor adults surveyed stated that they believed their lives would have turned out better if they would have had teachers who believed in them and treated them like they were "somebody." 98% of the respondents said that had they not been "pushed aside" and treated like they didn't belong by teachers and school administrators, they would have taken school more seriously. They would have enjoyed learning and had more self-confidence in pursuing advanced education and training.

Since teachers mostly come from middle class, their view of life and the world is through middle class lenses. Like the majority of others in the middle class, teachers have been socialized to believe the negative stereotypes about the poor promoted by the media. They think poor people are lazy, stupid, make bad choices, and are academically unmotivated. Teachers' lack of class consciousness made Dr. Beegle's respondents feel like they weren't wanted in school. Dr.Beegle's article *"Overcoming the Silence of Generational Poverty"*, which summed up her report, brought back painful memories for me.

People who struggle with poverty have had their voices silenced. They've been criminalized for their conditions of destitution. They "get it" — nobody cares about them. Nobody wants to hear about their problems. But Dr. Beegle's report gave those struggling in poverty a sense of recognition, of vindication, and of understanding. It is time to bring the social injustices of poverty and classism out of America's collective closet because it cannot be ignored anymore.

Generational poverty can best be described as something that had been fixed. When your grandparents, your parents, and you are all desperately poor, that is an example of generational poverty. Generational poverty is an economic prison because those stuck in it lack the means to escape. Many don't know anyone who has been successful in the job market. Everyone they knew worked hard but weren't paid enough to afford basic needs. There are no resources built into the lives of those from generational poverty.

Equally trapped are those who were foster children who "aged out" of the system at 17 or 18 years old. They're booted out onto the streets with no money, no health care, and nowhere to go. They don't even get a suit and $75 and a bus ticket like some felons get upon release from prison.

Poverty isn't an urban black thing or a rural white thing – it's a social injustice thing. It cuts across all religious, ethnic, age, racial and gender lines.

Although Dr. Beegle's work focuses on those from generational poverty, the common denominator of classism is experienced by those from different poverty situations. From the third generation kid in an urban housing project to the formerly middle class kid whose parents lost their jobs to the orphan who abruptly became destitute at age 13 and left to fend for herself in a male dominated society that does not care about her, or even acknowledge her existence – the injustices of poverty and classism are the same.

Teachers assume that all of their students have the same resources. They assume each child has a computer, Internet access, and a secure stable home with all the utilities on. When they make these assumptions, the expectation is that homework assignments requiring a computer will be completed on time. Many children don't have computers, Internet, or even a home. The only place available for the poorest of poor children to complete assignments is at the school during the day. That is the reality for children who have to go home to a cramped and overcrowded freezing house/apartment/trailer where the gas or electric has been shut off because mom couldn't pay the bill since she couldn't get a "man's job" to support the family; and the "father" cared more about getting a "men's rights" group to help him manipulate the courts into reducing his child support obligation than he cared about his own children and the woman who bore them.

It's hard to complete homework assignments when there is no quiet personal space in the home to concentrate on homework, where everyone is crammed into one room to keep warm around a space heater, and where there's no electric – never mind Internet! The only way for children (or anyone else) to become computer and Internet savvy is by having access to one at home to use every day. Learning comes by doing. And the Internet was supposed to be the great equalizer in our society. But many children in poverty lack this luxury that so many people take for granted.

When poor children are penalized for being unable to complete homework assignments on time, it sends the message that they can't win. Being ridiculed by classmates for not doing something that is "so easy that *anyone* can do it" creates aversion to education because it's not "so easy" if your home life is chaotic and you're in a poverty related crisis living on the edge waiting for the other shoe to drop.

By junior high and high school, kids form cliques and fitting in becomes a life and death matter. One Canadian parent expressed frustration about her teen being late for school regularly because her one and only Tommy Hilfiger sweatshirt was still in the clothes dryer and she refused to go to school without it. But this should not have been a surprise to that parent. The ability to socially fit in with others and your school experiences shape your relationships, educational opportunities, self-esteem, and forge the pathway to jobs in adulthood.

Adults are routinely denied good jobs because they can't afford the "right image." This concept of having the "right image" begins in junior high school and extends throughout life. Having the ability to afford the right stuff means far more than just being socially accepted by the other kids in junior high school. It means being able to participate as a member of society. It means being able to join extra-curricular activities and develop social capital. In adulthood, being able to afford the right image determines one's ability to socialize, find a mate, and getting (and keeping) a good job that makes middle class life and its attendant comfort possible. This is especially true for women since men can be uneducated, butt ugly and still get high paying jobs that don't require a college education.

Like the participants in Dr. Beegle's study, I recall the struggle of just getting to school on time because of not having basic physical and economic security. I remember being tired from delivering newspapers and being docked pay for customers who didn't pay their newspaper bill. I remember working late at McDonalds and having to go home to bed hungry and fearful of my sister's violent, unpredictable drug addict boyfriend who lived with us. I had to get a fake ID so I could get a "job" dancing naked for leering men who didn't see women as human beings — the only job opportunity other than prostitution available to poor young women from the urban underclass. Worrying about homework wasn't a top priority.

After my grandmother died, my sister was all I had and it was a choice of either living with her or going into the foster care system. And that meant if she was "in love" with the creep who beat her up and set our apartment on fire, I had no choice but to put up with him. But a foster home meant living among strangers and not being wanted except for the check the state would pay them on my behalf. The foster care system has always been known for abusing children and for its lack of accountability. It's better to go with the devil that you know instead of the devil that you don't know.

I remember my sister and I being told by landlords and employers that we shouldn't balk at their "generous" offers that amounted to a trade of sexual favors in exchange for getting hired in a low-wage job or getting a $10 break on the rent, because that was such a good deal for "girls like us." I'll never forget struggling to cope with having to live like that while trying to get through junior high and high school when nobody else had to live like that. With some things, there is no "getting over it."

Everyone else I went to school with had two parents and at least one of them had a good job. They didn't have to dance naked for men just to get money for rent and food. They didn't live in cramped roach-infested ghetto tenements, beholden to seedy slum landlords. They lived in nice houses where everyone had their own bedroom, everyone had closets for clothing, dental care was not a "luxury", meals were regular and orderly and everyone had plenty to eat. They had TV. If they needed any school supplies, their parents could afford to buy them. They didn't have to worry about anything, except being kids.

Poverty crushes self-esteem and makes it difficult to form friendships. Poor kids want what all the other kids strive for. They want to fit in, to be accepted, and to belong. Teen years are especially difficult. Teen years are stressful for "normal" middle class kids. For the child living in poverty, the stress from social rejection is overwhelming.

I learned by the 9th grade that I was expected to settle for less in life because I was poor, female, and didn't have a family. I was one of society's "throw-aways." I was "poor white trash" – therefore unworthy of a chance for anything in life. The public education system tracks poor kids, often placing them in special ed and slapping labels on them like "slow learner", "emotionally disturbed" or "learning-disabled" even if they're not.

I am mildly dyslexic, but not "slow", and not severely enough to warrant my placement in special ed. My dyslexia did not impede my ability to graduate from college in one of the most difficult majors of study. Some of the smartest people were dyslexic; Albert Einstein was.

For those whose learning disabilities are more severe, barriers to academic success are easily remediated through places such as the Sylvan Learning Center. But Sylvan costs a lot of money – money that poor families don't have. Middle and upper class families whose children struggle with learning difficulties can go to Sylvan, or even hire private tutors. Children from poor families or those in the foster care system struggling with learning difficulties get thrown in special ed where they're socially and academically discarded. The label of being a "special needs" student is a powerful social exclusion marker. The effects of social exclusion should not be underestimated.

Special ed classes frequently become dumping grounds for kids in poverty that middle class teachers don't want to deal with. Prior to the 8th grade, I was an honor roll student. My dyslexia did not prevent me from being successful in the classroom. I could not work out what was wrong when I was suddenly dumped in special ed. Something was not right. That "something", unseen by me, probably related to classism in the public education system. It set me back by defining my limits, crushing my dreams, and taking options away from me in my adult life.

I was the girl who wasn't one of the "popular" girls. The ones who were popular were always those from the middle and upper class families. They lived in the nicer part of town. They had the nicest clothes that were always in style. Often when middle class kids got cut from the gymnastics team, the swim team, varsity sports, majorette or cheerleading tryouts, etc., their parents flew into the school converging on teachers like a swarm of angry hornets whose nest got pissed on. They threw tantrums until they were placated with their child's acceptance in one of those activities. Middle class people have a sense of entitlement – they think they've got the right to bully their way to secure every advantage for their child, whether their child earned it or not.

Adolescent and teen years are hell. Whoever can't fit in is shunned, ridiculed, and bullied by everyone else in school. Adults who have the liberty to leave a toxic workplace rampant with bullying expect children to suck it up and take it within the environs of school. Kids cannot commit civil disobedience to protest the school. Unlike adults who can bring suit against employers for abuse and creating a "hostile work environment", children don't have the right to sue schools for abuse. Since primary education is compulsory they're forced to take abuse from peers that adults would never tolerate for a minute. If a victim of school bullying walks out of school when they can no longer tolerate it, they're punished. This remains part of their permanent school record and follows them into their adult life. When social exclusion and bullying reaches a breaking point, as it did for Eric Harris and Dylan Klebold at Columbine High School, the result is violence. The devastating consequences of social exclusion and bullying should never be underestimated. When adults in the school system allow or promote bullying and social exclusion while punishing those who stand up for themselves, children are not merely disappointed – they're told that they have no stake in society. The only lesson I learned in my 11th grade commercial art class was that I had no chips to play the game of life.

My "legal guardian" was my older half-sister who was a high school drop-out who had to work 6-7 days a week for $1.10 an hour plus sporadic tips as a waitress. Even if she would have had the economic security of a middle class job with paid personal days to deal with the problems I was having at school, she lacked the education and confidence to do it. She was ill-equipped to debate teams of condescending education "professionals." She was not on equal footing with college educated professionals whose jargon and elitist attitudes alienate the poor.

She could not take time off from her waitress job at the local greasy spoon to go to bat for me against educated adults who knew it was wrong to push a poor kid around. I was at the mercy of those who had no mercy. Any time I had some hope that I too could be "somebody" and have something, someone else extinguished that hope.

When I was a 15 year old high school sophomore, I wanted to fit in and be accepted just like any other teen. But fitting in is impossible when you are in a segregated class for learning-disabled students, sequestered from the other kids in the high school basement, where *everybody* knows that's the "retard class." I was pleasantly surprised when I was selected to be part of the test market for mainstreaming learning-disabled students into vo-tech classes. It was very exciting for me.

My vo-tech class choices were structured in the 10th grade year. I had to take agriculture, horticulture, commercial art and graphic design, masonry, and building maintenance. I enjoyed the commercial arts class immensely because I found out that I was good at it. The 10th grade commercial art teacher, Mr. Silvernell, believed in me and encouraged me to pursue commercial art as a major at vo-tech for my junior and senior years. Mr. Silvernell made learning fun. He made every student feel valued. He told funny stories centering on two fictitious characters, "Jake and Louie" in order to stress the importance of safety near the bindery equipment. Mr. Silvernell even extended his Jake and Louie tales to safe conduct while riding on the vo-tech bus:

"Jake and Louie thought it would be cool to throw a cantaloupe at the bus driver while the commercial art class was going on a field trip. I caught it as it just missed the bus driver's head. Things could have ended real badly if Uncle Silvernell hadn't stepped in."

I was the top commercial art and graphic design student. I won the first prize for the tri-county competition for a poster on Arbor Day. My competitors were sophomore, junior and senior art students from every high school in the tri-county area of Bucks, Lehigh, and Carbon counties. Winning first place in that competition boosted my confidence. By the end of my 10th grade year, Mr. Silvernell urged me to consider majoring in commercial art and graphic design for my junior and senior year. He also encouraged me to apply to the prestigious Philadelphia Art Institute after high school graduation, saying that he would recommend me for a merit scholarship at this Ivy League art school.

I was elated, but I was hesitant to pursue commercial art for my junior and senior vo-tech/high school years because the required commercial art tool kit cost $87 (this was in 1983, the equivalent of $200 today). There was no way I could ask my sister for the money to pay for it – she worked 6-7 days a week as a poor waitress to barely keep a roof over our heads. I had no way to afford an $87 vo-tech tool kit. (I hadn't begun strip dancing yet.)

Mr. Silvernell took me aside after class and told me that I should not let lack of money stop me from pursuing a talent. He said I had a lot of talent and that wasting it would be a crime. He told me that there was a grant fund available at the vo-tech specifically for the purchase of vo-tech supplies for promising students who were underprivileged. Mr. Silvernell told me all I needed to do was commit to the commercial art and graphic design program for my junior and senior years and keep up the good work. I smiled for the first time in years. I signed up for the program.

The following fall, I took my seat in the 11th grade commercial art class at vo-tech. The teacher for the junior and senior year was Mr. Maurer, a relatively young teacher in his early thirties. He had close-cropped dirty-blonde hair and a boyish face framed by stylish eyeglasses. On the first day of school, Mr. Maurer gave the class our first assignment as he passed out the brand new shiny orange art tool kits to the students. Mr. Maurer also reminded the class that everyone had to bring in their $87 for their tool boxes by the end of the first week.

Being a naïve 16 year old then, I thought Mr. Maurer "knew" about my situation. Lehigh County Vo-Tech was a small school and the art department had only three teachers. They all knew each other because they all worked together. I reasoned that Mr. Silvernell must have told Mr. Maurer that my tool kit would be paid for by the merit and need-based grant. I was wrong.

On Friday morning at the end of the first week of class, Mr. Maurer called the class to attention. He had an announcement to make. Twenty-five pairs of eager, young eyes were on Mr. Maurer as he stood in front of the classroom. Speaking in the authoritative tone of a Marine drill sergeant, he said, "Jacqueline Beckel, will you come forward please." Startled and confused, I got up slowly and approached the front of the classroom. What immediately followed hit me like a ton of bricks.

Mr. Maurer ordered me to face the class. Then he pointed at me and exclaimed, "Any student like Jacqueline Beckel whose parents can't afford $87 for their tool box doesn't belong in this class."

Life is hard enough for the teen who doesn't fit in, who is searching for acceptance in society while desperately cleaving to the belief that she can achieve anything she wants to because America is the "land of opportunity." For the poorest kid in a class of middle and upper class kids, the devastation from ridicule, rejection, and social exclusion is enormous. I fought back the tears that welled up in my eyes so that the rest of the class, who were snickering after Mr. Maurer's "announcement", would not have the satisfaction of seeing me cry. I walked past them with my head high, retrieved my "charity" tool kit, took it straight to Mr. Maurer's desk and set it down before him, and walked of the class without looking at anyone.

I was given a three day in-school suspension as punishment because leaving a class without permission is against the rules. Had I been a child from a middle or upper class family, the situation would have never occurred because the $87 tool kit would not have been an issue. If a teacher publicly humiliated a middle or upper class student, angry parents with plenty of social capital would have convened upon the school demanding action – and the teacher would have been disciplined.

The experience in Mr. Maurer's class was only one of many subsequent experiences that led me to believe that as one of society's "throw-aways", that I had no place in society. I didn't fit in, I didn't belong. I was made to feel that I didn't deserve a chance to participate in life, and that pursuing talents and goals were only for those who could afford that privilege. Being poor and from a dysfunctional family, I was nothing but "poor white trash" that wasn't good enough for anyone or anything. I was always wrong even when I was right. I was unworthy of a chance to be "somebody."

Being from the lower class meant I was defective. I even started to think that being an orphan was my fault. If only I had been "good enough", my biological dad would have stuck around and my mom would have wanted me.

I did not pick up a paint set since that Friday morning in Mr. Maurer's class in 1984. I had been made a fool out of deliberately. I was built up by Mr. Silvernell only to be knocked down and stepped on by Mr. Maurer. If that was how I got treated by Mr. Maurer for having to get my art kit on a small vo-tech grant, I could only imagine the horror that awaited me if I applied for scholarships and grants to attend the prestigious Philadelphia Art Institute. I switched to building maintenance and masonry halfway through my junior year.

When teachers give assignments that require the purchase of supplies throughout the duration of a course without any consideration for the student in poverty, they are fostering a hostile learning environment. They are promoting classism and fostering bullying. This environment stifles motivation for the student who is struggling in poverty because that student feels unwelcome and excluded at school. Teachers who do this are part of the problem, not part of the solution.

When those who have never been poor repeat the vicious canards about poverty being the result of "poor choices", and that those in poverty "chose" to give up; they don't grasp the definition of the word "choice." What choice does the disenfranchised youth have after being shoved aside because they weren't welcome in the education system – a system that was rigged against them from the start? If everyone is not starting out with the same chances and resources, can we really say our system is fair and based on merit? There's a big difference between starting out on third base and hitting a triple.

For poor kids who successfully navigate the unwelcoming high school environment with good grades and aspire to college, their efforts to attend college are often stonewalled. By lack of money alone, their options are restricted. They are denied the same college opportunities as the middle and upper class. Income and socio-economic class limits your choices severely when you're from the bottom rung. But it is not lack of money alone; it is also a hidden set of social class customs.

Consider the types of questions that are frequently found on admissions applications for elite colleges which are weighted more heavily than grades when determining acceptance. Questions on these admissions applications accord a certain number of admittance points that overwhelmingly favor the activities, affiliations, and social experiences that only the more privileged students would have. The following examples include some questions which were listed on applications from both Drexel University and Lehigh University – both expensive private universities in eastern Pennsylvania:

1. Which countries have you visited?

2. Which civic organizations are you a member of in good standing?
3. What is your family name?
4. Which extra-curricular activities have you participated in?

The first question assumes you had the luxury of being able to afford to travel. The second question assumes you had the privilege of free time and money to join and be active in civic organizations such as Rotary or the Junior League, which are socially necessary affiliations for upcoming affluent youth. The third question determines whether or not you can be admitted under a legacy admission; if either of your parents are wealthy alumni who contributed generously to the institutions coffers. The fourth question assumes you had parents that could afford to pay for music lessons, dancing lessons, horseback riding instruction – all activities exclusively enjoyed by middle and upper class kids. Awarding admission points based on your ability to participate in those activities excludes applicants from poverty because they could not afford those activities.

Few if any students from the underclass get admitted to Harvard, Yale, Princeton, John Hopkins, Carnegie Mellon, or University of Pennsylvania – even if they *could* get a full scholarship based solely on their high school grades. Their socio-economic background works against them. Poor people struggle just to be able to live. There's no money for life necessities, never mind for participating in any extracurricular activities or the leisure time to participate in civic organizations. Since there's no money to afford a vacation to Disney Land, it's fair to say that travel abroad is off the radar.

Poor people don't have the opportunity to travel abroad and visit other countries. That is a luxury frequently thrown in their faces by those who had that opportunity and who lord it over others as if to say, "I've done this, you haven't, so I know more than you." The privileged may know more about having the luxury of "slumming it" by visiting poor regions so they can feel better, and they may know more about traveling in style taking in the sights of the Louvre and the Eiffel Tower and European palaces than the poor who can't even afford a vacation to Disney Land, but that doesn't make affluent people the final arbiters of life's realities.

The only way poor people get to travel is if they join the military and risk life and limb when deployed to war zones; or if they're unembedded journalists traveling on sparse grant money to various conflict regions throughout the world to document human rights abuses and geopolitical upheavals that the mainstream news media ignores. Unembedded independent journalists risk life and limb, often without pay, doing what well-paid establishment "journalists" do not: serving as the watchdog of democracy rather than the lapdog of the elite. We must travel unarmed and we are at risk of being kidnapped, tortured, or even killed. The view of the world seen through the eyes of the unembedded journalist is not that which is seen by the wealthy whose only foreign travel experiences can be summed up neatly in a pretty Norman Rockwell picture.

To give a college applicant admission points based on extra-curricular activities that are rigidly stratified along social class lines is not affording an equal chance based on academic merit. The experience of answering such questions on college application forms is alienating and demoralizing to underprivileged applicants. They serve to reinforce feelings of shame and social inadequacy; a sense that their life experiences don't count. Not surprisingly, many underprivileged students rationalize that applying to a private college is a waste of their time. Instead, they "choose" to either go to a public college that's not their first choice, or they won't bother with college at all.

A lifetime of suffering deprivation where nobody helps and nobody cares while those who have plenty expect you to just go die quietly in some forsaken corner is enough to discourage the poor from trying. If those who have everything don't even want you to be able to live, why would they let you get an education?

Since federal and state student aid programs had been cut severely by the Gramm-Rudman Bill while I was struggling to get my degree as a destitute disabled woman, grad school was out of reach for me. After graduating with my Bachelors degree at age 34 in 2001, I had hoped to re-enter the workforce in a middle class job and eventually go to grad school. But that never happened for me. My last allowable student loan deferment expired three years after graduating from college. I was *still* without a job that would enable me to repay my student loans and be able to live. My student loans went into default – barring me from participation in *any* further career retraining and government job placement help or eligibility for aid to pursue grad school.

It should also be noted that a *summa cum laude* graduate from a public college is patently disadvantaged in the competition for good jobs when going up against an Ivy League graduate who barely skated by with a 2.0 GPA. Where's the meritocracy in that? Dude, where's the justice?

Chapter 6

"An imbalance between rich and poor is the oldest and most fatal ailment of all republics." ~ Plato

America's middle class hatred and social exclusion of the poor is rooted in deficit theory theology. Deficit theory blames the oppressed for their oppression, justifying greed for those who have everything. Deficit theory lets the abuser off the hook and unjustly puts the responsibility squarely on the shoulders of the victim. Deficit theory gives society a free pass for failing to hold the purveyors of social injustice accountable for their actions. In the US, deficit theory developed from a particularly obnoxious religion. Max Weber answers the question of why the American middle class hates the poor. The Dutch Reformed church and the Puritans of New England were the first European settlers in America. And they were all Calvinists. They follow the teachings of a 17th century Swiss theologian, John Calvin, who initially studied to become a Catholic priest.

Calvin taught a theology of predestination. When people are born, they're either predestined for heaven or hell, and there's nothing they can do about it — God ordained it and there's no way of knowing who is predestined for salvation and who is not. The "Elect" have already been chosen. Moral behavior is the barometer of your fate — as is prosperity and wealth. Greed, materialism, and oppression of the poor are rooted in the Protestant Calvinist doctrine. Calvinist doctrine basically holds that a person's salvation is predestined; that an infallible and omnipotent God had determined in His own time who would be saved and who would be damned, and that there's nothing anyone can do about it. The most influential Protestant Christian doctrines is Calvinism which basically holds that whatever happens to you is God's will. If you're poor or suffering from infirmity, it's because you were not favored by God.

There is something in Calvinism called "the Calling." It's a form of behavior where Calvinists teach each other, and everyone else, to work hard. What they were doing was trying to upstage their neighbors by showing them that they were headed for heaven. Weber said of a Calvinist, John Baxter, whom he met:

> "For in view of their neighbors, the appropriate sentiment for these Elect by God's Grace, it is not forbearing helplessness in the consciousness of their own weakness; but hatred and contempt for them as enemies of God who bear the mark of eternal damnation upon them."

People who are poor, disabled, non-Christian, or markedly different in any way are viewed by the middle class as reprobates; as "sinners" sentenced to eternal damnation. Calvinist capitalist America has always hated the poor and has a long-standing history of keeping its jackboot on the throats of marginalized people to keep them "in their place."

The Puritans who brought their social disease of oppressive theology to the New World despised the Native Americans whom this country originally belonged to. They viewed them as "heathens" and who were "agents of Satan." Although some European colonists thought that the Native Americans could become "good Christians" and trading partners, the Puritans distrusted the Native Americans and their self-concept as "God's Elect" reaffirmed that distrust. These Calvinists saw themselves as "chosen" people, as the "new Israelites" entering a land given to them by God through divine providence. They referred to the Native people as the "new Canaanites" and believed that God intended for them to slaughter these "heathen" and take the land for themselves, using biblical inferences of their colony a "city set upon a hill." Levitical Law (Mosaic Law) was incorporated into colonial laws in New England.

The massacres of the Pequot tribe on May 26th 1637 and on July 14th 1637 were carried out by the Puritans who believed they were directed by God and had a divine right to slaughter the "heathens" in the name of Christ if these "new Canaanites" wouldn't convert to

Christianity and hand over their homes and land to the Puritans. The Puritans were exceptionally cruel and brutal. They not only sought to kill the Pequot, they also relished in torturing them, as they did with one Pequot captive whom they "tore limb from limb" after which "Captain Underhill ended the victim's agony with a pistol shot. The body was then roasted and eaten by the Mohegans."[37]

The Puritans held themselves as enforcers of "law and order" due to their self-concept as God's "New World Zion" where the Indians were "Satan's horde" — thus justifying genocide, slavery, oppression, and land-grabbing. In one of the Pequot massacres of 1637, not only was the Pequot village set on fire, but the Pequot who escaped the flames were mercilessly gunned down. The rest had burned to death. Captain John Mason "gave full credit to God" for the massacre and Captain Underhill claimed that the Pequot were enemies of Christ and therefore had it coming. This same sentiment was later used to justify the American holocaust of Manifest Destiny, the "Business Plot" to assassinate Franklin Delano Roosevelt, abusive social and economic policies aimed at poor women with the Reagan Revolution, and the current trend towards a Christian fundamentalist theocratic takeover of Congress that seeks to conscript women into reproductive slavery while eliminating social security, the Civil Rights laws, the Equal Pay Act, food stamps, Medicaid and Medicare.

Calvinist apologists compared the Pequots to the Amalekites whose destruction was supposedly ordained by God. The Puritans were the antecedents of today's Dominionist, Kingdom, and Reconstructionist Protestant Christian groups. Religious justification for genocide, torture, slavery, oppression and misogyny — the Rosetta Stone of capitalism — is what this "land of opportunity" was founded upon. Calvinists are not ascetic. They are the opposite. They are conspicuous consumers in the hope of convincing their neighbors that they are successful by God's will and therefore headed for heaven. The American Dream of prosperity is a

---

[37] Alden T. Vaughan, *New England Frontier: Puritans and Indians 1620-1675*, pp. 141. ©1965, 1979

necessary illusion that Americans drag around them like a battleship chain.

Calvinist influence is imbedded in our culture and society today with America's hatred for its own poor. By hating the poor, the middle class derives a psychic benefit of superiority. The middle class openly talk of their hatred for the poor when they're amongst themselves. The middle class is the majority of this country. They despise the poor. Many won't even help their own family members if they fall into poverty. When people from other nations refer to the "ugly American", it is this classist and self-important face of America that they see.

No wonder our WASP[38] male dominated capitalist society has difficulty owning up to unearned privilege and acknowledging that it has any obligation to ameliorate the injustice of poverty created by imperialism, 300 years of slavery followed by racial segregation; and education and job discrimination against women (who comprise 84% of the poor). Women count for less than white male felons in this country. White male ex-convicts get hired in good paying union jobs with health and dental benefits at companies like Lennox or GE over poor women (many whom are poor single mothers) with clean records and a college degree. White women are *still* economically far behind both white and non-white men due to institutionalized sexism, misogyny, and capitalism — and poor women of color are even worse off. All of which are justified by "divine right."

A misogynist holding himself as an expert on God let those who have unjustly benefited from unearned privileges totally off the hook. John Calvin earned his theological spurs by justifying misogyny and the rapacious economics of patriarchal mercantilism to coincide with Reformation dogma, ignoring the Christian injunction of "sell everything you own, give to the poor, and follow me." This patron saint of American Protestant Christianity made cruelty and oppression fashionable for Protestants: he had Michael Servetus arrested and charged with theological "crimes" for which Servetus was burned at the

[38] WASP: "White Anglo Saxon Protestant."

stake. Calvin set a precedent for his followers: punitive measures should be carried out by God's "Elect" for the benefit of Christian social order, as ordained by God. The Republican Party driving American politics since the late 1970's have been using God as a battering ram. Unearned privilege is an entitlement because God said so – the gospel according to John Calvin, one of history's most influential racists, woman-haters and rabid anti-Semites. Apparently he didn't get the memo: If a perfect divine God exists, he would not need an editorial staff or a proofreading department.

Calvinism is the foundation of American classism: the middle and upper class white male notion of the "undeserving poor." It is the Calvinist "Protestant work ethic" that promotes and perpetuates classism, the false dichotomy that hard work and virtuous living is the reason why some prosper while others do not. And it is classism which ascribes stigma to poverty, propagating hatred for the poor and the negative stereotypes our society has about poor people today.

It is classism that provides justification in our "civilized" society for non-profit hospitals to dump indigent elderly and disabled patients out onto the street in front of homeless shelters if they're uninsured and can't pay their hospital bills. Such incidents were caught on the videotape of a Los Angeles Rescue Mission security camera and depicted in Michael Moore's "*Sicko*", a documentary about the healthcare crisis in America. Society allows this to happen by indifference, reaffirming the message that if you're poor, you're sub-human and not entitled to any basic human rights — not even the right to life. This is not surprising when you consider that Calvin's influence had permeated New England colonial society for almost a century before the American Articles of Confederation were scrapped in lieu of a Constitution – which excluded women and non-property owners from the full benefits of American citizenship.

In the 1700's, the Commonwealth of Pennsylvania had a law concerning the poor that said, "*If you are poor, you must wear a "P" on your sleeve whenever you leave your home. It must be 4 inches and be either red or blue.*" The idea that the poor should be punished for their poverty, rather than helped and uplifted is directly from the Calvinist Protestant influence shaping early American culture. It was thought that if the poor were made miserable enough, degraded enough, and humiliated enough that they could be shamed out of their poverty. That thinking isn't different from the present attitudes in the way poor people are treated under neoliberalism and the social policies of "compassionate conservativism." Not surprisingly, the neocon political movement in the United States is overwhelmingly sexist, racist, sociopathic and Christian.

But it does not matter religion people subscribe to. When people prioritize their own economic self-interest at the expense of others, that self-interest becomes the center of their religion and their lives. The way they practice their faith and view religious teachings changes to accommodate their socio-economic status. Compared to the traditional Jesus riding into Jerusalem on a donkey, the neo-Calvinist Reaganite Jesus rode into Jerusalem in a Rolls Royce wearing a Brooks Brothers suit and a Rolex.

Throughout the Inquisition and the Reformation, it was always poor women who suffered the most. Torture and forced conversions during the Inquisition were carried out by the Jesuit Order, a terrorist organization operating under the aegis of the Roman Catholic Church, targeted women with the College of Bishops' *Malleus Maleficarum*. The Roman Catholic Church is the world's oldest imperialism and the first multinational corporation. It was always the least empowered of the common people who were tortured into false confessions, forced conversions, and burnt alive at the stake for heresy – not the wealthy ruling class. And puritanical Protestants were no more benevolent towards the poor than their papal contemporaries. They were really Catholics who ran away from home (the Roman Catholic Church) and kept the elements of Catholicism's cruelty that suited them.

Wealthy nobility used the Protestant teachings to justify looting of cathedrals, stealing jewels and gold that had been fashioned into papist icons, and then throwing the landless serfs who were charity wards of the Catholic churches off of church property – leaving them idle, starving, and homeless. The rich have always used religion as a tool for subjugating the poor and social control to protect their own wealth and privilege and to justify greed. No matter which religious doctrine we examine, the "haves" twisted and manipulated religious teachings to justify economic cannibalism of the "have-nots." That is why classism remains deeply entrenched with us today.

An interesting observation of the bygone era of requiring the poor in colonial Pennsylvania to wear a "P" is the arcane medical practices. At that time, the educated male-only (women were barred from schools) medical establishment held some bizarre beliefs regarding personal hygiene. The highly esteemed medical constabulary of the 16th through the 18th centuries believed that the best defense against sickness, infection from sepsis during childbirth, and other deadly scourges was to refrain from bathing. They believed that "bad air" caused sickness and disease, but if you allowed a crust to build up over your skin by not washing you would be protected from the maladies carried by "bad air." Since that baseless notion went extinct by the mid-19th century, isn't it time we bury the 400 year notions about poverty as well?

By the mid-19th century, Great Britain and America had adopted very punitive attitudes towards the poor. Poorhouses, also known as almshouses or workhouses, were tax-supported residential institutions. Poor people were required by law to go there if they could not support themselves. These institutions were anything but charitable. They served to provide a pool of slave labor for the most miserable, low-paying and back-breaking jobs. Living conditions were similar to prisons except that the residents weren't shackled. The separation of entire families was unbearable and the squalor was so bad that most poor people resorted to the most dangerous of measures to try to get money to support themselves rather than go there.

Just like today, the majority of the 19th century's poor were women. Destitute women in the era of Charles Dickens often resorted to prostitution rather than turn to the local poorhouse. As a result, serial killer Jack the Ripper had no trouble finding victims when he unleashed his reign of terror in the fall of 1888 in the Whitechapel area in London.

The aristocracy didn't acknowledge that it was poverty and discrimination that drove women to desperate measures which put them directly in harm's way. Queen Victoria was reputed to have said that the only reason prostitutes engaged in their line of "work" was because they were over-sexed and lacked proper moral restraint. Considering Queen Victoria's panicked reaction upon being advised by her royal physician after the birth of her tenth (and last) child that her childbearing days were over. The royal arbiter of 19th century sexual morals exclaimed, "Oh doctor! Does this mean I can have no more fun in bed?" Apparently, getting to have sex was a class privilege.

It never occurred to the queen that the unfortunate women in London's impoverished east end were destitute and turned to prostitution in order to get money to survive and that because of a legacy of discrimination and paternalism, poor women had no other recourse.

Five of these poor souls paid the ultimate price for their poverty with their lives at the hands of Jack the Ripper. They were: Mary Ann "Polly" Nichols, Annie Chapman, Catherine Eddowes, Elizabeth "Long Liz" Stride, and Marie Jeannette Kelly. If the poorhouses were humane institutions, the unfortunate victims of Jack the Ripper would not have put themselves in harm's way in order to support themselves below subsistence levels.

The Victorian Poor Laws stated that the poor had to go request help from a local community-elected official known as an Overseer of the Poor, or Poor Master. Sometimes the poor were court-ordered to register with the Poor Master if they were caught begging in public, which was illegal (like panhandling is today). From there, they had to eak out dreary existences as slave laborers – overworked and abused by those who ran the poorhouses, often getting only stale bread and watered down broth.

Poorhouses in America were worse because they were run like prisons. They were set up to "reform" the poor and cure them of their bad habits and personal flaws that were assumed to be the cause of their poverty. A page from the rule book for the Orange County, New York poorhouse in 1831 states:

"All persons who are capable of working shall repair to their proper apartments or places allotted for them, ***where they shall work at such business and as many hours as the superintendents shall appoint****...Whereas some slothful persons may pretend sickness or lameness to excuse themselves from labour, such persons shall be examined by the physician, and if it appear by his report that those persons made false excuses, they shall be punished by confinement to a cell or some other solitary place, and fed on bread and water until they comply as the superintendents shall determine."*

Inmates in poorhouses could be worked until they dropped dead of exhaustion, hunger, or sickness. Poorhouse residents were always presumed to be feigning illness in order to get out of working. It was held that poor people were lazy and that's why they were poor. Society hasn't changed.

In sum, poorhouses were really a precursor to the Nazi slave labor and death camps — enriching the capitalist class by extermination through destitution and slave labor. And because it was mostly poor women and children who were treated this way, society didn't care.

The Workfare program implemented in the 1980's requiring welfare recipients to work for their meager welfare benefits, followed by the draconian Welfare Reform Act of 1996 was based on the very same premise as the 1831 poorhouse rule book: that the poor are lazy and don't want to work. Middle class people routinely accuse the disabled of "faking it" in order to get meager, inadequate SSI checks. According to middle and upper class Americans, poor people sit on their butts doing nothing but eating bon-bons while watching Oprah with their sweatpants stapled to the sofa. They think the poor just want to live large off the backs of those fortunate enough to have good jobs. The truth: no one wants to marginalized and excluded because everyone wants to fit in and be socially accepted. Most poor people want to work at jobs that pay a living wage with health and dental benefits where they're not abused, degraded, or insulted.

Sociologist Herbert Gans observed that the pejorative terms and negative labels ascribed to the poor serve as obstacles which impede their ability to climb out of poverty and join the ranks of the middle class[39]. Some may argue that labels are only harmless "sticks and stones." Labels are stereotypes which adversely affect one's life. While denigrating labels hold the poor back, the poor are expected to take advantage of the education, training, and job opportunities that are being denied to them; including those from which they've been barred by these very same damaging labels. Negative labels and stereotypes are powerful words are destructive "sticks and stones."

Labeling welfare recipients keeps them from getting an equal chance for middle class jobs – whether they have college degrees and training or not. How many poor single mothers in post-welfare reform America in need of living wage jobs after being cut from the welfare rolls have had their job applications discarded by human resource managers who think *all* poor welfare recipients "lack work ethic" and "soft skills" – and therefore don't deserve a chance for a job? How many poor women have been denied jobs because they "weren't a good fit" because they lacked a recent stable work history, even though the reason they lacked experience, stable job histories and employer references is because *no one* gave them a chance for a decent steady job? How many poor single mothers get denied the jobs they desperately need because employers claim that single mothers are less reliable as employees than single fathers, while forcing women to risk criminal neglect charges if they can't get anyone to watch a sick child that daycare providers and schools send home?

Negative attitudes towards the poor who are forced out of desperation to seek help are openly displayed by middle class social workers who get paid to help the poor. They assume that the poor have nothing better to do other than waste an entire day of their time, being

---

[39] "*The War Against the Poor*", by Dr. Herbert Gans

shuffled from one agency to another; each one giving them the run-around without helping them and sending them away to yet one more agency to be judged as "worthy" and sent away empty-handed – again. Many poor people give up. They would rather do without than waste their time begging for help that is either not forthcoming, or given begrudgingly - after having to wait in a crowded, noisy waiting room all day for their turn to be interrogated and having to bare their scars to strangers in order to prove themselves "deserving" of help only be turned away with nothing.

No Virginia, there really isn't "all this help out there."

As of 2007, only 14% of those eligible for help with subsidized housing (Section 8) can get it. That means that 86% of the poorest of the poor were turned away and *cannot* get it. Many of those in need of subsidized housing help are elderly and disabled people without families, trying to survive on less than $600/mo SSI. Applicants who *do* fit the "correct category" of poor eligible for housing help face waiting lists as long as ten years. Where can you get a one bedroom apartment and afford food and utilities on $600 a month without any help from Section 8? Subsidized housing programs for the poor fall miserably short, making it impossible for the poor to get any help. But nobody is talking about those in poverty who are turned away.

In Pennsylvania, poor people facing foreclosure can apply for emergency bail-out loans from the state under the PA Act 91 HEMAP Program. The intake interview process for determining if an applicant qualifies for help takes several hours during the day when most people have to work. It's very invasive having a stranger go over every aspect of your life with a fine tooth comb. In order to get help under HEMAP, applicants must show proof of adequate income proving that they can keep their mortgage payments current along with their HEMAP loan payments. But if they had adequate incomes, they wouldn't need assistance because they wouldn't be in foreclosure in the first place!

If an applicant's income is too low, they don't qualify for HEMAP help. Applicants are required to meet with a money management counselor as a condition of receiving help under HEMAP, *if* they qualify for help. Policymakers automatically assume that poor people don't know how to manage their money. It never occurred to them that you first need to have money in order to be able to manage it. Poor people have too little income as it is. They know *exactly* what everything costs, especially since they get charged more than the middle and upper classes for everything from utilities to auto insurance to basic checking accounts. The poor have to stretch their meager incomes like a mosquito's ass over a sugar bowl in a desperate struggle to survive.

Under the welfare reform laws, "Workfare" forced welfare recipients to work at various jobs in exchange for their welfare benefits, which amounted to less than the federal minimum wage. Conservative politics built on punishing the poor galvanized middle class voters into accepting a host of welfare reform laws that really promoted legalized slavery. The rhetoric of "no one is entitled to handouts" jelled with the middle classes. Middle class Americans resented anyone getting a handout, however meager, while not working. Whether the poor were getting chances for jobs or not didn't matter. The poor were painted as lazy bums and whores who "popped out babies just for the welfare check", and living large off the backs of middle class taxpayers.

Late president Ronald Wilson Reagan whipped middle class voters into a frenzy over poor single mothers buying fresh meat and produce with food stamps while the middle class scraped to buy Hamburger Helper. Reagan ignited middle class resentment with inflammatory remarks of "It's not fair that some healthy strapping young buck piles up his shopping cart with steaks that he pays for with food stamps while you're wondering how you're going to pay for a couple pounds of hamburger. It's time we ended welfare as an entitlement." But Reagan was not solely culpable.

Reagan had to work with a Democrat-controlled House of Representatives in Congress in order for his trickle-down policies and draconian cuts to social programs to get passed. There were <u>no</u> policies enacted during Reagan's two-term presidency that did not first meet the approval of the Democrat-controlled House. And these guys were not elected by some Fairy Godmother — middle class votes, many from white males in good-paying union jobs (that were and still are denied to poor women) put them in office based on their promise to cut already meager and inadequate welfare benefits which disproportionately hurt poor women, children, and the disabled. Blue-collar middle class union men drank the Kool-Aid, sucking up every word of Rush Limbaugh, an over-privileged gas bag who made his pile by peddling his gospel of hate for the poor — especially for women — from his media pulpit.

The middle and upper classes were Reagan's electoral foot soldiers. The 1980′s was a time when the young (Gen-Xers) comprised a greater proportion of people living in poverty than at any point after the Great Society programs of the 1960′s. Socialism became a dirty word and "entitlement" was code speak for welfare. About 400 government programs qualify as "entitlements." Most of the recipients are in the middle and upper classes.

Middle and upper class people resent meager entitlements for the poor. Ironically, it is the middle and upper classes that have benefited the most from entitlements. Telecommunications, the Internet, and other technologies were made possible through research and development that was funded by public tax dollars which provided the at-risk capital to for-profit privately owned companies that kept all the profits. Many who have enjoyed good jobs had employers that got "welfare handouts" in terms of tax exclusions, tax credits, price supports, loan guarantees, payments in kind, export subsidies, subsidized insurance premiums, marketing services, irrigation and reclamation programs, "enterprise zone" tax-exempt real estate, and research and development grants.

When it comes to entitlement attitudes, middle and upper class people think they're the only ones deserving of health care, educations, good jobs, and decent lives — claiming that nobody ever gave them anything, they "did it all on their own." Did it on their own my ass.

There's nothing as obtuse as the blindness of unearned privilege. A society that throws its poor, its excluded, and its marginalized to the wolves while guaranteeing wealth protection for the rich shields a lot of affluent people and corporations from having to compete in order to make money. This has had a deleterious effect on our economy, and on our society.

While middle class voters screech about "socialism" and called for the elimination of what few meager handouts existed for the poor, they conveniently ignored that socialist VA or FHA loan that helped them (or their parents) buy a nice house. They forgot about that socialist GI Bill that opened doors of opportunity for their fathers that were not made available to everyone else. They never mention the "handout" of a mortgage interest deduction that puts an average of $1,900 a year into the pockets of those lucky enough to have good jobs to able to afford to buy their own home. Many were employed by the "Big Three" auto makers and defense contractors like Lockheed Martin which got billions in public "handouts" in the 1980's and 1990's, benefiting middle class employees by proxy. They overlook how social security enables senior citizens to survive rather than forcing them to financially support their elderly parents.

In 1990, nearly one third of all veterans' benefits went to households with incomes above $50,000, as did one fourth of all unemployment benefits, one third of all federal civil service retirement pensions, and one half of all military pensions. Meanwhile, only one fourth of federal entitlements went to those at the very bottom who were economically discarded and unable to sell their labor in the market— the poor.

Slightly more than half of all US households have at least one member who is receiving a direct entitlement benefit from the federal government in the form of federal civil service pensions, veterans' disability benefits, and veterans' pensions. These households will collect on average about $2.4 trillion by the end of 2010.

They complain about paying for poor kids' subsidized school breakfasts and lunches, but they're silent about everyone else's taxes funding school choice vouchers for theirs. They object to subsidized housing for the poor who are financially excluded from the housing market, but have no problem reaping the benefits from taxpayer-subsidized federal flood insurance for their beachfront homes that no private insurance company would insure. Former president George Herbert Walker Bush benefited enormously from the federal flood insurance program when his vacation home in Maine sustained approximately $400,000 in storm damage in 1991.

The "entitlement" or "welfare handout" that everyone ignores is the $250 billion dollar a year tax subsidy for employer-sponsored health insurance. This history of tying health insurance to employment goes back to World War II when the government enacted wage controls. Employers were competing for workers and began offering health insurance because they couldn't offer higher wages than a competing employer. For some reason, this was not treated as taxable income to the employee. Middle class people who stockpile money in Healthcare Savings Accounts (HSA's) also get a line item tax deduction on their income taxes. So those who have *their* good jobs with health benefits and/or HSA's are getting theirs at the expense of *all* citizens — including the poor who aren't getting any access to medical, dental, and vision care.

When the middle class public hears stories of people left bankrupt, or disabled or dead from being uninsured, they see a lack of "personal responsibility" and virtue rather than a lack of good fortune and privilege. The idea that someone's misfortune stems from a lack of personal responsibility assumes that everyone has the same opportunities in life and that the poor squandered theirs. This is a common sentiment among right-wing middle and upper class white males that have always gotten everything by making sure women and minorities got nothing while having the moxy to crow about how "they worked for it."

Middle class Tea Partiers and "patriots" brandishing expensive assault rifles terrorized other citizens at Townhall meetings during the healthcare reform discourse, yelling that they refused to "pay for someone else's" health care. Those who begrudge the "undeserving poor" access to health care because they don't want to "pay for someone else" are getting subsidized while depriving the poor by refusing to extend that subsidy to everyone in the name of "freedom." Freedom to starve or freeze to death, or become disabled or die from being unable to afford medical care is no freedom at all. The backlash against real healthcare reform was never about "freedom." It's really about a false sense of superiority and classism.

The same people who killed any chance of universal health care are the same ones who hate the government's Cash for Clunkers program. Who had the clunkers? The poor. How could these well-off white males with their brand new Ford trucks feel superior to the poor if the government gives "those people" a little bit of money to buy a decent car? Like a decent car, they see access to health and dental care as a privilege that you're supposed to earn. It's a status marker, just like a new car or a home in an exclusive neighborhood. The middle class Tea Partier who takes his subsidy for his health care (or his job or business) is no better than the poor person who takes the government subsidy for a car when you frame it within the context of born-again Tealogic.

The threat to take away selective tax breaks and other "entitlements" for health insurance in *all* its forms would have been the best way to force the issue of real healthcare reform to the negotiating table. But Democrats in Congress, who get Cadillac health care courtesy of the public, fouled the ball. If the solution to health care is to let the poor, the weak, the pregnant, the old, and the unlucky die for lack of health care and let those who can afford it live healthy, happy and prosperous lives, what makes the US different than the Axis powers in 1930's Europe? The Nazi party rose to power by blaming Communists, Socialists, trade unionists, the disabled, and Jews for their social and economic woes. Their solution was to slaughter the people they blamed for their problems. It's very similar to the racist and sexist Tea Partiers who bring guns to Townhall meetings and protest rallies. Both were predominantly comprised of white middle class men.

Belligerent middle and upper class reactionaries denouncing "socialism" and "welfare handouts" for the poor have benefited far more from "socialism" than the poor *ever* have. And not one tantrum-throwing "self-made man" squawking about entitlements for the poor is willing to give *their* middle class job to someone in poverty that never got a chance so they could have a good job, thus reducing the number of those on the public dole whom they denigrate as "welfare parasites."

Corporate executives feel entitled to the tens of millions of dollars in salaries, stocks, and "golden parachutes" even if they steal from their companies and cause a national, or even a global, economic collapse. Poor people who kite checks to buy food or rob a 7-Eleven go to prison. CEOs get rich; poor people get the stinky finger.

Banksters and Wall Street crooks walked away with fortunes during the 1980's S & L scandal while the taxpayers paid the $500 billion dollar bailout tab. Thanks to Reagan's deregulation of the S & L industry, S & L's were allowed to take any investment risk they wanted with depositors' money with the understanding that any failures or bad debts would be subsidized by the public. 90% of those who were depositors had accounts worth more than $100,000.

US companies got $1 billion from the public dole through USAID from 1985 – 1995 to pay for shipping US jobs overseas to cheaper labor markets. USAID provided low-interest loans, tax exemptions, travel and training funds, advertizing, and "black lists" to weed out union sympathizers and organizers in other countries.

In 1995, over 40% of USDA subsidies and farm payments went to farmers with a net worth in excess of $750,000. Meanwhile, those of us on food stamps and WIC are begrudged nutritious food.

While Congress held hearings on "welfare dependency" and the impact of the "culture of poverty" on unjustly enriched "welfare queens", no hearings were held on the middle and upper class entitlement mentality regarding all the handouts *they* benefit from.

Do you have a 401(k)? If any of your portfolio's holdings include bank instruments, municipal bonds, Ginnie Mae's, or CD's, you're being enriched directly as the result of entitlement programs that have supported and bailed out those "malefactors of great wealth" that are privately owned. "Self-made" members of the investor class did not get theirs on their own. They got it off the backs of everyone else.

Any appreciation in your retirement portfolio's value from capital gains and increased dividend payouts on stocks came directly as a result of corporations realizing huge profits by "cutting costs" — a euphemism for slashing wages, benefits and permanently eliminating jobs. Those most likely to suffer from job loss, reduced wages and lost benefits are workers over age 40, who have been rendered permanently unemployable and have fallen into poverty after long-term joblessness due to age, gender, race, looks, and socio-economic class discrimination. Did you snipe at them for being on food stamps because you "worked for everything you got?" Newsflash: You didn't "earn" that wealth in your stock portfolio. You got it at the expense of others' loss. Have you thanked them for your economic success? No need for accolades, just support the restoration of something resembling a real safety net for those at the very bottom who got the least in terms of opportunity and societal benefits in "free enterprise" America.

The 1980's saw the economic decimation of family farmers, a lot of downsizing, deindustrializing, and unemployment. Cuts in social programs for the poor began under Jimmy Carter's presidency. Ronald Reagan and the Democrats along with social conservatives from the Religious Right escalated it. By 1985, a poor female high school graduate had almost no opportunity — CETA was eliminated. Rents skyrocketed and access to college was increasingly elusive for most poor youth under age 25. The prosperity of some came directly as a result of the social, political, and economic disenfranchisement of the many — those that were poor, non-male, and/or non-white. The poor were the biggest losers in the era of "family values."

Middle class voters were silent about welfare for the rich while they elected politicians who slashed meager subsistence benefits and other social programs that helped the poor. They cried foul about preferential jobs placement programs for the disadvantaged under CETA and Affirmative Action while they benefited from the biggest preferential job placement program of their own: middle class good ole boy nepotism. The middle class drank the Kool-Aid – they bought into the rich Republican's bogeyman: the "welfare queen" and the "able-bodied SSI cheat." Mainstream media promoted and fueled Reagan's demonization of the poor, sowing the seeds of "class envy" towards the poor among a Balkanized middle class voting public. This eventually brought us the Welfare Reform Act. But no voices were raised for the guarantee of a right to a living wage job and health and dental care.

While the middle class and the rich benefited and pointed to the mass line about "economic recovery in 1992-93 to invalidate the reality of the poor who were not making it, the US Census Bureau data for 1993 revealed that the national median income had declined by 7% since 1989. The Conference of Mayors' report cited a 15% increase in the number of poor people desperately needing food and housing — a large portion turned away from city shelters, food banks and soup kitchens because cities didn't have the resources[40], which were redirected to the rich and to middle class real estate investors that jumped on the gentrification bandwagon in the wake of privatization of subsidized housing financing through HUD.

The 1992-93 economic recovery bypassed poor women struggling to survive on AFDC and minimum wage jobs while House Speaker Newt Gingrich demanded more cuts to social programs for the poor; pounding his chest about the need to eliminate the "nanny state", cut welfare, and "get government off our backs" while perfectly content to let a right-wing government occupy poor women's genitalia under the "pro-life" banner. Gingrich used the words "nanny state" to bludgeon anything that helped poor women — access to abortion, subsidized contraceptives, Medicaid, Aid to Families with Dependent Children (AFDC), food stamps, and equal opportunity for training in good-paying non-traditional jobs — while his base in Cobb County, Georgia was the largest beneficiary of the "nanny state" through subsidies, "welfare handouts", and entitlements for rich white men at the helm of defense contractors, insurance carriers, and computer companies.

---

[40] Noam Chomsky and David Barsamian, *Class Warfare: Interviews With David Barsamian*, pp. 5-11. 1996

Cobb County's main employer was Lockheed-Martin, a defense contractor that benefited enormously from the largesse of taxpayer dollars flowing into its coffers through the Pentagon. Lockheed, insurance companies and high tech firms were heavily subsidized by the "nanny state." But not one Democrat in Congress countered Gingrich's war cry against the "welfare state" by pointing that out and mentioning that Gingrich's district got more federal subsidies than any other suburban county in the US. The "liberal media" was silent. So were the Democrats, out of fear of losing elections and control of Congress.

While rich white men were made even richer through welfare handouts from the "nanny state", poor women found their narrow escape routes out of destitution increasingly cut off and suffered record hunger and homelessness while AFDC, food stamps, and Medicaid were increasingly cut — along with need-based student aid for college and grad school, and rollbacks in Affirmative Action and other equal opportunity measures that could have enabled them to get into good paying skilled trades jobs and escape the living hell of poverty.

Middle class "soccer moms" and the rest of Clinton's cheerleaders proclaimed the 1992 elections and Clinton's presidential victory as the "Year of the Woman" while every last escape route out of poverty was blocked for poor women. And the petit bourgeoisie feminist organizations were silent. The miserable reality and increased suffering of poor American women wasn't an important issue. Somehow, the "trickle-down" of women's equality never made it past middle class women to their much poorer "sisters" beneath them on the socio-economic ladder. The spigot of prosperity and social justice had run dry; so much for the "Year of the Woman."

While William Jefferson Clinton presided over the passage of the Welfare Reform Act of 1996, it was a Republican-controlled Congress that propelled it under the direction of House Majority Whip Newt Gingrich. He knew exactly what he was doing when he placated the middle class with tax cuts that were paid for with spending cuts in domestic programs and the mother-mugging Welfare Reform Act. The middle class who typically vote for this brand of "compassionate" conservativism live in isolated suburban enclaves where all is good in their own little world. The middle class supported Welfare Reform because they viewed poor women as "lazy". They wanted to force poor women to get jobs and work, so long as it wasn't *their* middle class jobs.

Welfare reform punished poor women who sought to get educations to better themselves to get chances for jobs that would lift them and their families out of poverty. Attending college does not count as "work" or "acceptable vocational training." Poor single mothers like Dr. Donna Beegle ended up with their benefits cut and have even ended up homeless for daring to try to better themselves in accordance with the American ideal of a college education and the "Protestant work ethic." Middle and upper class people are entitled to a college education; America's underclass is not. Some animals are more equal than others.

Had Dr. Beegle not received the help of subsidized housing after her welfare benefits were cut as a penalty for attending college instead of making herself available for any minimum wage job as required under Workfare, she would not have been able to complete her Bachelors degree, let alone obtain her PhD. And she would not be a member of the upper-middle class today. Had she been childless, she would not have gotten the help that she did with housing since only certain categories of poor are eligible and she might not have ever made it out of poverty. The available help for certain categories of poor is grossly insufficient and for other categories of poor there is absolutely no help at all.

Since poor people are marginalized for their poverty, poor children internalize the negative opinions and stereotypes about them. Being poor means being inferior. Since poor people desperately want the same chances as everyone else so they can lift themselves up out of poverty, they often try to conceal their poverty to try to fit in with the middle class. They do it out of fear that any opportunity that comes their way will be taken away from them due to their low socio-economic status as "trash" in everyone else's eyes.

Poor American youth internalize their poverty because of the social rejection that accompanies poverty. In the middle class suburb of

Fremont, California hunger is considered "someone else's problem." High school students think of the homeless when they think of hunger in America. Due to all the negative labels and assumptions associated with homelessness, being homeless means "drug addict", "bag lady", or mentally ill. Poverty means "uneducated", the lazy "welfare queen" or able-bodied SSI cheat out to scam the system. The middle class kids in Fremont did not perceive those who are food insecure as people like themselves, their families, or someone in their community.

According to Alameda County Hunger Education Coordinator Jessica Bartholow, more than a third of the hungry live in suburbs like Fremont. More than half are white and come from working families. Ms. Bortholow was invited to speak to students in Fremont high schools to educate them about some facts on poverty that exist right in their community for the students' Hunger At Home project. The teens at Freemont's Irving High School were shocked to learn that their previous perceptions about poverty and hunger were wrong. They realized that the poor are not lazy, rather most are responsible people who need a little boost. The students formed a social action plan calling for free breakfasts and lunches for lower income students at the other California high schools which did not have them. The California state senate even thought the students' proposal was such a good idea that the legislature passed it, but the governor vetoed it.

The students at Irving High also realized that something was wrong at their high school even though Irving had a free/reduced cost breakfast and lunch program. Apparently, the cafeteria staff divided the students into two separate meal lines: one line for those paying full price and the other line for those getting free or reduced price meals. The low income students qualifying for the free/reduced meals keenly felt stigmatized. As a result, many low income students chose to go hungry – something that the subsidized meal program was supposed to prevent – rather than endure the social stigma of poverty. The pain from classism and social exclusion was worse than the pain of an empty stomach.

When the student activists participating in the Hunger At Home project questioned the policy of segregating students in the cafeteria lines based on socio-economic status, they got the typical bureaucratic response of "that's just the way it is because that's the way we've always done it."

Policymakers did not consider the stigmatization it imposed on low income students. They were only looking at the convenience it provided the administration in the meal program's implementation. But the student activists persisted and after several meetings with Irvin High School's administrators, the meal lines were merged. Lower income students could finally get their meals without fear of being labeled and ostracized. Imagine if young people in every high school across America were taught that classism and abusing the poor is wrong.

Kids learn from observing the behaviors of adults. Bigotry is learned. Some of the most highly respected adults in academia have benefited enormously from promoting classism like education "expert" Dr. Ruby Payne, who bills herself as a "national leading authority" on understanding poverty — even though she's never lived in poverty.

Ruby Payne asserts that children growing up in generational poverty don't succeed because they've been taught the "hidden rules of poverty" and not the "hidden rules of the middle class." She self-publishes her work through the company she owns called *Aha! Process, Inc.* That means her research does not have to be peer-reviewed. This is one of many reasons to question the validity of Dr. Payne's framework presented in her high-priced seminars and workshops.

Ruby Payne's book *"A Framework for Understanding Poverty"* contains deficit theory solutions to poverty that serve as the public education system's *deus ex machina*[41] under the constraints of No Child Left Behind. Her compiled "theories" are mental aroma therapy for the middle and upper classes to feel good about a false solution to poverty. It reinforces their collective comfort with the status quo. Society does not need to change; it's the defective poor who need to be taught how to get with the middle class program. Social and economic structures creating poverty and perpetuating classism don't need to be challenged.

---

[41] *Deus ex machina*: Latin, " a god from a machine"; a false hero.

Payne charges a princely sum to some of the nation's most economically distressed school districts for her workshops and seminars geared towards teachers on the "culture of poverty." Distressed school districts could put funds to more productive uses than for Payne's snake oil. This "culture of poverty", according to Payne, holds the poor back. This is a flawed premise on two counts. First, the reactionary behaviors, values, and norms exhibited by those in generational poverty did not cause the poverty initially. Exploitation, discrimination, greed and vulture capitalism caused it. Second, there is no universal "culture of poverty." There is no "hive mentality" shared by all poor people anymore than there is a culture of disabled-ness, of woman-ness, or of aged-ness.

"Framework" frames poverty as a personal character deficit of those who are struggling in poverty. She fosters the worst classist stereotypes of the poor. One teacher left a Ruby Payne seminar with having learned that poor kids "can't think abstractly", can't communicate properly, and are "prone to physical violence."

After Hurricane Katrina, Payne wrote the following commentary about the poor of New Orleans:

> "The violence was to be expected. Words are not seen as being very effective in generational poverty to resolve differences; fists are...Furthermore, to resolve conflict, one must have the ability to go from the personal to the issue, and the words are largely not there to do that...Additionally, in neighborhoods of generational poverty, two of the primary economic systems are prostitution and drugs. After Katrina struck, both of these economies were virtually wiped out overnight. Furthermore, individuals in jail were released because there was no plan about how to handle them..."

The gospel according to Ruby Payne targets and vilifies poor people, reaffirming that they are the "other"; something to be feared. Her quasi-intellectual drivel paints the poor as criminals who pose a physical threat to the safety and well-being of the "better" classes of people. Her theories about the poor are nothing more than inflammatory generalizations making it easy to see Ruby Payne exactly for what she is: an opportunist who profits from poverty and the strained budgets of

America's poorest school districts facing sanctions under No Child Left Behind (NCLB) by pedaling a gospel of prejudice, fear, and contempt by demonizing poor families under the false pretense of helping them. Promoting classism has been a very profitable endeavor for her. She has sold over four million copies of *Framework*, making her a multi-millionaire — not including what she's received in fees for her seminars and speaking engagements.

Ruby Payne will never admit that she has benefited from unearned social class privileges. She has enjoyed significant gain at the expense of those for whom the system is not working by promoting negative stereotypes. Acknowledging the systemic barriers of classism and poverty would force Payne into the uncomfortable position of having to admit she not only benefited from unfair advantages in our society, but also by profiteering from selling hate. And she would risk having her own unearned social class privileges scrutinized. Ruby Payne is looking out for her own economic gain and social class interests under the guise of helping underprivileged children to academically succeed. What she is really doing is ensuring that the status quo, which has benefited her at others' expense, remains unchallenged.

Payne tells her middle class audience that poor people lack books in their homes because they don't value education. Reality check: most poor people lack books because the time to read and enjoy them is a luxury that is out of reach for those who must spend all of their time dealing with one poverty-related crisis after another with no end in sight.

Ruby Payne has never had to deal with being one rent increase, one illness or injury, or one sick child away from homelessness. She has never had to try to live on a low wage job where a car breakdown can precipitate a cascade of problems that routinely plague those who have no resources. She's never been through an eviction and had to scramble on short notice to find another place to live on limited money with a poor credit report (which landlords use to select tenants) further restricting her options. She's never had to rush on short notice to get all of her possessions out of a rental unit before being padlocked out where anything left behind was either discarded by the landlord or sold at a sheriff sale. She's never had to try to get a job while having to face potential employers with visibly decayed or missing teeth for lack of money and health insurance to afford dental care.

This is the reality in which poor people have to live. Books are just one more thing you will lose if you are evicted and unable to pack and move everything within a week or less when you have no car, and no credit card required to rent a U-Haul truck. Books are one more personal possession that someone else will take away from you that you won't be able to replace.

Ruby Payne wrote in *"Framework"* that the poor are more apt to resolve conflict with their fists than through discussions and debate. According to Payne, the poor are incapable of resolving conflict without resorting to violence. Her seminars and workshops are a menagerie of fictional examples that draw on all of the negative stereotypes about the poor: welfare queens, uneducated drug addicts and alcoholics, convicted felons, and the mentally ill. Not one of her examples includes the millions of others who do not fit the derogatory stereotypes about poor people. Her examples don't include children who are orphans, or foster kids who have been discarded by society. Her "framework" doesn't include the disabled; or parents who work two minimum wage jobs (or more), leaving no time to help children with homework that the parents may not be capable of doing themselves.

Ruby Payne's cheerleaders claim that she is trying to help teachers in high poverty school districts reach their students in order to meet academic goals framed by the unfunded mandate of NCLB. Her credibility is circumspect because Payne operates from a deficit theory perspective. She disseminates partial truths, and *that* is what makes her dangerous.

She claims that the poor don't know the "hidden rules" of the middle class and that they need refinement. She uses the term "culture of poverty" to help teachers learn how to communicate with students struggling in poverty. *"Framework"* may provide some colorful insights, but it institutionalizes the very same stereotypes educators should be trying to dismantle.

Payne uses anecdotal examples of décor and food. She says that in poverty, the main issue is getting enough to eat; in the middle class, it's a matter of how good the food tastes; and in the upper class, how well the food is presented. Payne concludes that the poor lack good taste and refinement while she fails to address the fact that lack of money means a very real lack of minimum security and comfort – which severely restricts options and shapes taste.

Anyone can have good tastes if they have plenty of money. Payne's hypothesis is that class determines level of refinement. But money determines class. No amount of "hidden rule" mastery compensates for lack of money and unequally shared prosperity. Payne's *"Framework"* is a logical fallacy of *post hoc, ergo propter hoc*[42] by asserting that poverty is caused by a lack of "hidden rule" mastery.

Payne's work does not show an unbiased, un-cropped picture. If you are shown the picture of a supermodel's armpit you cannot say, "Wow, what a beautiful woman" because you cannot tell if all you see is an armpit. You need to see the whole picture. Ruby Payne fails to show the whole picture. She fails to acknowledge inequity in our economy, our healthcare system, and in our society. High poverty school districts lack facilities and structures conducive to learning. They lack computers, science labs, and some even lack basic sanitation.

Payne's work ignores the reality of poverty. She justifies classism. Her work legitimizes marginalizing those labeled as "trash." When questioned on where she got her data, she said it was based on her marriage to her commodities broker husband for 30 years who was temporarily poor as a youth, and that her research was her observation of his poor neighbors. Understanding poverty doesn't mean you go "slumming it" and then you're an "expert." Understanding poverty is

---

[42] *Post hoc, ergo propter hoc:* Latin, "after this, therefore because of this"; a logical fallacy rendering an argument invalid by assuming that because one event happens after another event, the two events were causally related.

contemplating what it does to someone who is told they are worthless in the grand scheme of life, that they don't count — in addition to all of the deprivation and having to live under daily economic terrorism.

Ruby Payne's critics say she's perpetuating offensive stereotypes, a charge she vehemently denies. *Framework* speaks for itself: "...individuals in poverty are seldom going to call the police, for two reasons: First, the police may be looking for them..."[43], and that poor people are "prone to settle disputes with their fists." If that isn't promoting stereotypes about the poor, then what is it? Payne denies the charge, saying she would be "heartsick if anyone used this information to stereotype." Yet her book is pregnant from cover to cover with negative stereotypes. Is this "leading expert" on poverty so obtuse that she's incapable of recognizing her own classism? How is painting a picture of *all* poor people as a bunch of broken misfit toys *not* stereotyping them?

Wordsmithing partial truths lead middle class audiences to false conclusions that shape their views and treatment of the poor. What they're *not* seeing is that the poor are often targeted by the police and subjected to police brutality and trumped up charges because they're poor, *not* because they're criminals. Ruby Payne's deficit theory view of the poor relieves the middle and upper classes of responsibility for classism, poverty, police brutality, and a broken judicial system that is classist and racist.[44]

2006 Fulbright Senior Fellow and 2008 Best Education Resource Award winner Dr. Paul Gorski, founder of EdChange, is a highly credible scholar and impassioned social justice activist on the battlefield of class justice. He is famous for his criticism of Ruby Payne's "work" for her failure to acknowledge the systems and structures of classism that perpetuate poverty. Gorski received a lot of feedback, including from Ruby Payne.

> "Ruby Payne threatened to sue me. I received a call from her attorney. Bill Sommers, one of her trainers, called different

[43] Ruby Payne, *A Framework For Understanding Poverty*, pp. 37-38

[44] Ibid; pp. 37-45 (refer to discussion on MOVE)

people at my university in an attempt to silence me. In fact, several times when I've been scheduled to speak at an event, Sommers has called the event organizers to try to convince them to uninvited me. I have received several other angry responses. What's been interesting is that none of these angry responses critiques my specific criticism of Ruby Payne's *Framework*. Instead, they attack me, like how dare I critique Ruby Payne. Payne's *Framework* is popular because it does not challenge the status quo."[45]

Anyone who subscribes to Ruby Payne's message is learning how to "other" poor people. Payne's work reaffirms the notion of the "undeserving poor" — a powerful tool used by policymakers to justify cutting funds for social programs designed to help the most vulnerable and downtrodden. The "undeserving poor" image convinces people that the wealth gap and class inequities result from poor people's personal faults rather than defects with the system that impoverished and excluded them. Reiterating the "culture of poverty" propaganda and peddling paternalism are time-honored tactics used by the elite for justifying the war on the poor and securing power to protect their wealth and unearned privileges.

Ruby Payne began her illustrious career as the nation's leading "poverty expert" after she moved to Texas in 1993. She read a New Age type of book, *Creating Money*, which is a guide to the "spiritual laws of money." It was allegedly dictated to its authors by two "spirit guides", Orin and DaBen.

Ruby said, "The book said, 'Make a list of what you want in your life and the universe will bring it to you.' So I did. I wrote: 'I want a life without financial constraints. I want a life without institutional constraints. And I want to make a difference with children.' And it happened!"[46]

---

[45]2007 Interview with Paul Gorski by Camilla Green; *Journal of the National School Reform Faculty*

[46] Paul Tough, "The Class Consciousness Raiser", *The New York Times*, June 10, 2007

So there you have it, boys and girls! Buy into some cosmic woo, jump on the feel-good bandwagon of supporting the capitalist status quo and your New Age fairy godmother will bend the laws of the universe to give you everything you want and if it doesn't work, it's because *you* didn't do it right!

According to a 2006 report from the Federal Election Commission, Ruby Payne contributed thousands of dollars to the Bush-Cheney campaign and the Republican National Committee. In June 2006, she gave $1,000 to the campaign of Texas senator John Cornyn whose voting record was very hostile to the poor, to organized labor, to women, and to public education. Ruby Payne is no friend to poor children.

Poor people need what everyone in this country needs: a real safety net and a guaranteed right to a decent education, a living wage job and access to health care; not personal value judgments from someone who makes $15,000 per day conducting seminars and speaking engagements about "fixing" the "undeserving poor."

Capitalism's winners will do anything to defend the savage realities of classism and poverty to preserve their own unearned privileges, including flexing their economic muscle to quell any criticism of their work — as Ruby Payne's for-profit company's retinue of attorneys and trainers have done to Paul Gorski after he conducted two presentations critically analyzing Payne's *Framework* at a national conference. Distressed school districts operating under severe budget shortfalls do not need to squander money by enriching right-wing "welfare queens" like Ruby Payne, a poverty pimp who profits enormously by promoting and reaffirming classism, racism, and sexism.

It is beyond arrogant for those who have received the most advantages and benefits from an entire system of unearned privileges to authoritatively proclaim that it's the undeserving, defective poor who need to be "fixed" and taught how to get with the middle class program, and then call such ideas "scholarship." There is nothing that remotely passes for intellectual and academic honesty in unreferenced research undertaken with confirmation bias reeking with the stench of classism. Poverty pimps who advance the "culture of poverty" school despite knowing better, do so to curry favor and receive social prizes and rewards from the corporate 'Massas' who endow their academic department chairs, fund their research, and pay them as "policy experts" in right-wing think tanks.

Capitalism is based on entitlement, and as you go up the economic ladder, attitudes of self-importance and entitlement increase. This naturally follows from the fact that as one goes up the income ladder, the rate of capital accumulation increases in a world with finite resources. But we never talk about the culture of greed and getting ahead at all costs that is so prevalent among the middle and upper classes who think they have a "divine right" to come first.

The notion that the misery and deprivation commensurate with grueling poverty is merely the "undeserving poor" getting their "just desserts" for being morally defective is not an original idea. The argument for the "culture of poverty" has been internalized these past 30 years by lawmakers from both sides of the aisle who say that social security is a "milk cow with 310 million tits"; that unemployment benefits (which only cover about 40% of the unemployed) makes the jobless "lazy" and encourages them to buy drugs; that the miserly inadequate food stamps allotment in post-welfare reform America makes the recipients rich and causes obesity; and that the solution for 50 million uninsured Americans, 44 million struggling in unrelenting misery below the poverty level, and for the 35 million ill-housed, are more vouchers, more "free market" capitalism, and more budget cuts for food stamps, Medicaid, and Medicare to pay for middle class unemployment benefits extensions — leaving the poorest of this nation's jobless to starve to death given that food stamps is the sole income for six million of the most disadvantaged and unemployable jobless.

As it stands, deregulation of utility monopolies in tandem with deep cuts to the already underfunded LIHEAP program, which provides very stingy and inadequate help to only 20% of the eligible poor while 80% of the poor are turned away, has resulted in over six million US households suffering without at least one life-sustaining utility. The increasing number of casualties among the poor from freezing in unheated homes and apartments or fatal residential fires caused by unsafe alternative heating methods in a desperate attempt to avoid freezing to death, evidences only some the fruits of this "culture of poverty" school's bitter harvest of classism.

The past three decades of abusive social and economic policies justified by the "culture of poverty" amount to one sordid continuum of human rights violations against the "undeserving" poor. For those who have unfairly benefited from a legacy of unearned privileges, including advanced educations at prestigious universities, to use their privileges like a cudgel to beat the poor into the ground and crush them underfoot for personal gain and accolades under the guise of "scholarship" is sociopathic.

We don't have a "culture of poverty." We have a culture of capitalism that promotes, perpetuates, and maintains classism — the least challenged bigotry that is responsible for the most social harm. We have a capitalistic society that touts greed and self-centered entitlement as a virtue. Capitalism is an architecture of aggression in which its biggest losers (poor women) are set up and labeled as "the Other", devalued, and unacknowledged.

This culture of capitalism is centered on the idea that wealth and privilege is sacrosanct. Only the "fittest" deserve anything and to hell with those of us who have been socially excluded and economically marginalized in order to make way for the overprivileged alpha dipshits of the world to grab everything they can latch their meat-hooks onto; without a shred of remorse for the human casualties they leave in their wake.

Since cultural norms, mores, and trends are largely defined by the higher status and more affluent classes, this "culture of poverty" was created by the privileged. The injustices and social ills framed by deficit theory thought are not caused by "just a few bad apples." They're caused by a cultural ethos; a sociopathic one that is reflective of the dominant class's "values."

It has not escaped the notice of those of us who struggle in poverty and who agitate for social justice that the government is described as "democratic" when it serves only the interests of the privileged and economically powerful elements of our society. In the words of Michael Parenti: we have a "democracy for the few." And whom this "democracy" serves was made painfully obvious by the absence of poor people's voices from these poverty "studies."

When poverty is couched in euphemisms that really mean race and gender, it's a deliberate attempt to justify classism and legitimize the economic terrorism and social repression visited upon the poor of all races and genders. Being black, being a woman, or even being a single mother doesn't make one poor — abusive social and economic policy and discrimination does.

Raising rhetorical questions associating crime and poverty in terms that label the poor as "criminals" is a deliberate promotion of prejudice. The poor are routinely denied employment opportunities because there is a widely held view among human resources personnel and corporate employers that the poor are a bad risk for hiring because they're likely to steal. Discussing why the poor "break the law with impunity" implies that they're not punished — an outright fraud when everyone knows that the poor overwhelmingly comprise the US prison population. It further ignores the fact that when people see those with lots of money and privilege breaking the law on a grand scale with impunity, there is a loss of respect for <u>any</u> law.

The "culture of poverty" claptrap also led to the assumption that poverty can be reduced to a lifestyle choice — something former House Speaker Newt Gingrich claimed from his bully pulpit during the Clinton administration as he cheered the Welfare Reform Act of 1996. The Welfare Reform Act of 1996 threw this nation's poorest and most socially disadvantaged families and individuals under the bus; 99% whom were women and children (only 1% of AFDC recipients were able-bodied men) under the guise of "personal responsibility" — a unilateral social contract best described as a policy of Benign Neglect in which the entire burden of poverty was dumped on the poor while society and government did nothing to guarantee poor women living wage jobs with health benefits, child care help, and assistance in obtaining reliable transportation.

Former Wisconsin governor and US Department of Health & Human Services Secretary Tommy Thompson [47]provided the template for the Welfare Reform Act of 1996. He is one of the "pro-life" religious conservatives who would deny poor women access to birth control and abortion while leaving poor single moms and their babies utterly destitute if society failed to provide the supports required for poor mothers to enter the workplace and guarantee them living wage jobs with health benefits.

Since the enactment of Welfare Reform, Tommy Thompson and other political leaders who swallowed the "culture of poverty" pablum spoon-fed by conservative Ivy League poverty pimps defeated measures to track the outcomes of all the poor women and children thrown off of welfare after exhausting their five year lifetime limit, regardless if they were able to get a job. Before the economic downturn began in the early 2000's with off-shoring white-collar jobs due to globalization, unknown numbers of "hard-to-employ" women in poverty ejected from the welfare rolls have been economically disappeared. There is a real social holocaust unfolding in America, but nobody cares until it hits them.

Are the promoters of the "culture of poverty" school proud of these "scholarly" achievements that encouraged nationwide mother-mugging by framing poverty as a "choice?"

There is something here that needs to be said about "choice." When discussing choice, it is important to also discuss a fundamental mathematical theorem that has been proven over 200 years ago, named after mathematician and clergyman Thomas Bayes, who studied how to compute a distribution for the probability parameter of a binomial

[47] http://www.sourcewatch.org/index.php?title=Tommy_Thompson

distribution. Bayes' Theorem treats conditional probability and the outcome based on the relationship of the conditional and marginal probabilities of events. The most simple and basic mathematical statement of Bayes' Theorem is:

$$P(A|B) = \frac{P(B|A)P(A)}{P(B)}$$

{Read as: "The probability of A given B is equal to the probability of B given A times the probability of A, all divided by the probability of B."}

where :

P(A) is the **marginal** or **prior** probability of event A. It is "prior" in the sense that it takes nothing into account of anything known about event B.

P(A|B) is the **conditional probability** of A, given B.

P(B|A) is the **conditional probability** of B, given A (also called the "likelihood")

P(B) is the **prior** or marginal **probability** of event B and acts as a normalizing constant.

Theorems analogous to this one cover situations entailing more than two events. Applying Bayes' Theorem to the existing axioms and theorems of calculus, we can describe the marginal probability distribution of a variable to a data set:

$$f(r|n = x, m = y) = \frac{f(m=y|r,n=x)f(r)}{\int_0^1 f(m=y|r,n=x)f(r)dr},$$

for ∀ x,y ∈ R

where the likelihood function is the probability of "y" successes in "x" trials for a binomial distribution, for all "x" and "y" in the set of all real variables. (The most common application is the study of voting patterns and employer drug testing).

More famous applications of Bayes' Theorem are the Monty Hall Paradox and the Principle of Restricted Choice, which proves with a mathematical certainty that making the "right choices" 100% of the time is impossible. The Principle of Restricted Choice states that the play of a particular card increases the likelihood that the player doesn't have another equivalent one. Invalidating classism and the injustice of poverty by claiming that poverty is the result of "choice" may be convenient politics, but it is a mathematical fallacy that defies logic and common sense.

It is therefore intellectually dishonest and morally bankrupt to frame the discussion of poverty in terms that blame the poor for their poverty by reducing it to "lifestyle choices" and the "culture of poverty."

It is no secret that middle and upper class people also frequently screw up and make the same "poor choices" as poor people. But the difference is that the outcome is totally different; such that it does not punish them with lifelong destitution and misery. It is also known that the middle and upper classes have a lot more options available to them while options for the poor are really a Hobson's choice (either way, you're screwed).

The way in which we speak about others, the words we use to describe others has the power to disempower and break, or to uplift and inspire. The power of life and death is in the tongue. The notion that words can't hurt is a fallacy. Words can not only hurt, they can kill. Words are powerful tools which human beings use in interpersonal relationships and in the organization of entire societies. Words can be inflammatory enough to start illegal wars – the Bush administration's false claim of Iraq's weapons of mass destruction comes to mind.

In examining deficit theory propagated stereotypes of poor whites, consider the following two "definitions" of "poor white trash" contributed by people in the online word definition source, urbandictionary.com[48]:

---

[48] http://www.urbandictionary.com/define.php?term=white+trash&page=3

Insectile, sub-human vermin from the Appalachian Mountains. Always drunk, always fighting, always stealing, always racist, always fucking anything that walks on two legs, always in jail; these are the products of 10 consecutive generations of brother-sister fucking with some barnyard animals thrown in to give their gene pool that extra spice. They can be identified as unbelievably macho, bullying, 300 pound trailer-living, bingo-playing, Elvis plate collecting, front teeth missing, Wal-Mart shopping, "ya'll" saying, cowboy hat wearing, Camaro driving, horribly hygiened, Bible-thumping, woman-beating, English butchering, meth injecting, beer guzzling, NASCAR watching embarrassment to carbon molecules whose only purpose in their obnoxious proto-human existence is human cockfighting on the Jerry Springer Show. They tend to drop out of school at 15 to spawn as many of their filth as they can (often with blood relatives) and because they have the IQ of a toilet seat, their banal, quacking conversations (or noise that passes for them) always revolve around fucking or kicking someone's ass. Nothing else. ...Uneducated and slow-witted people who lack the social graces and proper hygiene. Being judgmental is a white trash trait, as well as being selfish and verbally abusive to others. They love to make others cry and see them hurt. A white trash person is more likely to turn their back on their friends, stab them in the back, after using them for what they could get out of them. They tend to be social parasites and try to ingratiate themselves into social circles completely for their own personal gain without ever planning to give back."

If there ever was anything that fit the definition of "hate speech", that entry in urbandictionary.com is it. Such "definitions" are weaponized language. Words can cut deeply, leaving people emotionally scarred for a very long time, if not permanently. There is no excuse for deliberately inflicting cruelty and abuse to perpetuate unearned social class privilege at the expense of others.

Shaming or humiliating people for their poverty will not make them less poor. Punishing poor people for being poor will not help them to overcome the obstacles to education and good jobs and propel them into mainstream society. Instead of assuming that it is the poor who need to be “fixed”, we should assume that we have an obligation to fix the broken system of inequity and social injustice created by discrimination, misogyny, sexism, racism, and economic cannibalism. We cannot do this until we confront classism by unpacking the invisible knapsack of unearned middle and upper class privileges.

Chapter 7

"You're either part of the problem or part of the solution." ~ Eldridge Cleaver

The term "invisible knapsack" was originally coined by Peggy McIntosh in her brilliant exposé of white privilege. It can also be applied to unearned social class privilege, making class privilege visible. The invisible knapsack contains all of the unearned benefits and privileges that are automatically conferred upon the middle and upper classes.

In examining the knapsack's contents, we can see all the ways that ascribed characteristics (those one is born with) have been kept invisible to the point where we are blind to their effects and how they shape the outcomes in our lives – not seeing those outcomes as achievements of merit. By making class privilege visible, we are forced to admit that those at the bottom have been unfairly cheated and then blamed for their situation while those on the middle and upper rungs have received accolades for accomplishments that were not wholly earned.

Dr. Will Barratt from Indiana State University compiled a knapsack of middle and upper class privileges which benefit the "haves" at the expense of the "have-nots." This is not to say that no one in the middle and upper classes worked for anything that they have, rather it means that they had a head start in life and didn't have as many barriers to overcome as those starting out from behind the 8-ball. Dr. Barratt's class privilege knapsack inventory includes:

1. I don't have to concern myself with learning the social custom of others [my social customs are the dominant ones].
2. The "better" people are in my social class.
3. It is likely that my career and success will be attributed to my hard work.
4. People appear to pay attention to my social class.

5. When I am shopping, people usually call me “Sir/Ma’am”.
6. When making a purchase by check or credit card, my appearance doesn’t create problems.
7. When I (or my children) are taught history, people from my social class are represented in the textbooks.
8. I can easily speak with an attorney or physician.
9. There are neighborhoods I can move to where I feel “at home.”
10. There are places where I can be among those exclusively from my social class.
11. I can deny class privilege exists [and dismiss others’ views as argumentative]
12. Experts appearing on mass media are from my social class.
13. There are stores that market specifically to people of my social class.
14. I can arrange to protect myself (and my children) from people who might not like me (or them) based on my social class.
15. Law enforcement officials will likely assume I am a non-threatening person once they see and hear me.
16. Disclosure of my work and education may actually help law enforcement officials perceive me as being “in the right” or “unbiased.”
17. I can easily speak to my child’s college professors.
18. My citizenship and immigration status will likely not be questioned and my background will likely not be investigated because of my social class.
19. I can be sure that my social class will be to my advantage when seeking medical or legal help.
20. If I wish to give my children a private school education, I have a variety of options.
21. I can find colleges that have people from my social class as professors/students that welcome me (or my child.
22. If I apply for a prestigious job competing against people of a lower social class, my social class will be to my advantage.
23. The decision to hire me will be related to where I attended school.

24. When I watch TV or read the papers, I can see people of my own social class represented well.
25. The "newsmakers" are people like me.
26. I deserve my status because of my accomplishments [merit].

There are two major social class privileges that Dr. Barratt omitted that I will add:

27. The values, beliefs, norms, customs, and mores of my social class define those for everyone else (e.g. smoking bans, weight bashing)
28. My social class accords me the freedom to be rewarded for my creativity, and access to the resources required in order to secure residual rewards for my ideas, inventions, or designs and prevent others from taking the credit.

Let's examine these privileges starting with the last two. Over the past 20 years, wealthy powerful pharmaceutical interests and their well-heeled non-profit arms together with "Big Media" have launched an aggressive social engineering campaign to denormalize smoking resulting in the marginalization of smokers. Johnson & Johnson and other global pharmaceutical corporations were found to have used fraudulent studies to promote their agenda. The pharmaceutical giants want to exclusively control nicotine, reaping obscene profits from their smoking cessation drugs and anti-depressants. Smoking cessation drugs such as Zyban have common and fatal side effects; and anti-depressants such as Effexor are associated with severe weight gain. Not to worry: there's plenty of pills and expensive, risky medical procedures to cure you of all the fat that you gained from quitting smoking – "Big Pharma" and their evil twin "Big Medica" have seen to *that*.

The social exclusion of tobacco users has been incremental and began with seemingly reasonable restrictions such as banning smoking on domestic airlines during the 1970's. As of 2007, many states have adopted unconstitutional smoking bans prohibiting smoking in any establishment that extends an invitation to the public and which also allow local municipalities to ban smoking in certain private residences such as condominiums, apartments, and subsidized housing units. Elderly smokers and disabled vets in nursing homes and assisted living centers are forced to forego their sole comfort that they can still enjoy in their twilight years – or risk freezing to death in the middle of winter from having to traipse off the grounds just to be able to have a cigarette. This is not the freedom and liberty that our veterans fought for.

Opportunistic attorney John Banzhaf gleefully cheered, “No longer can anyone say ‘my home is my castle’, we have crossed the threshold there.” Banzhaf is a wealthy lawyer who made his pile from the largesse of tobacco company lawsuits and the notorious Master Settlement Agreement which was supposed to pay for the healthcare costs of sick smokers, but didn’t. The Master Settlement Agreement costs incurred by “Big Tobacco” were passed onto smokers. Tobacco is a legal product and smoking is a legal activity. But if you own a condo in Golden, Colorado or a home in Belmont, California, you can be evicted or excessively fined for engaging in the lawful use of this legal product on your own front porch if someone complains.

Smokers comprise 28% of the population, but are overwhelmingly represented among the lower social classes. Smoking was one of the very few comforts available to the poor. Since smoking is equated with low socio-economic status, no one thinks it’s unfair to throw smokers out in the cold in all kinds of weather if they want to have a cigarette, while benefiting from smokers’ tax dollars. The majority of non-smokers are upper-middle class. They demand smokers to “be considerate and step outside for 5 minutes” if they have to have a cigarette. Consideration is a one-way street: it is not reciprocated for the smoker.

Smoking bans force smokers to go out onto the sidewalk or street a minimum of 15 feet from the entrances of all establishments open for patronage. Smokers are relegated to unsafe areas and must leave their drinks unattended inside the bar in accordance with “open container” laws for alcoholic beverages. This places women smokers at the additional risk of having their drinks spiked with “date rape” drugs. The premise for these smoking bans is "public health." Those who make public policy, including policies of "public health", hail from society's upper echelons that fought against national health care.

The public health excuse for marginalizing smokers was brilliantly debunked by author and social activist Michael J. McFadden and retired chemist Dave Kuneman in their article *"A Study Delayed: Helena, Montana's Smoking Ban and the Heart Attack Study"*[49] which was published in the British Medical Journal. Michael J. McFadden is also the author of *"Dissecting Anti-Smokers' Brains"* in which he points out that chemicals in foodstuffs and vapors from a single martini pose more of a health hazard than second-hand smoke.

Executives that drink and smoke are not forced to submit to the indignity of invasive random alcohol, drug, and nicotine screenings by employers. Executives are not being thrown out of their jobs for having a couple of martinis while schmoozing at the country club during business hours. But peons at Weyco Pharmaceutical and Scott's Miracle Gro are unceremoniously fired after random nicotine testing reveals that they might have smoked cigarettes while at home during their own personal time. Corporate big shots are above having to submit to assaults on their privacy, but working class stiffs are expected to suck it up and take it. The war against smokers is a class war, make no mistake about *that.*

Not only are smokers being thrown out of their jobs, their homes, and made *persona non grata* everywhere, but they're also targeted for punitive taxation. The excessive "sin" taxes imposed on tobacco fund social programs that benefit the middle class such as SCHIP. Middle and upper class voters supported politicians' recent reauthorization of SCHIP – a federally subsidized health insurance program for uninsured kids whose parents are not poor enough to qualify for Medicaid. The taxes that fund SCHIP are entirely borne by smokers — a group which falls disproportionately into the bottom socio-economic rung by 75%. Cigarettes are a poor man's Xanax. A welfare program for the middle class is being funded by the poor.

---

[49] *American Council On Science and Health*, July 12th 2007, "Facts & Fears"; http://www.acsh.org/factsfears/newsID.990/news_detail.asp

Imagine if $10 martinis were singled out for excessive taxation to fund SCHIP? If the comforts of the middle and upper classes were socially penalized while being excessively taxed to fund SCHIP, that entitlement program would have never been funded – never mind reauthorized! Everyone is making out at the expense of the smokers except the smokers themselves.

"Big Pharma" interests such as Johnson & Johnson own exclusive patents for nicotine replacement therapy drugs (NRT). Their non-profit arm, The Robert Woods Johnson Foundation, heavily funds virulent anti-tobacco groups in the media for socially engineering public health hysteria against smokers. If these well-heeled drug companies get their way, they will exclusively corner the market for any nicotine product and NRT's with patents.

The patent system created and maintains class privilege. Right-wing politicians and their supporters justify our broken system of exploitation, greed, and discrimination by claiming that society's winners are merely being rewarded for their inventions, creations, and designs that benefit society. What they do *not* admit is that powerful elite interests have stolen credit for others' work and have benefited unjustly from a patent system that they've contrived to disadvantage the poor.

Patent protection allows you to be rewarded or compensated for something you design, create, or invent. Literary works, music, and film productions are protected by copyrights. But machines, household devices, tools, software, computer hardware, bio- chemical/engineering application methods, genetic alteration processes, chemicals, and pharmaceuticals are protected by patents. The costs for getting a patent are prohibitive and out of reach for the majority of Americans. Patents allow the claimant to artificially restrict competition by exclusive control over the production and distribution to manipulate and control the "free market", maintaining a monopoly on the rewards and privilege of residual royalties. The current fee and cost schedule for a utility patent is listed online at the US Patent & Trademark Office. The fees as of 2007 are:

- Mechanical or electrical invention of average complexity: $4,000 - $8,000.
- Complex computer or electronic inventions: $6,000 - $10,000.
- Biotech or chemical inventions are a minimum of $7,500 with the required DNA sequence listings.
- Internet business method inventions: $6,500 - $ 9,500.
- Patent Office Basic Filing Fee: $155.
- Patent Search Fee: $255.
- Patent Examination Fee: $105

Litman Law Office is the oldest and most reputable patent and trademark law firm in the US. According to attorneys at the Litman Law Office, there are fees that must be paid to a patent lawyer in order to thoroughly search patent office records to ensure your work is original and that there are no other existing patents for your creation. The fees charged by a patent lawyer to do a patent search run about $2,000.

Even if you can manage to scrape together the money for the patent office fees, plus another few thousand in patent lawyer fees, the game doesn't stop there. After your patent application is filed and granted "Patent Pending Status", you must pay a $300 fee to the US Patent Office for the mandatory filing of an Information Disclosure Form. The patent lawyer may require additional fees for the preparation of other documents after the initial filing, if any are required. The fee for that additional service ranges from $200 - $300. After paying steep costs to file an application for a patent, a bureaucrat known as the Patent Examiner may reject your patent application. All the fees you would have paid in connection with the initial filing amount to a small fortune and these fees are non-refundable.

The Patent Examiner rejects 85% of all patent applications. This rejection, known as an "Office Action", leaves you with two choices. Pay more money to the patent lawyer to appeal the Office Action which can run into another several thousand dollars in legal fees without guarantee of a favorable outcome; or chalk everything you've invested thus far into patenting your creation up to a loss and walk away. Most people can't afford to risk that kind of money. Most people don't have $10,000 - $20,000 on hand to pay for patent application fees to being with.

In the event you *can* secure the money for all of these costs and fees and actually get your patent, you still must pay periodic "Maintenance Fees" to the US Patent and Trademark Office to keep your patent from expiring. The fee schedule for that is as follows:

3 ½ years after patent date: $465

7 ½ years after patent date: $1,180

11 ½ years after patent date: $1,955

Unless you're wealthy and have a team of lawyers guarding your interests, holding a patent is no guarantee that you will get a worthwhile return for your time and money invested. Few individuals can afford to pursue legal action to collect monetary damages for patent infringement. And there's the chance that legal remedy will leave you unable to collect damages from wrongful infringement by a culprit without royalty compensation from them.

Countless ingenious "backyard inventors" who have come up with useful inventions lack the money to file an application for a patent. They're easy prey for hucksters. These companies claim that, for an affordable fee, they can patent and market your invention to big corporations who will pay you for your invention. But what often happens is that these unscrupulous firms drain several thousand dollars from unsuspecting inventors over time with false promises of getting them through the patent process.

Meanwhile, these "inventor firms" get copies of an inventor's design and the prototype by duplicity and bilk the inventor out of money while raking in more money peddling the designs and prototypes of inventions at global manufacturing symposiums where the big corporations get these inventions and designs without having to compensate the inventor. The wealthy and powerful corporate interests who *can* afford the patent application process get patents for others' ideas and work while the little guy gets nothing, except taken to the cleaners.

The exact number of new and innovative ideas that materialize into new products, applications and methods is very high. How many of these ideas and products were the actual work of someone of modest means? How many inventions were expropriated from the little guy? Plenty!

A minimum degree of economic security is required in order to have the leisure of free time to devote to creating and inventing something. When you're poor and struggling at the very bottom, you don't have that luxury. Free time is a social class privilege. Working sub-poverty wage jobs struggling to make it, or spending all of your time at various social agencies trying to get help consumes all of your time. Tools, materials, and a place in which to operate all cost money – a scarce commodity for those who are poor. Sufficient economic resources give the "haves" a huge unfair advantage over the "have-nots."

The poor are also up against the iron fist of government, which only protects the interests of the wealthy. Laws severely tilt the playing field in favor of the middle class and rich at the expense of the poor so the poor don't stand a chance. Wealthy corporate interests and their Commissariat squad whine about taxes. They complain about restrictive government rules that limit discrimination, worker abuse, and require a miserly inadequate minimum wage. But these same selfish interests have no problem when that same restrictive government allows them to artificially manipulate markets and monopolize the means and control of production with entitlements, IRS Code loopholes and the US patent system. By creating a system of red tape and unaffordable fees for obtaining a patent, "Big Government" is working far more in favor of the rich than the poor.

If we truly were a free market society, our patent system would not structurally exclude the poor, and mega rich corporations would not be able to flex their economic muscle to restrict the means of production to rig markets unfairly, and fix prices. This is why no one has been able to mass produce automobiles fueled by hydrogen to meet consumer demand and society's needs, given the unaffordable gas and oil prices. When OPEC sneezes, the poor get pneumonia. Market-rigging is why pharmaceutical giants can produce drugs for pennies on the dollar and gouge the American public with prices that are unaffordable for the majority of people.

"Big Government" also protects the interests of the rich by passing laws that make it illegal for Americans to buy their medicines at more affordable prices from outside the US. And this is one of many reasons why millions of poor Americans are unable to afford medical care. Millions of poor seniors and disabled people on low fixed incomes are forced to choose between food and rent versus healthcare and medicine. It is no wonder that 45,000 poor uninsured Americans died prematurely last year from easily treatable (if not entirely preventable) health problems.

The US patent system is not about ensuring that someone doesn't reap unjust rewards for another's invention or idea. It's about preserving social class privilege through artificial market manipulation. That is not a system of free enterprise; that's plutocracy. It's socialism for the rich and privatized risk for everyone else.

Do we really need to ask why those whose talents that *could* contribute society never get the chance? In sum, our system does not reward the creative and talented people who lack support, social standing and money. Getting any recognition, respect, and reward for your talents is indeed a social class privilege.

Let's examine the other social class privileges in Dr. Barratt's knapsack. The social customs of the middle and upper classes prevail and dominate the rest of society. The social customs of the middle and upper classes dominate and prevail. They're the trend-setters. They're the ones who determine the standard of beauty, the "correct" policies, and the level of credentialism. The values of the lower social classes are devalued and ignored. As Joe Bageant, author of *Deer Hunting With Jesus*, said: "politicians don't speak in born-again Bubba."

Successful people are always credited for their hard work, as having earned their success. In some cases, that's true. But for others, it's not and they never admit that they got where they got because of having benefited from unfair advantages. They claim that their successes are based solely on own merit. They claim that poor people who have worked harder, tried longer, and sacrificed more only to get nowhere lost out because they just weren't good enough to be able to compete. They also claim that America is a classless society. But if that were true, then Saks 5th Avenue would be Wal-Mart.

When shopping, it is not the well-dressed members of the higher social classes who have to think about whether or not their appearance will arouse mall security's suspicions. Members of the middle and upper classes are not stalked by mall rent-a-cops who automatically assume that they're going to steal. But that's precisely what poor people experience when they go into shopping malls and other middle class venues. Going to the mall just to "window shop" when you're poor will often get you ejected from the mall, even though you've done nothing wrong. The poor are automatically assumed to be thieves or pests who will bother shoppers by panhandling.

Meanwhile, someone who looks middle or upper class can "window shop" without being harassed. They get treated politely, while poor people don't get treated with any respect. Shopping malls aren't the only places that treat poor people badly.

When I traveled across state to cover the Bucks County murder trial of Richard Laird who was the subject of my second book, *"Eyes of a Monster"*, I was denied service at a full serve gas station in Doylestown because I was poor. Doylestown is the county seat for Bucks County – the wealthiest of Pennsylvania's sixty-seven counties. It is a small semi-rural "old money" town about 40 minutes northeast of Philadelphia full of historic stone homes, quaint specialty shops, oozing with charm. Doylestown also has a local ordinance prohibiting self-service gas stations, so all Doylestown gas stations are full-serve only.

On February 7th 2007, I pulled into the Gulf gas station on Doyelstown's Main Street, a few blocks from the Bucks County courthouse. My truck's gas tank was empty. While I sat and patiently waiting to be served several late model luxury sedans and expensive looking SUV's had pulled in, gotten served, and left while I still sat waiting to get my pick-up fueled. My pick-up is a large 1995 Ford F-150 that the gas station attendant had to walk past in order to serve the other customers. He had made eye contact with me. After waiting for 20 minutes when I was the only customer left, I finally gave my horn a light tap. The attendant snapped at me, "We don't need *your kind* around here. Go back to where you belong."

I was refused service at a business open to the public in an upper class town because I was poor; I didn't "belong" there. I'm not the "right kind" of white. I had to drive seven miles out of my way on fumes to another gas station, hoping that I wouldn't get stranded in the bitter February cold without the luxury of a cell phone plus extra money or a credit card to pay for a tow truck. Getting served at businesses open to the public is a social class privilege.

The ability to qualify for a credit card under favorable terms has always been a social class privilege. A credit card is a tool to handle expensive, unforeseeable emergencies. But being able to qualify for a credit card is anything but a social class privilege now, considering the increasing insolvency rates of consumers.

The next social class privilege Dr. Barratt mentions is the romanticizing of events in history books. Most whom are credited with the building of America as a nation were wealthy white men who stole others' land and took credit for others ideas. For years, men justified discrimination against women by claiming that if women were deserving of an equal opportunity for jobs and educations, then all the great scientists and mathematicians would not have been white males. What they refuse to acknowledge is that for centuries, women and other "minorities" were denied the same legal rights and societal benefits as wealthy land-owning white males.

Women were really no more than slaves. They were denied the right to retain ownership and control of any property or money (if they had any) when they married. They were denied an equal opportunity for an education and barred from admittance to the most "important" jobs. Women were still denied admittance to universities in fields such as science and engineering as of the 1970's. The reason why wealthy WASP male contributions and accomplishments are heralded throughout history texts while women and other "minorities" were relegated to obscurity is because they were denied equal rights as citizens and barred from opportunity.

Women's sacrifices in colonial America, such as dying in childbirth on westward bound wagon trains because they had no choice but to obey and follow their husbands are never mentioned, while the men who fought at the Alamo are held as heroes. The settlements of early American pioneers were not made possible by men alone. Women remain the unsung founders of the US to this day.

History is full of people who flocked to the "land of opportunity", who invented technologies but got cheated out of any reward for their contributions. Antonio Meucci invented the first electromagnetic telephone in 1856. But because he couldn't garner financial backing, including the $10 filing fee for a patent caveat for his "sound telegraph" (or *telettrofono* as Meucci called his device), he couldn't get his invention patented and reap the rewards for his idea. He was unable to sue Alexander Graham Bell for patent infringement in 1876 because he was bankrupt and couldn't afford to hire a lawyer. Meucci was post-humously credited with the invention of the telephone by the US House of Representatives on June 11th 2002 – 113 years after he died a pauper.

Throughout the 19th and early 20th centuries America has not been a "free market." It was one big free-for-all where "might made right." The "makers and shakers" of America's rising ruling class were no different than the "heathen" European tribes who pillaged every place west of the Carpathian Mountains; taking whatever they wanted by force. Yet, these "masters of the universe" are credited in history books for being the architects of national prosperity. The disenfranchisement of women, blacks and poor whites; the holocaust of indigenous peoples, exploitation of the poor, and institutionalized theft and discrimination justified by religious dogma is ignored as if everyone else sat idle, waiting for the genius of rich white men to bestow the gifts of civilization on this land.

Railroad tycoons like Cornelius Vanderbilt, John Jay Gould, John D. Rockefeller and others did not succeed by "free market" competition. They used political bribery, violence, and hired thugs (the Pinkerton Agency) to force poor people from their homes, expropriating their land. One of the victims of these robber barons was the widowed mother of Jessie James.

The investors and owners of the Union Pacific and Central Pacific railroads got healthy cash transfusions from Congress in 1862 pursuant to the Pacific Railroad Act[50]. Basically, the government paid these companies per mile of track laid. Union Pacific and Central Pacific took advantage of "corporate welfare"; their executives became unjustly enriched from the government largess.

Meanwhile thousands of poor Chinese, Irish, and Welsh laborers who were over-worked and risked injury and death (without compensation paid to their families) every day laying the thousands of miles of railroad tracks were paid sub-poverty wages in company scrip – redeemable only in company towns. Without these workers and their families who were viewed as nothing but disposable commodities, the transcontinental railroad would have never been possible.

Union Pacific and Central Pacific executives diverted funds from their corporations into their own personal coffers. Union Pacific created its own coal company, mining coal for $2/ ton and selling it to themselves at $6/ton – pocketing the profits. This scam, among others, was exposed in the Crédit Mobilier scandal. Union Pacific president Thomas Durant bribed Congressmen and other government

[50] *"American Railroads"*, by James Stover, 1961

bureaucrats[51]. Free railroad passes and Crédit Mobilier stock shares were given as graft to state and federal lawmakers. General William Tecumseh Sherman was given a cut-rate deal on a land purchase near Omaha, Nebraska which he was able to buy for $2.50/acre when the going rate was $8/acre.

The robber barons profited from exploiting the poor, feeding at the public trough and by using political connections to pass laws that prohibited competition. These guys weren't free market capitalists – they were political bandits. And we all know the word that Benito Mussolini used to describe the merging of state and corporate power. (Can you say "fascism"? I knew you could.)

The robber barons of the American rail industry have not faded away into obscurity. Deregulation resurrected them. In 1980, there were forty competitive railroads. Today, there's only five. And the railroads are exempt from anti-trust laws. The robber barons have returned – like Freddy Krueger.

Prior to rail industry deregulation in the 1990's, the onus was on the railroads to prove that their prices were fair and in keeping with regulations. Now, that burden has been shifted to the shipper. Captive agricultural shippers in the upper mid-west rightly claim regulator bias.

The General Accounting Office reports that 35% of America's grain harvest relies on rail transport[52]. Executive Director of Consumers United for Rail Equity Bob Szabo says, "The railroads have more monopoly power over shippers than they did in the late 1800's. They've divided the country." Szabo explains, "Let's say an ag elevator wants to challenge a rate that the railroads have imposed on him. He has to prove that he could build his own railroad and operate it at a price cheaper than what it's costing the railroad."

The Chicago School was wrong. Free market capitalism is a social disease.

---

[51] *"Entrepreneurs vs. the State"* by Burton W. Folsom, Jr.

[52] *"Railroading Ag"*, Matt Bewley, *Agweek*, December 8th, 2008

Clearly, the laws and the history books favor the “winners”, even though they won by violence and unscrupulous means. Those from the lower social classes are not represented well in history books, if at all.

The social class privilege of being able to get medical and legal needs addressed is not a social benefit that is available to all in our society. When those of the poor who are Medicaid-eligible try to get their health concerns addressed, they are often dismissed. Any care they might get is dragged out. They’re not provided with the options available to their middle and upper class counterparts. Cutting edge medical technology has no meaning for those in poverty; such benefits are only available to the affluent. Even the slipshod care available to the poor on Medicaid has dwindled because fewer and fewer doctors, dentists, and surgeons accept Medicaid patients. The few who *do* accept Medicaid are not far removed from the likes of Dr. Mengele.

In Erie County, Pennsylvania, there was only one root canal dentist that accepted Medicaid in 2004. His practice was located in the outlying region of western Erie County; inaccessible by Erie’s limited bus service. He also begrudged his Medicaid patients adequate pain relief such as Novacane for them to be able to tolerate a root canal procedure. He was indignant that I should expect Novacane for a root canal on an abscessed tooth, saying loud enough for his office staff and other patients to hear, “The whole problem with *you people* is that you rely on too many drugs to cope with pain and life in general.”

The only Medicaid-accepting dentist who did crowns, Dr. Michael Turner, was located in North East borough – about 20 miles northeast of Erie. Shortly after the loss of my briefly held job at Ion Health, I had the dubious honor of being graced with Dr. Turner’s “care.” It was a bitter cold February morning in 2005 when my husband and I braved a lake effect blizzard to drive all the way to his office in North East for my dental appointment. Dr. Turner arrived late. He loudly berated me for his having to come into his practice in the miserable weather while sick with a cold, yelling at me while I sat in the chair, “Maybe if you got off your lazy welfare ass and got a college degree, you wouldn't have problems with your teeth and you wouldn't be a loser."

Dr. Michael Turner did not realize that I *do* have a university degree, and that I am far from lazy – I pounded the pavements for 4 ½ years trying to get any job that paid a living wage with health benefits. But when no one wants to hire a middle aged woman for anything except part-time menial $7/hr supermarket cashier jobs, what the hell was I supposed to do? Ending up poor, on Medicaid and food stamps, and unemployable because of dental problems on top of sex and age discrimination despite having a "marketable" degree wasn't what I had in mind when I made enormous sacrifices (including steep student loan debt) to get the degree which was supposed to be my ticket out of poverty.

As a result of being punished for my poverty, I ended up being denied the proper care needed in order to save and restore my teeth. I eventually had to have my remaining teeth extracted due to an antibiotic-resistant abscess that infected my entire upper jaw. I was almost 40 years old by the time I could finally afford dentures; when I was "too old", too poor, and unemployed too long for any employer to want to hire me.

Technology such as dental implants, which are the closest thing you can get to your natural teeth, was not an option available to me. The extractions and upper denture cost $8,000. Dental implants would have cost me over $90,000. Those who are much poorer than I am cannot even get dentures at all if they need them because Medicaid won't cover dentures: they're not deemed "medically necessary" and are classified as "cosmetic." Apparently, poor people don't deserve to be able to chew and look normal so they can get a job before they're "too old."

When you present yourself to prospective employers (and the public at large) to apply for a job, even a minimum wage job as a sales clerk or a supermarket cashier where you have to face the public, no one will hire you when you have missing or rotting teeth. Access to good dental care is a luxury that only the middle and upper classes "deserve."

Instead of acknowledging the problem of lack of access to good dental care, the "haves" simply blame the poor: it's their fault that they lost their teeth because they didn't brush and floss properly. They didn't eat properly. They must have been doing drugs. They lost their teeth because they made "poor choices."

Then there are the Medicaid-accepting doctors who only care about padding the bill, bilking the system to enrich themselves while not giving a rat's ass about the poor whom they're paid to treat. The only primary care physician, Dr. Bradley Fox, accepting new Medicaid patients in Erie at the time my husband and I were on Medicaid was affiliated with Saint Vincent Hospital – a non-profit Catholic hospital. Due to my husband's terminal heart condition, we qualified for a "medical emergency" reprieve from National Fuel gas company so our gas wouldn't be shut off for inability to afford the bill on our low monthly fixed income.

But in order to get help with our utilities, Dr. Fox would first have to sign a "medical situation" letter for the electric and gas companies. Dr. Fox refused to do so – not because my husband's age and health problems weren't serious enough to merit it, but because it was against the Saint Vincent physicians' group's policy to sign such a form unless the patient is a small child with a respiratory condition. Middle aged and older poor people with serious health problems can just suffer and freeze to death for all the local medical community cared. The "good" Dr. Fox – a community pillar – certainly didn't care.

Taking two minutes to sign this form would have prevented additional health problems from having to freeze all winter without heat, hot water, or cooking fuel. But he didn't do it, despite knowing our situation. Hospital policy was his excuse. What kind of medical professional in the humanitarian field of healing the sick follows such policies? One can only surmise that all the trappings of affluence and success numb the consciences of those who promise to "first do no harm."

As a result of having to tough it out in the cold with no heat due to our gas being shut off, I came down with pneumonia – for the third time. Being cold weakens the body's immune system. It is more detrimental for people as they age because a 40 year old is not as healthy and strong as when they were 20. Senior citizens with heart problems (like my husband) are even more frail than a 40 year old with a history of pneumonia. The doctor knew that being without heat in the winter in Erie, PA meant a possible death sentence.

The only help we got was an annual $157 grant from LIHEAP, which was not enough to prevent our gas from being shut off. It wasn't even enough to cover one month's worth of gas bills during the winter. The LIHEAP grant was not enough to even put a tiny dent in the rising fuel costs that are unaffordable for us. (We are now off-grid). The utility companies and our welfare caseworker kept sending us back to the doctor for the letter of medical emergency – the doctor who refused to help us.

When doctors swear to uphold their Hippocratic Oath, it is obvious that "do no harm" only applies to middle and upper class patients, not the "undeserving" poor. Poor people get verbal abuse, denied pain relief, and suffer without heat in the winter and we're just supposed to take it on the chin. Nobody cares about poor people who are kept poor due to discrimination and lack of social class privilege. Social class privilege might not be immediately visible, but its effects and consequences *are*.

In mass media, middle and upper classes are represented as "normal', as the majority, as the "nice" people. The villains are always the unattractive looking and people who are poor. The only TV shows that depicted the lives of working class and poor people were *All in the Family* and *Roseanne*. The main characters in each were negatively depicted as uneducated, bumbling bigot and an opinionated overweight mom. Their flaws were exaggerated to feed into the stereotypes of America's lower social classes.

Compare *All in the Family* and *Roseanne* to shows like *Law & Order* and *Grey's Anatomy* where all the main characters are affluent, have perfect smiles, perfect bodies, perfect hair, perfect homes, and perfect lives. They always seem to know what to do about everything in any given situation. The middle and upper classes are never depicted as cold, calculating, greedy status-seekers who stab co-workers in the back, or as spoiled brats with entitlement attitudes who throw tantrums until they get their way.

At any given time in a capitalist society, there are always more job seekers than there are jobs. Hence, there will always be poor people because there were always people being socially and economically excluded. It was like that before globalization which has seen millions of living wage jobs leave America and where millions more can be off-shored to the lowest bidder in a minute.

Today, the number of poor Americans has increased significantly. According to the most recent US Census, 44 million Americans are classified as officially being in poverty based on austere and antiquated federal poverty guidelines.

- Of all the US poor, 84% are women and 63% are white.
- Of the urban poor, 44% are white.
- Of the rural poor, 39% are white.

The Harvard/McGill Survey conducted in 2007 studied 170 countries with specific attention to the lack of opportunity and support for women as a major cause of poverty. Of the 170 countries, only 4 don't have any form of national paid leave for new mothers: The US, Papua New Guinea, Swaziland, and Liberia. Over 140 other countries have a guaranteed minimum number of paid sick days; the US does not.

In the US, about 48% of private sector workers, and nearly 80% of low-wage workers, don't get any paid sick days for themselves, or to care for sick children. In the US, a baby is born without healthcare coverage every 41 seconds. Single mothers are 79% less likely to be hired than non-mothers. As of 2007, women are still paid only 73 cents for every dollar earned by men; single mothers – about 60 cents. As a result of job and pay discrimination against women, especially against single mothers, and a lack of family-friendly policies; many mothers are forced to leave formal employment when their children are young and they face a host of new problems when they later try to re-enter the workforce. Until these disparities are rectified, welfare reform remains an act of aggression in the War On the Poor, not a Contract With America. Welfare Reform delivered nothing but empty promises to go with the empty stomachs and empty wallets of America's poor.

There is another dimension to another aspect of poverty issues that needs to be rectified. And that is the problem of chronic poverty, which Dr. Donna Beegle refers to as generational poverty.

The sources of chronic poverty and the ways that it is perpetuated, be it Appalachia or in the ghettoes of rust belt cities, are characteristic of any chronically poor place in America. Chronic poverty represents long-term neglect and disinvestment. Capital disinvestment is not a happenstance; it's by design. It begins when those in power, local elites, employers, and lawmakers deliberately hold people back in order to keep the local labor pool vulnerable, docile, and powerless.

Part of controlling everything in a community includes not educating people. It is also controlling the ministers, the doctors, and other civic leaders to discourage workers' participation in community life by making the workers dependent on paternalistic employers for everything. This tactic worked well for the robber barons of America's Gilded Age and it remains deeply entrenched today. Chronic poverty is a legacy of deliberate underinvestment in order for an oligarchy to maintain control within a community, creating a permanently oppresses class of people. The result is high chronic unemployment, low educational levels, and high disability rates. This is the face of chronic poverty whether we're talking about Appalachia or the ghettoes of Detroit.

One of the prime reasons Lyndon B. Johnson's "War on Poverty" failed was because more needed to be done that wasn't. Johnson's "Great Society" needed to make government more responsive to the people, moving towards a fairer distribution of opportunity and access to societal resources. And fairer distribution has to do with the way a community works, i.e., social class connections and stratification. Individuals in poverty making bad choices are not the cause of chronic poverty. We all know that middle and upper class people screw up. But there's a way in which the family resources and community resources in middle and upper class settings are garnered to give middle and upper class people a second chance that is not available in low-income communities and poor families.

In regions of chronic white poverty, the middle and upper classes distance themselves from the poor. They don't include them and bring them into the middle class fold of social activities, or even into the same churches as middle class people. Isolation and social exclusion of the poor perpetuate poverty and restrict lifestyle choice. Those who are rejected and isolated live in a world of only the poor. They're repeatedly told that they do not belong in another group; that they're unwanted and unwelcome.

When you ask why regions of poverty persist, you need to examine the social dynamics of those areas. Look at the extent of trust in the community. Is one part of the community making all the decisions while the other part of the community is left out? Is the civic culture broken because things have been bad for so long and there's a deep distrust because of a deeply entrenched history of patronage, of getting chances for good paying jobs based on who you know or family name? Is there an ongoing anxiety over being associated with those labeled as "ne'er do wells"? If so, then there is a distancing where chronically unemployed poor people are socially and economically isolated, and are falsely made to feel that they deserve what they get.

I have drawn particular attention to the data of poor whites for the purpose of making classism visible. To be poor and white in America is to be a non-person. White people are assumed to be middle and upper class. It is assumed that the system works for all whites just because they have not experienced the racial discrimination that other minorities have faced. Professor Roberta Rosenberg described her experience in attempting to teach class consciousness to her English literature students who are largely from the middle/upper-middle classes. Assigned reading included Toni Morrison's *The Bluest Eye* and Carolyn Chute's *The Beans of Egypt, Maine*. Both novels center on poor young girls: one black and the other white.

In *The Bluest Eye*, poverty and marginalization is seen through the experience of a poor black girl, Pecola Breedlove. In *The Beans of Egypt, Maine* unfolds through the eyes of a poor young white woman, Earlene Pomerleau in rural Maine. The subject of incestuous rape and out-of-wedlock birth is treated in both books, as is the white middle class standard of beauty. Both stories end in tragedy. Rosenberg's students could empathize with Pecola Breedlove while they had nothing but contempt for the poor white women in *Beans*. Rosenberg noted that many of her students were able to accept cultural disparities when it was a matter of race, not when it was a matter of class. She ascribed a America's middle class hatred for the poor to the fact that sociologists and other "experts" from the ranks of the intellectual bourgeoisie define poverty by the deficit theory view — the "culture of poverty" — citing Barbara Ehrenreich's book *Fear of Falling*, which centers on middle class perceptions of the poor. She said that sociologists infantilize the poor by suggesting that the poor exhibit a "peculiar pathology", namely that "the poor person lives for the moment, unable to think ahead, to save or plan for the future…trapped in the past, unable or unwilling to 'grow up' as the middle class has."[53]

Rosenberg said that if American culture views poverty as something which is pathological, that explains her middle class students' visceral revulsion for *The Beans of Egypt, Maine*. The middle class values order and success, so the disorder and chaos that are hallmarks of poverty make the middle classes very uncomfortable around the poor; if not hateful towards the poor and downright disgusted by them for being what they view as stunted adults that cannot or will not grow up and join independent middle class mainstream society. The fictional characters in

---

[53] Barbara Ehrenreich, *Fear of Falling*, pp. 50-51; Roberta Rosenberg's presentation at the Milwaukee, Wisconsin March 1996 Conference on College Composition and Communication

Beans are members of the American underclass, a part of contemporary society that is permanently separated from the middle class dream of upward mobility (because of being marginalized), and therefore the middle class fear them.

One reason white poverty is kept invisible is because any recognition of oppression of white people by other white people is an open admission of classism and the failure of capitalism in our so-called classless society. There's a more sinister reason for the invisibility of white poverty. Racializing poverty justifies the "culture of poverty" defined by black urban poverty in a nation founded on the ideologies of racial and gender inferiority. It supports a legacy of injustice caused by imperialism, colonialism, feudalism, and capitalism. A racially unified poor people's movement fighting for social equality and economic justice is the elite's worst nightmare.

When competing against more and more people for fewer and fewer jobs, the middle and upper classes have an unfair advantage over the poor because their social networks include policy makers, alumni associations, and business executives. Their social networks also extend to rich white male dominated social fraternities and "secret societies" like the Freemasons. In any given town across America, there are families whose members always seem to get the good jobs with high wages and benefits. The frequent common denominator is that many with secure middle class jobs in municipalities and law enforcement are Freemasons.

In order to join the Freemasons, you have to be a white male and from a middle or upper class family. Women and blacks are excluded. Local Masonic lodges have a ladies' auxiliary, the Order of the Eastern Star, which is for the wives, sisters, daughters and mothers of Masons. But the Eastern Star really has no social clout – it's just a glorified hen's circle to mollify Masons' wives. There are also Masonic groups for teens: Rainbow Girls for teen girls and DeMolay[54] for teen boys. Upon

[54] Demolay is named after the Grand Master of the Knights Templar, Jacques de Molay, who was burned at the stake on March 18, 1314 for refusing to disclose the location of

age 18, DeMolay members can launch into the Knights Templar or the Freemasons.

Blacks can join the Prince Hall Masonic lodge. But Prince Hall lodges are not recognized or chartered by the Grand Lodge. "Separate but equal" did not die with the US Supreme Court's overturning of *Plessy v. Ferguson* in the landmark case of *Brown v. Board of Education, Topeka.* Segregation is alive and well – behind the locked doors of Masonic lodges where backdoor favors are routinely conferred with secret handshakes and esoteric rituals.

All chartered Masonic lodges in America fall under the aegis of the Grand Lodge of Free and Accepted Masons headquartered in Great Britain. Its membership boasts European royalty and it is (unofficially) over 1,000 years old; a long history of nepotism deeply entrenched in local governments and local economies. Most state lawmakers, sitting judges, and high ranking members of the American Bar Association are Masons. Given the unfair advantages in competing for life's social prizes and rewards in patriarchal capitalist societies where certain groups are perpetually favored at the expense of others, no one can honestly say that economic success in America is solely awarded on merit.

Masonic oaths bind the Mason to a loyalty to other Masons above all else – even above wives and children. The oaths obligate the Mason to aid another Mason even to the extent of circumventing the laws of this land. The Freemasons and their cheerleaders who tout the Masonic charities claim that the Freemasons are a benevolent social fraternity. But one must question whether their charity is worth the price of poverty and job discrimination rooted in unearned privileges and unfair advantages gained through backdoor patronage and favoritism.

The typical middle class white males who join the Freemasons do so in order to get favored treatment in the political and legal system, and preference in hiring at good jobs without having to compete against

---

Templar wealth to the Roman Catholic Church. The Knights Templar is an appendant Masonic body.

women and minorities. They're cheats with attitudes of self-importance and entitlement. Who loses out? Women and minorities.

Even though Affirmative Action opened the doors of educational and economic opportunity by a small crack so that a tiny percentage of women and minorities could get a chance, Affirmative Action accomplished very little in leveling the playing field. The result is a permanent underclass that will never be able to climb out of poverty no matter what they do — and whose lives are not substantially improved by a few charities that arbitrarily and begrudgingly dole out meager crumbs of help. Exclusive white male social fraternities that confer membership and a ticket to the American Dream go a long way in determining who gets a chance and who does not. It's no accident that poverty has a woman's face.

Due to social exclusion and isolation, the poor lack opportunity created by entrenched nepotism. The middle and upper classes only socialize with others in their own classes. No one from the lower social classes is ever a part of their social, educational, or professional circles. The middle and upper classes don't even want to have to look at poor people, let alone include them socially. They do not want their children associating with poor children (they're not "our kind").

The only time middle and upper class teens see a poor person is if they attend a public school or if they're doing their civic duty of occasional volunteering in the local soup kitchens. Even then, interaction with the poor is strictly limited and cross-class discourse never occurs. It is no wonder that so many middle and upper class kids grow up with entitlement attitudes, lacking a sense of social justice. They were never socialized to accept the poor as people in our "classless" society. Fifty years ago, sociologist and journalist Vance Packard made this point in his book *"The Status Seekers"* when he interviewed several individuals and families across the socio-economic strata in America.

Packard said that the status-striving upper-middle class sent their children to exclusive private schools because "it was socially necessary." They mapped out their children's future beginning as early as age six, and no later than age ten. Attending the right prep school, dancing lessons, music lessons, and horsemanship — are all rites of middle class passage that the poor couldn't afford.

Access to jobs and social mobility due to the workings of social class stratification mentioned by Packard was described by sociologist Max Lerner in his observations of civic organizations and social clubs. Lerner observed that upper classes and middle classes use social clubs for different reasons. Lerner said,

> "The upper classes use their clubs and association primarily as an instrument for the strategic manipulation of community resources through their control of country clubs, civic organizations, and fund raising drives. The middle classes use clubs and associations largely as a way for improving their social status and for training themselves in articulateness and leadership."

Among the individuals interviewed by Packard were three bank presidents: one form the Midwest, the northeast, and the south. The first one candidly stated, "And active banker belongs to every damned club in town. It is part of the game." The second bank president said, "We pay the dues of any banker who belongs to a good club and uses it for business." The third bank president was more elaborate stating that, "Our officers are encouraged to be active in clubs where they have contact with leaders of the community." He then proceeded down the list of his bank's officers in descending order according to rank. It was clear as he went down the list of executives, the prestige of the clubs they were permitted to join declined.

Packard also cited a study of friendship patterns conducted by Bevode McCall. This study was conducted in McCall's native Georgia town. McCall concluded that "the way people choose their friends is a part of the functioning of social class." McCall surveyed more than 2,000 people and asked them to name their "three best friends." The survey resulted in 5,200 friends listed. In most of those surveyed, the "best friends" were members of the same socio-economic class. McCall sorted the few who had been polled where the "best friends" crossed social class lines and checked the list of those listed best friends to see if the feeling was mutual. He found that only in 140 cases out of the 5,200 that there was a mutual choice of friends that crossed social class lines – less than 3%.

Although Bevode McCall's study was conducted almost 50 years ago, the invisible barriers between socio-economic classes are even more entrenched today. Social class barriers have become more rigid with the "white flight" of the well-to-do to the suburbs where the only other people they see and interact with regularly are those of their same socio-economic class. This has served to cement the social exclusion of the poor who remain isolated on the margins of society. Noblesse oblige is French, literally meaning "nobility obliges." Privilege entails responsibility, and America's "winners" have abrogated theirs.

A 2004 report from the Pew Charitable Trust, a non-profit public service and information organization, shows a dismal but realistic picture of the elusiveness of the American Dream. Upward mobility, the core tenet of the American Dream, is becoming unobtainable. According to the Pew report, 33% of working age Americans are doing worse economically than their parents. The Pew reports also show that:

- 42% of children born to parents in the bottom fifth of the income distribution remain at the bottom.
- 39% of those born to parents in the top fifth remain at the top.
- 50% of those born to parents in the middle income range have an equal likelihood of ending up in either the top or the bottom group – presenting equal promise or peril for those born to middle class parents.
- 5% of those born to parents in poverty ascend to the top income quintile.

When the requirements to get even an entry level job consist of 2+ years experience and perfect credit, the whole system is set up to provide a legal way to deny jobs to an entire class of people.

According to Leo Hindrey, Jr., the chairman of the Economic Growth/Smart Globalization Institute at the New America Foundation, the *real* national unemployment rate was 18.9% as of September 2010. The Bureau of Labor Statistics (BLS) uses a much lower number when reporting unemployment levels. The BLS uses only household surveys rather than much more accurate payroll data that Hindrey's group uses — which shows the under-employed, the marginally employed, and the very long-term unemployed (discouraged workers who have been jobless for longer than a year).

Decisions about job eliminations or permanent lay-offs don't consider skills of the workers or how hard-working they are. Entire departments and individuals get cut by a calculus of evil — anything to make the numbers work, to boost the corporate bottom line. Managers are mostly doing what they're told within the shortest time so that they can keep *their* jobs. The idea that employers won't get rid of their best and brightest is a lie promoted by delusional people convincing themselves of the validity and ethics of the corporate culture. Employers are like spoiled kids in a candy store. They want everything for nothing. It's "how can I hire the best for the least."

Most of the workers targeted for budget cuts and job obsolescence just so happen to be older workers. Age discrimination is a real problem that keeps getting swept under the rug and employers get away with so much illegal discrimination that the Civil Rights Act is a toothless shell of its former self, thanks to "At-Will" employment laws. Companies jettison single mothers and the middle-aged and a few months later, they post notices in classified ads and on Internet job search boards for positions with new titles but with the exact same duties associated with the laid-off workers' old positions, but at a lower pay. Employers are not allowed to say that they won't hire single moms or workers over age 40, but they *can* say that they aren't rehiring those who have been laid off and that they aren't hiring those with poor credit.

One of the most significant predictions of economic distress is if households rely on credit cards to cover non-discretionary living expenses. According to several 2005 national consumer surveys of debt-ridden Americans, 70% of low-income and middle class Americans reported using their credit cards as a financial safety net to meet necessary expenses such as car repairs, medical needs, groceries, and skyrocketing utility bills. Part of this is due to a real lack of disposable income from prolonged joblessness, low wages, and unaffordable fuel prices. The other part is due to predatory lending practices used by the deregulated banking cartels.

Greedy corporations and Wall Street banksters got richer by making everyone else poorer. In 2004, the average debt for those aged 65 and older was $4,000 – up by 89% since the previous decade. Most credit card debt owed by senior citizens was driven by healthcare expenses and skyrocketing utility rates and prescription drug prices. The average net worth of a 50 year old American was slightly under $40,000, *including* home equity.

The final trap for the average American which sealed the fate of the majority to lifelong insecurity, poverty, and debt peonage was the Bankruptcy Abuse Prevention and Consumer Protection Act of 2005. There is no "protection" for the consumer. It is a rewriting of the bankruptcy laws to reduce the ability of bankruptcy laws to protect the public from predatory lending practices by America's economic terrorists.

Capitalism leads to economic cannibalism. The top 10%, the super rich, own 70% of the nation's wealth. This wealth is blood money obtained by cheating the working classes and the poor. Meanwhile, the bottom 90% of the population have less than 30% of the nation's wealth (which they've produced) and owe 70% of the consumer debt. The rich got richer while everyone else got poorer.

This shouldn't be a surprise considering that all of the social programs and safety nets from Roosevelt's "New Deal" and Lyndon Johnson's "Great Society" have been eviscerated. The elimination of much of those social safety nets occurred during the global rat race to the bottom as corporations jettisoned 30 million middle class jobs since the 1980's while importing H1-B and L-1 foreign "guest workers" – those who replaced millions of American high tech professional workers. The importing of the foreign guest workers without restraint under the H1-B and L-1 visa program aided corporate fat cats in off-shoring most, if not all, of the good jobs to their overseas operations with minimal difficulty. Adding insult to injury, the displaced American workers were forced to train their foreign replacements under threat and penalty of being denied unemployment benefits and losing their severance pay.

While it is undeniable that college degreed IT workers got the shaft, I have a lot less sympathy for them than I do for everyone else who lost jobs due to off-shoring and NAFTA. They were the high-flying, high paid know-it-alls with fancy degrees in database engineering and information systems analysis who told the poor to "stop whining" and go to college to get marketable skills in order to be "worthy" of a chance for a good job in the new "Information Age Economy." They belittled those with "unimportant" college degrees and dismissed academic subjects such as history as "worthless."

But they should have studied history; their corporate slave masters did. America's fortunate sons studied Plato and Cicero while attending their exclusive prep schools and Ivy League universities – learning from history so that they could crush the common people in order to rule the world from their decadent thrones and gilded palaces of debauchery. If those IT professionals had studied history in depth from the fall of ancient Rome up through the American labor movement and the class struggle, they might not have been duped by the rich. You can't know where you're at if you don't know where you've been.

If those IT professionals would have had half the guts that the "uneducated" coal miners, textile workers, and railroad workers and all of history's unpaid and disenfranchised domestic reproductive slaves (wives and mothers) — whose sacrifices guaranteed the smooth running of our society — *maybe* there would be more good jobs in America today and NAFTA would have been fast-stopped instead of fast-tracked.

Before their jobs were outsourced to India in the late 1990's up through 2004, IT professionals thought they were better and smarter than everyone. They had little sympathy for dislocated middle-aged blue-collar union workers in manufacturing who lacked college degrees. And they had no sympathy whatsoever for poor women who never got any chances at all.

But unlike the blue-collar folks, these college degreed IT geniuses didn't even put up a fight. In fact, it was their political sway that brought leaders into power that facilitated union busting and globalization. They didn't organize and tell corporate big shots to go to hell, and that they were not going to train the L-1 and H1-B foreign guest workers who were their replacements and who were relocating our "information" jobs overseas. Instead, they dug their own graves. And for what? A couple more weeks on the job? A little bit of severance pay?

What they did was trade our collective birthright for a bowl of lentil soup – and it was poisoned lentil soup at that. American IT workers were instrumental in their own demise, and in the destruction of what remained of the American middle class and the promise of upward mobility.

Some people shrug and say, "oh well, life's not fair" in order to absolve themselves of having to do anything to help level the playing field and ease the suffering of the poor who have been crushed underfoot. But the only reason that "life's not fair" is because those with unearned social class privilege, wealth, and power make damn sure it stays unfair. The fairness in life (or lack thereof) is not a happenstance. It is by design.

There are several reasons why privileged people don't see privilege as a problem. They don't see their own privilege because they don't have to. Privilege insulates them from the consequences it poses for others. They think privilege is a personal problem and that individuals get what they deserve. Once those who are privileged are confronted with having to acknowledge their unearned privileges, they get angry because they're selfish: they don't want to lose the benefits they got at the expense of society's excluded. The system is working fine for them — too bad, so sad if it's not working for you.

They minimize the effects of stratification and deny the disadvantages imposed on others. They stubbornly cling to a 10 year old child's concept of fairness and justice, raising childish arguments to defend the indefensible. Whenever the issue of unearned social class privilege and the injustice of poverty in America is mentioned, the "haves" skirt the issue. They claim that America's poor (especially poor whites) are poor because they failed to take advantage of opportunity. But they have not removed the barriers they've placed blocking us from those opportunities.

They play the "education card", claiming that if you're poor and get a college degree you'd be able to get a good job. They point to immigrants who came here and made it. When confronted with objections due to the very real lack of jobs for non-traditional aged college grads (many are displaced manufacturing workers and middle-aged displaced homemakers), they say we're just "making excuses" and not trying. As for the immigrants who come here and make it, they get a lot more help and support than America's homegrown poor.

Sure, a college degree is (in theory) the social elevator to good jobs and a decent life. But there are many job seekers with the "right" degrees who never got a chance for a job that paid a living wage. A reader posted a response addressing this very issue to the online edition of the *Higher Education News Journal*. The journal published an article claiming that "the more educated anyone is, the higher the income, and the higher their income, the more financial latitude they have, placing them firmly on the road to "asset building." This reader responded with the truth:

"That is an outright lie and has cost more low-income families to be so debt-ridden that it's not even funny. Particularly low-income single mothers who were duped into that line of thinking and find themselves without good jobs and an astronomical amount of interest on student loan debt. Some are paying out of their SSI and living on the streets...

I don't make any more income now with four years of college than I did before college. The only difference is now I have $100,000 in student loan debt that I can't afford to repay, and it will just go up and up and up. I'm too old to donate/sell my eggs, too old to prostitute [although snuff films are an option], and too old to strip...

But here's the real clincher and why colleges need to STOP SELLING THE LIE, especially to lower income non-traditional aged students!

Corporations and companies do NOT want to hire 40 somethings just out of college – especially women.

That's just a fact and no amount of education will change that.

Statistically, if you do the research, it's amazing at how many student loan defaults are not young college grads but older non-traditional grads who find they can't get jobs...

So many have been told that education is the key to higher earnings but that's simply not the case...Education is not any guarantee of squat. I know people who have nothing but a 10th grade education that are doing better than me.

The only thing education has guaranteed us (my husband is in the same boat) is... that we are butt ass poor and in debt forever."

Tasha, @ 4:45 AM EDT on May 5, 2008

Tasha's situation is not unique. In 2004, New York City ran an ad on Internet job searching boards seeking people with a Bachelors degree in mathematics to teach high school math in economically distressed New York City schools facing funding sanctions under the No Child Left Behind mandate. Normally, one needs a Masters degree plus state teacher certification in the state one will teach in as a condition of being hired to teach grades kindergarten through high school. But New York City claimed there was a math teacher shortage and was willing to hire those with a Bachelors degree in mathematics and pay for the additional credentials for anyone holding a Bachelors degree in mathematics that was willing to teach in a rough urban environment.

I have a Bachelors degree in mathematics and I applied for a job. I was one of the candidates selected for an interview which entailed traveling from Erie, Pennsylvania where I live to New York City, which cost an entire month's income of my husband's social security check. After the interview, I learned that I was one of 26,142 candidates who interviewed for a total of 1,800 jobs. Being middle-aged with visibly decayed and missing teeth and no recent employer references as a long-term unemployed woman, I'm not surprised that I wasn't picked, given so many applicants competing for a far less number of jobs. This is the untold story of the jobless poor that never makes the news.

Most people who enroll in college do not major in mathematics or physics because those are the hardest areas of study. The coursework is very difficult, even for bright kids who were in the college prep track in high school. Math majors are a rare breed, almost an elite minority unless you're at MIT or Cal Tech. It is very telling about capitalism in the way our society steers people into certain areas in order to fill an alleged shortage when you've got 26,142 unemployed job candidates with Bachelor's degrees in mathematics vying for a total of 1,800 jobs for a salary that is not exactly the most rewarding. Regardless of what the media claims about a shortage of people with the "right" skills and the "right" degrees to fill vacant jobs, there really isn't enough jobs to go around for everyone —even for those with educations in one of the most "in demand" fields. And this was in 2004 *before* the economy was acknowledged as being officially in trouble.

Since student loan debt can no longer be absolved with filing bankruptcy, impoverished middle-aged job seekers owing student loan debt cannot get ANY relief or a bailout (unlike rich Wall Street banker crooks). Many have resorted to "dumpster-diving" for essentials because their paltry paychecks from minimum wage part-time jobs are eaten up in garnishments for outstanding student loan debt. Many are homeless and living in "tent cities." America's poor do not have it good, no matter what the "haves" claim.

Contrary to popular belief, the poorest of the poor in the US live in conditions of poverty very close to that in 3rd World nations. Countless poor people are going blind from untreated glaucoma and diabetes and suffering other kinds of permanent disabilities that would otherwise be preventable — all for lack of money and health insurance[55], because America's middle and upper classes hate the poor. They begrudge us our eyesight, our limbs, and our lives. Detroit, the working class's "ground zero", has a poverty rate of 50%. Roughly one third of the impoverished long-term jobless residents in Detroit – the poorest city in America – are without potable or clean running water because they couldn't afford to pay their bills and so their water was shut off, creating a real public health problem. In other metropolitan areas, poor people are without clean running water and garbage removal service, too – because they couldn't pay the bill. So trash gets piled up outside of their homes. If they're caught putting it in a dumpster someplace else, they get fined (and if they don't pay their fines, they'll go to jail on a bench warrant where they remain until they can pay their fines).

It's easy for the middle and upper classes to say, "being poor is no excuse for being dirty or letting your trash pile up in front of your place." But when your heat, hot water (or even the water itself) is shut off, how are you supposed to bathe? How are you going to have clean clothing? As for piled up garbage, where do you put it when your refuse service has been cancelled because you couldn't afford the bill and you can be prosecuted and fined if you try to take it elsewhere? When you're income is so low (if you have any income at all) that you have to choose between paying your rent and buying food, paying your water/sewer/refuse bill is not high on the priority list. America's poor are without basic utilities for the same reason: unaffordable rates, no money, and not enough help.

The maximum amount of help my husband and I qualified for under LIHEAP as a family of two without small kids was $157 for the whole year in 2006. The local gas company, National Fuel, has a budget

---

[55] Toni Martin, MD, "Going Blind On Our Watch", *Health Affairs*, 25, no. 4 (2006): 1121-1126, © 2006 by Project Hope; http://content.healthaffairs.org/cgi/content/full/25/4/1121

program called LIRA. Under the LIRA plan, our monthly gas bill skyrocketed from $79/month in 2004 up to $189/month immediately after Hurricane Katrina struck in 2005 – far beyond what we could afford on a total monthly household income of less than $1,000/month for two people, not counting the monthly mortgage payment of $541/month which ate up more than half of that total monthly income. We were shut off and left to freeze in the dead of winter in one of the coldest parts of the country: Erie, Pennsylvania. There wasn't "all this help out there" for us. There was NO help. There are many Americans living in 3rd World poverty conditions right here in the "land of opportunity."

While poor Americans are discarded, poor immigrants from other nations are not stigmatized and socially excluded like poor Americans are. Poor immigrants are given special assistance from welfare that our own poor are ineligible to receive. Immigrants are also given preference for jobs, which means there is even more competition for the crumbs at the bottom for poor Americans desperate for a job. The government does not care that eliminating social programs and adequate safety nets is essentially imposing a "death by destitution" sentence on those who have been economically marginalized and excluded. Our leaders are blind to the fact that discrimination, health problems, and age are barriers to adequate gainful employment – in addition to all the negative stereotypes that work against the poor.

Those who enjoy unearned privileges under the status quo refuse to acknowledge this. They ignore the issue of classism, they justify classism, or they deny the existence of classism. They say that workers *agree* to the wages offered by employers. Given the unequal bargaining power of the parties in question, can we really say this is fair? When you're poor and struggling to survive, you either have to agree to work for what an employer is willing to pay (if he hires you) under the conditions of the job, or you get nothing at all. Justifying classism is usually framed as, "We can't all be winners. Do you want everyone to have the exact same thing?" Capitalists cry that progressive taxation is punishing the rich and scream that it's not fair. "Fair" does not mean everyone gets the same thing. "Fair" means that everyone gets what he or she needs. And that includes an equal chance to use their talents to achieve their potential. Our system does not have to be a zero sum game. But any suggestion along these lines will precipitate screeching about "socialism" from people who benefited from capitalism's system of unearned privileges.

Beneficiaries of unearned privilege often usurp the victim status by claiming they're "sick and tired" of hearing about poor people's problems. If the middle and upper classes had to suffer a fraction of the deprivation and abuse that the poor suffer, they would be the first to whine and they would complain the loudest. Everything is always all about them. They never cared about anyone else except than themselves. And now they awaken from a 30 year slumber, wondering what happened to their country.

The canary in the coal mine was the way this nation, middle class and rich alike, collectively threw the poor under the bus — especially poor women — in the name of "personal responsibility and "family values." The main argument proffered against passing the Equal Rights Amendment in 1980 was that women would be drafted if we got equal rights. Today in 2010, poor single mothers are enlisting in the military out of economic necessity and are going to fight in an illegal and immoral war because we have a draft by socio-economic proxy.

And presidents are not figureheads serving as a tourist attraction. They have considerable power. As we have seen, the president can circumvent the law at home and abroad. In 1995, there were 470 statutes that enabled the president to claim potentially dictatorial powers. Those statutes have been expanded enormously (Patriot Act I and II). President Obama did nothing to repeal any of them.

While most of America's poor are women and one out of every four black men goes to prison, affluent liberals cheer that we've all finally "arrived" because a Harvard-educated black man in the White House can now legally commit the same human rights violations under the guise of "national security" in the name of fighting the "War on Terror" as rich white men previously could. Pour the hemlock for one last round, and let us raise our chalices in a toast to this "democracy."

Chapter 8

"You can't remain neutral on a moving train." ~ Howard Zinn

Linda Chavez, former nominee by President George W. Bush for Secretary of Labor, enjoys a cushy position with a well-heeled conservative non-profit think tank known as "The Center for Equal Opportunity." In a recent article titled "*Profits, Not Unions, Save Jobs*", Chavez wrote:

"It costs Chrysler $75.86/hr to employ each worker, according to the American Press, which is the highest in the American auto industry. The costs include not only what goes into the average worker's paycheck, just under $29/hr, but more importantly the contributions the company makes to employees' health and retirement benefits...Companies that lose money can't increase salaries, much less pay out billions in benefits to retirees. But unions rarely demonstrate an understanding of this basic economic fact... Even harder for unions to grasp is that there is no such thing as job security. Sure, a company can foolishly promise never to lay off workers, but it can't keep its promise if it doesn't make a profit. And unless productivity rises – which means producing with fewer workers – profits will decline...Unions would be better off abandoning their adversarial role and tying to become helpful partners with employers. It's in everyone's interest – from the lowest paid worker to the CEO – that a company maximizes profits."

Maximizing profits means "cutting costs", meaning the elimination of jobs and growing poverty while CEO's rake in tens of millions of dollars – a basic economic fact that Ms. Chavez demonstrates a failure to understand. Capitalists' profits gave us jobs? I'm sorry, but, no. Capitalism and corporate profiteering did not do that.

It was the working class and the poor who fought and died for democracy and workers' rights, including the (now obsolete) AFDC safety net, social security, the 8 hour day, child labor laws, workers' comp, and the federal minimum wage — all of which allowed the likes of Robert Rector, Linda Chavez, and the rest of the Commissariat to enjoy a middle class life.

Ever stop to think why Danes and Swedes don't work for 15 cents an hour like they do in Indonesia or Saipan? Ever wonder why *you* didn't have to work for that? Do you think it's because you are so much better and have so much more personal dignity that you could refuse to work for 15 cents an hour and not have to eat dirt cookies like the "middle class" workers in Haiti? Or is it because something forced political, social and economic changes here? Want to see how well workers live in capitalism's "free market" paradise? Look no further than Saipan or Indonesia where workers are paid 13-15 cents an hour making $1,000 Armani suits and $200 Nike sneakers where people, including children, work until they drop dead from exhaustion, sickness, and hunger before their 40th birthday.

What you may not know is that America was never the "land of opportunity" that extended the promise of "liberty" and the "freedom" of the good life to those who worked hard. In the 1820's and 1830's, one third of the population was destitute. Poverty and overcrowded living conditions brought malaria, scarlet fever, cholera, and typhoid epidemics throughout the 1830's and 1840's in New York City, Baltimore, Philadelphia, New Orleans, and St. Louis. The richest 1% owned 50% of the nation's wealth and the top 10% owned 80%. Everybody else was poor, despite working long hard hours and dying young from malnutrition, sickness, disabling and/or fatal workplace injuries, and from utter destitution. Adolescent girls worked from morning to midnight in textile mills for $3/week. Women fainted at their looms from heat, malnutrition, and exhaustion. Children worked 14 hour days all week and often fell asleep beside their machines, and frequently suffered from malnutrition, illiteracy, disease, and stunted growth.

As early as 1805, one century before the Industrial Revolution began, 8 shoemakers were arrested in Philadelphia for "conspiracy to raise wages."[56] Employers used the courts to punish the poor who fought for basic human rights, branding labor organizers as "conspirators against property and the US Constitution." Throughout the 19th and 20th centuries, untold numbers of poor people were killed by the rich through the wealthy's use of government to protect capital. The US was a 3rd World country throughout the 19th and much of the 20th centuries.

Instead of "promoting the general welfare" by protecting the people from the abuses of capitalistic social predators, the government persecuted the poor and the working class. The authorities always intervened on behalf of the rich using police, state militias, and federal troops — all of which were comprised by a willing and eager middle class — to crush the poor who struggled for daily bread, and worked hard but couldn't even afford to live. Scores of workers were killed and thousands were maimed and wounded as they were beaten up and jailed. The robber barons routinely called upon soldiers to crush the poor who attempted to negotiate for fair wages and humane working conditions. Some wealthy industrial magnets called for permanently garrisoning the industrial areas of the cities. Government responded by erecting armories as a measure of convenience for the deployment of troops against poor Americans at the behest of the rich to crush the working class.

High ranking government officials who used state legitimized violence against the poor workers were often very wealthy themselves. And they got their wealth by exploiting, abusing, and cheating women, minorities, and the poor out of anything and everything. President Grover Cleveland was a "deadbeat dad" who fathered an out-of-wedlock son whose poor mother — a 36 year old widow named Maria Halpin — never saw a penny in child support. Cleveland never admitted nor denied paternity. His idea of doing the honorable thing by "consenting to make provision" for the child and its mother whom he abandoned was to use his position and privilege to sweep the matter under the rug. Cleveland prevailed upon his friend, a judge named Roswell L. Burrows, to handle the embarrassing scandal. Burrows had Maria Halpin committed to the Providence Asylum for the "mentally deranged" run by the Sisters of

---

[56] Michael Parenti, *Democracy For the Few*, pp. 64-65

Charity and tool legal steps through the Overseer of the Poor to commit the boy to the Protestant Orphan Asylum at the board rate of $5 per week, which Cleveland was to pay through Judge Burrows. Cleveland went on to marry a 21 year old "hottie" in the Blue Room of the White House.

Cleveland's attorney general, Richard Olney, was a wealthy stockholder of railroad securities who used anti-trust legislation, mass arrests, labor spies, and federal troops against workers, workers' families, and early labor organizers. From the local sheriff and magistrate to the President and the US Supreme Court, the forces of "law and order" were used to grind the faces of the poor and dispossessed into the dirt with the brutal suppression of workers. The Sherman Anti-Trust Act of 1890, which was supposed to outlaw monopolies and capitalists' collusion in the restraint of "free enterprise", was mostly used against workers' rights and poor people's groups. The same wealthy robber barons that demanded "free market" capitalism used the government to restrict the market for the working classes. And this same cabal of criminals, who insisted that government stay out of the business of promoting the "general welfare" of the poor and providing minimal protection for them from economic terrorism, were themselves the heaviest users of government to protect their criminal wealth-grabbing activities.

The same elites who clamored for "free market" capitalism in a competitive society resorted to calling upon government to enrich them through tariffs, public subsidies, land grants, government contracts, and other "welfare handouts." The same government that did not have one dollar for the indigent (poverty was a matter best left to private charities and the church), coughed up $51 million in government bonds and gave 21 million acres of land to a handful of wealthy railroad financiers — most who got rich from the genocide of Native Americans and through the trans-Atlantic slave trade.

The wealthy manipulated the courts whose judges' interpretations of contract law were used to deny compensation to maimed workers and to poor widows and children of workers that were killed from unsafe working conditions. Employers were not held liable for workplaces that were deathtraps.

According to the 1900 census, there were 12 million families in the US, and 11 million of those lived in abject poverty. They lived in decrepit, conditions. Public education was rare. Here is what the "free market" capitalist paradise in 1900 America looked like:

- Typhoid epidemics in major cities
- Illiteracy
- Overcrowded living conditions as working class families doubled and tripled up to afford rents for hovels
- Child labor — most children had to work to help support the family, working 14-16 hours per day for six days a week with no opportunity for school
- No minimum wage
- No social security/widows' benefit/disability
- No workers' compensation
- No social programs or safety nets of any kind, outside of draconian "alms houses" which were run like prisons, and a few community churches that were barely equipped to meet the needs of their own congregants, let alone the nation's poor.

According to government data, 2 million children were forced to work 14 hour days six days a week to help support their families. In 1916, 35,000 workers were killed on the job because of unsafe working conditions; 700,000 suffered blindness and other permanent physical disabilities that were work-related.[57] The majority of Americans suffered the horrible, debilitating effects of 3rd World poverty. In 1928, Congressman Fiorello la Guardia said regarding his tour of New York's poorer districts, "I confess I was not prepared for what I actually saw. It seemed almost incredible that such conditions of poverty could really exist."[58] According to the Brookings Institute in the late 1920's, 60% of all US families did not get enough income to live on, covering their most

---

[57] Richard O. Boyer and Herbert M. Morais, *Labor's Untold Story*, pp. 184

[58] Howard Zinn, *A People's History*, pp. 376

basic human needs — excluding health care. These were also the hardest hit by the Great Depression and the 1929 crash.

The reforms that were attempted to reign and control the capitalist class's criminal behavior did not go far enough to substantially improve the lives of the poor. Workers' compensation laws place the burden of proof on the injured or disabled worker and provide no penalties when employers criminally suppress evidence. Before I moved to Erie and met my husband Donnie, he had suffered a permanently disabling back injury on the job at Tanner Manufacturing — the foundry where he worked in 1987 at a rate of $9.29 an hour (the most money he had ever been paid in his life). The most he ever made in one year was $20,000, including overtime pay. His health insurance benefits did not include any dental. And this was a workplace represented by a pretty decent union — the IAM. For the 10 years that he had to fight with the workers' compensation board and their flanks of middle class professionals who wield the power of life and death over the poor, he was followed and spied on by workers' comp insurance investigators who documented every trip he made to the supermarket.

The rich and middle classes have always benefited by depriving the poor of anything by claiming that the poor are "faking it" to "scam the system" for "free money" to get out of working in jobs that the middle class themselves would never do, while the upper classes are the biggest thieves, scam artists and criminals of all.

Workers' compensation laws also impose statutes of limitation that makes it nearly impossible in many cases for sick workers to collect anything for diseases that have a long latency period.[59] Only about 10% of all injured workers ever win any benefits, meaning that 90% get nothing and are forced to turn to welfare and SSI — which they must also fight for, and well-heeled lawyers grab 33% of any back-owed SSI award. Of those workers who eventually win some workers' comp benefits, the law forces them to forfeit their right to sue a criminally negligent employer. The workers' compensation system really only

---

[59] Michael Parenti, *Democracy For the Few*, pp. 110

provides protection for industry and shields the wealthiest companies from liability.[60]

The evisceration of miserly safety nets during the past 30 years of the War on the Poor and the disappearance of good paying jobs created a desperate labor pool willing to work on an "if-when" basis as contract workers who are exempted from protection of workers' compensation, unemployment benefits, and work credits towards social security. They're paid less and taxed as "independent contractors." They pay a higher income tax and social security and Medicare rate than big businesses and regular employees.

Independent contractors are treated as "self-employed", but they do not have the autonomy and free market privileges that are supposed to apply to independent contractors: their working terms and conditions are dictated by the employers who use "self-employment" statutes to get out of paying into workers' comp, unemployment insurance, social security and Medicare and liabilities for payroll taxes. When you're poor and desperate and in need of a job so you can live, what real choices do you have?

Smug upper-middle class professionals would rather slit their own wrists before giving one dollar to a poor person in need standing in front of them asking for badly needed help. They tell those in poverty to "help themselves." But how are the poor who are disabled, indigent, unemployed and undesired as employees, and uninsured supposed to "help themselves" when the middle class has done everything humanly possible to assist the rich and deprive the poor of what they need to do just that?

The only alternative left for those in poverty to "help themselves" — those of us who have nothing, no medical care, no hope, no chance and no way to "bootstrap" our way onto our own two feet — is an option that the middle class won't like.

---

[60] Mark Reutter, "Workmen's Compensation Doesn't Work or Compensate", *Business and Society*, Fall 1980, pp. 39-44

The large middle class was a phenomenon that enjoyed its season in the sun between 1946 and 1980 was not because of capitalism, but in spite of it. Capitalism's cheerleaders say "look how well Americans were able to live because of capitalism!" But what is ignored is the fact that it was only within the last 60 years for a 30 year window that there was a large American middle class, and while there was this large middle class there were still many suffering in poverty. Those gains enjoyed by the middle class were really the result of the poor and working class fighting the capitalists tooth and nail and fang and claw for those benefits — which the poor, who fought for them, did not receive any of. Wealth increases poverty and poverty feeds wealth.

Benjamin Franklin once said that a democracy was two wolves and one sheep deciding on what's for dinner. However, capitalism is a few wolves deciding how many sheep they're going to devour without regard for the sheep's deliberations. Capitalism is not an ethic, it's a process. It has no intention of ever providing equal opportunity for the same reason it cannot and will not ever provide 100% full employment at a living wage. Capitalism is not just an economic system. It's a whole social order that rigged the rules in favor of capital. The capitalist state has two functions: (1) Maintain and advance the interest of capital accumulation, and; (2) Protecting the capitalist system against the capitalists, i.e. "saving capitalism from itself." It is (2) where capitalism fails the majority of the people because it often fails to save itself from itself until it's too damn late and millions of people have already suffered irreparable harm and society has degraded past the point of no return. Cases in point: Argentina and Somalia.

In the post-Soviet era, most of the world is now capitalist. And most of the world is now poor and it's getting poorer. Free market capitalism is not "the rising tide that lifts all boats"; it's a rogue wave that overtakes all but the largest of nuclear powered Nimitz class aircraft carriers. So why credit the capitalist class for your middle class life when those are *precisely* the same people who fought doggedly to the death against the democratic social and economic reforms that your impoverished antecedents fought and died for? You should credit the poor and working class and thank us, not the rich.

So, Mr. Joe the (Self-Made Man) Plumber, listen up: If the world's capitalist class had its way, you would not have been paid well. You/your wife/your children probably would not be able to read and write, and you would not have a trade/profession enabling you to live a middle class life. You/your family would have died from some poverty-related malady before age 40 while working in maquiladora zone conditions without any of the middle class privileges and comforts you've enjoyed up to now.

Companies crying poor-mouth about being unable to afford to pay a living wage and health benefits to workers is the same drivel the rich have been spoon feeding the public since time immemorial. The rich always win at everyone else's expense. They never wanted the middle class to join them at the top. They never wanted the poor to have a chance to even reach the middle class. From the riots of Haymarket Square to the Pullman Strike, from the Molly Maguires to the Matewan Massacre, from the riots in Detroit and Watts; the working class and the poor have been fed the same pie-in-the-sky empty promise by the rich: "When we have made enough profits you will get yours. But now it's our turn."

Of course, the masses never did get *their* turn. When they finally did get to collect a small percentage of that long overdue IOU from the owning class, it was not without blood and bullets.

While impoverished workers were ill-fed, ill-clothed, and ill-housed during America's Gilded Age and lived in overcrowded, overpriced decrepit slums, the ultra rich lived in mansions that rivaled many European palaces from feudal times. None of the wealth from their vast fortunes ever "trickled down" to the poor.

Should people have to starve or die from lack of health care, suffer from cycles of unemployment and poverty, living in "tent cities" and in homeless shelters while CEO's live large in the name of "maximizing profits?" Why should anyone work if they can't afford the basic necessities of life on their wages when you can be just as poor *not* working?

Countless people who are homeless in America work at least one job, but their wages are not enough to afford shelter. Millions of Americans are food insecure at any given point in time, meaning that they routinely go hungry because there isn't enough money to afford groceries – even with help from food stamps and local food pantries. Is there really any "freedom" in starvation? Many of us from the underclass have been economically excluded for generations, prevented from ever getting a chance. How do you think we got this phenomenon referred to as "generational poverty?" Do you really think we *chose* to have to suffer?

What about all of the college-educated high tech professionals in the "Information Economy" whose jobs were off-shored to the lowest bidder? Was *that* the result of their piss-poor planning and "lifestyle choices?" They were ordered to train their foreign replacements, helping their employers to off-shore their jobs. Were *those* workers not being "helpful partners" with their employers? And what did they get for their helpfulness? They got discarded just as easily if they were "poor white trash" or poor people of color. They got a one-way ticket on the ride of the death spiral of poverty: loss of their jobs, dissipation of their life's savings, their kids' college savings, foreclosure, homelessness, and a lack of access to health care. Bear in mind that these were once upper-middle class people who believed in the "meritocracy" myth of the American Dream.

They thought they were indispensable, that they would be rewarded for their "helpful partnership" with the capitalist class. They bought into the capitalists' lies about "pulling yourself up by your bootstraps." They believed the wealthy's phony invitation to partake in the "ownership society" that the right-wing cult leaders of free market fundamentalism have been preaching since 1980. They thought that they could become the next Bill Gates or Donald Trump when all along the rich never intended to include them at the top.

If these fallen members of the Commissariat who call themselves the "99ers" because their unemployment benefits ran out after 99 weeks think they're hurting; it's *nothing* compared to the carnage wrought on the underclass whom they looked down on, who had been kept at the bottom all along, utterly marginalized and excluded — we've had to suffer in poverty without getting our needs met even during the "good times."

Corporate profitability failed to keep good paying jobs in the nation that enabled them to build their wealth because capitalists are loyal to no one and nothing – except their own wallets. The elite are emotionally retarded psychopathic liars who will sacrifice anyone – family and friends included – if it serves their own agenda. And these are the people whom the middle class have emulated and glorified, aspiring to become one of them someday.

Robert Rector of the right-wing think tank the Heritage Foundation claims that America's poor have it made. In his article, *"The Role of Parental Work in Child Poverty"* Rector said, "child poverty would be reduced by 72% if only the parents would work more."

Expecting parents (especially poor single parents) to work 24 hours a day 7 days a week while children are left to raise themselves as if they need no more care than a houseplant so the family won't be poor is insane. I have one simple question for Robert Rector, "Dude, where's the living wage jobs?"

Scores of poor families headed by women are living in cars, homeless shelters, and "tent cities" despite working more than one low-wage job. Many others have tried to get a job and simply could not get one at all. Tens of millions of good jobs conducive to supporting families and individuals have been off-shored permanently during the last 20 years, spurred by NAFTA, GATT, CAFTA, and other global "free trade" agreements. The majority of the jobs that remain are minimum wage part-time service jobs that you can't live on, and they have no health/dental or retirement benefits.

For migrant farm workers, waitresses, home health aides, and commissions-only paid sales workers, the pay is less than minimum wage. Those who work two or three minimum wage jobs still can't make it. Just how much more can anyone reasonably be expected to work so that they're not one footstep away from destitution? And what about those who *didn't* get a chance and who have been made poor because they got left out of this macabre game of musical chairs?

Robert Rector and Linda Chavez don't know history very well, and don't want you to know it either. Maybe it's time for a walk through American history, the real history of 90% of the US population.

During the height of America's Gilded Age, 90% of the population lived in poverty. Entire families worked (including children as young as age 6) in canneries, textile mills, coal mines, and sweatshops. Even with entire families working, they were barely able to afford food and pay their rent to slum landlords who threw them out onto the streets if they couldn't pay. The average life expectancy in the early 1900's was in the 40's and 50's with very few people living beyond that. This was not solely due to a lack of medical science advancement as much as it was due to lack of food, adequate shelter, sanitation, and access to medical care for the poor.

For the majority of Americans, life was a hardscrabble existence. Entire families worked hard, but they never got ahead. None of the wealth from the largesse of the elite trickled down to them. Robber barons, lawyers, and that den of iniquity known as Wall Street stole more prosperity from ordinary Americans with their pens and briefcases than Jesse James did with a gun.

As a result of entire families having to work, many children never learned to read and write or do basic arithmetic. High school was a luxury. Only those whose families could afford tuition and forego their children's sweatshop wages were able to send their children to high school. This was before compulsory education laws, child labor laws, minimum wage laws, public education, and occupational safety laws.

Did Robert Rector and Linda Chavez ever read *"The Jungle"* by Upton Sinclair or *"How the Other Half Lives"* by Jacob Riis? The "you won't be poor if you only work more" meme is a lie used to demoralize and degrade the poor, and to bribe the complacency of the middle class.

It's a lie used by the super rich to ensure their own privilege at the expense of everyone else.

It's a lie bought into by the middle class who have historically been whores for the rich. They thought if they identified with the rich by supporting laws and social policies that hurt the poor; they would find favor and be rewarded with security and comforts. They thought that they too would share in the prosperity of the chosen few. It was a lie then and it's a lie now. Yet, people keep falling for the same bait and switch. The American Dream was always a nightmare. You cannot be rich or even middle class unless others around you are poor — often directly associated with your efforts to get ahead.

From the 1940's through the 1970's, many Americans prospered and were able to live comfortably. There was a large middle class. This was due to four main factors:

1. Strong labor unions which fought for workers' rights; an acceptable living standard.
2. Franklin Roosevelt's Public Works Project to employ the poor and jobless in the wake of the Great Depression.
3. The Social Security Act which provides a safeguard against widows' poverty and old age destitution.
4. Lyndon B. Johnson's Great Society programs, including AFDC and CETA.

The inadequate and miserly safety net of AFDC that used to exist was no panacea. And there were many Democrats during FDR's day, including FDR himself, who were unsympathetic to the plight of the poor — especially poor women and minorities. FDR saw himself as the rescuer of capitalism from a pending socialist or communist insurrection as the discontent among the poor and the hardest hit victims of the Great Depression grew restive. The poor had been suffering in utter misery since the beginning of the 20th century with the Industrial Revolution. By 1932, they were fed up.

One third of the nation's population was desperately poor and couldn't "pull themselves up by their bootstraps" because they had no boots. They were ill-fed, ill-clothed, and ill-housed, and ill-employed. Another third, the higher paid (mostly white males) of the working class, were just barely getting by — although they were better off than working class blacks and women who were overrepresented among the ranks of the destitute, and underrepresented among the ranks of the steadily employed.

The first two terms of FDR's presidency are often referred to as the era of "the forgotten man" and the New Deal. But the New Deal mostly benefited upper-middle class landowners and corporate agricultural producers at the expense of the poor tenant farmers, sharecroppers, and the working poor who struggled just to afford food.

The New Deal was more dedicated to business recovery than socio-economic reform. The first New Deal component implemented was the National Recovery Administration (NRA) which set up "code authorities" that were mostly comprised of corporate leaders in industry to restrict production and set minimum price requirements — the results far more benefited big corporations than smaller competitors. The Democrat majority and Republicans both acted in unison in Congress during Roosevelt's time — pouring large sums of public money into the coffers of the moneyed few.

Within nine years, the Reconstruction Finance Corporation lent $15 billion to big businesses. While one third of the nation was ill-fed, ill-clothed, and ill-housed due to lack of income and lack of affordable housing, and lack of adequate job opportunities, the federal housing program stimulated private construction with subsidies and profit protection for bankers and mortgage brokers through the loan insurance program — all of little to no benefit for the millions of homeless, jobless, and poor whose hardest hit victims were women, the disabled, and minorities: those were the very members of the working class least likely to get adequate employment opportunities in those industries.

The New Deal aided Big Ag with price supports and production cutbacks while sharecroppers and poor tenant farmers were evicted when federal acreage rental programs took land out of agricultural use.[61]

FDR finally created a relief program in the face of massive social unrest to ease only some of the suffering of the poorest, most excluded of the working class with the Social Security Act of 1935 — its Title IV component, which was AFDC, provided subsistence anti-starvation aid to destitute women and children and that has since been eliminated with the Welfare Reform Act of 1996. AFDC was a miserly allotment and you had to buy your food stamps. The poorest could not get them because they had no money to buy them. Many poor women and children in poverty, especially in Appalachia, literally starved to death in this country until Lyndon Johnson made food assistance a human right and an entitlement.

Under FDR, the Civilian Conservation Corps (CCC) provided jobs at near-poverty wages for 250,000 out of the 15 million jobless poor. At its peak, the Work Project Administration (WPA) employed 9 million of the 15 million desperately poor and jobless, leaving 6 million of the poorest and worst off with nothing. Of those helped with WPA and CCC jobs at 40 cents an hour or less, only about 500,000 were helped by the new minimum wage law.

The Social Security Act of 1935 barely covered half of the working class population. No provision was included for national health care and income protection against illness or injury before retirement. Old Age social security pensions and unemployment benefits applied only to those (mostly white males) who had enjoyed steady employment in *select* occupations while millions of other workers (mostly women and minorities) further down on the economic ladder weren't covered at all.

Even though welfare programs and other government interventions were terribly inadequate for meeting the needs of the most vulnerable and destitute, they achieved notoriety, which served to diffuse

---

[61] *Regulating the Poor*, Frances Fox Piven and Richard Cloward, pp.76; *The New Deal*, Barton Bernstein, pp. 269-270

discontent. After the threat of civil unrest subsided, federal relief for the most disadvantaged and destitute was slashed in 1936-1937, plunging families into destitution and leaving them worse off since the 1929 crash.

The initiatives FDR and both political parties in Congress enacted were half-assed, half-hearted, half-measures — typical of "priests of half-truths." The New Deal failed to solve the problems of economic depressions. It failed to uplift the impoverished. It failed to redistribute income and provide genuine equal opportunities for everybody. It failed to promote equality and ensure that everybody — regardless of race or gender — had a guaranteed right to a living wage job and/or an equivalent income guarantee. It failed to make business accountable for the social welfare or address business's preeminent political power in the very nation that enabled them to get rich and powerful in the first place — at the expense of exploited and disenfranchised groups.

Although FDR's New Deal produced some economic gains, it was largely a middle class with an overwhelmingly white male face that benefited; while the poor, with an overwhelmingly female or minority face languished from deprivation of human needs in Third World poverty up through the 1960's. And even the Great Society expansion of AFDC benefits was not adequate. Giving the poor food stamps instead of a minimum guaranteed income to budget for their needs accordingly was merely a kiss-off along the lines of "we don't trust poor scum with money, but here you go beggar— use these food stamps so you won't starve and come after us and kill us to steal from us to survive."

Before unions, the New Deal, and Johnson's great Society programs, America was not the "land of opportunity" for a better life for the working classes and the poor – the majority of the people. Due to a legacy of discrimination in a nation founded on the principles of racial and gender inferiority, America was not the "land of opportunity" for the poor, for blacks, or for women after the New Deal. Roosevelt's New Deal actually did not go far enough with reforms and it had done more to help the capitalist class than it did for poor and marginalized groups.

1900 was the age of robber barons. While a handful of Americans such as John D. Rockefeller, John Jacob Astor, Jay Gould, Cornelius Vanderbilt, and Andrew Carnegie (to name a few) were obscenely wealthy; very few Americans were middle class. Most Americans were very poor despite the fact that entire families – including women and children – went to work in the factories in the cities. The dichotomy between the "haves" and the "have-nots" was an impassable gulf. These conditions gave rise to labor unions. The class struggle for fairness, dignity and basic human rights was a difficult one.

As an aside, some important things need to be said about organized labor. Unions in the US in general overall have failed to address sexism, discriminatory training and hiring practices, and the impoverishment of women caused by the gender division of labor and the devaluing of "women's work." This turned a lot of dispossessed and marginalized people off to unions as union workers became part of the privilege middle class. Discrimination against women and the undervaluing of "women's work" is not a position that unions should be maintaining and defending as agents for economic justice. That has greatly undermined *all* members of the proletariat.

In France when the poor were treated half as shabbily as we are, the French citizenry shut down the whole country. These are people who made change happen by guillotine rather than begging their leaders for change. The French enjoy a better quality of life because they drew the line on acceptable minimum standards. President Sarkozy does not own the streets of Paris — the people do. France is a country where the working class and the poor have resorted to the "guillotine solution." Compare that to the US where middle class people obediently beg for crumbs from the table of their corporate overlords and call that "freedom" while looking down their regal noses at the poor.

Journalist Chris Hedges ascribes this to the abysmal failure of what he calls the "liberal class" to stand its ground against abusive social and economic policies that benefit the capitalist class at the expense of workers, consumers, and the marginalized. The liberal class encompasses institutions and organizations that had been the traditional agents of social change and economic justice; unions being a prominent force.

The bifurcation of the liberal class from its core ideology led to it becoming an apologist for the expansion of discrimination, repression, cruelty, and exploitation. This has been in the making these last 40 years. They made a deal with the devil on the devil's terms, thinking they could prevail through pragmatism. This alienated them from their core allies — Communists, Socialists, women's rights groups and criminalized minority movements (AIM, MOVE, Black Panther Party, etc.) — because we saw that nothing was really gained. Compromise after compromise chipped away at what few social and economic reforms that the liberal class previously took credit for.

Societies that cannot, or will not, regulate capitalist forces collapse and cannibalize themselves. With the failure of the liberal class, particularly unions, to vigorously abolish discrimination and restrain capitalism's abuses and the hijacking of democratic governmental processes comes a void. That void will not be filled by educated progressive leaders agitating for social justice; rather it is being filled by hate-filled apocalyptic demagogues from the religious right like Glenn Beck and the Tea Party movement who call President Obama "Hitler" and clamor for supplanting the US Constitution with Levitical Law (which is the same as Sha'ria Law).

Throughout the last 30 years, there should have been members of the liberal class — whether in the press, organized labor, or academia — who stood firm on the core values of social equality, aggressively calling for the abolishment of training and job discrimination against women in *all* arenas and demanding an adequate non-punitive safety net for the poor, the elderly, and the disabled. Their voices were silent on the matter of a guaranteed right to a living wage job and health care for all Americans, regardless of race, age, or gender. They should have spoken up three decades ago. But they didn't. They only looked out for themselves while they threw the poor under the bus.

The ghettoization of women into minimum wage low-valued service occupations causes women to be a lot poorer than men. Even if there is union representation in some of those occupations, it is weak and ineffectual for securing a living wage and favorable working conditions. And the total exclusion of the disabled ensures that injury or sickness will leave anyone, no matter what other unearned privileges they may have otherwise had, utterly destitute.

By failing to address these and other broader social issues, unions have gone the way of the dodo bird because they became bastions of middle class white male privilege. Unions are the domesticated house pets of the capitalist class, along with the rest of America's "liberal" organizations. Even the Democratic Party is against the poor, and has been for the past 30 years as policies of Benign Neglect were enacted with their complicity.

Benign Neglect is a policy (or set of policies) of ignoring a situation instead of assuming responsibility for managing, fixing, or improving it. The Welfare Reform Act of 1996 is just one example of Benign Neglect. What Welfare Reform really was, was the repeal of Title IV of the Social Security Act of 1935. It removed welfare (AFDC) from an entitlement status to something arbitrary and capricious. It replaced the entitlement to subsistence with a lifetime five year limited and a horrendously slashed welfare benefit, and tethered it to a unilaterally stringent work requirement as condition for receiving those time-limited benefits.

The New Deal philosophy held that society had an affirmative duty to keep poor women and children from starving to death, especially since women were economically excluded from most jobs that paid enough to live on. Welfare Reform placed the burden of poverty squarely on the shoulders of the poor by insisting that adults on welfare "move from welfare to work" without any guarantee that opportunities for education, vocational training, and access to jobs would be made available; and without any stipulation requiring employers and unions to welcome poor welfare recipients as employees so they *could* become economically self-sufficient.

Our welfare "reform" came directly out of meetings between government and corporations, in which corporations bitterly complained about the lack of "affordable" (cheap) labor. Back in the 1980's, the public was told that "spoiled, lazy Americans" were demanding "outrageous" wages and job protections and this burden was "forcing" businesses to flee the country or shut down. "Lazy Americans" refused to take horrible jobs that didn't pay enough to live on and welfare gave vulnerable people a safety net as an option and *some* protection from the brutal exploitation of rapacious capitalism. Employers that paid poverty wages and/or kept dangerous working conditions couldn't find or keep enough workers *precisely* because people had an option and this fact helped protect the wages and working conditions for *all* workers. The solution: get rid of "welfare as we know it" and people will be desperate enough to take whatever they can get.

The tragedy is that so many Americans fell for propaganda used to gain their approval of redirecting public money from poverty relief to corporate "tax relief", including very lucrative "non-profit" groups. No one addressed the fact that the existence of welfare effectively protected workers and provided a solid floor for a blue and white collar middle class. Not only did welfare protect wages, it also prevented people from homelessness if they lost their jobs. Now, thanks to Welfare Deform, you might (or might not) be able to get a few pennies of aid under the TANF block grants to the states if you lose your job and can't get re-employed after exhausting any unemployment benefit you might (or might not) be eligible for. Middle class Americans swallowed the anti-poor pablum shoveled at them since the 1980's and they were actively complicit in enabling policies of Benign Neglect. Welfare Reform has been the single most powerful tool for suppressing wages, getting rid of unions, and creating a very large domestic 3rd World workforce. As a result, Americans have gotten poorer while corporate profits soared.

While everyone "knows" of "welfare queens" wearing diamonds and fur coats driving their Cadillacs to supermarkets, an invidious embellishment spouted by sexist and racist class bigots that the middle class convinced themselves to believe; *no one* acknowledges the fact that US companies have laid off entire chunks of their workforce and replaced them with slave labor under Welfare Reform's Workfare component for less than half of the federal minimum wage. The mythical bejeweled "welfare queen" wearing a fur coat loading expensive steaks into her Cadillac is as elusive as Bigfoot. No one has any authentic pictures of this creature, and it's always somebody who knows someone else that saw this "welfare queen." If anyone captures living proof of the existence of this rich "welfare queen", they'll probably find her hanging out with Bigfoot.

Welfare Reform could not have happened without the manufactured consent of the public by getting them to see America's poor as sexually immoral "freeloaders" living large off of "good" hard-working Americans, turning the working poor against the poorest.

Remember the right-wing claim that "generous" welfare entitlements were wrecking our social fabric and our economy at the expense of the working class? Fact: US welfare allotments under AFDC were 100% *below* the outdated austere poverty line. Remember being told that welfare "created a culture of dependency?" Fact: those on welfare were those who had been impoverished by a combination of conservatives' assault on poor women's access to birth control and abortion; and a legacy of discrimination and economic exclusion in a patriarchal capitalist society that *still* denies poor women opportunities for good-paying jobs in the skilled trades while "women's work" is invalidated, unpaid/underpaid, and devalued. (This is known as the "gender division of labor.")

Those least able to leave welfare were women with learning disabilities, women with disabled children, and/or women from generational poverty who lacked the personal safety net of a middle class family willing to help them.

Liberals refused to address these issues. They were complicit in scapegoating the poor for political gain; first to build a conservative movement on working class resentment, then to transfer public welfare dollars into the bank accounts of the rich. This divide and conquer strategy ensured that there would be no uprising, no mass protests interrupting the wealth redistribution to the top.

Welfare Reform promoters were indifferent and outright callous to the wellbeing and needs of the poor. They knew that the draconian law would not make for a more independent, prosperous underclass and move them into the middle class.

They knew that employers and unions providing good jobs with dignity, a middle class wage and health benefits would not hire poor women being thrown off of welfare and that their male employees would not accept women as equals, as co-workers on the job.

They knew that under our capitalist system, there are never enough jobs to go around for everybody and that *somebody* always has to get left out.

They knew that many women, children, and marginally disabled people would end up tossed out onto the streets because they weren't desirable employees.

Although Senator Daniel Patrick Moynihan was a disciple of the "culture of poverty" school and was no friend to the poor, he was reticent to go along with Welfare Reform once he saw the implications for poor children:

> "The essential problem with this legislation is that it imposes time limits without any real provisions for the heroic efforts that are required to take people who have been on welfare for a long while, get them off and keep them off, to put a time limit on, when you do not have a provision for seeing that people have work is to invite an urban crisis unlike anything we've ever known since the 1960's...We will be making cruelty to children an instrument of social policy. No child in America asked to be here. Why then are we determined to punish them?"

And punish poor children America did — as well as poor women by depriving them of access to reliable contraception and abortion to teach the low-class "sluts" to keep their legs shut in the name of "personal responsibility" while the co-conceivers were exempted from the "tough love" of welfare reform's "personal responsibility." Instead, men were given the green light to be sexual criminals that impregnate and then abandon their bed victims at will with no concern for the needs of the woman whose body, health, life, and emotional well-being is 100% at risk in any pregnancy. Getting to have sex is not only viewed as a male privilege, it's also a class privilege: middle and upper class women can always get their choice reliable contraception, and they can afford to travel to get a medically safe abortion if their birth control fails.

But the petit bourgeoisie feminist groups said nothing these past 30 years about the deprivation of the right to bodily autonomy for poor women until the Stupak Amendment threatened middle class women's access to reproductive choice. Nothing is said when Viagra is given out for free to poor men like water at a marathon while RU 486 (Mifepristone) is withheld from women when that could be just as easily dispensed as Viagra. This shows just how deep the hatred is for the poor — especially poor women. There is a general consensus that the poor don't deserve anything. Not access to good jobs. Not education. Not health care. Not food. Not access to any societal resources. Not even acceptance and love. It's as if we owe the self-important middle and upper classes a debt for being born into *their* world.

Welfare Reform was not the "Contract With America"; it was a Contract On America. The middle class never wanted poor women to join their ranks. Poor women — who often get *no* opportunity for making a living outside of the seedy exploitative sex industry — are nothing but "trash" and "gold-diggers" whose hopes, dreams and aspirations don't matter. Poor women aren't good enough to "deserve" to be loved, married, and supported by the sons of middle class families — we're just "losers" who don't have anything worthwhile to bring to the table because we don't have money, social status, or any other cultural capital. Yet, we're not deserving of opportunities to enter a skilled trades' union apprenticeship and work in a skilled trade for middle class paychecks in jobs with dignity so we can earn our own way because that's "taking away a man's job"; never mind the fact that we don't get to pay less to live than men. We're the most disposable class in "pro-life" America.

Millions of middle class white males share Rush Limbaugh's sentiment: poor people shouldn't even get food stamps to have access to nutritious food. Instead, we should eat out of dumpsters. This is not just a matter of greed as a cultural imperative. It's a serious sociopathic pathology. There is no other way to describe a geopolitical and economic climate where the working class and the middle class begrudge the less fortunate jobless poor any adequate support so we can get our needs met and live with just a little bit of security and dignity after we've been involuntarily excluded and marginalized, and denied any *real* equal opportunity throughout most of our lives in a job market within the capitalist construct that *never* delivered 100% full employment.

Credentialism and structural unemployment serve to keep the majority of entire groups permanently unemployable and excluded — not because they're "losers" or "rejects" that have nothing to offer, but because of capital's need to suppress wages and remind comfortably off middle class workers: "if you don't like the workplace bullying, the unreasonable demands from that new manager, the increased co-pays in your employer-provided health insurance, or other terms and conditions of your employment, there are 100 extremely desperate poor people who will gladly take your job."

And if you're unemployed and over 40, especially if you're female, lots of luck trying to get another job that pays enough to be able to live plus repay your student loans you might have had to incur for a degree in order to be "worthy" of a chance for a job to begin with. Those who are middle-aged and long-term unemployed are facing being permanently excluded; that is to say, permanently unemployable until they "age out" of the labor market and can begin drawing social security (hopefully). And they may not even get social security if Scrooges in Congress get their way.

For everyone who got lucky in getting a chance for a good job, even one that puts you on the lowest rung of the middle class (not to be confused with the working poor), there are many others out there who got denied your seat. They got denied chances for a good job and got sent away poor and empty-handed. Every economically excluded fellow citizen that you begrudge health care, a decent guaranteed income or job, is your place-keeper. Whether you want to admit it or not, the fact is that you were afforded the opportunity to be able to participate and have a decent life at the expense of somebody (or a lot of somebodies) that was not.

Most of those who face permanent economic exclusion are the long-term unemployed middle-aged job seekers over age 40 while age discrimination is understated as a problem. Their résumés get tossed in favor of younger job-seekers[62]. And many among the middle-aged and unemployable didn't get chances for good jobs with retirement plans and health benefits when they were younger because capitalism has never provided enough jobs and opportunity to go around for everyone. And they don't have a lifetime of accumulated middle class toys to sell on eBay to get money to carry them through until they can get a minimum wage job as a Wal-Mart greeter (which isn't enough to live on), or begin drawing social security and get Medicare at age 67. Meanwhile, the bureaucrats at state unemployment centers across the US tell the poor with the greatest need of a chance to make a living that "no one owes you a job."

The poor who are disabled who are among the lucky ones to get SSI (many more are denied and have nothing) — are struggling to survive on $600/month SSI, which isn't enough to live on anywhere in the US. This portion of the disabled population provide hefty subsidies for the rich through exploitative "special minimum wage waivers." These are "workshops" that do the jobs subcontracted from some of our biggest, wealthiest corporations and the jobs in these workshops filled by the disabled are mostly assembly line or piece work. Any disabled person who ends up in one of these workshop jobs can be paid as little as $1.50/hour. Technically, the wages are supposed to reflect the actual rate

---

62 Mokoto Rich, "The New Unemployables: Workers Over Age 50", msnbc.com, September 20th, 2010; "For the Unemployed Over 50 Fears of Never Working Again", *New York Times*, 2010

of prevailing wage a non-disabled worker doing the same job would be paid. But in reality, the employer gets to decide whatever wage he wishes to pay.

The formula used by the government by which these slave wages reduce a disabled person's monthly SSI benefit is such that if the disabled worker's job stops abruptly, there wouldn't be enough left in SSI benefits alone to even cover rent for a place to live. After a disabled worker's employment ends at one of these sweatshops, it takes up to six months before their full SSI benefits are restored — which effectively keeps the disabled trapped in slave wage jobs programs.

America's poor today have higher disability rates, lower life expectancy rates and higher maternal and infant mortality rates than people in many 3rd World countries due to a real lack of access to health care and no real safety net. But the poor (you know, us "stray animals that will only breed if fed") aren't reproducing a large enough reserve army of surplus labor and aren't dying off fast enough to suit capitalism's winners. And there are fewer and fewer winners and more and more losers in this No Pea shell game of a Serengeti economy than at any other point in history since the Great Depression officially began 81 years ago. Yet, those who are smug with their luck of good health and opportunities have the moxy to look down on those of us who got left out and deprived of everything. They sneer at the poor begging for help at "charity" medical clinics and food stamp users in supermarket checkout lines.

If you think it's so easy for the jobless poor on SSI or welfare (which pays a benefit no more than what the AFDC benefit was in 1984) to "just get a job", give some jobless, poor and hard-to-employ person *your* good job and health benefits so they can have a job and a chance for once in their life while *you* go get another comparable job if you think it's so damn easy. (Don't like that idea, do you?)

President Obama rode the election into the White House on tough talk on "change" and the promise of hope. Within weeks of his inauguration, he morphed into a wimp, snivelling that he and Democrats in Congress had to make "compromises." Whenever our government leaders talk about "compromises" and the need to make "sacrifices", they mean <u>you</u>.

And yet, nothing was heard from the AFL-CIO regarding an adequate safety net for *all* of the jobless poor, including those "discouraged workers" who were not eligible for any unemployment benefits. Instead, they only talked about unemployment benefits extensions for the "99er's" who had already gotten 99 weeks of unemployment compensation during 2009-2010 while 60% of America's jobless have nothing — many whom are destitute, sick, homeless, and in the most need of an economic lifeline. In the end, after the 99ers helped push through legislation favorable to the AFL-CIO big shots, they were discarded and like the underclass, their needs were compromised. Like the rest of the liberal class, the union leadership and membership bodies ignored the lessons of the class struggle in history and sold out society's least fortunate. The working class fight for social and economic justice was in the past, a past that they chose to ignore at their own peril.

The Pullman Palace Car railroad workers lived in a paternalistic system of welfare capitalism.[63] They were held in debt peonage to their employer and much of their compensation was in the form of fringe benefits. In reality, they were little more than slaves. Pullman workers were required to live in Pullman City, the company town, which was a settlement of cheap housing provided by Pullman for his workers on the 3,000 acre tract of land he owned. This requirement of Pullman's workforce to live and pay rent for housing in his company town was a common condition of employment imposed by industrialists during the Industrial Revolution.

Treated like errant children, every aspect of Pullman workers' lives were micromanaged by their employer, George Mortimer Pullman. Workers were even fined by their employer for "poor housekeeping" habits! Workers were also expected to accept pay cuts and not complain about their workload, even though their rents were not likewise

[63] *Welfare capitalism* is the practice of businesses providing welfare-like services to workers in lieu of adequate wages paid in US currency; also known as paternalism.

decreased when their wages were cut. Pullman charged his workers fees for use of the library in Pullman City. Clergy even had to pay rent for use of the company town's church. Even to worship, Pullman workers had to pay.

Eugene Debs worked on the railroad as a fireman and saw the working conditions of his fellow railroad laborers. He saw men working for paltry pay; many whom were injured or killed because of unsafe equipment and management's cavalier attitude in viewing the workers as disposable commodities. Debs founded the American Railroad Union (ARU), which most railroad workers joined in an attempt to able to exert some leverage in order to improve working conditions. The ARU was very weak in its infancy stages. Corporate fat cats like George Pullman held all the cards. The masses were kept poor and demoralized and shackled in debt to company towns.

In 1893, factory wages at the Pullman Company fell by 25%, but the rents George Pullman charged his workers for their housing did not decrease. If a Pullman worker incurred debt as a result, the worker's paycheck was garnished by Pullman to repay the debt at high interest. Workers were paid inadequately to support their families and risked disability and death on a daily basis on the job. The drastic pay cut without a commensurate rent decrease proved to be the match that lit the tinderbox.

On May 11th 1894, 3,000 railroad workers for the Pullman Palace Car Co. (named for its founder and president George Mortimer Pullman) went on a wildcat strike – a work stoppage not authorized by their fledgling union, the American Railroad Union (ARU). It began with a walkout after negotiations over declining wages failed. The workers appealed for support to the ARU, which argued unsuccessfully for arbitration. On June 20th, the ARU gave notice that as of June 26th its members would no longer work trains that included any Pullman cars. The work stoppage and boycott of trains with Pullman cars was centered in Chicago, but it crippled railroad traffic nationwide until the federal government intervened with a comprehensive injunction forbidding all strike activity followed by a declaration of martial law in which federal troops were dispatched.

The ARU members refused to allow any trains with Pullman cars to move – except those carrying US mail. Meanwhile, the railroad company owners formed a clique of their own: the General Managers Association. There were 24 railroads that were a part of the General Managers Association, which boldly announced that no one was going to tell them how to run their businesses. They threatened to fire any switchman who refused to move Pullman rail cars. In response, Debs's union announced that if any switchman was fired because of refusing to move Pullman cars, all ARU members would walk off the job. By June 29th, 50,000 men walked off the job. Railroads began recruiting workers from the ranks of America's destitute and jobless to work as strike-breakers (scabs) and riots ensued. Railroads appealed to the government authorities for intervention.

Illinois governor John P. Altgeld did not want to involve US troops because he felt that the workers should enjoy the same rights as their bosses. The General Managers Association resorted to the tactic of character assassination by flooding the press with embellishments that made Eugene Debs look like a dangerous radical and the ARU as a band of violent, lawless thugs. Illinois Attorney General Richard Olney sided with the railroads saying that if the ARU members disagreed with how they were treated, they were free to quit their jobs. (Does this sound familiar?)

But the railroad workers really weren't free. Kept in debt peonage to company towns, beholden to employers for their company-owned housing and having no money they could not just up and quit and go work for someone else. In free-market America, the working class and poor were free to starve, free to be homeless, and free to die – that's about all the poor are free to do.

Striking railroad workers began burning rail yards. On July 2nd 1894, an injunction from the federal court was handed down saying that the strike was illegal. President Grover Cleveland sent in federal troops and martial law was declared to forcibly subdue the striking workers and their sympathizers. On July 7th 1894, a mob of rail workers and their supporters confronted the federal troops in an attempt to stop a train that the troops were escorting. Gunfire from the soldiers erupted, killing many innocent unarmed civilians as well as the striking workers. By July 10th 1894, the Pullman strike had ended and the workers gained nothing. ARU founder Eugene Debs was jailed for six months for tampering with the US mail as a result of the strike.

While the Pullman workers didn't win that battle in the war for fair pay and working conditions, they won in the court of public opinion. It was an important step towards securing adequate wages and tolerable working conditions for America's working class. Americans began to resent corporate fat cats who tooled around in luxury while claiming they couldn't afford to pay their workers a living wage so that the workers and their families could live with a little bit of dignity, security, and comfort. George Mortimer Pullman was seen by the public as a greedy intolerant ogre, not as an enlightened employer who took care of his workers. He was the quintessential "benevolent slave master." He was offended by his perceived ingratitude of his workers and was always paranoid that the "unwashed masses" were out to steal from him.

Many railroad company owners, like Franklin B. Gowen, also held interests in land leasing companies and coal companies. Gowen was the president of the Philadelphia & Reading Railroad and also of the Reading Coal & Iron Company. He had ruthlessly driven out smaller independent coal operators and after taking over their mines, he treated the workers brutally. Gowen owned two thirds of southeastern Pennsylvania's coal mines. In addition to being a greedy coal kingpin and railroad robber baron, Franklin B. Gowen was also the district attorney for Schuylkill County, Pennsylvania.

The rail and coal industries were interconnected. Not surprisingly, coal mine workers were treated no better than railroad workers. In fact, miners were treated worse.

Coal miners were not paid an hourly rate or a salary. They were paid piece rate, and they were paid in company scrip – not US currency. Like the railroad workers in Debs's union, coal miners had to live in ramshackle dumps owned by the coal companies in company-owned towns built on company-owned land.

A band of disgruntled miners who later became known as the Molly Maguires took matters into their own hands after Gowen slashed the miners' wages by 28% during the winter of 1873-1874, owing to a nationwide financial panic. The Molly Maguires, or "Mollies" as they were called, were members of a secret Irish fraternity: the Ancient Order of Hibernians – a "benevolent" Irish Catholic social fraternity with origins in Ireland. The Ancient Order of Hibernians was heavily entrenched throughout the coal region of eastern/central Pennsylvania. Violence ensued in Pennsylvania's anthracite coal region, which comprises the counties of Lackawanna, Carbon, Luzerne, Columbia, Northumberland, and Schuylkill in the eastern/central part of Pennsylvania. It was not just the cut in pay that ignited the "big trouble" in Pennsylvania's anthracite coal region. It was a series of injustices suffered by mine workers caused by their employer prior to 1874.

On September 6th 1869, a fire claimed the lives of 110 miners at the Avondale mine in Luzerne County. The victims' families rightfully blamed the greedy coal company for its refusal to install secondary exits for the mine. In Schuylkill County alone, 566 miners were killed on the job and over 1,655 were seriously injured over a seven year period. Their widows and children received no compensation from the coal operators and there was no Social Security benefit back then. Miners' widows and children were left destitute without means to economically fend for themselves – on top of the devastation that accompanies the loss of one's love, one's husband, one's father and one's best friend.

After the Avondale Mine disaster, John Siney of the Workingmen's Benevolent Association addressed a crowd of several thousand miners from surrounding communities, "Men, if you must die with your boots on, die for your families, your homes, or your country. But do not consent to die like rats in a trap for those who have no more interest in you than in the pick you dig with." Thousands of miners joined the newly formed United Mine Workers union (UMW) that very day. Over 85% of Pennsylvania's anthracite miners belonged to the UMW.

But a vulture capitalist like Gowen was determined to break the union by forcing a financially crippling strike and a showdown, deliberately provoking violence and bloodshed. In the winter of 1873-74, over one fifth of Pennsylvania's miners were unemployed due to a nationwide depression. Gowen slashed wages of those still working by 28% - without reducing the rents he charged for his company housing (which were worse than slave quarters on plantations of the antebellum South), or the price of food and clothing in the company stores he owned. The Mollies retaliated with work stoppage.

In Schuylkill County, striking miners and their families were starving to death – literally. One miner's account as documented by historian Andrew Roy had written a letter to a friend about the bleak conditions he faced which were like those suffered by many other miners and their families:

> "Since I last saw you, I have buried my youngest child, and on the day before his death there was not one bit of victuals in the house with six children."

Gowen employed the Pinkerton Agency to subdue the striking miners. Pinkerton thugs shot and killed some of the striking miners, and in one case, even shot the wife of one of the miners. She was unarmed. The Mollies killed most of the Pinkerton goons. In the end, six Molly Maguires were arrested, tried, and convicted and sentenced to death by hanging for their brand of vigilante justice in the shooting deaths of the Pinkerton men.

Four members of the Molly Maguires, Alexander Campbell, John "Black Jack" Kehoe, Michael Doyle, and Edward Kelly, were hanged on June 21st 1877 at the Carbon County prison in the town of Mauch Chunk (renamed Jim Thorpe in 1953). Just before Alexander Campbell went to the gallows, he slapped his muddy hand on his prison cell wall and swore, "There is proof of my words. That mark of mine will never be wiped out. It will remain forever to shame the county for hanging an innocent man." Despite efforts to remove the handprint, including tearing down and rebuilding the wall, the handprint remains in the same spot – serving as a spectral indictment of a justice system corrupted by wealth.

Twenty men were hung in connection with the Molly Maguires – the innocent along with the guilty. The UMW was not disbanded, however and gained strength. And Gowen went down in history as a disgusting, selfish elitist. Almost eleven years to the day of Molly Maguire member John "Black Jack" Kehoe's hanging death, Gowen took his own life. He committed suicide in a Washington DC hotel room.

Even after the miners had a strong union, not all mines were unionized by the 1920's. The bituminous coal fields in central Appalachia were the last stronghold against unionization. The isolated rural communities nestled among the mountains on the southern West Virginia coal beds were really systems of feudalism run by vulture capitalist non-union coal operators. Feudalism exists when free people have to work for a single employer, or not work at all. Those who worked for the mine owners were paid slave wages in useless scrip money and were subjected to unimaginable abuses. This was the situation endured by those living in West Virginia's Logan, Mingo, and McDowell counties. The most compelling cases for keeping corporate greed in check balanced with workers' rights and environmental laws is the Matewan Massacre and the Battle of Blair Mountain.

In Mingo County, West Virginia the coal mines in the sleepy town of Matewan were operated by a ruthless coal operator – the Stone Mountain Coal Company – that resorted to hiring a private police force, who were really nothing more than armed thugs, to kill union organizers who tried to help miners join the UMW. The Stone Mountain Coal Company owned everything in Matewan. Its owners were like feudal lords ruling as petulant monarchs over the fiefdom of Matewan. Theirs was the only game in town – a town in which they owned everything, even the church pulpits that Sunday sermons were preached from. The miners were beholden to their employer for expenses – their tools, train fare, tool repair, fuses, caps, and powder – all of which the company-owned stores sold them at hyper-inflated prices. The little remaining wages left were paid in company scrip, a non-negotiable currency good only at the company store for non-work items essential for survival: food, clothing, and household goods. Additionally, the miners were forced to work under duress. They were under constant threat of violence from the Baldwin-Felts Agency – a ruthless outfit of mercenaries for hire on the payroll of the Stone Mountain Coal Company to protect its monopolistic interests and maintain feudal paternalism.

The only option the working class residents had was to flee penniless to the mountains if they didn't like the yoke of serfdom imposed on them by the coal company. Although a rugged, independent life free of servitude to greedy coal barons would have been preferable, it was a choice that did not come easy to make.

Classism was present even in the heart of Appalachia: the miners looked down on those whom were derided as "trash." This sort of caste system was a very effective form of social control. It served to restrict the miners' options by being a strong social deterrent to simply leaving.

When the UMW escalated its campaign to unionize the mines in Logan, Mingo, and McDowell counties, coal operators retaliated by hiring the Baldwin-Felts Agency thugs to stifle all union activity. Those who did try to join the UMW were evicted from their company-owned homes with no money and nowhere to go; forced to seek refuge under crude canvass shelters in the hills. The coal company's hired mercenaries shot at those encamped in the hills.

Matewan Police Chief Sid Hatfield sympathized with the miners and rightfully viewed the actions of the coal companies as reckless and in violation of the law. When thirteen "detectives" from the Baldwin-Felts outfit stepped off the train in Matewan to evict the miners from their homes, Sid Hatfield stood ready to arrest them for illegal eviction papers. The confrontation proved fatal. Shots were fired as the miners of Matewan returned the favor, giving the Baldwin thugs a "lead diet" of their own. Twenty people died on May 19th 1920 in the Massacre at Matewan, including Matewan's mayor Cabell Testerman.

Sid Hatfield had previously been called as a witness by the Senate committee appointed to investigate the conditions in the coalfields of Mingo County. Hatfield and several Matewan miners were indicted for the shooting deaths of at least three of the Baldwin-Felts goons, one of which was the brother of Tom Felts – partner/owner of the Baldwin-Felts Agency. Sid Hatfield was ordered to stand trial in the neighboring McDowell County, which was known to be a lot more sympathetic to coal mine owners than to the miners. But Hatfield never made it to his trial. On August 2nd 1921, Sid Hatfield and his right-hand man, Ed Chambers, were gunned down on the McDowell County courthouse steps by Baldwin-Felts agents. Hatfield and Chambers were unarmed. But it wasn't over. Minister John E. Wilburn said, "It's time to lay down the Bible and pick up the rifle."

On August 20th 1921, over 600 armed men gathered in Kanawah County. By August 24th, their ranks swelled to 13,000 miners and their sympathizers – including the notable Mary Harris Jones, the patron saint of working class America. The miners proceeded to march towards "Bloody Mingo." They donned red bandanas to differentiate who was on their side and who was for the coal company, thus earning the nickname of "rednecks."

The Boone County sheriff let them walk right through his county without incident. But Logan County sheriff Don Chafin saw things differently. His deputies, together with Baldwin-Felts mine guards – a total of 1,500 company men – dug trenches and encamped on Blair Mountain waiting to open fire on the miners. A few skirmishes broke out between the two factions on August 27th, but by August 29th a full scale war erupted.

The Battle of Blair Mountain was the largest armed insurrection since the Civil War. President Warren G. Harding declared martial law and sent in US troops and Air Corps to quell the insurrection. The US government dropped bombs on Blair and the neighboring town of

Sharples. By September 3rd 1921, federal soldiers arrived to find the miners leaving. Most of the miners had served in the US military in World War I and were not inclined to shoot at fellow veterans – even if they were on opposite sides of the Battle of Blair Mountain.

Ironically, the historic battleground and grave site of Blair Mountain faces a different battle involving greedy coal operators: permanent destruction from mountaintop removal. This socially irresponsible tactic for getting all the "black gold" out of Appalachia threatens the drinking water of southern West Virginia and its neighboring states as well as the entire ecosystem of the mid-Atlantic and eastern United States. Once mountains are blown up, they're gone for good. But greedy coal operators and the land leasing companies don't care. To them, the communities, the flora and fauna, the delicate balance of nature and the ecological stability provided by the Appalachian Mountains are as disposable as the people who live there.

Although the coal company succeeded in keeping the union out temporarily, it was a Pyrrhic victory just as in the case of the Pullman strike. The public resented greedy corporate fat cats who felt they could treat everyone any way they pleased. But the railroads and coal mine outfits were not the only corporate elites whose blood-stained wealth and lavish lifestyles were bought and paid for with the blood of America's poor.

The garment and textile factories in the big cities were sweatshops that had no regard for fair play, or for the safety and well-being of the millions of poor women and children who toiled in them for barely enough pay to help support their families.

Women and children employed in the sweatshops were paid piece rate. They had to work 50-60 hours per week. They were required by their employers to pay for the electricity used to power the sewing machines, which they also had to lease from their employers. They were even charged a fee for the use of their stools and work benches at which they sat to work! These factory workers were also required to take work home with them for completion that could not be done on the sewing machines (buttons, etc.). Just as with coal operators and railroads, greedy factory owners used threats, physical abuse (beatings were not uncommon) and any other means necessary to intimidate the women and girls to dissuade them from joining a union.

The women and girls were subject to daily searches to ensure that they were not stealing anything from their employers. Workers were docked pay if they went to the bathroom. Leaving the assigned work station was prohibited; any worker who did so was fired. It should be noted that the humiliating indignities of random employer searches and docked pay for going to the bathroom have made their ugly resurgence by employers today. Workers were also locked inside the factories with no provisions for exiting in the event of emergency, such as fire or earthquake. The most horrific result of this practice was evidenced in the infamous Triangle factory fire.

On March 11th 1911, a fire broke out in the Triangle Shirtwaist Company located on the 8th, 9th, and 10th floors of the Ascher Building in Manhatten, New York. The fire was caused by faulty wiring in an electric motor in one of the sewing machines. The only exit was the elevator, but the fire blocked the path and interfered with the elevator's operation. The factory doors had been locked to prevent the workers from leaving. A total of 146 desperately poor workers, most of whom were women and girls, perished. They plunged ten stories to their deaths as they jumped from the windows trying to escape the inferno. Those who did not jump burned to death inside.

When the owners of the Triangle Shirtwaist Company were investigated under an inquest, they were found "not guilty" of any wrong-doing and agreed to pay the victims' families $75 each. When the factory bosses were asked about the locked doors and other policies that physically prevented workers from being able to leave the premises in the event of an emergency, their response was that those practices were to prevent employee theft. Corporate policies just like that have re-emerged in low-wage America today, as evidenced by the recent case involving Wal-Mart. (Poor people have always been stereotyped as thieves.)

The growth of unions gradually helped improve the lives of some of America's working class, but not all. Well into the 1930's, many working class Americans still lived in poverty and insecurity without any safety net if something happened to them. Safety nets were non-existent until President Franklin Delano Roosevelt's "New Deal" programs that put the destitute to work in the Public Works Program during the Great Depression and the Old Age Security Act (social security) so that workers (and widows) wouldn't suffer the indignity of destitution in their twilight years. And even that didn't go far enough because it failed to encompass all of the jobless poor. The Republicans, the political party of the rich who decry safety nets for the poor as socialism and who beat their "personal responsibility" drums, have been endeavoring to dismantle social security for America's old, widows, and the disabled ever since.

Chapter 9

"To write is to wage a war." ~ Voltaire

After World War II, unions had gained a strong toehold. More Americans were able to live comfortably, realize upward mobility, and send their children to college than in previous decades. The prosperity of the post-war years was largely due to labor unions which fought for a living wage, acceptable working conditions, and the 40 hour work week with mandatory overtime pay. Unions and Roosevelt's "New Deal" programs also eliminated child labor. No one under age 16 was allowed to work more than part-time and all children up to the age of 18 had to attend public schools.

But the elite had a different agenda. The victories gained by unions, resulting in a large prosperous middle class, threw a monkey wrench in their designs. It took 30 years for the super rich to implement their global wealth hijacking scheme.

During the 1950's, the government focused on fighting the spread of Communism. Even though Soviet Russia had been our ally in World War II against fascists in Nazi Germany, they suddenly became our deadly enemy. Since fascism and Communism are diametrically opposed political systems, the enemy of our enemy became our "friend." At the end of World War II, it was agreed that Soviet Russia could take over the Balkans. Croats, Serbs, and Bosnians learned to live together in relative peace and the birth of their new nation was Yugoslavia, presided over by Josip Broz Tito. The Allied Forces were agreeable with this arrangement. But almost immediately, the Cold War was on as the world's capitalists' fight against Communism began in earnest.

The "Red Scare", resulted in countless entertainers, movie producers, intellectuals, and writers getting blacklisted if they openly espoused any opinions supporting social programs for America's poor and measures of social equality between races and the sexes. Senator Joe

McCarthy stepped up the efforts of the House Committee on Un-American Activities.

Any sympathy for the poor, for blacks and women who were being discriminated against for educations and good jobs, any peep against segregation was silenced with the cudgel of "Communist." You were un-American if you held such views. If you were suspected of being "un-American" you were thrown out of your job and blacklisted from getting another. You could even find yourself imprisoned on trumped up criminal charges. In extreme cases you could even end up accused of espionage for selling atomic bomb secrets to the Soviets and executed for treason – like Ethel and Julius Rosenberg.

The "evidence" against the Rosenbergs was more flimsy than a used Kleenex. Of course, the Rosenbergs were poor and staunch anti-capitalist in their politics. The Rosenbergs met their deaths in the electric chair at Sing-Sing prison, leaving their two young sons, Robert and Michael, orphaned. Because of who their parents were, many suitable adoptive parents within the American Jewish community were reticent to take the Rosenberg children in until finally Ann and Abel Meeropol adopted the sons of Ethel and Julius Rosenberg. Sympathy for America's disenfranchised is as un-American as the "godless Communists."

In 1959 when America saw a burgeoning middle class, 30% of Americans still lived in poverty despite the gains and social progress made by unions and Roosevelt's "New Deal." This was largely due to sex and race discrimination which kept good jobs out of reach for women and blacks. Women fared the worst. It took the Civil Rights laws during Lyndon B. Johnson's administration to gain a very small measure of equality for women and for blacks. It took Johnson's commitment to picking up where the "New Deal" left off, giving birth to a new vision: the "Great Society." Although Johnson did compromise a lot with Republicans and agree to a "guns and butter" agenda, and although his measures were paternalistic the Great Society programs saved countless poor people's lives and brought hope for the first time to America's poor.

Lyndon Baines Johnson was an ornery cuss who liked his whiskey and told it like it was. He didn't take any crap from anybody and sometimes he had to kick some asses to get stuff done. But for all his flaws, he tried his very best to be fair. The principle of fairness was important to Johnson. Coming from very humble roots, he knew firsthand the social injustice of poverty. This was why John F. Kennedy chose him as his Vice President. When Kennedy was assassinated, Johnson was sworn into office.

However, unlike Kennedy, Johnson wanted to tackle the issues of poverty and discrimination head on –not in a half-assed, half-hearted effort. He wanted to grab the bull by the horns and get to business. This earned Johnson a lot of political enemies.

Johnson experienced poverty firsthand, having grown up in rural Texas during the Depression. He knew what unfairness and injustice was and how crushing poverty can be. He came up the hard way and went to a public college. He resented the Kennedys who had never known poverty while proclaiming to be the mouthpiece for social justice in America. The Kennedys attended elite private schools and lived like royalty. Johnson felt that they were not doing enough to help alleviate crushing poverty in America. Johnson once said to Ambassador Carl T. Rowan in reference to Robert Kennedy, "When's the last time that son-of-a-bitch ever had to miss a meal?"

After Johnson declared war on poverty from the broken steps of a front porch in the heart of Appalachia, he was a force to be reckoned with. Anyone in his cabinet suspected of dragging their feet on the important goal of poverty reduction was promptly given "the Johnson treatment" – some forceful motivation framed in terms that were not polite.

Under Johnson's watch, programs such as AFDC (welfare) and Medicaid were created as entitlement programs to provide *some* bare minimal support for America's poor – those who had been economically excluded during the New Deal era and throughout the rising prosperity brought by unions in the 1950's. Programs such as Head Start, which provides preschool to countless low-income children, were implemented. Other Great Society programs included Job Corps, which provided paid training and GED preparation for disenfranchised youth from dysfunctional homes, and CETA which provided subsidized employment for the most socio-economically disadvantaged members of society. The GI Bill of Rights was extended to include something new: the Pell Grant and the Guaranteed Student Loan program to ensure that lower-middle class and poor people would have a chance to go to college and better their lives.

Johnson also cracked down on banks' practices charging excessive fees for basic banking services. He also implemented the Truth in Lending Act, bringing the banksters to heel. The Truth in Lending Act, known as Regulation Z, required banks to fully disclose to consumers in understandable terms all costs, fees, and conditions in connection with getting a mortgage. Johnson's administration was also responsible for passing laws prohibiting usury and for protecting consumers against unsafe products and corporate fraud.

Unfortunately, the Vietnam War debacle cost Johnson politically. It raised the ire of middle and upper class college kids because of the draft. Consequently, Johnson's popularity waned. It should be noted, however, that if it was only the sons of the poor who served in Vietnam only to return missing limbs or in body bags instead of America's fortunate sons, there never would have been a peace movement in this country. In fact, the only time a conservative administration ever ended a war was when Nixon brought the troops home from Vietnam in 1974. Do you think that would have happened if those sent to fight in the hellholes of southeast Asia were all poor, inner-city youth whose only real "career opportunity" was enlisting in the military during a time of war?

For all of his policy flaws, Lyndon Baines Johnson was the best president the middle class, the working class and the poor ever had. Poverty in America had been reduced from 30% in 1959 to an all time historic low of 11% by the time his term ended. Unfortunately for America, Lyndon B. Johnson's Great Society never got the full chance necessary to eliminate poverty and social injustice. His programs were cut short within less than a decade after Johnson left the oval office. In 1968, America got a new president: Richard "Tricky Dick" Milhouse Nixon, whose conservative agenda and cloth coat sporting wife made Protestant austerity and uncharitable treatment of the poor popular. Nixon began his administration by promptly dismantling some of Johnson's anti-poverty programs.

Corporate elites did not suffer hardship due to Johnson's Great Society programs. The rich always lived well. But they still weren't happy that workers had to be paid a minimum wage (a middle class wage if they were union). They found a new way to generate obscene wealth for themselves without having to work for it, without having to produce or create anything to earn it. Part of their plan was to create a desperate workforce and the only way to do that was to cause more poverty to ensure that there would never be enough jobs to go around for everyone who needed one and to depress the wages of existing jobs. By creating massive poverty, they could create unprecedented and unimaginable wealth for themselves. This plan took 30 years to unfold.

The execution of this plan picked up steam after late former president Ronald Wilson Reagan, a one-time B-rated ham movie actor. It began with Reagan's slashing of federal funding for the social programs implemented by Johnson to help the poor – those least able to economically fend for themselves. It was Reagan's emotive propaganda that turned public sentiment against the "undeserving" poor included the mythical "welfare queen" – a black woman decked out in designer clothes and jewelry loading up her Cadillac with the best foods in the supermarket while working class stiffs scraped to afford Hamburger Helper.

Reagan also used effective race-baiting in justifying cuts to the CETA programs like the Job Training and Partnership Act (JTPA), VISTA, and Job Corps. He implied that only able-bodied black men benefited (at everyone else's expense) from subsidized employment and job training programs. Reagan referred to young inner-city black males as "strapping young bucks" who didn't need a taxpayer handout and preferential treatment in getting chances for jobs. It did not matter that economically disadvantaged white people also benefited enormously from the CETA programs. These Great Society programs gave underprivileged and disadvantaged job seekers a chance where they otherwise had none because they lacked access to middle class familial support and social networks.

The funding cuts to CETA were implemented during one of the worst job markets in American history: the recession of the 1980's. Since classism fueled racism and sexism, and has always permeated American society, turning public sentiment against the poor was easily accomplished. Reagan single handedly created a homeless population never before seen or imagined in America when he slashed the budget for the Department of Housing and Urban Development (HUD) by 75% from $32 billion in 1981 to $7.5 billion by 1988. HUD was the main provider of subsidized housing for the poor. By the end of Reagan's second term in 1988-1989, only one quarter of all poor US households got any kind of housing subsidy. Of the very few poor who get rent vouchers, half of them returned the vouchers unused because they couldn't find any affordable housing.

Reagan overhauled the IRS tax code to reduce incentives for developers to create low-income housing for poor families and individuals. Under the direction of "Silent" Sam Pierce, Reagan's HUD appointee, the lion's share of HUD funds were redistributed from low-income housing to the private sector for the enrichment of developers, banks, and real estate investors while the poor didn't get any decent affordable housing at all. The number of people living below the federal poverty line rose from 24.5 at the beginning of Reagan's term to 32.5 million in 1988. But no one cared. Blue-collar middle class union workers applauded the cuts in programs for America's poor and most vulnerable. Democrats helped drive the Reagan Revolution and never restored the budget cuts to undo the misery inflicted on the poor.

The Democrats haven't just turned their backs on us after the most recent election of President Obama and an overwhelming majority of Democrat Congressmen. This has been going on for over 30 years since the Reagan Revolution. The Democrats didn't just sit on the sidelines hand-cuffed to the bench as helpless bystanders while conservatives in Congress and the Reagan administration played a game of "let's make the poor even poorer and more degraded and miserable."

Reagan had to work with a Democrat-controlled House of Representatives in Congress in order for his trickle-down policies and draconian cuts to social programs to get passed and enacted. There were <u>no</u> policies enacted during Reagan's two-term presidency that did not first meet the approval of the Democrat-controlled House.

And these guys were not elected by some Fairy Godmother — middle class votes, many from middle class white males in good-paying union jobs (that were and still are denied to poor women) put them in office based on their promise to cut already meager and inadequate welfare benefits, which disproportionately hurt poor women and children and the disabled. Blue-collar middle class union men who drank the Kool-Aid as they sucked up every word of Rush Limbaugh, an over-privileged gas bag who made his pile by peddling his gospel of hate for the poor, for "illegal" immigrants, and for women from his media pulpit.

The middle, upper-middle, and upper classes were Reagan's electoral foot soldiers. The 1980′s was a time when the young (Gen-Xers) comprised a greater proportion of people living in poverty than at any point after the Great Society programs of the 1960′s.

After Reagan's two terms followed by Poppy Bush, the network of safety nets for America's poor was unraveled. From 1980-1991, social programs for the poor (as miserly and inadequate as they were) got defunded and were subjected to brutal budget cuts:

- 14.7% from maternal and child health care.
- 69% from job training and subsidized employment programs (CETA) for the most socio-economically disadvantaged of any race, age or gender.
- 94% from rural and urban community service grants.
- 81% from subsidized housing (HUD) for the poor.

- 100% blanket denial for SSI benefits for low-income elderly and/or disabled whose earnings and social security credits are insufficient to qualify for regular social security.

Ironically, the same white male blue-collar middle class union workers whose votes for Reagan supported cuts to poor welfare mothers were the same men who dodged their child support obligations. They were also the same men who discriminated against women for equal opportunities in male dominated jobs that paid a decent wage, and who were too selfish to marry and financially support the women they claimed to love as they strung them along for years in relationships that never seemed to go anywhere while dangling the commitment carrot. I know because I lived through this and I observed this hypocrisy first-hand as the only woman in the local plasterers' union from 1989-1991. Male chauvinism and classism cloaked by the "respectability" of socially conservative ideology is enough to turn any poor woman into an angry cynic.

I heard the men I worked with constantly complain about the paltry child support payments they resented making because it took away from their beer and entertainment money. I heard them advise each other on how to get out of paying support; how to skip state and stay under the radar. These same men who didn't want poor women to have an equal chance for a good job in the construction or manufacturing union jobs in order to support themselves, begrudged poor women the benefit of economic support through marriage and commitment. They also begrudged poor women any miserly welfare benefits and child support for the children they abandoned — along with the women who bore them.

During the mid to late 1980's when the war against poor women and children began in earnest, a poor single mother with 2 kids (like Dr. Donna Beegle) got a whopping $408 a month in welfare cash benefits in addition to food stamps and Medicaid. Since food stamps can only be used for food, that paltry monthly welfare check had to cover the rent, utilities, transportation costs, and toiletries. The average rent for a small two bedroom apartment back then was $395 a month, leaving whole whopping $13 left over for the entire month to pay the utilities, buy soap, tampons, and toilet paper. Minimum wage "pink collar" jobs without benefits did not – and still do not – pay enough to afford these basic needs. Most men never cared if women and children starved and died out on the street with nothing.

Reagan was successful in demonizing the poor and the mainstream media did more than its fair amount of conning the majority of blue-collar middle class voters into accepting the gutting of safety nets for the poor. After those of us in poverty were thrown to the sharks, Reagan turned his demagoguery against the blue-collar middle class by taking aim at unions. Reagan fired all the unionized air traffic controllers who were on strike. He claimed that unions were too greedy; that union workers were "lazy" and that unions were corrupt and interfered with freedom and liberty in America – the land of the "free market."

Reagan, the mouthpiece for America's rich and shameless, told white-collar middle class professionals that in order for every American to prosper, we had to move towards a merit-based society and away from unions and welfare handouts. He passionately intoned that we needed to untie the hands of the corporate elite so that they could create more good jobs and make college-educated middle class workers even more prosperous. He claimed that this had to be accomplished by lifting the restrictive laws that had given too much power and control to the unions. Reagan insisted that unions protected those who did not contribute to the making of America's wealth – that most union members were slackers and goldbrickers.

White-collar middle class workers bought into it hook, line, and sinker. They fell for the classic carrot on the stick; the false promise that if they were highly educated with marketable skills, there would be room for them in the promised land of wealth and prosperity. This is the oldest con job since the dawn of civilization, and America's "best and brightest" fell for it. They drank the Kool-Aid. It was an elaborate form of bait and switch – and it worked. The white-collar middle class was at loggerheads with the blue-collar middle class and both were firmly pitted against the poor.

The Baby Boomers who had been the free love; the peace, pot and microdot indulging, body painting, anti-war draft card burning protesters of the 1960's and 1970's exchanged their idealism for materialism in the 1980's. The only peace they cared about was getting their piece of the American pie, at anyone else's expense. They swapped their ponytails for Armani suits, and traded their tofu for country club memberships.

This same generation that had been the hippies, the provokers of social consciousness, became the shallow, self-centered yuppies of the 1980's and 1990's. The same people who fought for the passage of *Roe v. Wade* so women had the same sexual freedom as men with choices regarding unintended pregnancies; voted for two conservative presidents in a row whose policies and US Supreme Court appointees led the attack on reproductive choice, and slashed funding for birth control pills and abortions for poor women – those who can least afford to get pregnant and dumped. Medicaid funding for abortion was eliminated. This left poor women who found themselves pregnant – even from rape – without any options outside of forced birth.

But the men responsible for being the co-conceivers faced no consequences, and suffered none of the social ostracism suffered by the women and their children. Why isn't there any outcry and stigmatization of the selfish "pump and dumpers" that got women pregnant after lying to them just to get into their pants, and then abandoned them and their unborn babies? Women have less access to abortions because well-heeled churches backed the "moral majority" of the conservative party, which holds that life begins at conception. These wealthy powerful groups poured billions into political campaigns to take away women's human rights, draped in the habiliments of "pro-life family values." But their treatment of women, their social policies in particular, reek of sadism and misogyny. Life begins at conception but ends in the hospital delivery room – as evidenced by the Welfare Reform Act of 1996. If the "sanctity of life" means so much, why aren't poor women compensated decently for being forced to give birth (even in the event of rape) without any regard for how the "reproductive livestock" feels about it and for the risks of whether or not they survive the ordeal undamaged?

Those Boomers who lived in hippie squats in their youth, who protested the draft during the height of the Vietnam War; had no problem with social injustice for up and coming generations. They didn't care if America's poor and underprivileged were deprived of opportunities to get college educations and were disproportionately sent off to war because the only jobs available to them offering any health and dental benefits were in the US military. So much for the Boomers' legacy of anti-war, equal rights for women, and bold anti-establishment activism: Greed and the culture of "me-ism" prevailed.

My generation was outgunned at the voting booth by Boomers whose votes elected Reagan (twice) followed by George Herbert Walker Bush whose policies of "voodoo economics" resulted in the foreclosure of the American Dream. My generation's concerns for affordable college educations and enough good jobs for everyone and help for the poor were dismissed. No one cared. In the wake of rampant corporate downsizing and age discrimination in a depleted job market, many Boomers are finally seeing the light. The economic, social, and trade policies set in motion during the 1980's and 1990's are now coming back to bite the self-indulgent spoiled Boomers and the rest of the upper-middle class in their egotistical asses.

So now the chickens have come home to roost. The formerly middle class "99ers" are whining louder than anybody about the unfairness of their newfound poverty, after decades of telling those of us in poverty to "stop whining" about our problems because "nobody wants to hear it." They cry how they can't take a minimum wage job because it pays less than their unemployment benefits, yet they expected poor women who never had anything and whom they've helped pitch off of welfare to work at those same minimum wage jobs without health benefits and pensions that aren't enough to live on since the beginning of the War On the Poor began in 1980. They cry the loudest about the raw deal they're now getting while never giving a damn about those of us who were far worse off than them all long. The only sympathy they'll get from me is out of the dictionary: between "shit" and "syphilis."

The nefarious plan of poverty by design and the subsequent hardships suffered by the lower classes with assaults on social programs for the poor and attacks on workers' rights was referred to by the heavy metal band *Megadeth* as the "foreclosure of a dream." The 1980's launched a new era: the "Me" era. It's fuck your buddies; use, abuse and dump poor women, and send your mother a card once a year on Mother's Day – it's all shit.

The white-collar middle class, who have always been the status-seekers and social climbers, were blinded by their own classism. They didn't need much convincing to go along with the program because they thought there was something in it for them. They jettisoned the blue-collar middle class whom they had always looked down on with contempt. They voted along the same lines as the elite, resulting in NAFTA, GATT, and CAFTA and other globalization "free trade" treaties which cost millions of Americans their jobs. Their votes eviscerated safety nets for the "rabble" and promoted globalism to our national detriment.

While many older workers from Mack Truck, Bethlehem Steel and countless other factories had vested pensions and enough economic security built up over the years to maintain their middle class lifestyles, many others did not. They were caught between the devil and the deep blue sea because they were in their 40's with 25 years to go until they could collect social security, but they were not welcome in new careers when joblessness forced transition on them. They were too young to retire and collect social security, but too "overqualified" for getting hired anywhere else – except as minimum wage Wal-Mart greeters.

When they complained about their lack of economic security and the financial dire straits they found themselves in, they were told by affluent college educated elite to "stop whining." They were told that if they couldn't get good jobs, it was their own fault for being too uneducated to be able to compete. But none of the "experts" had an answer for this dilemma: Not everyone can be a doctor, a bank president, a lawyer, a NASA scientist, a computer guru, a college professor, or a CEO. So what are the rest of us supposed to do? How were we supposed to live?

There weren't enough jobs that paid a living wage and had health benefits to go around for everyone before all the off-shoring began. Entire groups of people were economically left out and hence, were poor. In the wake of globalization and elimination of welfare entitlements for the poor, the "great unwashed" is even more desperate. With fewer and fewer jobs to go around now more than ever before, and more and more job seekers competing for each job, how is a trade or a college education going to solve *that*?

The "experts" also overlooked the fact that a country without a strong manufacturing base, a nation that puts the employment of illegal immigrants and foreign "guest" workers ahead of its own poor and jobless citizens cannot adequately support a service oriented economy. It doesn't matter if things made in the maquiladora zones and other nations overseas are cheaper. Do you really think that matters to the growing numbers of Americans struggling in abject poverty that they can get a $3,000 laptop computer for only $700 when even $700 is out of reach for them? It doesn't matter if you don't have a job because you could never afford the $700 computer anyway.

Many displaced blue-collar workers had to downsize every aspect of their lives and settle for a lot less just to be able to survive. They sold the homes they loved, their second cars, their swimming pools, and many of the nice things they acquired after a lifetime of work. They raided their kids' college savings just to be able to keep afloat and not end up homeless, bitterly telling their kids that they were on their own to pay for college. They took jobs that previously would have gone to disadvantaged youth and adults, bumping those out who had the least security in society and who had suffered the worst under Reaganomics. Many of these downwardly mobile workers weren't gracious about it. Being middle class, they were infused with entitlement attitudes – they felt they were owed the good life while others are not. They felt that the low wage jobs without health benefits and pensions weren't good enough for them – even though they had no problem taking those "survival jobs" away from the poor (who got shoved out).

The poor weren't getting any chances for jobs at all. The poor felt entitled to just be able to live because nobody asked to be born into this society. In their view, these ungrateful middle class workers were taking the "survival jobs" away from them while those same middle class workers complained that the jobs weren't good enough for them. The downwardly mobile middle class often collected more in unemployment benefits than the working poor earned by working 50 hours a week at Wal-Mart's. Not surprisingly, the long-term jobless poor who had never gotten any chances at all resented the downwardly mobile middle class for whining when the middle class never had any sympathy for those of us who know what it means to have nothing.

Corporate elites further demoralized the downwardly mobile middle class workers by throwing it in their faces that if they didn't like their new digs in low-wage America; a hundred poor people stood ready take their place in a minute. The creation of massive poverty, a desperate workforce struggling to survive is a social Darwinist society called "free market capitalism."

By the late 1980's in throughout the 1990's, the white-collar upper-middle class saw their stock portfolios grow as corporate profits surged from all of the elimination of good paying blue-collar jobs that had been off-shored. The "greed is good" attitude had taken a firm root. America degraded to a hedonistic society with fewer morals than jackals; a law-of-the-jungle society of "every man for himself." Those who weren't able to get a chance and make it were spit on and discarded.

Homeless shelters and soup kitchens began seeing an influx of more people daily that were not the stereotypical homeless person. The "new poor" were not bag ladies, drug addicts, alcoholics, or mental patients. These over-burdened private charities were seeing a lot of families – mostly women and children – from the lower social classes who just couldn't get a chance. Lyndon B. Johnson's "Great Society" lost out to greed. Previous generations who cared enough about the poor no longer saw it as society's obligation to help those who weren't getting a fair chance and consequently, who could not economically fend for themselves. America went from a society seeking to attain fairness for all to a nation that worships at the altar of Mammon.

The middle and upper classes elected Reagan twice because they wanted a Congress and president who would undo the safety nets for America's poor. They hated the poor and sneered that if they were suffering it was their own fault. They told the poor that the ticket out of poverty was a college education. Meanwhile, Reagan's policies followed by those of his successor George H.W. Bush, favored the rich by sticking it to the poor. College was made unattainable for the poor and put further out of reach for the lower-middle class with the passage of the Gramm-Rudman Bill.

The Gramm-Rudman Bill slashed funding for Pell grants and student loans. This act of Congress also restricted Pell grants and student loans to certain post-secondary institutions, the amounts of student aid were capped and time limits were established that effectively put grad school out of reach for the majority of America's poor. The ability to get student loan debt discharged under a bankruptcy was eliminated in the event a college grad was unable to get a job that paid enough to be able to live plus repay student loan debt – which disproportionately hurts those among America's ranks of underprivileged the worst. All of these assaults on the middle class and the poor transpired during a time when a college education was becoming increasingly vital for obtaining employment in jobs that pay enough to lift individuals and families out of poverty.

In conjunction with the ramifications of Gramm-Rudman, banks and lending institutions were deregulated – bringing back the usury practices and abuses seen prior to Johnson's passage of the Truth in Lending Act. As a result of deregulation, banks were allowed to charge exorbitant rates and fees for home mortgages and set the interest on student loans much higher than Johnson's Guaranteed Student Loan program had ever intended – putting college further out of reach for the lower half of society.

Meanwhile the cost of a college education soared, surpassing the increasing cost of living. The poor were told to "pull themselves up by their bootstraps" by starting their own businesses or by getting educations in order to be "worthy" of a middle class life; never mind the fact that it takes money to start a business and most small businesses fail within the first two years. But until now when the economy collapsed in 2010, nobody wanted to hear it.

Many poor people (mostly low-income women) who *did* go into unaffordable college loan debt ended up strapped and trapped in poverty's vicious cycle. Many never got chances for a good job at all despite "doing all the right things." Their student loans went into default, destroying their credit, barring them from most jobs above minimum wage, and even resulted in garnishments on the social security disability benefits for those were disabled. Student loan defaults also barred them from eligibility in many state funded job placement programs that sprung into existence – after the loans defaulted from long protracted fruitless job searches.

The chasm between the "haves" and "have-nots" grew wider. Upward mobility had ended. Recent data showed that the likelihood of success and access to the good jobs were high for those hailing from affluent households, but were slim to none for those at the bottom. The competition for white-collar jobs requiring a college degree grew fiercer. Employers began requiring a Bachelor degree for jobs that only required a high school diploma 30 years ago.

The elite created even more unearned wealth for themselves by creating a bigger poverty trap for everyone else. They off-shored white-collar jobs just as they previously had with manufacturing. Tens of millions of jobs in high tech and finance were off-shored to foreign nations whose impoverished workers could afford to undercut our workforce because they had a much lower standard of living than Americans. By the late 1990's into 2001, countless computer programmers, software engineers, and database analysts were without jobs as a result.

Carly Fiorina, former CEO of computer giant Hewlett-Packard, led the rush in off-shoring good paying high tech jobs. During a Congressional hearing on off-shoring held on January 7th 2004, Fiorina addressed Congress members saying that, "There is no job that is America's God-given right anymore. We have to compete for jobs as a nation." The global rat race to the bottom was well under way, amidst tax cuts that disproportionately benefited the super rich that were paid for with cuts in spending for social programs for the poor to the point where any remaining help is practically non-existent. People with impressive degrees in information science and mid-level managers found themselves in the same boat as the uneducated blue-collar union workers whose American Dream was stolen out from underneath them. Ironically, these are the same people who still look down on the very poor and begrudge us access to health care and any adequate safety net.

The ranks of America's poor swelled as more and more formerly well-off highly skilled and well-educated people were downsized from a disappearing middle class. Today, one in four jobs are low wage jobs lacking health benefits with paychecks that are insufficient for lifting people out of poverty. The promise of the American Dream, that if you try hard enough and are willing to work hard enough and "live right" then you will be able to support yourself, has become a pipe dream. It's a dream because you have to be asleep to believe it.

One in four workers earn less than $8.70 an hour in jobs that provide little to no healthcare benefits, sick pay, paid vacation, or pension. And this is the lot for those who have not been completely shoved aside and economically excluded because of age and sex discrimination. For those who have been completely excluded from any adequate employment at all, the conditions of poverty are far worse because there are no safety nets remaining anymore to spare unemployable people from homelessness and destitution.

In spite of all this, the upper social classes still expect those struggling lower social classes to be responsible for saving money for emergencies and to accumulate enough wealth to be able to live during their old age years. They want to dismantle social security – the *only* means of preventing the majority of America's elderly, widows, and disabled from being utterly destitute. The premise is that during your younger working age years, you're supposed to set aside enough savings from each paycheck for your old age.

But just how are you supposed to be able to do that if you don't have a job, can't get one if no one will hire you, or if you don't make enough money working at some low wage job that doesn't pay enough to be able to cover rent, food, utilities, transportation and health care? Sure, saving is great – if you're one of the lucky ones to have a good job and if you can afford to save without having to live in a dumpster, a "tent city", or crammed into an overcrowded apartment with half a dozen of your low-income friends.

When workers are struggling between temp job assignments and can't get anything better, something is drastically wrong. When workers are struggling in jobs that pay a dollar or two an hour above the federal minimum wage and can't afford food, clothing, medical and dental care, and a modest roof over their heads, there isn't any money left over to save for anything. When those struggling in minimum wage jobs are living in "tent cities" and homeless shelters, society needs a wake-up call. If there was ever a time when our government needed some "Johnson treatment", it is now.

For those who are lucky enough to have even a low wage job as opposed to having nothing, there are minimum costs just to be able to go to work. First you need reliable transportation – your own car. This is especially true for those workers registered with temp agencies where each new job assignment varies in location and the shifts are not all 9-5. Many places are not located in areas accessible by bus and are in rural areas without any public transit system at all. Then there is the cost of having to get the proper clothes employers expect you to wear for the job. You must also be able to afford a phone. You can't get a job if you can't get phone calls for interviews, short notice hiring for temp assignments. Many employers demand that workers be available "on call" and that the workers be flexible enough to change scheduled work shifts on a moment's notice. This is impossible when you don't have a car, a place to live, and a telephone.

For those who are homeless, not having a place to bathe properly and keep their clothes clean presents an additional barrier to getting a job. But the average rent for a two bedroom apartment is well beyond reach for anyone making less than $8.70 an hour based on a 40 hour work week. Many workers are struggling trying to cobble together a living working two or three 15-25 hour a week jobs and find that work schedules often conflict. Try pulling yourself by your bootstraps under that scenario when you've got health problems. Try getting a job when you've been reduced to homelessness and have nowhere to go, can't bathe regularly and a trip to the Laundromat is a luxury that you don't have. Then come back and tell me that you wouldn't "whine and complain" if it was *you* that had to live like that.

Working parents need to be able to pay for daycare or after school care for their children in order to work – leaving children unattended carries the criminal charge of child neglect.

Low-income workers who are single are the sole breadwinners in their lives. Even though they may have only themselves to support, if something happens to them that takes away their ability to earn a paycheck, there is no spouse's income or child support check to fall back on – there's nothing. And there is no program to help them because people without kids rank lowest on the scale of "worthiness" for any help. One car breakdown, one illness or one injury and those who are all alone without any family network or spousal support safety net are sunk. Single people without kids are also taxed more heavily than any other group and they do not get the benefit of the generous Earned Income Tax Credit (EIC) that people with children get to offset their expenses of job training, undertaking an active job search, or getting to and from work.

Since Hurricanes Katrina and Rita devastated the Gulf Coast in 2005 combined with the ongoing Iraq War, gas and oil prices skyrocketed by an average of 41% within a single year in Pennsylvania alone. This priced millions of poor people out of being able to afford winter heating fuel and gasoline to put into their cars to get to and from work and afford food. Heating fuel prices are rising again. Those who have jobs are finding that they have to choose between food and gasoline in their old used cars for getting to their low-wage service jobs.

For those who are involuntarily jobless but not counted among the ranks of the officially unemployed, there is no income to be able to afford to sustain a long and fruitless job search. There are inherent costs associated with applying for jobs and going on interviews, even in an attempt to get hired in the most menial low paying jobs.

Making matters worse, Congress voted in 2006 to cut spending for the underfunded Low-Income Home Energy Assistance Program (LIHEAP) program in order to pay for tax cuts for the wealthy. The sparse remaining help available for poor people who are unable to afford their utility bills, is insufficient to prevent utility shut-offs. Countless more poor people who are LIHEAP eligible are turned away and cannot get any help at all. Gas and oil prices eat up so much of a poor person's income (for those who *do* have any income at all) that anyone not employed full-time making at least $15 an hour will not be able to afford to go to work.

A car is necessary for getting to school, job training, work, medical appointments, and the grocery store. Many areas across America are rural and have no public bus service. But it is not only the cost of oil, gasoline and periodic preventive maintenance and inspections fees that pose a hardship for those in poverty. There is also the cost of mandatory auto insurance which most poor people cannot afford, especially since auto insurance companies charge the poor more because of credit scoring in their rate tiering.

It is illegal to drive without insurance in every state except New Hampshire. Many states fine scofflaws heavily and even suspend the drivers' licenses of those who are caught driving without insurance. Since the price of auto insurance is higher than what the poor can afford, many working class people and unemployed job seekers hope and pray every time they get behind the wheel that they won't get caught because they've been forced to choose between car insurance and gasoline – both needed to get to work. For low-income people, there is no extra money to afford a savings account, a checking account, a 401(k) or an IRA. There isn't even enough money to afford all of life's most basic needs.

When too many people are hurting and can't afford anything, entire communities suffer. Small businesses fail, and the small business owner who finds himself or herself without a livelihood doesn't qualify for unemployment. Those struggling to make a living as self-employed are hit the hardest. They're simply shit out of luck. But our state and federal agencies have made no provisions to help them during tough economic times. And most of them cannot easily get hired at good jobs because being self-employed doesn't count as "real work experience" in the eyes of employers and corporations.

The fact is that there are not enough living wage jobs with any kind of security for every man and woman who desperately needs one. Browbeating poor people for being "losers" and telling them to "stop whining" won't make them less poor or lessen their hunger, illness, or homelessness. Just how are those without any money and jobs supposed to get a job when there aren't enough living wage jobs to ensure they'll get one? What good does it do to tell someone who's poor who *does* have an education (for which they can't repay their student loans) to get *more* education in order to get a job when they're being economically excluded because of age discrimination?

Many who have been economically left out *did* get college educations, trade school certificates, and job training – only to get denied chances for good jobs due to age and sex discrimination, in addition to classism and poverty profiling. When middle-aged job seekers are discarded like used Kleenex and no one will hire them, how are they supposed to be able to live? Just what exactly are you supposed to do when you've got 15-25 years to go until you can draw on the poverty level subsistence of social security?

One desperate geriatric gentleman from Columbus, Ohio held up a bank just so he could go to jail where he'd have a hot shower, a warm bed, and be assured of a meal until he could begin drawing on his social security benefit and get a modest apartment. On October 13th 2006, 62 year old Timothy J. Bowers quietly handed the teller a note demanding $80, then immediately handed the money to the security guards and sat down, politely waiting for the police. He had been unemployed for five years at this point. His meager life's savings had run out and he had lost his home while desperately trying to get another job. He saw no other alternative.

It's fine to tell poor people with varying levels of skills and educations to get a job – if the jobs are there for them and *if* the jobs paid a living wage. Thanks to corporate greed in the global theater, this is not the case.

The social and economic devastation visited upon American workers by greedy, megalomaniacal, globalist corporate big shots did not stop at increasing poverty and misery in the US by off-shoring most of our good paying jobs. The dystopia that America has become is a microcosm of what is unfolding around the world today. After the ultra rich were given the blessing by our complicit middle class and our sell-out government to siphon all of America's wealth upward in a reverse Robin Hood sort of way here in the US, the elite took their classless act (pun intended) of avarice and lust for power to the world marketplace. The working class and the poor in Greece, Germany, Great Britain and France are having "austerity measures" imposed on them.

Throughout the 1990's, petroleum giant Unocal (the company's orange and blue "76" logo is often seen at truck stops) gained enormous wealth in a little known Southeast Asian country known as Myanmar (formerly called Burma). Unocal paid the Burmese military, well known for its human rights abuses, to help Unocal and its partners forcibly remove peasant farmers from their lands without compensation in order to get 39 miles of land for running a gas pipeline. The pipeline was constructed by Burmese slave laborers who were forced to work under gunpoint and torture by the Burmese military. Punishment for attempting to flee and escape forced labor was torture and murder of the slave worker and his entire family.

International human rights lawyers filed suit based on the forgotten law drafted by our nation's founding fathers known as the Alien Torts Act of 1789 on behalf of eighteen Burmese peasant farmers. The Alien Torts Act of 1789 allows foreign nationals the right to sue for redress in US courts in the event of wrong-doing by American interests. The Karenni villagers of Burma told horror stories of abduction from their huts by the Burmese military, forced at gunpoint to "clear land mine areas" by running through rice patties where forgotten undetonated land mines were lodged, many losing their legs or their lives in the process. They testified how they were forced by soldiers to work without compensation clearing trails and building helipads on Unocal's pipeline project. They described in vivid detail how the Burmese military tortured and killed anyone who resisted. One woman testified that her husband tried to escape forced labor and as punishment for his attempt, she and their baby were thrown into a fire – resulting in permanently disfiguring injuries to her and the death of her baby.

Unocal claims no knowledge of these atrocities. However, remember that IG Farben, which benefited from Jewish slave labor and genocide in Auschwitz, also claimed no knowledge of genocide in the Holocaust. Human rights attorney Paul Hoffman didn't buy it. His position is that Unocal directly promoted, used or otherwise benefited from the Burmese military's atrocities committed against the people of Burma and that Unocal executives knew that slavery, property theft, torture and murder were occurring – and approved of it.

Another bad actor in the global "free market" is Chevron-Texaco. The gas and oil giant provided helicopters to Nigerian forces and helped plan an assault on unarmed, non-violent protesters on an oil platform nine miles off the Nigerian coast. Chevron-Texaco denies all allegations. No surprise there!

George W. Bush sought to repeal the Alien Torts Act. The president who called America's affluent "his base" had shown us the real evil-doers: America's corporate elite. America's ruling class wants to absolve itself of any liability and consequences for human rights violations committed in the name of "progress" and "free trade."

The super rich will never change. They will never be fair to the working class and the poor of this world without government intervention to keep their activities in check. They view the needs of the people as an economic nuisance. Since they could care less about the pillaging, torture, rape, forced labor and murder of poor Burmese or Nigerian villagers, do you think they give a damn about *you*? Do you think that without the restraint of government that they wouldn't do the same here on American soil if given the chance?

Why should you believe them when they say cheap foreign labor makes necessities affordable for you when they've already priced you out regardless because you no longer have a job or a chance of getting a job to be able to afford their crap in the first place? Give more to the ultra rich and it will eventually trickle down to you sometime during your lifetime? Newsflash: what trickles down on you won't be green!

The economic abuse of stealing people's land and homes by the robber baron class of the Gilded Age has returned with the infamous US Supreme Court case known as *Kelo v. New London, CT*. The premise that the robber barons of yesteryear stole people's farms and land via eminent domain abuse was the fact that railroads were providing a service to the public: the transshipment of goods. Therefore, it was seen as being for the "common good" of the people. In *Kelo*, a wealthy real estate developer was able to get restrictions of eminent domain use bent to his favor. In doing so, he used eminent domain to force several lower-middle class homeowners from their homes for a song – he didn't want to pay fair market value for prime land. He won and got the properties for a song. He erected a fancy office for some private enterprise and luxury condos for the rich. That is not justification for property grabbing under the guise of a public or common good. The US Supreme Court's vote 5-4 in the developer's favor rendered the 5th Amendment of the US

Constitution impotent and toothless. We can expect to see more abuses along this vein if justice is not restored to this nation.

If it were not for the "New Deal" programs, the gains in workers' rights made by unions, and Johnson's Great Society programs, poverty rates in America would be higher. And with the attacks on much of those over the last 30 years, abject poverty and 3rd World misery is rearing its ugly head on American soil and it is now harder to hide the truth, despite the blackout by mainstream media.

The same bad actors that siphoned America's wealth upward in a macabre reverse Robin Hood scheme during the Gilded Age are the same bad actors who off-shored jobs over the last 20 years to 3rd World countries without workers' rights or environmental laws where they routinely abuse, torture, maim and kill those nations' disposable impoverished workers. Do you really think the rich value your life better? If you believe that by supporting the agenda of the capitalist class that you will be invited to join them at their great table of wealth and prosperity, you're an idiot who ought to be arrested for possession of brains with intent to use. Just ask the Burmese victims of "Big Oil" cartels like Unocal.

Without the Alien Torts Act, the world is sent the message that American society condones rape, torture, slavery, and murder (in addition to the wanton destruction of clean water and farmlands) in the name of "free trade" in the global marketplace. And the fossil fuels cabal is not the only offending group.

Sweatshops in Indonesia and other forgotten corners of the world force poor workers to work until they drop dead from exhaustion – literally. Women and young girls are literally chained to their machines. They're paid an average of 34 cents an hour for making Armani suits and other high end designer clothing sold here in the US for prices only the rich can afford. How many middle and upper class people who can afford to buy high end designer clothing ever think about *that*? Do they ever think about the untold cost in terms of social misery and human casualties at which their wealth came to them when they look at their stock portfolios and see the burgeoning profits evidenced by stock appreciation of the underlying companies? Or do they brush that aside because all is fine in their own little worlds?

In order for there to be winners, there has to be losers. And the middle class never once felt they had an ounce of obligation to the losers. And now with the worst job market since the 1930's and a collapsing economy, many of these fortunate sons with their 401(k)'s are crying about how their retirement plans lost value in Wall Street's casino economy.

Capitalism by its nature and definition *must* exploit the environment and labor for profit. This leads to booms and busts — overproduction followed by underproduction in a cycle that has oppression, marginalization, exclusion, discrimination, poverty, and joblessness built into it. Capitalism is a self-devouring beast that cannot police itself, and, as the past 30 years have shown us, cannot be reformed. Any time throughout history where reforms were implemented, they were rolled back by the capitalist class.

Middle class Johnny-Come-Latelies need to take a good hard look in the mirror. They need to be a little less smug, a little less egotistical, and a hell of lot more humble. They need to see that they're now suffering the fate that they've condemned the poor to — the jobless poor as well as the working poor.

It was *you*, Middle Class America, who have always been the "king-makers." As a class *you* set up the criteria, the credentialism, the "charitable assistance" guidelines, the tests, the profiles for success and it was *you* who determined the "punishment" for those whom your beloved capitalist system failed. It was *you* who served as the taskmaster, the gatekeeper, the overseer, the gears driving the bureaucracy machine that runs the world on behalf of the rich.

Lack of access to housing, food, health care, and good jobs was never on your priority list before now because it never bothered you so long as it was "someone else's" problem — those of us in poverty who never got chances before being cut down by illness, injuries, and preventable disabilities from lack of access to health care these past 30 years. You didn't care when it was only the "undeserving poor" that were suffering. Instead, you told us to "pull ourselves up by our bootstraps." You said it was our own damn fault if we weren't making it and you told us to "stop whining" because you "didn't want to hear it."

Take some of your own "advice" that you've doled out to us all these years: accept your *nouveau pauvre* lot as the result of your "bad attitude" and if you change your attitude to a more socially acceptable one, you might be welcomed with open arms back into the middle and upper class fold. If you can't cope with your newfound miserable lot in life, the mind doctors are there to help you cope, adjust and accept your deprivation, losses, suffering and abandonment by society — a society which was of your making when you were a vacuous capitalist cheerleader defending the rich, who no longer have use for you.

What a travesty that the decimation of the middle class is newsworthy when it happens to people who previously cashed in on the unearned privilege system all these years at my expense as a poor woman from the underclass. You didn't have a problem with the injustices of capitalism until you were the ones staring down the barrel of capitalism's firing squad; after you got done making sure that I couldn't get what I needed, and after making life even more miserable for my impoverished "sisters" of color. And now, with the global economic jihad launched by your klepto-plutocratic free market gods, you're finally hurting and seeing capitalism for what it truly is in its ugly naked form after decades of being seduced into complicity by the beautiful side of evil.

It has not been presidents or lawmakers or even US Supreme Court judges who have historically secured any real freedoms, economic or otherwise, for the American people. They merely rode on our shirttails after all the head-busting, jailing, fighting, blacklisting, and dying was suffered by the rest of us. Those who fight for social justice have never been able to get that good job or become a politician. It has always been the poor who are the first to fight and die for the benefits that disproportionately accrue to the middle class, which the middle class is now rapidly losing. Yet, the poor never got as much as a 'thank you' from the high and mighty middle class. The only thanks we ever got was Welfare Reform, "Three Strikes" laws, mandatory minimum sentences, "faith-based" initiatives, no respect, no health care, no equal opportunity, and no guaranteed right to a living wage job.

What we got was punished for our poverty as we were kept poor and told over and over that weren't wanted in your neighborhoods, in your houses of worship, in your schools, or in your workplaces getting the same opportunities and making decent wages and getting the same decent health and dental benefits as you and your families got. While your children got to go to Disneyland, ours got sent to Prisonyland. While you traveled working for the Peacecorps feeling good about yourselves for all the "good" you did for poor brown children in countries that were victims of capitalism, we got sent to Iraq to kill other brown children at the behest of your capitalist gods. While you got your nice houses, nice clothing, new cars, and your health and dental needs met, we got to suffer and do without while being told how undeservedly large we were living off of your tax dollars.

What's happening to the middle class now is unquestionably horrible. But it is no more horrible than what the middle class condemned me to by virtue of its role as an enabler, apologist, justifier, enforcer, and reinforcer of capitalism. And throughout the entire time, you, Middle Class America, thought you were so smart and so special and so much better than someone like me — a "poor white trash" woman from the ranks of the underclass. And now you're finally starting to "feel the love" you've dished out to the poor and you're crying foul. In case you didn't get the memo: The owning class isn't all that into you. You're not special. You never were anything more than a number in their calculus of evil.

Anyone who thinks that poverty wasn't a problem after the New Deal and the post-war boom before now needs to research the state records of vital statistics where poverty-related deaths, such as treatable disease and starvation, claimed the lives of those in poverty that were not economically included in America's "almost golden" age of prosperity.

More than 30% of Americans were still living and dying in 3rd World poverty.

In the 1950's and early 1960's the state of West Virginia alone, which had been beleaguered by two centuries of paternalism by ruthless coal companies, reported approximately 200 deaths per year due to starvation. People actually starved to death in the US during the height of middle class prosperity. Deaths from sickness and starvation throughout Appalachia were directly the result of poverty from deliberate disinvestment and a manipulation of the labor market by greedy timber barons and coal operators who suppressed industry and opportunities for other jobs for the people by keeping other businesses out.

Comparisons between lawmakers' attitudes about the current poverty rate and that in 1965 when president Johnson launched the War On Poverty from the heart of Appalachia demonstrate just how far to the right political consensus has moved. No Democrat today in 2010 proposed even the slightest measure to alleviate the social holocaust of the burgeoning poverty ranks, never mind a serious mobilization of the nation's resources. Middle class "progressives" took 30 years too long to decide with team they were batting for. They tried to take the easy way out through pragmatism, thinking only of feathering their own comfortable nests within the capitalist paradigm while leaving the poor hanging out to dry.

In an updated Pew report[64] released on October 7th 2010, researchers found that 30% of the unemployed had been jobless for a year or longer. Based on the official unemployment rate, that translates to about 4.4 million people — roughly equal to the population of Louisiana. Most of these discarded workers were age 35 and older.

When President Obama was asked about the problem of growing poverty in the US during his September 24th 2010 press conference, he answered by parroting straight from the Reagan playbill, saying that "the best anti-poverty program is a job" — meaning that nothing should be

64 Pew Fiscal Analysis Institute, Addendum to "A Year Or More: the High Cost of Long-Term Unemployment", October 7th 2010

done to help those for whom the capitalist system could not and will not provide adequate employment. If the American people have any hope of getting real change, it won't come from the Madison Avenue false reality makers who have packaged Obama as the savior of the world.

Neither wing of the Capitalist Party proposed any policies for directly creating jobs for the unemployed, many whom the private markets won't hire: older workers, the very long-term unemployed, women, the poor, and job seekers with less than perfect health and less than perfect credit. Neither the Republicans nor the Democrats proposed anything to provide relief for the growing number of poor and unemployed people, or to alleviate the scourge of mounting utility shut-offs, hunger, and homelessness.

The Heldrich Center for Workforce Development at Rutgers University released a study on September 1st 2010 which revealed that among the jobless:

- 86% cut back in their family's spending
- 63% exhausted their retirement savings
- 60% had been forced to borrow from family or friends

How many jobless poor have no family to turn to for help, either because their families are also poor and unable to help, or because they have no living family left? How many jobless poor have selfish middle class families that won't lift a finger to help them because they don't want their resources being drained? Growing "tent cities" and the number of people that shelters must turn away because they're full provide a good clue. The US is one big plutocratic cesspool. Pragmatism by "progressive" politicians brought nothing but three decades of compromises in which it has always been the needs of the poor that were compromised.

Chapter 10

"If you can find money to kill people, you can find money to help people." ~ Tony Benn

People who have never been terribly poor over many consecutive years are not only blind to their own privilege; they're in denial about the reality of poverty. They think that "there's all this help out there" for the needy. But there isn't. Welfare caseworkers are actually paid to *deny* help to the poor, forcing the poor to fight for negligible aid. The safety nets have either been eliminated or had their funding slashed while need grew. Since only 20% of those who destitute enough to be eligible are getting helped, 80% are turned away. But nobody talks about those who are turned away.

Dr. Beegle pointed this out during her interview with Northwestern Regional Education Laboratories (NWREL). As long as the public thinks there are programs out there to help the poor, the public doesn't feel obligated to do anything. Many also feel that poverty is not *their* problem – it's the fault of the poor; the only group in America that is expected to take personal responsibility for everything that happens to them.

One of the main reasons the issues of classism and the social injustice of poverty are being examined now is because of the stalwart efforts by people like Dr. Donna Beegle. Another reason is that more and more formerly middle class people have fallen into poverty in this global rat race to the bottom. Dr. Beegle came from poverty. She now holds a PhD and works as a paid consultant to educators who find themselves stonewalled by the implications of "No Child Left Behind" (NCLB) mandates in high poverty school districts.

Under NCLB, school districts are penalized with funding cuts for schools whose standardized test scores fall below the levels mandated by NCLB architects. Educators face a no-win situation when they can't reach the students who are struggling in poverty because too many poor kids in crisis will drag down the overall test score for a particular school.

Since educators and administrators have not lived the daily crisis that living in poverty entails, they often don't understand why poor kids aren't able to complete homework assignments and focus in class, or why they miss a week of school at a time. They either don't make the connection or they don't care that the family in poverty doesn't have adequate living space so the child can have a stable and quiet place to do homework. Families in poverty have chaotic lives. Mom and dad are not able to take time to help with homework when every waking moment is consumed with just trying to survive. When you're scrambling to find/maintain shelter, put food on the table and keep utilities from being shut off, homework isn't a priority. Many poor families are doubled up in overcrowded living quarters – an environment not conducive to learning and academic success.

Dr. Beegle points out that poverty means that one thing going wrong triggers an avalanche of problems that compound and snowball. She cited the example of a school counselor doing home visits to a pair of elementary school twins that had missed nine consecutive days of school, and therefore falling hopelessly behind in class. The family was very, very poor and in a crisis. It began when the mother was pulled over by police for a burned out tail light while on her way home from her 3rd shift job at a donut shop. The mother's car insurance had lapsed for non-payment of premium, a common occurrence among low-income workers who are forced to choose between car insurance, gasoline to get to work, or the rent. Because the mom was caught driving without insurance, her car was impounded and her drivers' license was suspended. She was also fined heavily. As a result of losing her car and her drivers' license, she couldn't get to work and she lost her minimum wage job – her sole source of income. As a result of losing her low paying job, she was unable to pay the rent and the family was evicted.

The crisis and turmoil this family was in stemmed from just one problem: getting caught driving without insurance because the woman couldn't afford it in the first place, even though she needed to drive in order to get to her low wage job because there was no public transportation available and the woman had no other job opportunities that paid more. The end result was the children missing school after the family became homeless. Situations of desperation like this are not uncommon in post-welfare reform America.

The counselor and Dr. Beegle brainstormed. Dr. Beegle asked the counselor who she knew and how they might possibly be able to help this family, thus helping the kids stay in school and not fall even further behind. It turned out that the counselor's husband was the town's chief of police. Dr. Beegle asked the counselor to write a letter to the judge explaining the poor mother's situation emphasizing that the woman had no money to pay the fines and the severe hardship imposed on the family by the loss of her car and drivers' license, which is how the family ended up homeless and the children's education was jeopardized. The counselor wrote to the judge.

What Dr. Beegle did was ask this counselor to "open up her network" to the poor single mother who had no network, no social standing in the community. Since much of social class privilege hinges on whom you know, opening up networks is vital because poverty is socially isolating.

Beegle drove that point home when she emphasized her own elevated socio-economic status enabled her to open doors of opportunity for her son who had an avid interest in all things golf. Beegle pointed out that had she not been in a position to rub elbows with the right people, her son would not have been able to pursue his golf interest and turn his interest into a lucrative career designing golf courses for the municipality. But how would that scenario play out for those who are poor, who lack affluent social connections and clout?

The contact between the "haves" and "have-nots" is very limited and restricted. The only people those in poverty know and can socialize with are other poor people. The local bank president doesn't socialize with the janitor or the waitress at Dunkin Donuts. They live in different neighborhoods, have different entertainment options, and move in different social circles. The upper classes never wanted to rub elbows with the lower anyway.

The "haves" don't understand how lack of enough help to mitigate one problem leads to a cascade of more severe problems for those in poverty. When everything else goes wrong as a result of an initial or "trigger" problem and the shit really hits the fan, middle class people claim that there's all this help out there. The truth: there's not. The poor exist on the margins of society; reviled, ignored, and forgotten.

If there truly was enough help out there and if capitalism's system of unearned privileges weren't the problem, we wouldn't have so many Americans (mostly the elderly and the disabled on low fixed incomes) dying each winter from the cold because their utilities have been shut off for inability to afford the rates.

Deregulation of the energy industry has not only resulted in exorbitant prices, it has also resulted in utility companies' concealment of the number of shut-offs because they're no longer held to strict reporting standards. But the facts can only be obscured and hidden from public knowledge for so long before they surface.

As of 2002, a report from the Joyce Foundation showed that in the wake of welfare reform, the families who left welfare were still poor – if not poorer – than they were when they were on welfare. In Michigan, more than one million people fall within the federal poverty guidelines. The Joyce Foundation report showed statistics of both the working and jobless poor in America's Rust Belt show high percentages of people whose basic utilities had been shut off as of 2002:

- 15% of Wisconsin's poor
- 15% of Ohio's poor
- 25% of Indiana's poor
- 11% of Michigan's poor

The statistics for individuals and families who regularly go without food in order to pay unaffordable utility bills is triple that of those whose utilities had been shut off. In 1988, 37% of the poor got energy assistance from LIHEAP and what they got was enough to stave off shut-offs. In 2000, that percentage was less than 20% due to LIHEAP funding cuts – ironically at a time when more and more Americans were falling into poverty. The sharp rise in energy and fuel prices vastly outpaces the amount of help from LIHEAP and left more people with their utilities shut off.

According to the Rhode Island State Office of Energy Resources, the Division of Public Utilities and Carriers:

- Utility shut-offs in Rhode Island in 2007 reached a record number of 29,970 households.
- The cost to heat a typical home with oil this year is estimated to be $2,069.
- The estimated cost to heat with natural gas this year is $1,485.
- 24,000 – 25,000 households are expected to receive federal heating assistance from LIHEAP this year
- Households expected to receive help through the state's new heating assistance program: 0

In Pennsylvania, which has brutally cold winters with single-digit temperatures, extremely low-income disabled and elderly people who have been shut off must pay 50% (or more) of their past due balance to get service restored. The help they can get from LIHEAP isn't enough to cover that amount or even one month's worth of heating bills in the winter. And the increased rates are far more than their incomes can bear.

As of 2007, Pennsylvania Power & Light (PP&L) reported a 111% increase in the number of shut-offs while Met Ed reported an increase of 50%. For the winter of 2008-2009, the price of both natural gas and home heating oil will increase by another 30%, according to a Fox News report on Channel 43 in central Pennsylvania.

In 2002, nearly 30,000 households in Wayne County, Michigan suffered gas and electric shut-offs. The increasing number of people suffering without heat and power is due to deregulated utility monopolies, government's failure to protect the public from price-gouging, increased unemployment, and draconian welfare reform measures that severely reduced government assistance for those in crisis. During 2002, Michigan utility companies discontinued the Vendor Pay Program which protected the poorest of Michigan's poor from utility shut-offs. The Family Independence Agency which administered this program paid a portion of your utility bills until you were back on your feet again. Without this safety net, more and more poor people quickly fell behind on their utility bills and were left to freeze in the dark.

The numbers of people in crisis has risen after the unaffordable utility rate hikes in 2005 after Hurricanes Katrina and Rita. In 2007, oil and natural gas prices skyrocketed again; hurting even more Americans and this was caused by the greed of wealthy energy speculators and commodities brokers. But our government does nothing to protect the public from this sociopathic greed. It would rather wage illegal wars and make Haliburton executives richer, and bail out Wall Street financiers than spend one dime of taxpayer money on helping the most vulnerable and poor Americans who have been involuntarily socially and economically excluded.

Maureen Taylor, the State Office Chair of the Michigan Welfare Rights Organization told staff writers at *Critical Movement* magazine, "Being poor in the richest country in the world should not deny you the right to life. It does not justify you being killed in a house fire or freezing to death in the cold. These are crimes of poverty, and they happen every year."

In Philadelphia, Pennsylvania alone, 7,700 more households have been without heat since November of 2006. That month, 24 Philadelphians died of causes linked directly to gas shut-offs by Philadelphia Gas Works (PGW). PGW spokesman Doug Oliver blamed the rate increases on Hurricanes Katrina and Rita. Oliver whined, "We can't give away free gas." No one was asking PGW for free gas – just don't raise the rates so high that poor people die as a result of shut-offs from inability to pay unaffordable utility bills.

In February 2009, the *Erie Times News* ran a biased article denying the severity and frequency of utility shut-offs and the full impact on northwestern Pennsylvania's poor. The article only cited spokesmen for National Fuel, the gas utility monopoly that serves northwestern Pennsylvania — including Erie, half of whose population struggles to live on less than $20,000 a year. National Fuel's PR spin doctors lied, claiming that National Fuel does not, and has not, shut off service to those unable to pay their bills in the winter. They also claimed there was "plenty of help for those who are unable to afford their bills", citing LIHEAP and Greater Erie Community Action Center (GECAC) and National Fuel's LIRA plan (a miserly discounted gas bill whose reduction amount is based on the discretion of LIRA administrators). This left readers with the false impression that there's "all this help out there."

The article reeked with an odor of mendacity. The Erie newspaper never investigated the thousands of residents in Erie, Crawford, Mercer, and Warren Counties who have had their gas or electric shut off in the winter and who have not been able to get service restored once terminated. The *Erie Times News* failed to include stories from the region's poor who have suffered through Erie winters without heat, hot water, power, and cooking fuel. Winter house fires are reported as to being caused by kerosene heaters and lack of a smoke detector; not as a result of a lack of utility service.

GECAC is the main Erie social agency charged with dispensing help with utility bills through the Customer Assistance Program (CAP) program, the Neighbor-For-Neighbor Fund, and weatherization assistance for low-income homeowners. They always run out of funds, leaving many otherwise eligible applicants without any help. But no one is talking about those who are turned away, the ones who aren't getting helped.

Local news media whitewashes the reports of house fires that are directly related to utility shut-offs from unaffordable rates and a very real — not hypothetical — lack of adequate help. Poor adults without children rank lowest in priority of getting helped, including the disabled and elderly. Most are turned away. Many poor households with young children also don't receive adequate help due to funding shortfalls and capricious mechanisms for triaging the help that exists. One woman, wishing to remain anonymous said that she was offered three dollars from GECAC as help toward her electric bill. For many Pennsylvanians, the protection of final resort against either dying from the cold or in a house fire from unsafe alternative heating was Pennsylvania's winter shut-off moratorium. That moratorium was law until November 2004.

Act 201 (also known as SB 677) was passed by Pennsylvania lawmakers and signed into law by Democrat governor Ed Rendell on November 14th 2004 without the public's awareness. Act 201 removed the winter moratorium on utility shut-offs, leaving Pennsylvania's poor and most vulnerable citizens without any safeguard against losing life-sustaining utility service in the winter.

Two months before Hurricane Katrina, national Fuel raised its rates significantly. After Hurricane Katrina struck in 2005, the gas utility rates skyrocketed again by another 41%, pricing out Pennsylvanians on low fixed incomes — the disabled and senior citizens on social security. My husband and I were two of capitalism's victims from deregulation's unaffordable energy costs. With no unemployment benefit for me, no income at all other than my husband's $937/month social security check plus food stamps, we have been without our gas since October 31st 2005.

Before the rate hikes in 2005, we struggled to afford our monthly budget plan payment to National Fuel of $79/month for our gas for heating, hot water and cooking. After the rate hike, our payment on the LIRA plan shot up to $189/month, which we couldn't afford. The mortgage and tax escrow payment on our modest home in the poor side of town took $541/month out of the $772/month total household income we were getting at that time (as of 2008, the COLA adjustments on his social security brought us up to $937/mo which has not been raised since). We tried to get help, only to get nothing but our time wasted.

My husband salvaged a propane stinger from a gas grill we got from scavenging other people's garbage for scrap metal. He pulled the guts out of the natural gas hot water tank and replaced those parts with the propane grill stinger, which we have hooked up to a small propane tank —the kind you use with a gas grill. Since there is no way to automatically shut the propane off once the water inside the tank heats up, we must constantly watch the hot water tank so it doesn't explode. It takes about 2 hours in the summer to heat the water so that we can get a shower and do dishes. In the winter time when it is 40 degrees in our basement, it takes about 4-5 hours to heat the tank, and we have to set the alarm clock in case either of us falls asleep and the tank overheats and explodes.

There is no such thing as being able to jump in a hot shower on a moment's notice to bathe properly for an impromptu job interview (which I've had none). And since propane isn't cheap, we can't afford to bathe every day which makes me feel extremely self conscious about being in public around other people. Hot water is good for my back problems, but a hot sit-down bath is a luxury that I haven't been able to afford since our gas got cut off.

Since we couldn't afford to finish badly needed home repairs through my long-term joblessness (which I've resigned myself to the fact that, as a middle-aged woman, will be permanent), we couldn't afford to get our chimney relined at a cost of $8,000 plus pay for a wood or biofuel fireplace insert. Nor could we afford to install a solar energy system. Instead, we had to make do with a second-hand antique wood-burning cook stove that we got for $200 at an estate sale. We had to rig a metal stovepipe/chimney through our kitchen window to the outside and all the way up the side of our house to the third floor. This stove was not meant for heating a house. It takes only one or two small blocks of wood at a time — meaning that during the winter, we get no sleep except for one hour cat naps because we must constantly feed the stove every hour so we don't freeze to death. We also can't leave the house except to buy food because we always need to keep an eye on the wood stove. Kerosene isn't cheap and one 5 gallon can only lasts two days in our kerosene heater on the coldest winter days when we need to run the space heater in addition to the wood cook stove. We only buy kerosene when the temperatures go down into the single digits because we can't afford it on our income.

Being poor and having to live like this took a toll on our health. It aggravated his heart disease and he had already had one triple bypass in 1996. In March of 2010, he almost died from exhaustion just from trying to help me keep us both from freezing to death and having burst frozen plumbing. This is how we have to live. And nobody cared — including my husband's middle class step-siblings who never even bothered to check on us after our phone got disconnected.

Instead, we get told by sanctimonious middle class progressives how "lucky" we are to be poor in the US instead of in some other country and how privileged we are because we're white, and that we "need to learn how to help ourselves" rather than ask for any help from those who are clearly in a position to give a real helping hand. Stories like ours across America are ignored because middle class America hates the poor. The middle class never wants to hear about our problems or give us anything along the lines of real help that mean the difference between life and death.

Since charities and social agencies always run out of money, more than half of those in dire need don't get helped. Of those who do, the help is not enough to stave off shut-offs. The average LIHEAP grant for Pennsylvania's poor seniors and disabled adults on SSI with no children was a mere $157; which doesn't even cover one month's worth of winter heating bills. I know because we got LIHEAP before the 2005 utility rate hikes priced us out, and the little bit of help we used to get from LIHEAP wasn't enough to make home energy affordable for us.

People told the National Fuel executives all of this at the public hearing right before the 2005 rate hike went through. Citizens gave personal testimony on their incomes and how these rate hikes would impact them. National Fuel executives, members of the Public Utilities

Commission (PUC), and members of Pennsylvania's state legislature were present. They ignored Pennsylvania's poor, saying "there's help out there for those who can't afford their utilities."

One utility executive quipped that people "can get a second job" to pay their bills; disregarding the fact that northwestern Pennsylvania has been hard hit by permanent job losses and many are lucky if they can get one minimum wage job, never mind a second one. He disregarded the disabled and seniors who are least likely to get hired in any job, especially in tough economic times. During the best of economic times, the unemployment rate for the disabled is 96% despite the passage of the Americans with Disabilities Act because employers won't accommodate disabled workers.

Another National Fuel spokesman said that the utility company does not shut off utilities for low-income people with medical problems if they provide the company with a letter from a doctor. But the reality is that the region's few doctors who accept patients on Medicaid are unwilling to provide such letters. All of this was ignored by mainstream news media.

Doctors in the St. Vincent Physicians Group, affiliated with Erie's Catholic "non-profit" hospital — St. Vincent Health Center — have a policy of refusing to sign letters of medical emergency except where the patient is a child with a respiratory ailment. Poor older adults who are disabled, who have heart disease, or a history of pneumonia are left facing a death sentence for the status crime of living while poor. Hospital admissions from existing health problems exacerbated by utility shut-offs makes *them* more money: such patients will need more aftercare, routine blood work and check-ups. The working class is apparently good enough to provide St. Vincent's doctors with a bourgeoisie lifestyle in our for-profit health care system, but if you fall into poverty from job loss, disability, pregnancy and childbirth, or age discrimination, *your* right to life is null and void.

According to the head of the Pennsylvania Consumer Advocate Office, Sonny Popowski, a survey of LIHEAP recipients by the National Energy Assistance Directors' Association issued in September 2005 (a few weeks after the post-Katrina rate hikes) revealed that:

- 73% of the respondents reported that they had reduced expenses for household necessities because they did not have enough money to pay their utility bills.
- 19% reported that they kept their homes at temperatures that were unsafe or unhealthy due to unaffordable utility bills.
- 24% reported that they used their stove or oven to provide heat.
- 20% reported that they went without food for at least one day per month to try and meet utility bills and avoid shut-offs.

A February 2006 report from America's Second Harvest, the nation's food bank network, found that 45% of their clients reported that they had to choose between paying for food and paying for utilities.

Sonny Popowski also gave testimony before the Pennsylvania senate regarding Chapter 14 of Act 201, which replaced a large number of provisions regarding utility service rules; namely, terminations and reconnections that had previously been the subject of PUC regulations contained in Chapter 56 of the PUC Title in the Pennsylvania Code. With respect to terminations, the PUC statistics show that there was a dramatic jump in the number of terminations by Pennsylvania's electric, natural gas, and water utilities — from 152,000 in 2004 to 242,885 in 2005.

According to the PUC winter survey, the number of Pennsylvania households that were without heat due to loss of electric and/or natural gas service rose from 15,005 in 2004 to 17,057 in 2005; while the number of households who either had no heat or were using unsafe alternative heating methods increased from 17,654 in 2004 to 21,063 in 2005. As of February 1st 2006, there were 14,533 households that were not restored and that had no heat.

Chapter 14 modified a number of provisions from the PUC regulations regarding grounds for termination, notice, and timing of terminations — this contributed to the increase of terminations in 2005. "Indeed, it is otherwise hard to explain how or why a company like American Water Company increased its terminations by 211% from 7,502 in 2004 to 23,302 in 2005," Popowski said, objecting to the manner in which Chapter 14 removes the discretion over utility service rules from the PUC and gives that discretion instead to the utilities themselves. Chapter 14 put the fox in charge of the chicken coop.

After the run-up in wholesale natural gas prices before Hurricane Katrina and subsequently thereafter, utility bills more than doubled. Governor Ed Rendell initiated the Stay Warm PA program which helped instigate the appropriation of Pennsylvania's first state supplement to LIHEAP and called on regulators to take steps to protect customers. In October 2005, Governor Rendell announced, "We need to set reasonable standards for customers who are terminated. I will ask the utilities to agree not to charge more than $50 upfront for a reconnect fee and no more than $100 for a deposit for those being reconnected for any family under 250% of the federal poverty level. If utilities don't agree to voluntarily establish such reasonable levels for this winter, I will look to the PUC to use its powers to make this happen."

It is five years later and Pennsylvanians still don't have this "reasonable protection." This is directly due to Chapter 14 of Act 201. Under Chapter 14, the PUC has no "powers to make this happen" unless the utilities agree to it.

§1407(c)(2) of Chapter 14 under Act 201 explicitly allows a utility to refrain from restoring service to low-income or payment troubled customers who defaulted on two prior payment agreements — even though these payment arrangements and monthly budget plans are more than what low-income customers can reasonably afford to pay — unless the customer pays the full reconnection fee and security deposit allowed under §1404, plus the full outstanding balance upfront in cash.

Since this is embedded in statute and not in regulation or Commission Order, the PUC is powerless to change it; even in the face of emergency anticipated from skyrocketing rates and surges in wholesale prices. Pennsylvania senator Mary Jo White attempted to address this specific issue through the introduction of SB 1005, but that bill never advanced.

§1404 of Chapter 14 states that "the PUC commission shall not prohibit a public utility from requiring a cash deposit equal to two months of estimated bills." This deposit can be required from "any applicant or customer who is unable to establish creditworthiness to the satisfaction of the public utility through the use of a generally accepted credit scoring methodology." Further curtailment of the PUC's authority governing the business practices of utilities that contraindicate the public's best interests in what the market (the people) can reasonably bear is listed throughout Chapter 14 of Act 201.

The PUC's hands are also tied regarding the types of termination notices that were previously required of utilities. §1405 (b)(2) states: "The utility shall not be required by the Commission to take any additional actions prior to termination."

The average back due gas bill of disconnected Pennsylvania's poorest customers was between $800 and $1,000 as of 2004. In the spring of 2004, Philadelphia Gas Works (PGW) shut off the gas of 15,798 customers for non-payment. Some got help from the LIHEAP crisis grant in 2005. But there are new rules. Residential customers must pay 100% of their past due bill plus a $123 reconnection fee. Extremely poor people on very low fixed incomes couldn't afford their bills after the rate 2005 hike to begin with. They certainly couldn't afford to pay the full arrearage plus a $123 reconnection fee plus the $372 fee assessed by PGW for gas customers whose gas had to be shut off at the street.[65]

---

[65] *People's Weekly World*, Philadelphia, Pennsylvania, January 5th 2006 edition

Community Services lawyer Jonathon Stein said, “Thousands of Philadelphia’s low-income residents are without heat. They can’t afford to pay their bills, let alone these fees.”

Since utility rates had already priced out Pennsylvania’s poor, they cannot keep utility payment arrangement plans because they can’t afford it. The poor are the ones most heavily penalized with excessive rates and fees. Kensington Welfare Rights Union spokesman Galen Taylor said, “Safe housing and heat are human rights. Act 201 must be repealed.”

Sonny Popowski testified before the Pennsylvania legislature on December 4th 2009: “As many of you are no doubt aware, the rate caps that have protected many Pennsylvania customers from increased electricity rates for the last decade are coming off at the end of this year or at the end of 2010. For residential customers of PP&L, which serves much of central and northeastern Pennsylvania, we know that average bills for residential customers will be increasing by approximately 30% beginning on January 1st 2010.”

This in conjunction with the imposition of the global carbon fuel tax, which is a regressive tax (however cleverly cloaked with a cap and dividend shell game) that disproportionately hurts the working class, will slap a "death by destitution" sentence on America's poor: the disabled, elderly, unemployable jobless pregnant women, children, and the involuntarily jobless long-term unemployed middle-aged workers. This isn't just class warfare; it's class genocide. Make no mistake about it.

This is not isolated to just the US. It is part of a global jihad against the world's have-nots with the imposition of "austerity programs" and the global carbon fuel tax.

As an aside, many gas and electric utility companies across the US collect billions of taxes from their customers for the utilities’ corporate taxes – which the utilities keep instead of sending in to the government. Surprisingly, this is legal in most states (including

Pennsylvania). Minnesota Attorney General Mike Hatch explained, "Essentially, utility customers pay twice: once through the utility bill and again through the lost revenue to government. That means either higher taxes for them or less government services."

When desperate poor people do what they have to do to survive, they're accused of utility theft. But when rich utility monopolies extort tax money from customers that they don't turn over to the government, and when they price gouge the public, it's called "free market capitalism." It's time to fight the economic terrorism wielded by this criminal cabal of economic cannibals and it's time to place human rights above the "rights" of social predators to get rich from policies resulting in the deaths of the poor.

The days when the utility industry was part of the social contract with the public, including those of the lowest economic strata of society, are gone with the wind. According to the Public Utility Commission (PUC) required Cold Weather Survey, PGW had terminated heat-related service for non-payment to 37,000 customers in 2006. PGW's payment agreement terms for disconnected customers were prohibitive for those customers – over half have incomes at 125% below the federal poverty line.

The situation was even worse in Detroit – the poorest city in America. In 2001-2002, Detroit Water & Sewer had shut off running water to over 40,000 low-income residents.

With lost jobs and cuts in aid for America's poor, Detroit's poor were left without any means to afford the bills for the most basic of life-sustaining utilities. Detroit's main utility company, DTE Energy, had shut off gas and electric service to 6,620 inhabited residences within the city of Detroit since March 31st 2002. Of those 6,620 households, 4,518 had the electric shut off and 2,092 were denied gas service. Additionally, 2,520 senior citizens on low fixed incomes had both their gas and their electric shut off because they couldn't afford the price-gouging rates that have far outpaced their incomes. During this same timeframe in 2002, DTE Energy merged with another utility giant, MCN, and posted a revenue growth that went from $1.84 billion to $2.4 billion dollars – driving up the 2002 first quarter profits by 45%, which created even more wealth for America's investor class at the poor's expense.

When poor single mothers like 29 year old Sylvia Young of Detroit have to lose what little bit of nothing she had in a deadly house fire that claimed the lives of three of her seven children because her utilities got cut off — we know exactly what supporting faux democracy under capitalism ultimately means for us.

When that man working for DTE, enjoying *his* middle class union job with benefits enabling *him* to afford health care, a home, good food, and *his* utilities, went to cut off Sylvia Young's gas and electric on March 2nd 2010 in Detroit's frigid winter temperatures, he spoke with her less than two hours before her children died in the fire from a space heater. He saw her children. He knew that cutting off her gas and electric was a death sentence for her and those children. And what did he do? What was his response to the pleas of a poor single mother who *didn't* have a good job? "Sorry, I've got to do my job."

How nice for him that he's got *his* good job and that it's not *him* being slapped with a death sentence for the status crime of living while poor and female in our wonderful "democracy." Were the deaths of three poor children, the destruction of a poor family, worth it? Did he sleep comfortably while the tiny pink and blue caskets for 3 year old Selena Young, 4 year old Fantasia Young, and 5 year old Trávion Young were paid for by community donations from other poor people?

Let's compare the current corporate fascist state of America to the deadly corporate fascist state of Nazi Germany 70 years ago. In both cases, the poor and marginalized groups were targeted as disposable "surplus population" that are "useless eaters." Both used illegal war and the invasion of other countries as a pretext to further the capitalist expansionist agenda. And both have their water boys who are overwhelmingly among the ranks of the middle class that were willing to carry out the dirty work of the owning class by deliberately killing the poor and unwanted. Both have used media propaganda to dehumanize their victims.

It was the predominantly middle class trade unionists and social Democrats who allied themselves with Germany's industrial bourgeoisie. They distanced themselves from Germany's Communist Party (KDP). Their support for "reform" rather than overthrow of an oppressive capitalist/imperialist system allowed the Nazi horrors to unfold, plunging Europe, Japan, and America into World War II and culminating in Hitler's "Final Solution." The "Final Solution" could not have been carried out without a large complicit middle class.

Three engineers — Fritz Sander, Kurt Prüfer, and Karl Schultze — working for Topf and Son designed, patented, and built the continual feed industrial strength crematoria *specifically* for use in the Nazi death camps. They willingly installed these ovens of destruction and performed routine on-site maintenance from 1941-1945. They witnessed their "creations" in use in the liquidation of innocent women, children, and elderly or disabled men that were "unfit" for slave labor.

After the war ended when these three men testified at the post-war trial in Erfurt, they were asked why they approached the SS and secured for their employer the exclusive contract for supplying the death camps with these crematoria that had to be specially outfitted to the gas chambers. They were asked why they *willingly* designed, patented, built, and maintained this machination of genocide. They didn't say it was because they hated Jews. They didn't say it was because they were afraid of their Nazi government. They didn't say it was because they feared reprisal from the SS. They said it was because they didn't want to lose their middle class positions[66], that they were "just doing their jobs" and supporting their lawful government.

Similarly, middle class union utility workers who shut off poor people's electric, water, and gas claim they're "just doing their jobs." They've got families and a middle class lifestyle to maintain after all —

---

[66] Quoted from the interrogation transcripts by Professor Gerald Fleming from the University of Surrey

to hell with the poor. They know that by cutting off poor people's utilities, they're causing the deaths of vulnerable people who are dying from the cold, or in residential fires as a result of desperate and unsafe alternative measures.

If you are a utility worker who ignores the pleas of a poor woman as you shut off her gas and electric, you're nothing but a cold-blooded murderer for hire. Is that little bit of extra comfort and middle class privilege you're enjoying worth killing the poor — disabled, elderly, long-term unemployed, women and children — as part and parcel of having *your* good job really worth it? What makes *your* middle class status and *your* nice life so more important than someone else's human right to life? Poor people have just as much of a right to live as you. We didn't ask to be born in this country and we don't deserve to have to suffer because of others' greed.

Here is only a very small partial list of casualties in the War On the Poor who died (or who were injured or left homeless) as a result of unaffordable utility bills and a lack of adequate social and economic support. In Pennsylvania since 2005, the price of natural gas more than doubled for Pennsylvania's residential customers. More than 242,000 Pennsylvania households had their utilities shut off for being unable to afford their bills.

Dauphin County — Swatara Township:

- Britton Donachy, age 2
- Onna Donachy, age 18 months

Died in a fire caused by a candle after PP&L cut off their electric.

Cambria County — Hastings:

- Delores "Dee" Holland, age 50
- Jordan English, age 3
- Alisha McConnell, age 15
- Lindsey Depto, age 14

Died in a fire caused by a candle after Penelec shut off the electric in the rented home of Dee Holland and her 57 year old disabled fiancé Jack Sexton; and Dee's daughter, a poor single mother who, like her mother, worked at a minimum wage job.

Lancaster County — Lancaster:

- May 3rd, 2008; nine tenants were left homeless after a fire caused by a candle destroyed the apartment building after PP&L cut off the electric to the apartment of Kenneth Yaw in April of 2008
- August 9th 2009: Cynthia Glassman (age unknown) died in a fire sparked by a candle after PP&L cut off her electric the day before. She struggled to afford PP&L's payment arrangement plan, but was short $7 for the "late fee." Her electric got cut off and she lost her life for lack of $7.

Jefferson County — Brockway: Ten people died in a house fire that broke out on April 3rd 2008. The fire was caused by a space heater. National Fuel had cut off their gas in 2005 and they had been without gas since May 2005. The only survivors were 20 year old Elizabeth Peterson and her father, Douglas Peterson II. Killed in the fire were three generations of the Peterson family:

- Kimberly Peterson, age 40 (mother and wife of Douglass Peterson II)
- Rebecca Peterson, age 17 — a poor single mother
- Douglas Peterson III, age 13
- Isaac Peterson, age 8
- Grace Peterson, age 6
- Lillian Peterson, age 11 months
- Domanic Delullo, age 4 (Elizabeth's son)
- Desiree Delullo, age 2 (Elizabeth's daughter)
- Jason Mowry, age 19 (Elizabeth's fiancé)

Philadelphia: More than 8,800 Philadelphia households had their gas shut off in the winter of 2009. On December 26th 2009, seven died in a single house fire after the gas was cut off. The fire was caused by a kerosene heater that exploded after fuel for the heater caught on fire:

- Ramere Dosso, age 8
- Mariam Dosso, age 6
- Zyhire Wright-Teah, age 1
- Elliot Teah, age 23 (Zyhire's father)
- Jennifer Teah, age 17 (Elliot's sister)
- Vivian Teah, age 25 (Elliot's sister)
- Henry Gbokoloi, age 54 (neighbor)

California: More than 288,000 California households have had their utilities shut off. Four children died in a single apartment fire sparked by a candle after PG&E cut off their electric when their parents, two sisters who were both poor struggling single mothers, couldn't pay the electric bill.

- Natalie Rogers, age 2
- Nevaeh Nunn, age 2
- Keviana Morgan, age 1
- Robert Charles, age 4

Michigan: More than 400,000 Michigan households had their utilities cut off because of unaffordable utility rates, with over 221,000 of those terminations in Detroit.

Bay City:

Marvin Shur (93 year old World War II vet) died of hypothermia after Bay City Electric restricted his utility service with a limiter, causing his furnace to shut down. Hypothermia is a very slow and extremely painful way to die.

Detroit (July 2009):

Four members of the Reed-Owens family died from carbon monoxide poisoning caused by a generator they were using after DTE cut off the family's electric. The wife, Marquetta Ownes, and one of the children, was asthmatic and relied on a nebulizer to breathe; which requires electricity.

- Vaughn Reed, age 46

- Mar'Keisha Reed, age 17
- DeMarco Owens, age 12
- DeMonte Owens, age 8

Detroit (Februrary 2010):

- Marvin Allen, age 62
- Tyrone Allen, age 61
- Lynne Greer, age 58

The Allen brothers were both disabled and couldn't walk. They were struggling to survive on SSI. Lynne Greer, Tyrone's long-term unemployed girlfriend, paid DTE the $108 fee to get service restored, but DTE never restored service. Three poor older adults died in a house fire started by a kerosene heater.

Detroit (March 2010):

- Trávion Young, age 5
- Fantasia Young, age 4
- Selena Young, age 3

Three of the seven Young children died when a space heater ignited a fire after DTE shut off the gas to the rented home of Sylvia Young, a poor single mother struggling to survive with seven children on $675/month welfare cash assistance. Her rent was $500/month. The fire broke out only a couple hours after Sylvia Young pleaded with a DTE worker to not shut off her utilities. With no car, she had to trudge through ice and snow on foot to the nearest Dollar Store to buy an additional space heater so she and her children wouldn't freeze to death. Since she had no car and it was bitter cold, she couldn't drag her small children with her, so she left them in the care of her oldest — her 12 year old son. She was only gone for about a half hour when the fire broke out and ravaged the home. But the worst came after the fire when Michigan's state agencies, Governor Jennifer Granholm, Detroit's mayor David Bing and the mainstream media in concert with DTE Energy launched a massive attack on Sylvia Young; and brought criminal child neglect charges against her and took custody of her surviving children. The mainstream media didn't wait for the smoldering embers to die before seizing the opportunity to vilify a poor black single mother on welfare with a very misleading article about the fire, stating that the fire broke out while Sylvia Young went to a "party store", leaving her children unattended.

During that same month, David Fox of the National Low-Income Energy Consortium said that prior to funding cuts to LIHEAP this year, the program was grossly underfunded so that at maximum, only 20% of all eligible needy households were able to be served. The number of LIHEAP recipients will shrink more for the winter of 2010-2011 with the 2010 LIHEAP budget cuts of $1.8 billion that have been enacted. Meanwhile, the number of people in need is skyrocketing due to the worst economic crisis since the Great Depression. Approximately 10 million poor households will be without their winter heating utility and/or electric by the end of 2010. Given the number of long-term unemployed whose unemployment benefits ran out in 2009 or early 2010 who have no income and who have been unable to get jobs in addition to the 5 million jobless poor who weren't eligible for any unemployment benefits at all and whose sole income has been food stamps, the actual number of households that will be without life-sustaining utilities will probably be much higher than the projected 10 million.

According to the annual survey conducted by the National Energy Assistance Director's Association (NEADA), 60% of LIHEAP recipients couldn't pay their utility bills because they lost their jobs or had a reduction in income. NEADA said in its September 2010 letter to Congress that LIHEAP funding cuts target the poorest and most vulnerable layers of society: 92% of LIHEAP recipients have an elderly person, a disabled person, or a child in the home. Additionally, 21% suffer from severe respiratory ailments, including chronic bronchitis; 51% have a heart condition, and 46% have severe asthma.

Other consequences of utility shut-offs include homelessness, heat stroke, poor child development, and the disintegration of families. According to the National Fire Protection Association (NFPA), the link between utility shut-offs and deadly fires is clearly established. When utilities are cut off, people resort to unsafe methods such as space heaters to stay warm and candles for lighting. NFPA data revealed that from 2003-2007; space heaters were involved in 72% of fire deaths and 62% of injuries related to home heating and 24% of fatal candle fires occurred when electricity was cut off. Many families who have not yet been shut off use these methods to reduce unaffordable utility bills.

According to data supplied by the Michigan Public Services Commission, 300,000 Michigan households have had their heat and/or electric cut off for nonpayment, and over 221,000 of those households were in Detroit which has a real unemployment rate close to 50%. On October 30th 2010, DTE Energy requested a $253 million dollar rate increase from the Michigan Public Services Commission. On that same day, DTE reported an increase in its third quarter profits from $151 million in 2009 to $163 million in 2010. On November 4th, Detroit's ABC news affiliate carried an exposé on "illegal hookups." NPR ran a program two days prior on November 2nd exploring the depth of the "energy theft crisis" in Detroit. [67] The NPR reporter ignored the fact that the existence of unauthorized hookups is the result of desperate poverty, the absence of significant aid, and unaffordable utility rates compounded by the $1.8 billion dollar funding cuts to LIHEAP.

There is a direct relationship between unaffordable utility rates, deadly fires, and poverty. If the utilities were not unaffordable, people wouldn't have their utilities cut off for nonpayment and the preconditions for these fatalities, injuries, and property damage would not have been created. And some of these fires cannot be blamed on "energy theft." Illegal hookups exist because utility rates are unaffordable and because utility monopolies shut off service to the poor. These casualties occur because our capitalist government — a product of our narcissistic "me first" capitalist society — allows utilities to influence residential zoning laws, then charge exorbitant rates and shut people off because they have no money because they couldn't get jobs that pay a living wage, and have no adequate social safety net either.

---

[67] CAUS, November 2010, vol.1

The Sonderkommando in Nazi death camps at least had an excuse: they were forced under the barrel of SS guns to do the dirty work of their Nazi bosses. But they never once said of their less fortunate prisoners that "they deserved it" for being "losers" for not lucking out in the death camp lottery calculated by the devil's arithmetic.

The "I was only doing my job" meme didn't wash at the post-World War II trials and it doesn't cut it today. If you're a Medicaid-accepting doctor, it's because you want the status and privileges and comfortable living that being a doctor provides for you. If you're a union utility company worker, it's because you want a middle class life and all the comforts, money, benefits and 401(k) stock portfolios that comes with it. You're not forcibly conscripted for that job. No one is holding a loaded gun to your head and forcing you to collaborate with your capitalist bosses in what amounts to the holocaust of America's poor. You don't have to kill the poor just to get ahead. It's called morals. It's called ethics. It's respecting others' human rights, which don't have to be sacrificed on the altar of the Almighty Dollar just so you can have your middle class toys and status. You live in a society where other people have needs and rights, too. Everything isn't all about you.

In oil-rich Texas, the impact of utility company deregulation hit low-income people especially hard. The utility companies established multi-tiered rates based on customers' payment histories. In essence, multi-tiered rates punished the poor by charging those who had the most difficulty paying their bills on time the highest rates. Wealthy Republican Senator David Sibley co-sponsored the Texas utility deregulation bill. Sibley's response to consumer advocate groups' criticism of the bill's unfairness to the poor was, "People who do not pay their bills are not going to enjoy the same rates as everybody else. We wanted them [the poor] to have electricity, but they don't have the right to electricity at the same rates as everyone else."

Other unfair pricing policies aimed at hurting the poor include exclusionary credit policies, prepayment meters, lesser quality service and service-limiting adapters. Inadequate (and rapidly vanishing) amounts of energy assistance for poor seniors and disabled people will disappear completely after the energy industry becomes fully deregulated. Those who have the least income to afford anything are socked with utility rates that are 25% - 50% higher than the rates enjoyed by those who aren't poor and who can easily afford their bills.

Utilities for residential heating and cooling costs eat up an average of 20% of the annual incomes of those in the bottom economic quintile. In contrast, the same utility costs consume only 3% of the annual incomes of the households that aren't poor. If those with incomes of $50,000 a year had to shell out 20% of their annual incomes for basic life-sustaining utilities, they would be paying $10,000 a year for the luxury of not having to freeze to death in the winter or drop dead from heat stroke in the summer.

As an aside, many gas and electric utility companies across the nation collect billions of taxes from their customers for the utilities' corporate taxes – which they keep instead of sending it to the government. Surprisingly, this is legal in most states. Minnesota Attorney General Mike Hatch explained, "Essentially, utility customers pay twice: once through the utility bill and again through the lost revenue to government. That means either higher taxes for them or less government services."

There's not only a very real lack of help due to the government slashing funds for aid for America's poor, but the government is also a co-conspirator in league with greedy rich utility monopolies and fossil fuel cartels. It was the state and federal governments that allowed utility monopolies like National Fuel, UGI, PGW, First Energy, Penelec, PP&L, and countless others to raise their rates by a whopping 41% within weeks after hurricanes Katrina and Rita ravaged the Gulf Coast in 2005. But the electric and natural gas providers who raised their rates were not as affected by the hurricanes as they claimed. Most derive their fuel from the bituminous coal beds in Appalachia. So what's their excuse (other than greed) for raising the rates and pricing out the most poor and vulnerable?

Massey Energy is the fourth largest coal producer in the US; its mines yield about 40 million tons of coal each year. Massey controls a third of all central Appalachian coal reserves – about 2.2 billion tons of coal. Massey Energy is also public enemy #1 to environmentalists, workers' rights groups, and consumer advocacy groups.

On October 11th 2000, the hamlet of Inez, Kentucky was besieged by a coal sludge flood from a failed coal slurry impoundment that was equivalent to the volume of 306 Olympic lap pools. The toxic pudding containing chemicals and heavy metals from coal waste poured out like black lava sparing nothing contaminating everything in its path. The slurry made its way downstream through Coldwater and Wolf Creeks and into the Tug Fork, flooding two tributaries of the Big Sandy River along the West Virginia – Kentucky border. Within ten days, the sludge reached the Ohio River, leaving a 75 mile long path of destruction and contamination in its wake. The spill killed 1.6 million fish, contaminated the water supply of 27,623 people, contaminated the soil of hundreds of acres of homeowners' properties, and washed away roads and bridges. The Environmental Protection Agency (EPA) said the spill was the worst in the entire history of the eastern United States. The Inez disaster was nearly 30 times larger in magnitude than the Exxon-Valdez oil tanker spill that dumped 11 million gallons of oil in Alaska's Prince William Sound.

The coal company that owned the failed impoundment was a subsidiary of Massey Energy. And Massey Energy, specifically its CEO Don Blankenship, has friends in high places – from the halls of Congress to the Bush administration.

Massey Energy contributed heavily to the Republican Party and was especially generous to the presidential campaign of George W. Bush in both the 2000 and 2004 elections. In a questionably legal *quid pro quo*, the Bush administration returned the favor by appointing coal and timber barons to key government positions within watchdog agencies such as the Mining Safety and Health Administration (MSHA) and the Department of Labor. Bush put foxes in charge of the henhouse. Bush appointed James "Big Buck" Harless to the president's task force on energy and Elaine Chao, wife of Sen. Mitch McConnell (R-KY) as the Secretary of Labor. Harless had raised $275,000 for Bush's 2000 election, given $5,000 for the Florida recount, and contributed $100,000 to Bush's inaugural fund. Harless told reporters for the *Wall Street Journal* that, "We were looking for friends, and we found one in George W. Bush." And Dubya was a very good friend to rich and powerful interests. He appointed Stanley Suboleski, a long-time Massey Energy executive, to the position of Assistant Secretary for the US Department of Energy (DOE).

The coal industry raised a record $3.8 million for Bush's 2000 election, of which 88% went to the Republican Party. A few months after Bush took office, the annual meeting of the West Virginia Coal Association was held. The group's director told an audience of 150 coal company executives, "You did everything you could to elect a Republican president. Now you are already seeing in his actions the payback." Wealthy coal barons had given Bush something and they expected (and got) something in return. Through the flexing of their economic muscle, coal barons got MSHA's Mine Safety Institute's most respected engineer Jack Spadaro run out on a rail by Bush's newly appointed head of the MSHA: Dave Lauriski, a former coal industry executive.

The coal industry didn't like Jack Spadaro because he is a man of integrity whose principles are not for sale at any price. Spadaro had uncovered evidence that the Inez disaster was not an "act of God" as Massey claimed; rather it was the result of gross negligence and deliberate corner-cutting on the part of the coal company[68]. According to Spadaro, Dave Lauriski came into his office and demanded that Spadaro sign off on a white-washed version of the investigation report – a version that absolved the coal company and let the MSHA off the hook. Spadaro refused and went public about the whitewash and started an investigation of no-bid MSHA contracts doled out to Lauriski cronies. Jack Spadaro was harassed and then railroaded out of his job over a disputed $22.50 in

68 http://www.cbsnews.com/stories/2004/04/01/60minutes/printable609889.shtml

cash advances on his government agency-issued credit card. His investigation was buried.

Spadaro's quashed investigation concluded that the Inez impoundment had previously had another spill in 1994. Massey Energy claimed it had taken measures to ensure it wouldn't happen again. But a Massey engineer told Spadaro's investigative team that the problem had never been fixed and that both he and the company knew another spill was inevitable. The engineer told Spadaro that at least 5 others in the company knew it. But Massey didn't want to spend the money to find another impoundment site.

The reason the Inez spill in 2000 was inevitable is because there was only a very thin layer of rock at the bottom of the reservoir that contained the coal slurry. But that's not what Massey Energy told the government. Massey told the government that there was a solid coal barrier at least 70-80 feet wide between the mine workings and the bottom of the huge slurry pond. But they lied. The barrier was only 20 feet wide. Massey Energy misrepresented the facts in order to fraudulently get the impoundment permit. Massey cut corners where safety was concerned and Bush's appointees in government watchdog agencies knew it, too.

Spadaro's investigation was cut short when Bush campaign contributors and Republican Party donors were appointed to the very government agencies that are supposed to protect the public from corporate fraud, abuse, and safety violations. Had Spadaro not been canned and his investigation not been sabotaged, Massey Energy would have faced criminal charges and hefty fines for 8 major violations. But Massey ended up with only 2 citations for lesser violations, resulting in a total of $110,000 in fines. Apparently, "personal responsibility" only applies to the lower social classes. The elite are insulated from the consequences of their actions.

Bush-appointed Secretary of Labor Elaine Chao backed the crony-contrived falsified Inez report. Chao refused to be interviewed by *60 Minutes*, as did Massey Energy executives and MSHA's Dave

Lauriski. It is no surprise that mining deaths and toxic disasters have increased since wealthy powerful coal interests were able to buy the government lock, stock, and barrel – from the Oval Office to every watchdog agency charged with protecting public interest and worker safety. Even the judgeships in state and federal courts are for sale. Massey Energy, under the direction and leadership of CEO Don Blankenship, financed and engineered an election victory for West Virginia State Supreme Court judge Brent Benjamin, a Republican and corporate lawyer based in Charleston. Benjamin was no friend of the common man. He made his pile by sticking it to the "little guy."

In West Virginia, state Supreme Court judges are elected; not appointed. Just as Massey and the rest of the coal cabal bought the White House and wielded their economic might to transform the MSHA, the US Department of Labor, and the US Department of Energy from watchdogs into lapdogs, Massey CEO Don Blankenship singlehandedly bought West Virginia legislature seats and the bench of the state's highest court.

Massey Energy is the most socially and ecologically destructive coal baron. It is the biggest, most aggressive practitioner of mountaintop removal in its endeavors to extract the "black gold" out of West Virginia hills – permanently destroying the greatest biodiversity in the US[69]. Mountaintop removal is the blowing up of mountains – blowing their tops off. Giant earth moving equipment is then used to scoop out the coal at about 100 tons per scoop. Any sediment that is not coal is then dumped into the valleys and freshwater streams below. To date, 479 mountains and over 1,200 miles of freshwater streams have been permanently destroyed this way. Some of the blast sites have been "reclaimed." But this reclamation is not full restoration of the once clean freshwater streams and replanting of the indigenous hardwood forests and 1,500 species of the world's best medicinal herbs such as black cohosh and ginseng native to Appalachia. Reclamation is really a half-assed re-vegetation effort of introducing foreign invasive species of vegetation and genetically modified fast-growing grass commonly used

---

[69] http://gristmill.grist.org/print/2007/12/19/11262/475?show_comments=no

on the putting greens of golf courses. No matter what Don Blankenship and Massey Energy claims, reclamation is a joke. Once mountains are blown up and their structural integrity is breached by weakened slurry ponds, they don't grow back and the soil and water is not cleansed of the coal waste toxins. The ecosystem is not adequately restored.

Don Blankenship attempted to defend Massey's mountaintop removal activities, claiming it was actually good for the environment saying, "low cost electricity, the creation of energy, of jobs, of an economy, ultimately leads to an improvement in the environment. There is no place in the world that has a good environment where people live on $2 a day with no electricity." Yet there are numerous impoverished West Virginians who *do* live like that due to the feudalism of "King Coal" and its stranglehold on communities throughout central Appalachia. And anyone familiar with the environmental, geopolitical, social and economic destruction of diamond-rich Africa at the hands of DeBeers Corporation knows how bad the situation is for the poor of Angola, Liberia, and Sierra Leone. It's easy to see Blankenship's defense of environmental and economic rape for the lame excuse it really is.

Massey's safety record at its underground mines is abysmal and far fewer miners are killed at mountaintop removal sites. But that's only because very few miners are employed there. Most of the work is accomplished with automation. And this is why there's been a steady sharp decline in mining jobs in regions where coal mining is the only industry – the only source of jobs at all. This explains why West Virginia's biggest coal producing counties have persistent abject poverty. In McDowell County alone, 37% of the residents live in poverty comparable 3rd World conditions. The poverty rates for Mingo, Logan and Boone counties are not much different.

In areas of aggressive mountaintop removal activity, the destruction to air, soil and water quality is so devastating that it prevents other businesses and industries from investing in West Virginia and sustaining healthy and wholesome communities. Impoverished residents are trapped because they're stuck with homes and land with contaminated soil and water that no one else can use or would want.

Health problems, disabilities and premature death galore abound as a direct result of chemical and heavy metal toxins that cannot be affordably or easily removed from the soil and water. The cost to properly treat the water supply makes safe, clean running water unaffordable for a significant number of West Virginians.

A lack of viable industries and businesses means a lack of jobs. Lack of alternatives for sustainable communities and jobs is the cause of poverty in Appalachia. Worse, this poverty was deliberate. It was created by design; perpetuated and worsened by interests like Massey Energy and greedy sociopaths like Don Blankenship whose iron grip on West Virginia keeps its citizens poor and sick.

Don Blankenship is a West Virginia native from Mingo County. He reportedly came from very humble origins as the son of a poor single mother. In his ascent up the socio-economic ladder up through the ranks of Massey Energy, he forgot where he came from. His reputation for ruthless miners' union suppression is unparalleled; resorting to any means necessary to keep workers insecure and vulnerable. Only 3% of Massey's workforce is unionized.

Blankenship threatened and bullied his critics, even assaulting an ABC News reporter. He threatened to shoot the unarmed cameraman in response to the reporter's polite request to interview him. Blankenship's legal "dream team" assert that the ABC News reporter "pushed his camera closer to Mr. Blankenship's face without having identified himself or his news organization." But the tape of the incident revealed otherwise. The reporter twice identified himself as being from ABC News as he approached Blankenship. The tape also showed that Blankenship threatened the reporter without just cause or provocation, stating, "If you start taking pictures of me, you're liable to get shot."

The altercation between Blankenship and the reporter occurred around the same time that news photos surfaced depicting Blankenship and West Virginia's state Supreme Court chief justice Elliott "Spike" Maynard vacationing together on the French Riviera while a multi-million dollar suit against Massey Energy was pending. Blankenship claims each man paid for his own trip and meals, insisting that no impropriety occurred.

But it doesn't matter who paid for what. Blankenship isn't fooling anyone. Social class nepotism and backdoor deals are the only believable reasons two rich white heterosexual men on the older side of middle-age from the same local "good ole boy network" would vacation together in the romantic exclusive French Riviera, cavorting as dinner dates. The fact that one of the men is the chief state Supreme Court justice posed to reside over a multi-million dollar class action suit against the other man's corporation is not mere coincidence. Blankenship has not been very discreet in buying judges and manipulating the West Virginia legal system.

In 2004 during the election of state Supreme Court judges, Blankenship financially mounted a vicious smear campaign to unseat Justice Warren McGraw in retaliation for previously ruling against Massey Energy, replacing the well-respected jurist with an unknown challenger: Brent Benjamin, a corporate lawyer from Charleston who is no friend to the common man. The campaign wasn't merely financially loaded; it was a bloody character assassination of McGraw who was targeted by greedy mining executives, corporate interests, and affluent physicians' groups. Beth White, spokeswoman for West Virginia Consumers for Justice, a coalition of labor and consumer advocacy groups, said, "It proves that West Virginia Supreme Court seats were for sale." Considering that Blankenship spent $3.5 million to get Brent Benjamin elected, "justice for sale" is an accurate description.

Massey Energy's prior verdict as the losing party in a $50 million dollar lawsuit brought by Harman Mining Corporation was overturned by "Massey's court." Brent Benjamin was one of the judges responsible for overturning the lower court's ruling and reversing the verdict against Massey. Brent Benjamin stated he has no plans to recuse himself for propriety's sake from Massey Energy's pending litigation, despite some strong nudging by his fellow jurists. Maybe money can't buy love, but it sure can buy a hell of a lot of justice and your way out of a ton of trouble in our allegedly classless society. And it can buy the means to create trouble for anyone who opposes your agenda.

The tentacles of Don Blankenship's power and wealth have West Virginia in a death grip. Anyone who dares to cross Blankenship or his company can expect financial or political repercussions. When West Virginia governor Joe Manchin vowed to keep a closer watch on Massey Energy's activities, Blankenship sued Manchin. Blankenship was represented by one of the most high-powered lawyers money can buy – Robert Luskin, the same lawyer retained by Karl Rove[70].

Blankenship pours millions of his wealth into political graft; keeping West Virginia poor with low taxes on coal kingpins, miserly social services, and lax safety and health regulation enforcement. But when it comes to paying his personal maid a living wage and benefits for her hard days' work, there's no money to spare. And it's not just the low pay and lack of health and dental benefits his maid received; it's also the verbal abuse and physical assault he subjected her to for that measly pay.

The stress from the abuse Blankenship heaped out regularly forced Deborah K. May to ultimately quit her job. Her claim for unemployment benefits was denied on the grounds that she "voluntarily quit" her job. May was paid a paltry $16,000 a year with no medical and dental benefits at her job as Blankenship's maid, which entailed her having to take care of several of his homes.

During the course of her employment, she was the recipient of his unpredictable outbursts and violent tantrums. Her unemployment benefit appeal stated that Blankenship subjected her to intolerable treatment, including an incident where he trashed a closet over an incorrectly hung jacket. May's claim also described an episode where he manhandled her and threw his McDonald's breakfast around the office because the order was wrong. On another occasion, he flipped out and demanded a detailed written report from May explaining her refrigerator stocking technique after he couldn't find his favorite flavored ice cream

---

[70] Luskin represented Rove in the White House debacle known as "Plame-gate", entailing the scape-goating of Scooter Libby as the fall guy.

because it wasn't where he thought it should be. Destructive, violent temper tantrums are not cute when coming from a 10 year old child. It's definitely not cute coming from a middle-aged man who is the coal industry's highest paid executive, and who holds himself up as a community pillar.

As part of this phony image, Blankenship paints himself as a nice guy who "gives back to the community." He doles out 2 toys and a turkey to 3,000 select poor children from Mingo County, West Virginia and Pike County, Kentucky every year at Massey Energy's "Christmas Extravaganza." The $200,000 annual charity event is nothing more than a high profile publicity stunt featuring social parasite Don Blankenship as the star.

Blankenship said he "wished there wasn't a need for it, but there is" regarding the poverty and the charity event he uses to polish his image. He says "it makes him feel good to give back" as he hands out gifts to those whom he's impoverished, whose soil and water he's contaminated, whose health he's ruined, whose children he's poisoning and whose future he's killing.

Maybe Blankenship really believes he is a nice guy. But nice compared to whom? The Burmese military? The Taliban? Pol Pot? Idi Amin? Foday Sankoh? If he's such a nice guy whose company has been unjustly targeted and smeared by "greeniacs" and "Communists", he wouldn't use his wealth to subvert the laws at the expense of other people's lives. If he thinks that Massey's failing coal slurry impoundments and toxic waste injected into mine shafts are truly that harmless, he should build one of those coal waste sites on his own soil next to his own home and let it seep into his own drinking water.

Government complicity with ultra rich fossil fuel plutocrats is not merely in the passage of laws that allow the rich to hurt the poor; it is also in the suppression of public investment in alternative heating fuel, electricity, and vehicles that are completely independent of oil, gas and coal cartels. As long as "Big Coal" and the "seven sisters" oil and gas cartels go unchallenged, the consumers have no choice but to pay whatever prices are set by this Axis of Evil – whether they can afford it or not.

Buzz Pitman and his father of Daytona Beach, Florida had produced a car engine that runs on water several years ago. They were not the first to do so. Their lives were threatened by very powerful interests who made it clear that they would be disposed of if they tried to patent and mass produce their engine.

Another brilliant inventor who was a threat to the entrenched elite was Bruce DePalma, brother of movie producer Brian DePalma. Bruce DePalma invented a device he called the "N-Machine" which generates free electricity using geomagnetic forces – a kind of perpetual motion device. DePalma was exiled from the US, after which he continued his research and development in New Zealand. Just as he had his device ready for mass production with patents pending, he died under very suspicious circumstances.

In his paper, *"Free Energy: The Political, Social, and Economic Implications of the N-Machine/Space Power Generator"*, DePalma wrote:

"If energy and transportation costs were zero, society would center on quality of life, small communities would form in which all basic life necessities would be met locally. Money would still be required to purchase manufactured high tech items and money could be earned through the sale of community grown or manufactured goods."

DePalma envisioned a society where the common man and woman were independent and truly free instead of being enslaved by debt peonage to a bloated over-class. His vision entailed an economy that was not a zero sum game and instead, everyone could live decently and with dignity. Is there a better way to eradicate poverty and social injustice?

According to the 2004 census data, 60 million Americans live on only $7 a day. But they are not "poor enough" to qualify for help. There are 44 million Americans who are officially classified as poor according to the US Department of Health & Human Services. That is roughly $1/8^{th}$ of the US population. And that is using the antiquated federal poverty guidelines that fail to take daycare costs, healthcare costs, and other factors of today into consideration. Throughout the US, 6 million households – not individuals – have had their utilities shut off for inability to afford the bills. Many of these people work. Many others want to work, but haven't gotten job opportunities. Others are seniors and the disabled whom no one will hire. According to the Center on Budget and Policy Priorities, 3 million workers were still jobless after their unemployment benefits expired as of 2004. That number has increased significantly since then. Many more poor people have been jobless for a lot longer but are not counted among the official unemployment stats.

I applaud Dr. Donna Beegle for admonishing the affluent to "open up their networks" to the poor. But those in the middle and upper classes really don't want to "open their networks" to the poor – a group of people whom they've collectively marginalized since this nation's founding. Middle and upper class people have deeply ingrained entitlement attitudes. They want to keep the poor isolated and excluded. If those who are affluent were truly interested in "opening their networks" to help the poor, they would not have retreated to their exclusive suburbs and gated communities with the intent of keeping the poor out of sight and out of mind. Why would the middle class suddenly be motivated towards removing the systemic barriers that keep the poor at the bottom when they hate us? And make no mistake about it; the middle class really does hate the poor.

All of the people whom the middle class don't like end up in the lower classes because they're denied admission to the middle class club. Now that the middle class is being decimated, they are getting a dose of their own medicine and howling the loudest about how unfair it is — ironic, coming from the very class who constantly heaped their personal value judgments on the poor as they told us to "stop whining" when we were suffering more than anybody else under capitalism these last 30 years.

The Gilded Age (1870 – 1900) was the era which saw the purest form of capitalism in America. It was also the most violent. Robber barons called on government to mass murder workers who tried to form unions. Rockefeller had the Colorado National Guard shoot strikers at his mines. Carnegie had Fiske use violence on workers in Pittsburgh. The list of mass murder by the capitalists is long and ugly. Some estimates hold that the robber barons killed more people than Stalin. From 2000-2008, George W. Bush gave public money — your tax dollars — to these religious institutions to keep this Calvinist Protestant hatred of the poor alive and well through "faith-based" initiatives which were never about helping the poor, rather they were about sheltering money for those with a vested interest in maintaining an unjust patriarchal capitalist system that favors them at the expense of women, minorities, and other disadvantaged groups. Our government worked hand in glove with influential Christian institutions, protecting capital and the capitalists so that the rich can rob the poor. Even atheist robber barons like Andrew Carnegie gave tremendous amounts of money to religious organizations and Protestant churches; all of which are Calvinist at the core (except for the Lutherans). They did this to monopolize the geopolitical sphere and keep the poor down with their faces in the dirt.

Capitalism's apologists claim that our capitalist society protects the rights of individuals from the tyranny of a majority. If that is so, then where are the protections for the equal rights of women as citizens and as individuals? How does capitalism, which protects property rights, protect the individual rights of the poor? What property does a poor person own? If someone owns property, then he or she by definition is not poor. Proponents of capitalism say that capitalism works. But what they leave out is whom it works for and whom it does not. They paint a rosy picture of capitalism that glosses over the fact that it devalues and oppresses women. Capitalism is, essentially, a gender war. The only women who seem to get ahead under capitalism are those who act like ruthless alpha-males.

Women's work is not considered "work" and that is an ideological attack on women that falls somewhere between insanity and stupidity. The entire welfare reform debate was based on the idea that raising children, taking care of a home, or serving as an unpaid caretaker for adult family member isn't work — yet, speculating on the stock market is. The woman who is taking care of a child isn't doing anything while the day trader flipping stocks in his Ameritrade® account is "working" (and therefore entitled to get rich) but the poor single mother is "undeserving" of economic support from a society that is benefiting by her role as a caretaker and which will further benefit by her child's future labor.

Domestic work altogether isn't considered "work" because women have traditionally done it. Devaluing women severely distorts the whole picture of the capitalist economy. It amounts to transfer payments from women to others. You don't get social security, health benefits, a pension plan, a paid vacation or paid time off or even a paycheck for being a caretaker and a housewife. You also don't get to punch out at the end of an 8 hour shift and go home and relax and do what you like. Raising children is a full-time round the clock job, leaving you no time for yourself and if you're married, no sex life either. The main reason why capitalism looks so successful is because it has always had a lot of slave labor — from half of the population. What women have been doing has never been counted. Not one voice from feminists or any other group in the liberal camp was ever heard raising this critical issue. Oddly, the only progressive voice that did raise this issue came from a man — Noam Chomsky.

With more men assuming this unglamorous and thankless duty as they lose their "real jobs" if wives/girlfriends are lucky to retain theirs, men should be speaking out about this because organized labor and feminists won't. The only "working" women feminists recognize are CEO's and professionals with the "important" jobs. Feminist organizations and labor unions have been co-opted by the bourgeois a long time ago. And the bourgeois has always been violently opposed to the interests of the proletariat.

It is admirable that Donna Beegle attempts to encourage the middle and upper classes towards humane treatment of the poor by trying to get them to see us as human beings who matter and who deserve to live just as much as anyone else, but most of her wisdom probably falls on deaf ears. She assumes that most middle class people care about fairness, that they're really humanitarians who just need to gain some perspective of the obstacles those of us in poverty face who never got a chance to make it. She assumes that the middle class simply doesn't understand. But she's mistaken: they *do* understand. They're the ones who erected those barriers on purpose in order to secure their own comfort and status within capitalism's hierarchy of unearned privilege because they emulate the rich, whom they hope to join. They didn't do it by accident.

For all the claims to the contrary, it's been my experience that the majority of the middle and upper classes hates the poor. This has also been the experience of others in poverty, too. They never really cared about us, much less wanted to help us. They wanted to help themselves. Cancer patient and lifetime resident in "the Other America", Lillian Hanson, felt the same way (as do a lot of other people who've been poor all their life):

I have never heard a middle class person express one sincere iota of concern for a poor person, whether they be a man, woman, or child, unless they felt fear or a threat from them, real or imagined. So getting the middle classes to feel genuine concern for the poor won't likely happen, unless something directly affects them. ~ Lillian Hanson

After 30 years of deindustrialization, off-shoring and insourcing, and 40 years of stagnant wages, the middle class has finally met Apollyon. No longer does a college degree confer a ticket to the middle class. Even accountants and medical professionals are losing their jobs. The safety net for the poor, which was never adequate, is now gone and social security for seniors and the disabled is next on the chopping block. The "low taxes, small government" middle class folks who told the poor to "pull yourself up by your own bootstraps" these past 30 years are now losing everything. Many are among the over age 50 group who got to live the middle class American Dream. They previously had everything and thumbed their noses at those of us in poverty that never got chances for anything. And now that they're losing everything, all the things those of us in poverty never got to have, they are the ones crying the loudest. (How's that "bootstrap" thing working out for you?)

The week before Thanksgiving of 2010, Democrats in Congress declined to renew the Bush tax cuts for the rich. The corporate class howled, saying that they dare not hire any new employees with the uncertainty over not getting their tax cuts. But this announcement from Congress didn't discourage the rich from luxury spending. Instead, luxury spending by the filthy rich is booming.

Corporate profits soared to a new American record of $1.6 trillion. Neiman Marcus sold 100 Limited Edition Camaros at $75,000 a clip within three minutes of the news on the non-renewal of tax cuts for the wealthy. Christy's reports high end shoppers are pouring in. Goldman Sachs chief Lloyd Blankfein's favorite fancy restaurant reported a business increase of 10%. While sales were down at mid-range stores catering to the middle class such as JC Penney's and Kohl's, Tiffany's reported a 3rd quarter profit of $55 million — up by 27% according to the Wall Street Journal, even though sales of items under $500 are down. All this profligacy abounds among the rich while 1 out of 5 Americans has to use food stamps to buy groceries. Yet, neocons in Congress claim that the economy can't get going again while the rich languish in anxiety and uncertainty over whether or not they will get their extension of the Bush tax cuts. The filthy rich who say they can't afford to create good jobs for all of the American people in poverty have no problem affording luxury toys that those of us in poverty can't even afford to dream about.

Pulitzer Prize winning Syracuse University College of Law professor and tax reporter David Cay Johnston said in response to MSNBC's Keith Olbermann's question on the wealthy's "uncertainty and anxiety":

> "The uncertainty is the millions of people out there who don't know how they're going to feed their children because of the disappearing jobs — all the jobs that are being destroyed by the machinations of Wall Street. We talk about Goldman Sachs as an investment house. 90% of its revenue comes from non-

investment house activities, principally trading derivatives and actions that are making the people at Goldman Sachs and the other Wall Street firms incredibly wealthy by destroying wealth and by destroying jobs and people's lives…A hundred years ago when most people worked in factories, there was a man named Taylor and he had a little stopwatch. There was something called "the speed-up" to get more work out of people. What they've done now is persuade people that 'you better work a lot of unpaid overtime and come in on Saturday or your job will disappear.' In effect, they are stealing an enormous amount of labor from people without paying for it."

Companies will be sitting on about $2 trillion in cash by the end of 2010 when the 4th quarter reports come out. Johnston says that "they aren't putting it to work because people don't have money to buy their goods and services."

The rich already have everything. They've got all the money, more than they could ever spend on themselves within their lifetimes. They don't need the American middle class anymore now that the middle class has outlived its collective usefulness as selfish, heartless capo pricks to keep the poor at bay so that the rich could keep accumulating more capital. The malefactors of great wealth have already fled the "great temple" of our society. They've made plans to flee American soil before being physically attacked by hordes of formerly middle class people, enraged at being betrayed, can team up with the poor and mount a full scale attack on those responsible for destroying other people's lives for perverse amusement.

The middle and upper classes justified their hatred of poor people by claiming that the poor will steal their "stuff." They build "McMansions" in gated communities to warehouse their "stuff." They pay monthly fees for home protection and security services in order to protect their "stuff." They buy cars and laptop computers equipped with Lojack – a GPS tracking system – so that their "stuff" can be quickly recovered in case of theft.

But the reality is that most poor people never wanted your "stuff." Why would we want someone else's "stuff" when all we got all our lives was other people's hand-me-downs? We wanted a level playing field so we can get our own "stuff", but you made sure we didn't get anything. Any measure that ever gave the poor a leg up was derided as "special treatment" and you helped dismantle what little bit of "special treatment" there was for us just so that you would not have to compete with us for good jobs that you felt only you were entitled to. And so you made damn sure we never got a chance. Bravo!

If only the poor are "most likely to steal", how do you explain the fact that some of the biggest thieves and worst social predators in American history were filthy rich Wall Street executives? Why do you aspire to join them and live in exclusive gated communities among the rich to get away from the poor when the poor have been more sinned against than are sinners?

Do you remember Enron and MCI WorldCom? Ken Lay, Jeff Skilling, and Dennis Kosloski were rich successful CEO's. They had second homes in the Dutch Antilles. They sipped $25 glasses of champagne on the French Riviera. Kosloski spent $6,000 on just a shower curtain in his posh upper-west side Manhattan condo. How about Bernie Maddoff? He was already rich, and he made himself richer by stealing from the very class of people who move heaven and earth to keep the poor at bay so we don't "steal their stuff." Why did Maddoff do it? Why did they bankrupt their companies by stealing from shareholders and employees alike when they had more than enough money to buy whatever they wanted? They didn't steal because of "class envy", out of wanting someone else's "stuff." They did it because they could and they thought they wouldn't get caught — like most psychopaths.

Most poor people are not criminals. But statistics have shown that the poor are more likely to be victims of crimes. Poor people who are violent are people who did not accept "their place" by sitting on the margins suffering quietly, depressed that no one cares. They're enraged and resentful. It's not class envy; it's class hatred. Have those who are comfortably off ever wondered why such social ills exist? Have they ever thought that maybe disenfranchised youth who become violent offenders are angry?

Look at the crime of carjacking. It's not just about taking your "stuff." It's about rage – lots of it. If it was only about taking your "stuff", carjackers would wait in hiding until you've parked your car. Then they would steal it while you weren't looking – and while no one else was looking, either. That would minimize the chance of being identified. Being identified means getting caught and sent to prison. Thieves don't want to get caught.

Carjacking is extremely violent. It is very in-your-face and personal. The carjacker does not merely take your car. He points a loaded gun in your face, roughs you up, and screams at you ordering you to get out of your car before he takes it – in the middle of the street in front of plenty of witnesses. Carjackers demoralize and terrorize their victims. They don't just take your "stuff." They let you know you've had your ass handed to you.

Have society's "winners" ever thought *why* the poor might be angry and surly in the first place? Could it be because sometimes poor people exhaust every last ounce of emotional capital struggling just to survive while getting heaps of abuse, but never getting basic human needs met in a selfish society that doesn't care about poor people's human rights? Could it be because those who act out in the extreme are reacting to the overload of the violence of sheer physical and psychological torture that poverty itself imposes and the stress of that alone, all the social isolation and rejection notwithstanding, surpasses any reasonable tolerance limits?

People do not only require their physical needs to be met; they also need love and social acceptance as well. People are social beings. When you're constantly economically terrorized and socially devalued, disrespected and excluded for the status crime of Living While Poor, wouldn't *you* be angry? How would *you* feel if *you* were treated as sub-human, had every ounce of *your* personal identity and self-worth chipped away with every deprivation and social injustice doled out to *you*? People are not born angry and pugnacious.

It's not crime and social deviance that the higher social classes fear. They fear that if they "open up their networks" to the poor and create a level playing field, they wouldn't have a group to feel superior to. And they fear fair competition. You don't have capitalism without competition. But the competition that drives the gears of capitalism is coercive and unfair. Those who live to compete against others love capitalism. They love it because they know they have advantages from unearned privileges, which they don't want to relinquish.

The only person motivated by competition is the person with a reasonable expectation of winning. If you're a teacher and you use competitive learning tools like spelling bees, the only person you're motivating is the good speller — the kid who's already motivated in that area. The kid you're *not* reaching is the one you're trying to reach. World renowned special education expert Rick Lavoie observed that for the most part we do our best work and that we're the most productive when we're competing against ourselves, not against others. Yet the entire American school system is based on head-to-head competition. The justification for that is that we need to "prepare kids for the real world." Since American values center on capitalism, kids learn at a very young age that it's in their best interest if their friends lose because their success depends on others' failures. What does the lead to in adulthood?

Given that we created and maintain a society based on the head-to-head competition of capitalism even though people do their best work when they're not competing against others, can we honestly say that this is the most productive and healthy construct for society?

The child in poverty learns very quickly that she can't afford to take any risks, since living in poverty is living with a lot of pain, rejection and a high likelihood of failure because the system is rigged. If she doesn't feel that she has a realistic chance to win, she won't want to compete because she doesn't see that it's worth the risk.

Living in poverty is not just being the kid who gets used donated toys, or who goes hungry, or who is being evicted and living in chaos. It's living with all that while being told you've got nothing to offer and that your place in the grand scheme of things is always at the bottom. Kids in poverty learn they've got no chips to play the game of life long before they learn their multiplication tables. And they learn it at school — a middle class institution where they don't fit in, where they're not welcome, and where their parents are belittled and judged.

Most of the fault for the dystopia our society has become lies with those who own the capital and means of production and their middle class capos. It is the elite who have no interest in seeing true 100% employment with at least an acceptable minimum standard of living to which we are all entitled as human beings. The elite fear loss of power. They fear loss of control over their monopoly of the world's resources and over other people's lives.

The rich maintain their control over everyone else by means of artificial market manipulation and wage suppression to keep poor people downtrodden, demoralized and crushed underfoot while fooling the middle class into believing that the poor are the enemy. They also conned the middle class into acquiescing to an unjust status quo by dangling the Horatio Alger carrot on the stick – but now there is no carrot and most people know it. Blaming the poor for society's ills gives those responsible a free pass. Clearly, it is poverty, not poor people, which is the problem. They claim that the poor have "class envy"; that the poor resent others for their success. What poor people resent is unfairness and injustice.

Make no mistake; the *only* class warfare being committed is by the haves against the have-nots. The only class envy that exists is in the insecurities and fear among the middle class who think that the poor being uplifted will somehow take something away from them. This fear was ignited and fueled by the rich to keep the masses fighting amongst themselves for token crumbs.

It's up to you to decide what sort of society you want, what sort of hope and future will be in store. If you're happy with the status quo and don't care about a fair or shared society, then continue cruising through life on autopilot and don't do anything. You can eventually die leaving all of your toys behind that you can't take with you, knowing that you chose to be part of the problem instead of part of the solution. But if you *do* care about raising the floor to a minimum acceptable standard, if you truly care about a society that is fairer for everyone, then do something to help achieve that. You cannot change everything in society all by yourself, but you are not exempt from doing your part – and no part is too small and unimportant. We all have something of value to offer.

Examine who you know and open up your network to help someone less fortunate than you. And above all, be willing to fight in the trenches. The solution will not come from voting because a vote for the lesser of two evils is still a vote for evil. What's the point in voting in a system set up to always favor those with privilege, money, and power who frequently use that power to abuse people and the environment in order to get whatever they want?

Democrats are more anti-woman and anti-equality and more pro-corporatist today than the Republicans were during the Eisenhower era. Voting for any candidate that is backed by either wing of the corporate-owned capitalist government is still a vote for the status quo. The Greens are no better. They're nothing but petit bourgeoisie liberals wearing an environmental label. Consenting to support the political fig-newton follies in this fetid capitalist sepulcher decaying from within from its own greed and misogyny is employing half-assed, half-hearted half-measures promoted by "priests of half-truths" (to quote Leon Trotsky); and will solve absolutely nothing.

Thanks to the party of "Yes, We Lied", the malefactors of great wealth are calling all the shots and have absconded with the entire nation's wealth that rightfully belongs to "we the people." The Democrats in Congress and in President Obama's executive commissions were not ham-strung into proposing cuts to social security, Medicare, and

Medicaid which has already impacted poor seniors. Their ranking party members like Steny Hoyer and Al Simpson led the parade!

In 2011, it will be the second year in a row that the elderly and disabled on social security did not get any cost of living increase, which is only a 2% raise, but every penny is desperately needed when the cost of everything else is skyrocketing.

So far, all the talk of "sacrifice" by the party of Neocon-lite has been along the lines of starving the poor to death, upholding second-class citizenship and childbirth chattel slavery for poor women, and pulling the plug on grandma with cuts to the very social programs that are needed to keep grandma alive.

None of these overpaid overprivileged gasbags in the DC Beltway are imposing these sacrifices on themselves — they'll never be poor and starving, or end up destitute from a disability or dead from lack of access to health care. Their wives and daughters won't ever be forced to carry a pregnancy to term that resulted from a rape, nor will they lack access to birth control or abortion in the event of contraceptive failure. They're getting their Cadillac health care coverage and pensions from the public dole without any intention of giving up any of those benefits.

It doesn't matter who we vote for or if we vote at all because "we the people" always lose as long as we're in a klepto-plutocracy capitalist society. It's a matter of recognizing that both political parties serve only the interests of the rapacious owning class, and most members of Congress are among its ranks. Voting isn't a "civic duty", it's a three-ring circus where you only get to vote for those that the elite prop up and allow you to vote for. Not a single member of Congress, except for Maxine Waters, is from deep poverty. You have to have a lot of money to run for office. Whose class interests are served by such a shambolic system? It matters not what race or gender a politician is; what matters is whose class interests are being served.

Anyone who believes that any of these political leaders and candidates are going to govern in the people's best interests rather than the sociopathic oligarchs' interests is either willfully ignorant or painfully naïve. Both the Democrats and the Republicans are visibly batting for the same team: the economic terrorist class and wealthy misogynistic theocrats at the helm of mega-churches.

It does not matter who caused the current economic crisis — what mattered is how it was handled. Both parties have rewarded those responsible for it with the biggest no-strings attached welfare handout in this nation's history. Meanwhile, the so-called party of the "forgotten man" who rode into office on an election landslide gave no bailouts to the people who are suffering the worst and who are in the most need of an economic lifeline. Instead, they cut the throats of the poorest of the poor (most whom are middle-aged women) — the "99er's" in addition to those 6 million jobless from the underclass who are extremely long-term unemployed without *any* income at all except food stamps, and who happen to be the most disadvantaged job-seekers in any job market.

Billions of dollars in welfare for billionaires, tax cuts for the middle class, and an unemployment benefit extension that helps only a small fraction of the unemployed was all paid for with cuts to Medicaid and the slated elimination of food stamps by 2012 — leaving 44 million Americans struggling below poverty to starve to death, suffer without health care, and with no bailout in the form of a real "right to life" safety net.

Did anyone in the Democratic Party in Congress who went along with these measures have any concern for all the poor, unemployable pregnant women who won't have food, who probably won't survive pregnancy and childbirth due to poverty, malnourishment, and lack of access to decent medical care? Did they care when they voted for these cuts and a shambolic health reform bill that only helps *some* members of the middle class and further enriches insurance companies and stokes the egos of misogynists who prefer to use fetuses to maim, injure, or even kill poor women?

Poor women are at the bottom of every pile. We're not even afforded equal rights as people, as citizens of this country. What do we gain by voting for those who have thrown us under the bus? We're just as downtrodden either way. The party of "change" has not done anything to make our lives just a little bit less miserable, degraded and hopeless. And we're supposed to be *grateful*?

Being deprived of personal liberty, of the sovereignty of bodily autonomy, for any other group of Americans would be considered a gross violation of their 13th and 14th Amendment rights. But for poor women, the most heinous form of slavery — forced breeding against our will at peril to our health, wellbeing, and lives — is acceptable because it's deceptively draped in the habiliments of "pro-life" family values and "morality." Poor women have nothing to gain by voting for the same party of sell-outs who dispossessed us of even our most basic human right to have control over our own reproduction, our own bodies. The outcome was the same for us under the party of Neocon-lite as it was under "the other guys." Neither party enacted measures that value *our* lives, or the lives of poor children who have been likened by South Carolina's Lieutenant Governor Andre Bauer to "stray animals that will only breed if you feed them."

Affluent citizens (who have no real concept of the harsh economic life for the rest of us — we're just statistics), actively deliberate the necessity and obligation of providing assistance for the least fortunate — the very poor that they themselves have helped create. "Free trade" agreements, tax breaks, corporate subsidies (welfare), bailouts, etc. are bastions of built-in inequity. That's why we're seeing the destruction of the middle class and increasing wealth for those who are already rich. Less for you means more for them. It's nothing personal, it's just business (you're just "human capital" after all). The rich created the poor and the middle class helped keep the poor down while claiming it's "not their problem." Their patriotic defense is: "I've got mine (no matter how I got it), now you go get yours (if you can, but I'll make sure you can't because I don't want competition)." And they make sure not to feed the "stray animals" that they themselves bred and turned out.

In his eloquence, America's most famous political prisoner and radio journalist, Mumia Abu-Jamal, summed up the true state of the American political machine:

> "Neither serpentine politics, nor sterile economic theory which treats them...as mere economic units, offers much hope. For the very politicians they vote for spit in their faces, while economists write them off as non-persons. It must come from the poor, a rebellion of the spirit that reaffirms their intrinsic human worth, based upon who they are rather than what they possess. From death row, this is Mumia Abu-Jamal."

We do not need a prison-industrial complex to create jobs anymore than we need child pornography to create jobs. We do not need to spend tax money on Halliburton's no-bid contracts to benefit a few rich people with the war in Iraq over oil. We do not need to reward those on Wall Street who caused the Great Depression II. Demand a government that won't reward those who have trashed the environment and deliberately impoverished entire communities. Demand that money be invested in making sustainable alternative energy affordable for everyone – and the creation of "green" jobs that pay a living wage be equally open to workers of all ages, races and genders who currently jobless and poor but who are willing to roll up their sleeves and get the work done.

Obliterating farmlands and mountains to build subdivisions of gated communities in order to hide from poverty won't solve anything. Penalizing people for their conditions of poverty by denying them opportunity after cutting social programs is not the answer. You cannot punish people out of poverty (Beegle, 2007).

Social mobility is the engine that enables a society to evolve. It drives society towards progression and improvement. The more rigid a society's mobility becomes, less progress is made. Studies have shown that in the US, someone who falls into poverty due to divorce, illness, injury, or job loss has a considerably slimmer chance of climbing out of poverty than their counterparts in other wealthy western nations.

When the viscosity of the fluid of upward mobility in a capitalist society breaks down to the level where it no longer exists; the engine of that society will founder. When the engine of a car seizes, there are two options: rebuild it or scrap it. It is often impossible to rebuild a seized engine, depending on the extent of the damage on all of its components. In that case, the only choice is to send it to the salvage yard for scrap metal. But when rebuilding the engine is possible, the cost is astronomical – almost as much as simply getting a brand new engine. In most cases, engine seizure can be prevented by spending a little money and time performing regular routine preventive maintenance. The cost of regular tune-ups and fluid changes is far less than the cost of having to rebuild or replace the engine.

Similarly, the cost of performing regular routine maintenance on our society in ways that actually help lift people out of poverty pales in comparison to the cost in terms of human casualty if things remain unchanged. Permanently lost potential, increased suffering, hopelessness, despair, diminished quality of life and ultimately the destruction of society is too high of a price.

A society is far more complex and dynamic than a car engine. Broken people and ruined lives are much harder to fix than a broken cam shaft. Therefore, doesn't it make sense to take better care of people and help everyone regardless of age/sex/race/disability, to climb out of poverty and reach their fullest potential with the talents and abilities they have? Isn't it time we evolved from the current "me" society into more of a "we" society?

Free enterprise apologists diminish, and even justify, the harm inflicted on the poor by the "sacred cow" of capitalism, claiming that capitalism is the great liberator. Whenever people whine about Communism or Socialism, they always raise the same old tired arguments. "Communism does not work because it killed 60 to 100 million people" and "Socialism removes people's incentive to strive more." They cite the Cultural Revolution or the starving of the Ukraine, which had nothing to do with classless societies but instead had everything to do with a cult of personalities and despotic authoritarianism. And even with all of the atrocities under Stalin, the Bolsheviks did for violently oppressed women in the Soviet East what no Western capitalist society's feminist group had ever done: abolished child bride purchases and horrific human rights abuses against the women and girls in Turkmenistan, Uzbekistan, and the Northern Caucasus.[71] Within less than one generation of the October Revolution, women in the Soviet East went from being sold as illiterate child brides into polygamous marriages to the highest bidder where they were starved and worked to death; from abused reproductive chattel forced to give birth on top of dung piles in frigid temperatures across the desolate frozen tundra of Siberia to being fully equal citizens with equal human rights. They went almost overnight from being reproductive chattel to university professors, pilots, collective farm managers, and Soviet government representatives — while their American counterparts were still fighting for the right to an education, a paid job, drive cars, and have control over their own bodies.

Before the 1990's Balkans war, socialist Yugoslavia was able to provide jobs and health care for everyone outside of the for-profit capitalist paradigm. Socialism works. And because it worked so well in Yugoslavia whose citizens enjoyed a much higher quality of life than we ever did, the world's moneyed elite stamped it out by using their brutal enforcement arm, the national security state.

Putting aside the fact that the Vatican backed the fanatical Catholic state of Croatia and was complicit in the horrors of Jasenovac and Croatia's Ustăse were resurrected under Tuđman; putting aside the fact that Bosnia's Alija Izetbegovic was a fascist and a fundamentalist Islamic hardliner who was an active Nazi in the Waffen SA during WW II who openly called for his praetorian guard of elite Bosniaks to resurrect the SS Handzar and used his own people as human shields (the staged "Breadline Massacre" of May 27, 1992) in the 1990's Balkan Wars by detonating a bomb and blaming the Serbs; putting aside the fact that Tito was a Catholic Croat and merely a puppet "dictator" who was only a tepid Communist; putting aside the fact that the US and NATO

---

[71] Fannina Halle, *Women In the Soviet East,* 1938

backed a known narco-terrorist Hashim "The Snake" Thaci, the Albanian leader of the KLA who has been directly tied to black market organ harvesting (murdering Serbs for their body parts) in the province of Kosovo; putting aside the fact that Slobodon Melosevic was a Serb nationalist who used rape camps as a weapon of warfare; putting *all* these things aside, the truth often gets left out in the discussion on socialism and the capitalist involvement in the planned breakup of socialist Yugoslavia.

Before Yugoslavia disintegrated into a hellhole of economic strife and civil wars, the people there had a very good standard of living. Sarajevo, the most cosmopolitan city of Eastern Europe with the richest of histories, was a cultural jewel known as Eastern Europe's "Jerusalem."

But some (like many in the East Bloc Warsaw Pact nations) saw American capitalist consumerism as this exotic gem and they wanted it, thinking that they would get to keep the security provided by their socialist system (their national health care, their generous unemployment benefits, education system, the guarantee of living wage jobs with paid vacations, generous pension benefits, etc.) and get this whole new glittering jewel of materialism on top of all that. They didn't get it. Now they do — they got that red, white, and blue "free market" capitalist dick shoved right up their collective ass.

After the fall of Communism in the former Soviet Union, the US seemed to have all these "enemies" all of a sudden — all these "enemies" who can't wait to attack us because they "hate our freedoms." That's the mass line used to cover up the class line. In fact, Joseph Schumpeter made the same observation in his analysis of the fall of the Roman Empire. Fact: the American ruling class viz a viz the national security state created those "enemies." (Why aren't there "enemies" waiting to pounce on Denmark?)

As Ramsey Clark said, Yugoslavia was built upon an idea. The idea was that the southern Slavs would not remain weak and divided people falling out among themselves, or falling prey to some imperialist outsiders. They would join together and have a territory that was large enough and strong enough to become a viable nation with its own development. After WWII, multi-ethnic socialist Yugoslavia was a post-war industrial power, a viable nation and an economic success.

Between 1960 and 1980, Yugoslavia experienced one of the most vigorous growth rates, a decent standard of living, socialized medicine and education, the guaranteed right to a job, one month's vacation with pay, affordable public transportation, housing, and utilities. Its literacy rate was over 90%. Life expectancy was 72 years in Yugoslavia between 1960 and 1980 — higher than in the US, where close to 50 million Americans lack access to health care.

The bulk of Yugoslavia's economy was in the public, not-for-profit sector. It was the type of country that global capitalists would normally not tolerate. Yet Yugoslavia *was* tolerated because it was seen as a buffer to the Soviet bloc, the Warsaw Pact nations. At the same time, efforts were made by the world's capitalist class to undermine Yugoslavia's socialist economy. Yugoslavia opened itself up to American capitalism as early as 1968, making the same mistake that the Polish Communist party leaders made: they borrowed from the West.

But that came with IMF penetration into Yugoslavia's economy and enormous debt. And with this debt came IMF demands for "restructuring." Restructuring is a euphemism for the imposition of harsh austerity measures which, by intent and design, disproportionately crushes the working class. Austerity programs means you cut safety nets for the poor and force the people to work harder and longer for less; and with the savings procured from these measures, you pay off the interest that's accumulating on that IMF debt.

There was a very conscious and deliberate plan to break up Yugoslavia, with full *priori* knowledge that it would cause bloody civil wars in the 1990's.

In November of 1990, President George Herbert Walker Bush ("King George I") pressured Congress to pass the Foreign Appropriations Act that called for the cutting off of all aid and credits to Yugoslavia. Trading without credits is fatal for any nation that doesn't have a hard currency, so this had a very devastating effect on Yugoslavia. This law also demanded that if any republic in Yugoslavia wanted further US aid, they would have to break away from Yugoslavia and declare their independence. (Foreign aid is when the poor in rich countries are forced to send money to the rich in poor countries.)

This law also required the US State Department's approval of election procedures and results in every one of the Balkan republics. It required that the republics do not hold national elections, but instead hold elections only in their own republics. Then the aid would go to those republics, if and only if they met the US definition of "democratic" — meaning small, ultra right-wing nationalists and fascist parties.

The elite's goals were to break up Yugoslavia and turn it into a fractured region of weak, helpless banana republics; privatized, de-industrialized, and demoralized. At that, capitalism was a resounding success. International bankers — the stakeholders in the IMF, World Bank, mining companies, and Federal Reserve — aided by their henchmen in US and Western European governments, decided to destroy Yugoslavia in the 1980's when it became evident that it was the one remaining Eastern Europe nation that would not relinquish what remained of its socialist system. It was the one country trying for economic independence outside of the global "free market" Third Worldization process.

The global capitalist class wanted a Yugoslavia whose rich resources would be at the disposal of rich multinational corporations, whose population would work for sub-poverty wages and not have health care or access to an education, and whose economy offered no competition with *existing* capitalist producers — only new investors. They wanted to dismantle Yugoslavia's petroleum, mining, auto and engineering industries. And they wanted to eliminate Yugoslavia's public sector and social programs. There was also an ideological component and motive behind Yugoslavia's destruction in which the Vatican was not merely tacitly complicit, but an active participant (which I treat in my book *Divine Right: The Truth is a Lie*).

In Serbian Bosnia, the last remaining radio station was a Serbian station. It was a dissident station whose broadcasts were critical of NATO and Western policies. UN "peacekeepers" went in and shut down the station.

Before the NATO bombings of Belgrade, before the assault in Yugoslavia by Western financiers, Slobodon Milosevic's parliament had more opposition representatives than any other European nation's government. Milosevic was elected three times in elections that foreign observers affirmed as having met the West's definition of "democratic", and therefore compliant with US demands. Yet, Milosevic was labeled a "war criminal" and a "dictator." The Hague War Crimes Tribunal requested that the US produce documentation of the war crimes Milosevic committed so that they could indict him as a war criminal.

In 1992, the US imposed a trade embargo against Yugoslavia. The result: economic devastation and social disintegration from which the region has still not recovered to this day in 2010. There is mass unemployment up to 80%, starvation, hyperinflation, and the health care system has completely collapsed at great cost to the population. With trade sanctions, the civilian population is not "collateral damage" — it's the primary target.

To justify these atrocities to the gullible American public, Western corporate-owned media launched a propaganda campaign which utterly demonized the Serbs to the American public for ten years (at least). Charles Boyd, former Deputy Commander of the US-European Command wrote in the September/October 1994 issue of *Foreign Affairs*:

> "The popular image of this war in Bosnia is one of unrelenting Serbian expansion. In fact, what the Croatians call "the occupied territories" is land which the Serbs have held for more than three centuries. Most of the same is true in Serb land in Bosnia."

So it was admitted in 1994 that the smear campaign against the Serbs, and against Milosevic (although he was no angel!), was all part of an elaborate propaganda scheme to foment hatred and disgust in the hearts and minds of the American and Western European people and turn them against the Serbian people by manufacturing consent for imperialist-driven genocide. It's easy to destroy a nation and kill its people when you can convince the rest of the world to despise them and view them as "less than."

Boyd also wrote (in that same article):

> "The US has punished one side in this war unfairly. It has supported the legitimacy of a leadership in the Bosnian Muslim government that has become increasingly ethnocentric in its makeup, single party in its rule, and manipulative in its diplomacy. We say we want peace, but we have encouraged a deepening of the war."

The American ruling class initially got a guy who they decided would be their boy in breaking up Yugoslavia. He was a banker. He was described as charismatic and charming. His commitment to Communism was milquetoast at best. He was the ideal man for the job. His name was Slobodon Milosevic. But instead of being a tool, he became an obstacle.

Serbs comprise the ethnic majority. For all the scuttlebutt about Serb atrocities, remember that atrocities were committed on all three sides — the worst were committed by the fanatical Roman Catholic Croatian fascist Ustăse.

Mainstream media is the stenographer of power. Well-paid journalists working for the establishment wrote stories that suited the interests of that power — that velvet glove that clothes the iron fist of the National Security State. They're not the watchdogs of democracy and truth; they're the lapdogs of the elite. They are well-kept mistresses among the billionaire Koch brothers' harem (CNN, Fox News, Bill O'Reilly, and Tea Potty drama queen Glenn Beck).

Class and ethnicity were not mutually exclusive factors in terms of either one or the other in understanding the breakup of Yugoslavia. Ethnic tension (like race, gender, and religion) is commonly enlisted by the rich to serve their own class interests. Generally, when there are different racial or ethnic groups living in a society where there's some measure of hope, security, and prosperity, they tend to get along. They mingle and inter-marry.

But when the economic shit hits the fan, when you've got trade sanctions, cuts in vital social programs and high unemployment, things unravel fast. People get desperate, and that's when people begin closing ranks along racial/ethnic/religious and lines. They also go hyper-patriarchal and it's *always* the women and children who end up suffering the worst: physically, politically, economically, socially, and psychologically.

It is the rich capitalists, and their middle class economic hit-men, who have the "class envy", not the poor — they don't want the poor and working class masses of the world to having anything.

In the heart of Eastern Europe sat this large country where 80% of its economy was publicly owned. It had a standard of living that was higher than ours with an elaborate system of human and social services. Now it has been splintered into small right-wing fascist republics. Everything is deregulated. Everything is privatized. And everybody is now poor. They're poor in Bosnia. They're poor in Montenegro and Serbia. They're poor in Macedonia. And they're poor in Croatia. They're poor in Albania. Poverty. Privatize. Deregulate. Crime. Black market organ harvesting. Narco-terrorism. Religious fanaticism. Militaristic fascism. Get 'em down to being peasants so they'll be stepping on each others' necks to line up to work for 15 cents an hour like the slave laborers in Indonesia, Saipan, and the Philippines. That's the goal of "free market" capitalism, which American middle class capitalist enablers and enforcers call "freedom" — the "right" of a privileged group to oppress the non-privileged and take away *their* freedoms, even their lives.

On September 27th, 2000 in Sofia, Bulgaria, the US-backed "Democratic Opposition" Party of Serbia met with representatives of the World Bank, NATO officials, and representatives of the International Monetary Fund (IMF) to sign a "letter of intent" pledging that when they came to power, they would raise prices and privatize state industry and dismantle what remained of Yugoslavia's free health care system. One month later in the same ancient Balkan city, an anti-fascist coalition that included members of the New York-based International Action Center (IAC) testified before an international tribunal about the price in terms of human casualties and social setbacks that had been imposed on them by Western European powerhouses, the Wall Street interests of the US, and NATO as punishment for rejecting the IMF's "economic restructuring" plan.

Yugoslavia was besieged with trade embargos, Western-backed right-wing fascist despots and civil wars, and a 78-day "humanitarian bombing" campaign launched by NATO. Before the assault on socialist Yugoslavia began, Bulgaria was seduced by the West's false promises of "freedom" under capitalism. For Bulgaria's cooperation, Bulgaria suffered IMF "shock therapy" that was imposed by the same type of "pro-democracy" leaders that the US and Western Europe backed in Yugoslavia. In 1990, a US-funded movement seized power in Bulgaria after a well-orchestrated campaign of destabilization. As of October 2000, the average Bulgarian was struggling to live on 58 cents a day.

Dr. Mimi Vitkova was Bulgaria's Health Minister from 1995-1997. She told the tribunal that from 1990 to 2000, life in Bulgaria for the majority of the people "has been a catastrophe." As a testament to capitalism's "freedom", she said:

"We never were a rich country, but when we had socialism our children were healthy and well-fed. They all got immunized. Retired people and the disabled were provided for and got free medicine. Our hospitals were free. Today, if a person has no money, they have no right to be cured. And most people have no money. Our economy was ruined. We had a lot of industry, but after privatization, many plants shut down. We lost our trade with the Soviet Union, with Africa, Latin America, and, of course, Yugoslavia…At least 1 million of our most educated people emigrated abroad. We were promised if we 'privatized' we would get access to West European markets, but it never happened. Instead, we got tiny loans from the IMF. Our organization is made up of people who swore to never allow fascism to return. Bulgaria was one of the few countries where all Nazi collaborators were punished. But today the pro-NATO regime is trying to clean up history, saying that Bulgaria never had fascism."

Another Bulgarian who testified was Blagovesta Doncheva, a former schoolteacher who was once an anti-Communist "dissident." She is no longer. She is now an anti-NATO activist and a defender of socialism. As an ex-member of Bulgaria's Union of Democratic Forces (UDF), she said, "The Bulgarian UDF was flooded with money, cars, trucks, computers from the CIA and the Soros Foundation. They made big promises and we believed them. Then the IMF and the World Bank destroyed the very fabric of our society. Our industry was shut down, our pensions were taken away. Earlier, women could retire at age 55 and men at 60. Now, no one can retire. Our seniors are eating out of garbage bins and children are dying from malnutrition."

Whatever else can be said about socialism, the erstwhile East Bloc countries and the former socialist republic of Yugoslavia managed to do what capitalism cannot, and has no intention of ever doing: providing a guaranteed right to a living wage job, social equality, universal health care, a guaranteed old age income, free education all the way up through the university level, and adequate food, clothing, and housing for all citizens — in countries that were never as rich as ours.[72]

While many Americans say that capitalism is not the problem, that it was intended as the proposed solution to the problem which has always been survival, the fact remains that capitalism in and of itself is a huge problem. The center of its ideology is dog-eat-dog competition; the antithesis of civilization under the guise of providing goods and services and encouraging innovation. But the sum total of prosperity cannot be

---

[72] Michael Parenti, *To Kill A Nation*

measured in terms of high tech toys and the GDP. It is measured by the lives of the people. And many Americans are dying from poverty, from lack of access to nutritious food, health care, adequate housing, and corporate toxic pollutants — all of which are directly caused by capitalism.

As with America's poor and oppressed groups that are frequently told to "leave if they don't like it", Bulgaria's poor are not able to emigrate. They're not welcomed as political, economic and social refugees into the bosom of Western Europe or other countries where they might have a chance. None of the rich "democracies" of the world want to help uplift poor, disadvantaged refugees who are over age 35 and lack a PhD plus job experience in an "in-demand" specialized field. Like our Bulgarian contemporaries, America's poor and disenfranchised are not able to "leave America if we don't like it" unless we have a boatload of money if we're unable to meet other Western nations' immigration point systems that are centered on adequate funds for self-support, level of advanced education, and age. We're stuck. We're unable to leave and we have very few allies or support from other corners of the world. The only help we get is a lot of finger-wagging and lip service. Meanwhile, America's insecure and downwardly mobile middle class — particularly those members of the dominant group that unjustly benefited from a legacy of unearned privileges — calls for actions that will save their comfortable lifestyle at the expense of America's "undeserving poor." Little do they realize that by voting for politicians whose sentiments mirror their own, they are voting to accelerate the Third Worldization of America and are quite happy to see poor homeless pregnant women, poor children, the disabled, and the elderly foraging for food in dumpsters like they do in "free enterprise" Bulgaria.

Capitalists use their power and influence to corner markets and drive out competition; destroying livelihoods and lives. Capitalists have certain personality traits that ensure that they will rise to the top in an economically predatory system. And like excrement, they float to the top. When capitalists talk about "free markets", they mean the freedom to exploit the finite world's limited amount of resources, including people, with no oversight. When plants close and jobs are off-shored and labor is insourced through "guest worker" visa programs, Americans lose their livelihoods — many are left permanently economically excluded and lose everything and there is no way to "bootstrap" your way back on your feet when you're in your 40's, 50's and 60's and suffering from untreated health problems without an income and access to medical care. But CEO's and the investor class, including those who can afford stock portfolios and 401(k)'s, prosper.

The function of markets requires that both the "buyer" and the "seller" in a transaction become better off as a result of the transaction. But that doesn't happen in a "free market" capitalist system. An essential principle of capitalism is a formulation of injustice. The rich get whatever they want; the poor get nothing. Under the religion of free market fundamentalism, you and your possessions become an island separated from everyone else. Capitalism became a moral theory in which the only people deemed deserving of being able to live are those who are economically successful because under capitalism, the primary purpose of the individual is his or her acquisition of wealth — which means others around that person have to be made poor in a finite world with finite resources.

Poor people aren't the problem; poverty is. "Class envy" is not the issue; classism is. For the price tag of the Iraq war, the $700 billion Wall Street bailout bonanza, and the tax cuts for the rich we could have invested in our infrastructure, forgiven all student loan debts for the poor and unemployed, and funded an income safety net for the economically excluded and marginalized, and implemented single-payer national health care for every citizen. We could have moved forward with alternative energy and made it accessible for every American. We could have invested in the economic needs of our own people and communities so that we could all have a decent life. Do you want to be part of the problem or part of the solution? The choice is yours. Be the change.

Works Cited

(2003). *Southern Rural Sociology , 19* (2), pp. 153-175.

(2004). *20/20.* ABC.

(2006, January 5). *People's Weekly World* . Philadelphia, PA, US.

Ashworth, K., & Middleton, S. (1999). *Social Security, Poverty, and Social Exclusion Survey of Britain.* University of Strathclyde.

Ashworth, K., & Middleton, S. (2005). *Study On "Unattractiveness" and its Socio-economic Penalties.* University of Strathclyde.

Beck, A. J., & Harrison, P. M. (2001). *Prisoners in 2000.* Government Report, US Department of Justice, Bureau of Justice Statistics, Washington, DC.

Beegle, D. M. (2007). *See Poverty - Be the Difference.* Oregon, US: Communication Across Barriers.

Bernstein, B. J. (1968). *The New Deal: The Conservative Achievements of Liberal Reform.* New York, NY, US: Pantheon.

Bewley, M. (2008, December 8). Railroading Ag. *Agweek* .

Boyer, R. O., & Morais, H. M. (1979). *Laobor's Untold Story* (3rd Edition ed.). United Electrical, Radio & Machine Workers of America.

Carroll, J. (2010, November 8). The Prison Boom Comes Home To Roost. *The Boston Globe* .

Chomsky, N., & Barsamian, D. (1996). *Class Warfare: Interviews With David Barsamian.* Monroe, Maine, US: Common Courage Press.

Couture, M. (2010, July 30). *Classism Exposed.* (B. Leondar-Wright, Ed.) Retrieved from Classism.org: http://www.classism.org/us-social-forums-a-sour-taste-of-classism

DeNavas-Walt, C., Proctor, B., & Lee, C. (2007). *Income, Poverty and Health Coverage In the United States.* US Census Bureau.

Drewnowski, A. (2007). The Real Contribution of Added Sugar and Fat to Obesity. *Epidemiologic Reviews , 29.*

Ehrenreich, B. (2005). *Bait & Switch: The Futile Pursuit of the American Dream.* New York, NY, US: Metroploitan Books, Henry Holt & Company, LLC.

Ehrenreich, B. (1989). *Fear of Falling: the Inner Life of the Middle Class.* New York: Perennial.

Evans, L., & Goldberg, E. (1999). *The Prison-Industrial Complex.* Oakland, CA, US: PM Press.

Fellows, M. (2006). *The High Price of Being Poor.* The Brookings Institute.

For the Unemployed Over 50: Fears of Never Working Again. (2010, September 20). *New York Times* .

Fulsom, B. W. (1989). *Entrepreneurs vs. the State.* US: Young America Foundation.

Gans, H. (1996). *The War Against the Poor: The Underclass and Antipoverty Policy.* New York, New York, US: Basic Books.

Halle, F. (1938). *Women in the Soviet East.* (M. Green, Trans.) New York, New York, US: E.P.Dutton & Co., Inc.

(2004). *Maternal & Infant Mortality In the US Report to the UN.* World Health Organization.

Nord, M., Andrews, M., & Carlson, S. (2007). *Household Food Security In the United States.* US Department of Agriculture.

Packard, V. (1959). *The Status Seekers.* New York, New York, US: David McKay.

Parenti, M. (1995). *Democracy For the Few.* New York, NY, US: St. Martin's Press.

Parenti, M. (2002). *To Kill A Nation.* London/New York, UK/US: Verso.

Payne, R. (2005). *A Framework For Understanding Poverty.* Corpus Christi, TX, US: Aha! Process, Inc.

Pennsylvania Food Banks. (n.d.). *Pennsylvania Food Banks Report.* Retrieved from http://www.pafoodbanks.org/PARF_Site/Archived_Articles/Trainer

Peters, A. (2010). Washington Cuts Funding For Emergency Utilities Assistance. *CAUS , 1* (3), 1-2.

Pew Charitable Trust. (2010). *A Year Or More: High Cost of Long-Term Unemployment.* Addendum, Pew Fiscal Analysis Institute.

Piven, F. F., & Cloward, R. A. (1993). *Regulating the Poor* (Updated ed.). New York, NY, US: Vintage Books.

Reutter, M. (1980). Workmens' Compensation Doesn't Work Or Compensate. *Business and Society* (Fall), 39-44.

Rich, M. (2010, September 20). The New Unemployables: Workers Over Age 50. *msnbc.com* .

Riis, J. A., & Leviatin, D. (1890, 2010). *How the Other Half Lives* (Second Edition (September 22, 2010) ed.). New York, NY, US: Bedford/ St. Martin's Press .

Rosenberg, R. (1996). *Conference on College Composition.* Milwaukee.

Source Watch. (n.d.). Retrieved November 27, 2010, from Sourcewatch.org: http://www.sourcewatch.org/index.php?title=Tommy_Thompson

Stover, J. F. (1997). *American Railroads.* Chicago, IL, US: University of Chicago Press.

Today's Workplace. (2003, August 21). Retrieved 2010, from todaysworkplace.org: http://www.todaysworkplace.org/2003/08/21/confusing-job-market-for-older-workers

Martin, Toni M. (2006). Going Blind On Our Watch. *Health Affairs , 25* (4), pp. 1121-1126.

Tough, P. (2007, June 10). The Class Consciousness Raiser. *The New York Times* .

Vaughan, A. T. (1995). *New England Frontier: Puritans and Indians 1620-1675.* OK, US: University of Oklahoma Press.

Zinn, H. (2005). *A People's History of the United States.* New York, NY, US: Perennial Classics.

CPSIA information can be obtained at www.ICGtesting.com
Printed in the USA
BVOW041807101011

273288BV00002B/20/P

9 780981 567914